Also by James Taylor and Martin Davidson
Spitfire Ace

Also by Martin Davidson
The Consumerist Manifesto
Decisive Weapons (*with Adam Levy*)
A Visitor's Guide To A History Of Britain

James Taylor
and Martin Davidson

BOMBER CREW

HODDER &
STOUGHTON

Typeset in Monotype Sabon by
Rowland Phototypesetting Ltd,
Bury St Edmunds, Suffolk

Printed and bound by
Clays Ltd, St Ives plc

Hodder Headline's policy is to use papers that are natural,
renewable and recyclable products and made from wood
grown in sustainable forests. The logging and manufacturing
processes are expected to conform to the environmental
regulations of the country of origin.

Hodder and Stoughton Ltd
A division of Hodder Headline
338 Euston Road
London NW1 3BH

Contents

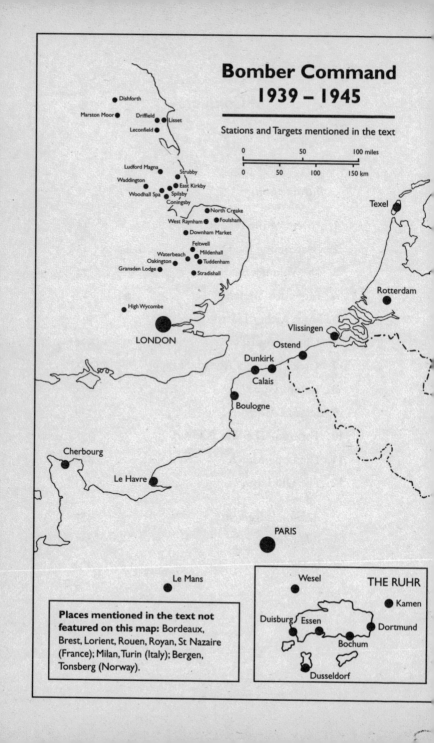

Bomber Command
1939 – 1945

Stations and Targets mentioned in the text

Dishforth

Marston Moor
Driffield
Lisset

Leconfield

Ludford Magna
Strubby

Waddington
East Kirkby

Woodhall Spa
Spilsby

Coningsby

North Creake

West Raynham
Foulsham

Downham Market

Feltwell

Waterbeach
Mildenhall

Oakington
Tuddenham

Gransden Lodge

Stradishall

High Wycombe

LONDON

Texel

Rotterdam

Vlissingen

Ostend

Dunkirk

Calais

Boulogne

Cherbourg

Le Havre

PARIS

Le Mans

Places mentioned in the text not featured on this map: Bordeaux, Brest, Lorient, Rouen, Royan, St Nazaire (France); Milan, Turin (Italy); Bergen, Tonsberg (Norway).

THE RUHR

Wesel

Kamen

Duisburg
Essen
Dortmund

Bochum

Dusseldorf

Introduction

In the summer of 1940, the RAF secured its famous victory against the Luftwaffe in the Battle of Britain. The nation could at last breathe a collective sigh of relief. Months of 'Phoney War' had been followed by a Blitzkrieg offensive that had rapidly subsumed most of continental Europe under Nazi rule. Norway, Denmark, Belgium, Holland and finally France had all fallen within a matter of weeks. The Battle of Britain marked not only Britain's own resistance to Hitler; it was also the first active check on the Third Reich's ambition. Led by the 'Brylcream Boys', the RAF had ensured that Operation Sealion, Hitler's planned invasion of Britain, had at least been postponed. This, however, was only the beginning. Britain had given itself a respite; it hadn't secured its peace. Most of the continent remained occupied; Hitler was still dominant in Europe. So the question now was, 'What next?'

It wasn't just a question of securing Britain's peace. The defensive role of Fighter Command would now need to be matched by an offensive campaign, and that would have to come from the fighter boys' RAF counterparts in Bomber Command. The role of the bomber in modern warfare had long been predicted, and occasionally glimpsed, not least in Blitzkrieg itself. Now the bombers alone provided the hope of bringing the war to an eventual end. There were, of course, those who advocated some kind of truce, but when Churchill had roused the nation with his 'never surrender', he hadn't simply meant that Britain should retreat into its island fortress and sit out the war, like some kind of Atlantic Switzerland. From the start of hostilities he had been one of the few to realise that the threat posed by

Hitler's Germany went way beyond simple military aggression; Nazism meant total domination of Europe, and with it the enslavement of her peoples. That was explicitly Nazism's intention in the east, the conflict that had, after all, pulled Britain into the war in the first place. Anyone putting their faith in the western nations being somehow exempt from this fate was living in a fool's paradise. Churchill had realised too that nothing short of total defeat would suffice. Hitler was never going to be half beaten. Nor was there any point looking to the Germans to help unseat their Führer. The whole world could see the unprecedented levels of popular support enjoyed by Hitler, a euphoric solidarity turned fanatical on the wave of early victories enjoyed by his armed forces. Hitler had transcended the vicissitudes of party politics; he was so triumphantly safe in the support of his people he had far less need of the kind of terror apparatus used by Stalin. Not even the Nazi hierarchy, so bitterly engaged in internecine rivalry, would ever have dared challenge Hitler's preeminence. He was a demigod to his people, not just a dictator.

Recognising the unique enormity of the threat posed by Hitler and the Germany he had roused from its post-Versailles slumbers was one thing. The idea that Churchill, or the British, were in any position to do something about it was quite another. The Battle of Britain had deprived Hitler of his European grand slam; but for Hitler this was a very temporary setback, of no long-term strategic significance. The arrogance of this view didn't seem misplaced; taking Britain out of the war remained, very firmly, work in progress. Still, Churchill refused to yield, or even dilute his commitment to Britain going on to the offensive, even with so much stacked against him. He never wavered in his belief that endurance was not enough; the only way to deal with the menace of Nazi Germany was the complete decimation of its ability to wage war. For a nation reeling on its back foot, this was either indomitable will-power talking, or sheer hubris.

So, how was this fight to be undertaken? The army, in post-Dunkirk disarray, was in no state to take on the Wehrmacht. The

Royal Navy could hardly fight a major continental land war. That left only one service: the RAF, and in particular its fledgling bombers. This was why it would be their job to justify Churchill's belligerent belief that this was a war that had to be fought, and had to be won. So the RAF set about establishing a new front, a front that would witness some of the most vicious fighting of the war, and would last until the very end of hostilities. This was a front that would sustain one of the most extraordinary escalations in technology and military devastation the modern world had ever seen, and whose legacy remains with us to this day. It would be established in the skies over Nazi Germany. For all his prophetic powers, Churchill could have had no idea in 1940 of what this aerial war would involve. By 1945, the war waged by Bomber Command had taken an utterly unforeseen form, in size, scale and ferocity. The firestorms of Hamburg and Dresden were simply inconceivable in 1940. By 1945 they bore testimony to an extraordinary overcoming of obstacles – of technology, will, strategy and, above all, human ability – achieved by Bomber Command. Perhaps no other arena of warfare in the Second World War moved so far from disastrous beginnings, or was so relentlessly honed and perfected against such apparently insurmountable opposition.

None of this – the aircraft, the munitions, the electronics – would have meant anything without the men who actually flew the bombing operations. It was they who had embarked on this long journey, from the early days of nuisance raids flown in aircraft dubbed 'flying coffins' by their crews, all the way to the Second Front's final stranglehold over Nazi Germany in 1945. A total of 55,570 men failed to return, an attrition rate unequalled by any other arm of the British war effort. The odds against survival were so great that surely nobody taking part in these raids could seriously have entertained any great hope of making it through the war. Yet still they flew, night after night after night. There were some extraordinary accounts of human endeavour to emerge from Bomber Command. One rear air gunner, occupying the most perilous post on a heavy bomber, flew on ninety-nine operations. He baled out six times during the war from burning aircraft, and on one occasion escaped from the Bavarian Gestapo before embarking on a long walk home. Not atypically, his post-war experiences reflected the thoughtfulness that many in Bomber Command possess about their contribution to the war. He lived in Germany for over a decade, using his engineering background to help adapt cars for use by the disabled. It wasn't an act of contrition – he had nothing to be sorry for – but recognition that after the destruction the world needed creation and healing. He combined great pride in the sacrifices he and his generation had made, helping rid the world of Nazi terror, with a rueful awareness of the obligations placed on victors and defeated alike, to move forward, and to help ensure that this time it really wouldn't happen again. His was only one of thousands of extraordinary stories to emerge from Bomber Command, however. This book, and the television series it accompanies, is based on interviews with twenty-five veterans, but informed by the recollections of nearly three hundred veterans we've spoken to in a bid to capture the experience of being a member of Bomber Command.

By the end of the war, Bomber Command had flown hundreds of thousands of sorties. Its aircraft had attacked an enormous variety of targets across occupied Europe. Many of these sorties involved not just scores but hundreds of aircraft, and the thousands of aircrew needed to fly them were supported by the many thousands more people in Britain helping ensure their operational success. In Germany many thousands of people were employed doing their utmost to destroy them. It was a drama that was played out with remorseless repetition, the ultimate war of attrition. Other campaigns flared into life, peaked and then fell away in significance, but the bombing campaign, once started, never let up for a moment. Furthermore, these sorties concentrated into the span of an eight- or nine-hour operation a lifetime of drama and incident of every imaginable sort. Perhaps no other arena of the war required the same rhythm of fear as was demanded of the bomber crews; its ritualised rise and fall before and after operations, the crescendos and climaxes during the missions themselves. The more usual battlefield experience of long periods of tedium culminating in short bursts of surging adrenalin and terror was never the way of the bombers. The demands placed on the psyche of these young men borders on the incomprehensible. Their Browning machine guns, their 20,000 feet of hard-maintained altitude, the sheer numbers in a typical bomber stream, the darkness of the night-time sky – all these gave the crews some protection. But they all knew only too well the fate that threatened so many of them: the Flak, the spotlights, the night fighters guided in on radar, and the fact that, unlike the fighter pilots of the Battle of Britain, those forced to bale out faced years in a prisoner-of-war camp if they survived.

Yet even before the war had ended, the bombing campaign had become embroiled in controversy. The devastation reaped on Dresden in the notorious raid of February 1945, in particular, led to a re-evaluation of the Allies' moral and strategic position at the highest level. When the final victory was celebrated in 1945, just about every section of the Allied forces was fêted, but little mention was made of the bomber crews. Their part in the defeat of Nazism has remained an uncomfortable element of the Allies' war ever since. Individual airmen were decorated; Peter Baker, Leonard Miller, John Whiteley and Tom Wingham, four of the veterans featured in this book, all received the Distinguished Flying Cross, while Ricky Dyson was awarded the George Medal for helping his surviving crew members when his aircraft crashed just after take-off. There was, however, no campaign medal for the veterans of Bomber Command per se, an omission that is felt bitterly to this day. In the years since, the contribution of the 125,000 airmen who flew in the bomber crews has been often ignored, and frequently condemned.

It is now sixty years since the war ended. There have been many debates about the moral and ethical dimensions of the bombing, but few attempts to understand what it meant for the airmen themselves. We wanted to move beyond the policy to obtain an insight into what thousands of men and women had contributed to, and sacrificed for, the Allied war effort. We weren't alone. Those who survived the war are, at the very least, grandparents, if not great-grandparents. Many of their grand-children are now firmly established in adulthood, and hungry to establish some kind of link to these unthinkable events, across the bridgehead of family memory. In many cases, this is made even more poignant by the fact that so few of those grandfathers are still alive. So many share a regret that they didn't find out more, earlier; that they were too young, and their grandparents too reticent, for real dialogue to have taken place. So we made the decision early on that, for the television series, our quest to capture some small aspect of the experiences endured by the men and women of Bomber Command should be enlivened by that family connection. What we wanted was the chance to bring these family memories to life, not just for the individuals taking part in our series, but for the wider public too. So we decided to find five grandchildren of Bomber Command airmen, themselves now approximately the same age their grandfathers would have been at the time, and give them a taste of the rigorous train-ing programme that had turned their grandfathers into bomber crews. They would get to contemplate the wartime careers of their grandfathers while wrestling with the very same equipment, disciplines and frustrations as their predecessors. They would get to climb aboard the very same aircraft, make the same calcu-lations, and in one case even take the controls of the mighty Avro Lancaster. Over the course of a few short weeks, our five would come as close as it is possible to get today to forming an embryonic bomber crew.

It was a remarkable journey, not just into the personal histories of five grandfathers, but into the wider history of Bomber Com-mand. James Smith, now thirty-one, was aware that his grand-father had been part of Bomber Command, but had had little opportunity to learn what that meant. He had been close to Harry Smith, a wireless operator on Lancasters in the final months of the war, but was just ten years old when his grandfather died. He had his grandfather's flying helmet, and had seen his medals. Harry Smith had been a noted artist after the war, and much of his work was influenced by his time in Bomber Command, so the images of aerial warfare were prominent. Yet still there were many gaps. The experience of being in Bomber Command had haunted Harry Smith, so James Smith's family told him. Family records on their own provide few answers, but as we come to grips with the wider history of Bomber Command, many of the underlying psychological scars start becoming all too visible.

As a commercial airline pilot, James Smith is familiar with the demands of flying large aircraft, but the difference between controlling modern airliners and Second World War heavy bombers quickly became apparent. 'The hairiest moment I've ever had is a loss of hydraulics, which is a very minuscule thing now as we have many back-up systems. In those days they didn't have any back-up systems, so the slightest problem could destroy an aircraft.'

It isn't just the technical differences which stand out. 'We're looking out of the window thinking, What a nice view! They would have been looking out of the window thinking, I hope we come back and we see it again.'

The airmen from Bomber Command were drawn not just from Britain but from across the world. Tanya Marriott, twenty-five, was born and brought up in New Zealand, but was keen to find out more about her grandfather. Tanya had barely known Fred Logan, who had been raised in a Devon seaside village before training as a mid-upper gunner. He had been part of the crew flying the last Lancaster to be shot down during the war. Following a divorce years later, the Logan family became separated, Tanya's grandmother moving to New Zealand while Logan remarried and stayed in Britain. Thousands of airmen had come from New Zealand in the 1940s, as well as from every other country in the Empire. It was part of a huge operation involving not only 125,000 airmen and the thousands of aircraft they flew, but the infrastructure that supported them: the ground staff and WAAFs running nearly a hundred stations, sending out several hundred aircraft each night; the aircraft factories; the training schools. The daunting size of the heavy bombers, of which the Avro Lancaster is the best known, was particularly striking for Tanya Marriott. 'I saw one as a kid, and things are supposed to get smaller as you get bigger, but this one's got bigger. It's the wheels that get me: they're my height, absolutely huge. It's a ton of weight when it takes off, and the aircraft doubles its weight when it's fully loaded.'

Ivor Chambers never flew the Lancaster, but was familiar with three other aircraft that were integral to Bomber Command: the Wellington, the Halifax and the Mosquito. His grandson, Tim Chambers, welcomed the opportunity to learn something about a grandfather who died long before he was born. At twenty-two, Tim is following in the family tradition of flying, having completed sixty hours as a pilot, but he's already older than Ivor Chambers was when he had completed his first tour of operations. The vintage Second World War aircraft, such as the Beech and Harvard, used for training during the war made an immediate impact on Tim, who had previously flown only on contemporary light aircraft. 'The smell is absolutely fantastic, like an old MG, and you smell the aviation fuel as they fire the engine up. With the sound, you know there's the power, and the feel of it is just really solid, although when you get onto the controls, they're very light and very precise. You feel the air and wind through the aircraft when you slide the canopy back just before coming in to land.'

Having familiarised themselves with the single- and twin-engine aircraft of the period, our twenty-first-century crew went on to experience flying in the four-engine heavy bombers. With only two airworthy Avro Lancasters left in the world, we chose to do much of our filming on 'Sally B', the last remaining airworthy Boeing B-17 Flying Fortress in Britain. Sally B has become an important symbol, not only of the USAAF's contribution to the bombing campaign in Europe, but also as a reminder of the close cooperation that existed between the USAAF and the RAF in the latter years of the war. While Bomber Command made some use of the B-17, it was the sight of the thousands of Flying Fortresses taking off from the USAAF's air bases in East Anglia which was the more familiar wartime sight. The USAAF also bore heavy losses, with around 26,000 of its airmen never returning.

Although John Nolan had known his grandfather, and indeed had been particularly close to him, it was only after his death that he learned some of the real detail of his wartime experience. When he was a child, John had been taken to the leading air museums by his grandfather, and they spent hours together as John learned about the principles of flight. It fostered a lifelong passion for aviation in John, twenty-five, who recently soloed in a Tiger Moth, the aircraft in which many Bomber Command pilots flew for the first time. But while Stephen had been happy to share with his grandson all the technical information at his disposal, this willingness didn't extend to talking about his own wartime experiences. 'If I asked him about an aerofoil section or what a trim tab did, he'd willingly explain it, and he'd explain what it felt like to fly the Mosquito or the Oxford or the Blenheim. But if I said to him, "Did you ever crash?" or asked for any anecdotes, he'd clam up, and it wasn't until he died that we found out a lot more about his flying career through his logbook and diaries.'

Those logbooks and diaries reveal a fascinating service career, first with the Coldstream Guards, and later in the RAF's Volunteer Reserve. His decision to join the air force had followed the evacuation from Dunkirk. John recalled his grandfather telling him that he hadn't wanted 'to sit at home waiting for the invasion'. Stephen Nolan had been particularly reticent about his last operation in April 1944. Having being briefed for a raid on Berlin, Nolan and his navigator had set off in their Mosquito, tanks full of fuel and loaded with 4,000 pounds of high-explosive bombs. As they taxied out to take off at their allotted time, the aircraft swerved and Nolan was unable to correct it. The wing tip hit the ground, causing the aircraft to burst into flames. Stephen Nolan was dragged unconscious from the aircraft just as its bombs exploded. Miraculously, both pilot and navigator survived, but the accident scarred Stephen Nolan for the rest of his life. His diary entry is a model of 1940s reserve, simply stating, 'Don't really want to fly Mozzies again, feeling a little rotten.' He came out of the RAF as quickly as he could, and despite having been an enthusiastic pilot had little to do with aviation for the rest of his life. It had been a brush with death too close for comfort.

While most airmen chose to keep their experiences very private, revealing little even to their closest family, Luke Alkemade's grandfather found himself in the public eye in the years after the war. Nicholas Alkemade had one of the most remarkable experiences to emerge from the war. Like thousands of other Lancaster crews flying over Germany, his was attacked by German fighters; their aircraft alight, the captain gave the crew the order to bale out. In the rear gun turret, Alkemade found himself unable to reach for his parachute beyond a wall of flame and faced a terrifying dilemma: either be burnt alive in the aircraft, or jump out from 18,000 feet and fall to a certain death. Alkemade chose to jump, and remarkably his fall was broken by the branches of fir trees covered in thick snow below. Against all the odds, he had survived. It was a story familiar to Luke Alkemade, now a chef, who was aware that the experience of baling out from a burning aircraft changed his grandfather considerably.

I know that after the war my granddad was haunted for quite a time. He had nightmares, and a bad shrapnel wound on his leg that caused a lot of pain for a long time afterwards. When he came back from Stalag Luft III, he was something of a celebrity. A lot of people wanted to speak to him but I think that affected him, and it was very hard to deal with the fact that out of all this rubble and death came some kind of celebrity status. After the things that he'd seen, he didn't consider himself such a special man.

As our contemporary crew became familiar with the aircraft and equipment of the time, and learned more about the role of Bomber Command, the respect they already had for their grandfathers only deepened. Luke Alkemade's reaction was typical. 'The things that we have done have definitely enlightened me as far as the skills and stresses that they must have been put under. Even firing a Browning machine gun, for instance; I would never have thought that it would have been so loud and so powerful.'

They also quickly discovered that being in a bomber crew involved a lot more than flying skills, in themselves demanding enough on the four-engine heavy bombers. If a crew was going to survive a tour of thirty operations, teamwork was crucial. As James Smith realised, 'They knew they were all there to help each other, to keep each other alive.'

So all five came to appreciate, as never before, not just what it was their grandfathers had done, but also what a generation had contributed to securing victory over Nazism, and the sacrifices that had been made. Tim Chambers is full of admiration for the Bomber Boys. 'There's been a chequered press on Bomber Command but people need to look back and realise that you need to sometimes make very hard decisions, and it's not always as black and white as people think. Thousands and thousands of men and women gave their lives so we can live how we live today. It's just a fantastic thing they did.'

What follows are the stories of the men who fought alongside these five grandfathers and, through them, the stories of the many thousands who never made it back home to start families of their own. They did not set out to be heroes; they were just ordinary young men, many of whom volunteered to serve when they were just eighteen or nineteen years old. Yet what the airmen of Bomber Command endured and achieved during these five and a half years of war was extraordinary, and an integral part of the Second World War.

1

Advent of the Bomber

'The bomber will always get through.
The only defence is in offence.'

Stanley Baldwin, November 1932

Ricky Dyson in 1936, shortly after joining the RAF. Initially he was ground staff, but would later serve as a rear air gunner.

It was only his seventh operation. Alan E. Bryett, a twenty-one-year-old bomb aimer, was approaching the target along with the other six members of his Halifax crew. Their target that night of 23/24 August 1943 was Berlin, the capital and epicentre of Hitler's Germany. Bryett and his crew were becoming confident practitioners in the bombing raids that were taking the war to the Nazi homeland. They had already taken part in the raid on Peenemünde, a research establishment on the Baltic coast, where scientists had been developing and testing the V2, a deadly new form of rocket bomb. They had helped bomb the city of Hamburg, a raid that had produced the deadly 'firestorm' that had devastated great swathes of the city. They had even bombed Italy, flying in a raid on Milan that had contributed to the eventual Italian surrender.

Four years into the war, Bomber Command was finally beginning to fulfil the war-winning promises made by its supporters. It had been a long time coming. At the start of 1942, the bombing campaign had looked in tatters. The Butt Report, commissioned in late 1941 to investigate the efficacy of the early bombing raids, had merely confirmed what everyone already knew. The RAF's bombers were too slow, too small and too often lost to deliver any real and lasting damage. Within six months, Bomber Command had been overhauled. It had a new commander, Arthur Harris, blunt, focused and entirely unsqueamish about what would need to be done to make bombing Nazi Germany work. By the end of the war, few Allied commanders would be able to take such personal and, in the end, controversial credit for so much physical and widespread damage inflicted on the enemy.

Bomber Command also had a new aircraft, the peerless Avro Lancaster, which could fly higher, longer and with more bombs than any of its rivals. Soon there would be better navigational aids too, such as *Gee*, which meant that Bomber Command now had the wherewithal to find its targets with more than just educated guesswork. The blindfold that had so hampered the early raids was off. So too were the early restraints. Harris wasted no time in bringing it all together in his first headline-grabbing 'Thousand Bomber Raid', the first real indication to the world that British bombing was here to stay, and that entire cities would now become his battlefield.

Nowhere provided as decisive a target as Berlin. The symbolism was potent; so too was the belief that a genuine blow could be struck against the Nazi leadership, and its government apparatus. So as Alan Bryett made his approach, he knew the significance of the task that lay ahead of him. As Berlin drew closer, it was time for Bryett to prepare for the bombing run. It would be his job, as bomb aimer, to take command of the aircraft, directing the pilot on the course to take, ensuring as accurate a bomb drop as possible; 'Left-left, right, steady' were the commands he would bark over the intercom. It was always 'Left-left', never simply 'Left'; repetition of the words, scrambled by interference and assailed by the noise of engines and flak, would help prevent the pilot misunderstanding his instructions. As the Halifax came within about 50 miles of the target, Bryett got himself ready for the bombing run, the climax of what would be a ten-hour operation.

Within about fifty miles, you put your parachute on because if you were going to have to use it, it was going to be over the target. You'd already have your parachute harness on. The parachute harness was rather like a Victorian lady's corset and the actual parachute was like a small suitcase. You had two hooks in the front of the harness you'd got on and you clipped the parachute onto the hooks. You couldn't have the parachute hooked on to you while you were flying because you could hardly move around the very cramped space.

Having secured his parachute in place, Bryett manoeuvred himself into position.

I would move down into the front of the plane and I would lay on my belly and get the bomb sight ready. The navigator would be feeding me the wind direction and the pilot would be giving me his speed. Within four or five minutes I would see that we were moving towards Berlin. The navigator would say, 'Are we all right moving for the target?' I'd reply, 'Yes, that's fine, we're doing fine.' Then the navigator would say, 'Four minutes and we shall be over the target, bomb aimer, four minutes,' and he'd give perhaps a slight variation of wind or the pilot would give us a slight variation of height. The last part would be visual, because the Pathfinders, who were the very exclusive, very experienced bombers, had gone ahead and had dropped markers, rather like huge fireworks on the ground.

The Pathfinders had been another key innovation of 1942. They were an elite force designed specifically to drop not bombs but flares that would help guide the main force to the correct target, especially in conditions of poor visibility. This was bomber flying at its most demanding, both of navigators, who of course would have no flares to guide *them*, and of pilots, who needed to be capable of flying their Lancasters and Mosquitoes at very low levels to guarantee the accuracy of the target markers. Their role was vital. All too often, the only thing visible to the main force would be these Pathfinder flares, lighting up the carpets of cloud that all too often utterly obscured the targets from those flying 20,000 feet up. There was even a complex system of colours to guide the main force all the way in.

At the briefing we would have been told, for example, to make for the green markers which would be on the northern part of the city. I would say, 'I can see the green markers,' and begin to position the pilot up and he would fly towards the green markers and I would be saying, 'Left-left', and get him on to the target. Then 'Steady-steady', and once you were on steady he would keep you on that. He didn't want to stay on steady for too long because you were very vulnerable to the German fighters who might be watching you, and while you were flying straight and level you were going to be shot down. So you'd steady-steady for as short a time as possible and then you'd press the button. 'Bombs gone!' and at that point he would quickly move away, and move out of his height level.

Having dropped the bomb load, crews would now aim to get away from the target area as quickly as possible.

I would come away from the bomb-aiming position, and go up to my seat which was second at the side of the pilot. You'd race away from the target because you knew the German fighters were all round. They were above you and you couldn't see them. You'd hear the anti-aircraft fire and by then the secret was given away where we were bombing, so German night fighters from the surrounding bases would be making towards Berlin. You were really in dead trouble if you didn't get safely well away.

No crew was totally safe until it had landed back on its home base, but for Bryett and his crew at least the worst should soon be over. The bombing had been completed, the aircraft was mercifully lighter, and therefore more manoeuvrable. Now it would be a race back the way they had come.

It was a case of 'Let's get away, let's get back to England, bacon and eggs, quickly as we can.' 'Give us a course for home, navigator', and there was an air of exuberance. We were always warned not to let the exuberance take over because by that time the German fighter defences knew exactly where you'd bombed. They knew you were going back to the eastern part of England, they knew roughly what your course was going to be, and you'd got to be on the alert the whole time.

In fact, it was the most dangerous part of any raid, even successful ones, and this was no exception. Already Bryett's crew could see that some of the other bombers were in trouble. 'A number of aeroplanes were damaged, not necessarily grievously but they were damaged, over the target, and they had one hell of a long way to come back. You had to fly back over the North Sea, which is a very inhospitable place and a huge sea to fly over if you've lost an engine.'

But they didn't have the luxury of simply watching these dramas unfurl; they too faced very real dangers, not least the sobering fact that attacking Berlin required one of the longest journeys home. Over 600 miles separated them from safety, and even on heavy bombers such as the Halifax and Lancaster such distances required careful calculation.

'As you began to get away from the target, the flight engineer's job was really watching the dials and making sure that you'd got your petrol. He was feeding information through to the navigator that your petrol tanks were all right, and the navigator would be saying to the pilot, "Fly on, sir, we've got enough petrol to get us back home to base, flying at X speed," and everyone was still very much on the alert but not slacking off.'

There would be no bacon and eggs for Alan Bryett that morning, however. 'It was at that point where we were moving away that the searchlight caught us.'

Searchlights terrified bomber crews, and in Berlin the searchlights were at their most intense. For Bryett the contrast with other targets he'd seen was immediately apparent.

The one thing which I found really quite worrying as you got towards Berlin was that there seemed to be hundreds of searchlights on the ground. They were flicking across the sky, just waiting, knowing that there were hundreds of aircraft, about eight hundred aircraft in a raid timed over twenty-five minutes. It was extremely difficult to get out of a searchlight. If one searchlight caught you, they were coordinated on the ground and within a matter of three or four seconds, we found we'd got five or six searchlights coordinated by telephone on the ground, all onto us.

Bryett and his crew now found themselves exposed to the enemy, and unable to escape the startling power of the searchlights. 'You were in a thick band of light, maybe six or eight hundred feet thick. The band of light was quite terrifying because you felt naked, you felt as though you were in a crowd of people in the middle of Piccadilly Circus and you were the only person there who was completely naked. You knew everyone there was looking at you, and all going to have a go at you.'

Lit up by the searchlights, this aircraft was now easy prey for the German night fighters circling around Berlin. Bryett knew only too well what would happen next. 'All of us knew within a matter of seconds that the German fighters above us were going to start diving down, realising that we were all virtually blinded by this terrible white light, and that was quite alarming. You could look out but you couldn't really see anything.'

It was essential to try to get out of the searchlights, and there was one tactic that could save them. The rear gunner shouted, 'Corkscrew.' A corkscrew was the most violent and desperate manoeuvre in the bomber pilot's arsenal; the instant he heard the word, he would throw his control column as far to the side as it would go, sending his aircraft into a vertiginous dive to right or left, twisting like a corkscrew, often repeating it three, four, even a dozen times if necessary, to shake themselves clear of either searchlight or probing night fighter. Rivets would scream in protest, but there was no room for tentativeness in executing the corkscrew. It required brute strength – there was no power assistance to help the pilot – nerves of steel and great skill not to simply plough into the ground or flip the aircraft over. For the rest of the crew there was nothing for it but to grab onto the nearest handhold, and try not to be sick.

On this occasion, though, it wasn't enough. The beam of light was too broad, and the hold it had acquired on the Halifax too tight for the corkscrew manoeuvre to evade. For six operations Bryett's crew had succeeded in slipping through the cordon of night fighters, but now, lit up by the searchlight, they were a sitting duck. Nothing had prepared them for what came next.

The next thing we knew, the German fighters were coming, spraying the aeroplane with incendiary bullets. When we were over Milan, we saw a German night fighter which came quite close to us and turned away! Over Berlin the operation before we were coned, you could see one or two night fighters. But the only night fighter we really saw close up was the one that shot us down, which came in remarkably close. The fighters were blacked out, but you saw the effects of them inasmuch as a plane would be shot down. You'd hear a machine gun going and see an RAF plane being shot down, but you didn't really see the fighters, only if it was too late.

Bryett remembers the moment of the attack vividly.

The sound in the aircraft when you're attacked is terrifically loud. You've got the noise of the engine, which is pretty deafening anyway, and which even affects speaking between crew members, but the noise of the anti-aircraft guns and the noise of the German shells from the fighters is quite terrific. It's the noise of absolute mayhem, which isn't too worrying until you realise that some of this mayhem is actually doing your aeroplane damage and there's a little fire coming up here and another fire there. The pilot is desperately trying to move the aeroplane about to get out of range of the fighter which is firing at you.

The pilot was unable to escape, with terrible consequences for the crew. 'The two gunners were killed, and then three of the fellows went out on parachutes fairly quickly. It was obvious the aeroplane was doomed. The pilot and myself were left in an aircraft which was burning furiously and losing height rapidly, spiralling to the ground from twenty thousand feet.'

There was no option now for Bryett, who was still barely old enough to vote, but to escape from the aircraft himself. Even though he had taken the precaution of putting his parachute on, just getting out of a Halifax was a Herculean struggle.

I got to the escape hatch but I couldn't get it open. It was a trapdoor rather like the trapdoor you have in the loft of a house and it was jammed. The pilot came down from his controls, got the escape hatch opened and pushed me out saying, 'I'm coming.' By then we were perilously low. We knew we were low but we didn't know how low. I pulled my parachute cord, and my parachute opened. I was on the parachute for two or three seconds before I landed in something soft, which seemed like bushes. I was still blinded by the searchlights. When my sight came back after maybe twenty minutes, to my horror I found I was in a forest of trees about eighty feet up and the plane had crashed quite near by. Eventually I got down to the ground with some difficulty. I didn't break anything, but I was badly covered in blood. I got to the ground and the trees had broken my fall. I landed, but the aeroplane had crashed and the pilot hadn't got out. He got me out but he couldn't get out.

The horror of that occasion has never left Bryett's mind. Over sixty years later, he is only too aware of how a pilot saved his life, but sacrificed his own to do so. 'The pilot couldn't get out, he couldn't pull his parachute and he couldn't save his life and he gave his life for me. It's something I think about every day. The whole of the last sixty years is through him, in that one moment of time, when he did what all captains of aircraft would do. He saved his crew but he lost his own life.'

It wasn't supposed to be like this. It was a time when the reality of war was learned only through the experience. For the airmen of Bomber Command, mostly in their early twenties, some still in their teens, a blind self-confidence had masked the appalling fate that all too possibly awaited them. Of course the airmen knew that there were losses, considerable losses. They knew that they were risking their lives, but quite simply they believed it was never going to happen to them.

> It never struck me that we were going to be shot down. When you were flying on operations, you would see aeroplanes shot down by anti-aircraft fire or by German fighters and it was always the attitude 'Poor chap, but it's not us, so don't worry too much about it.' I think the real point of the seriousness of it happened when we were over Berlin and the rear gunner shouted out 'Corkscrew' to the pilot and the aeroplane was riddled with incendiary bullets. The rear gunner was killed and the mid-upper gunner was gravely injured and there were about ten little fires going on all over that Halifax aircraft, because every incendiary bullet had started a fire. At that point the seriousness and the horror of it hit very suddenly, but up to that point I would say that it was always the attitude that not many people finished a tour of operations but we were going to be the ones who did. Our morale was high and we were doing all the right things and we were cautious and careful and were keeping our eyes open and we were going to be the ones that finished a tour.

Alan Bryett didn't finish his tour. Instead, like nearly ten thousand other Bomber Command airmen, he would spend the rest of the war in a prisoner-of-war camp. Perhaps Stanley Baldwin had been wrong, then. Maybe the bomber *didn't* always get through.

The prospect of bombs falling on civilian population areas had terrified Britain since the end of the First World War. It hadn't taken many years after the epic ingenuity of the Wright Brothers had created man's first powered flight in 1903 for the aeroplane to be turned into a forbidding weapon of war. As early as 1908, H. G. Wells was prophesying catastrophic aerial warfare in *The War in the Air*. It was only science fiction, and must have seemed a far-fetched notion to most of his readers, few of whom would have appreciated that they would see many of his predictions come true during their lifetimes. By 1912, the aeroplane was being used in army manoeuvres. In a war game exercise played out in East Anglia, an airship and twenty-four aircraft were deployed by officers to identify groups of 'enemy' troops and predict their movements. It was clear to the Director of Military Operations that the new technology of air power could be of great assistance in any future conflict. In a memorandum, he wrote, 'There can no longer be any doubt as to the value of airships and aeroplanes in locating an enemy on land and obtaining information which could otherwise only be obtained by force ... Though aircraft will probably have several uses in war, their primary duty is searching for information.'

During the First World War, the use of air power would indeed be pretty much limited to obtaining information and observing the enemy, as had been predicted, but nevertheless a handful of pilots engaging in dogfights acquired a reputation for the fledgling RAF of heroism and gallantry. There were rapid developments in the technology, making the aircraft faster, sturdier and more reliable, while the weapons they carried became more powerful. What began the war as a modest Royal Flying Corps, boasting just sixty-two aircraft in 1914, became the Royal Air Force of 1918, a complex organisation of around 300,000 men with 22,000 aeroplanes and 100 airships at their disposal. In a war that was characterised by the bloody stalemate of the trenches, air power represented chivalry and honour, and a series of quick and transparent victories over the enemy.

Yet the First World War also gave the first glimpses of a far more sinister employment of air power, a terrible forewarning of what was to come. The first bombs to be dropped by aircraft had in fact fallen before the Great War, during the Italo-Turkish war of 1911, when spherical bombs were dropped on Turkish troops controlling Ain Zaia, a town in Libya. Despite causing no injuries, and making little impact on the town, these very first air raids were seen as a particularly dastardly departure from civilised notions of the conduct of war, and there were howls of public outcry. A few years later considerations of 'gentlemanliness' were even less apparent. In January 1915, German Zeppelin airships, followed by Gotha and Giant bombers, began a bombing campaign on British cities and coastal towns that petrified their civilian populations. In a series of 103 raids, a total of 1,413 people were killed, all but 300 of them civilians, and around 3,500 were injured. In one particularly shocking incident in 1917, a daylight raid on the centre of London killed eighteen children in a school in Poplar.

The legacy of these raids was immense. For the British, the experience had been utterly traumatic, going far beyond the actual numbers of those injured and killed. Aircraft and bombs represented a whole new order of wartime horror. In the years after the war the concept of the strategic destruction of cities by large bombers became an RAF priority, even an obsession. The image of smashed London homes, and lines of burnt corpses, was a terrible omen of things to come. The result would be the creation not only of Bomber Command, but also of the four-engine heavies that would come to dominate Allied air power in the next war. The Germans, however, drew very different lessons from the episode. They saw the raids as largely ineffectual. The damage caused had been slight, the Zeppelins unwieldy and unconvincing war-winners. The Luftwaffe would be encouraged to take a very different course when, during the 1930s, it came to rearm. Their bombers would be twin-engine, medium-range machines whose job would be to support the army in Blitzkrieg attacks, not on their own to reduce enemy nations to smouldering rubble. They never built large bombers, and would find their own attempts at area bombing during the Blitz highly hampered by this fact.

Throughout the 1920s, therefore, the British would routinely make more and more alarming predictions about the future power of bombing. In 1925 the Air Staff forecast the possible consequences of prolonged aerial warfare, and suggested that a raid on London would produce 1,700 dead and 3,300 injured in the first twenty-hour period of conflict alone. Bombing would become central to all future wars. In a report for the Cabinet on air organisation, Lieutenant General Jan Smuts, later prime minister in South Africa, summed up the fear: 'The day may not be far off when aerial operations with their devastation of enemy lands and destruction of industrial and populous centres on a vast scale may become the principal operations of war, to which the older forms of military and naval operations may become secondary and subordinate.'

Such predictions did not translate, however, into substantial investment in the RAF. After 1918, the RAF was reduced in size considerably and left with just thirty-three squadrons. The public mood hardly favoured maintaining the high levels of military expenditure that had been necessary over the previous four years, and besides, there were many other demands on a post-war economy that dictated frugality as far as the air force was concerned. Nevertheless, one man continued to advocate the importance of air power. Hugh Trenchard, who had been instrumental in turning the Royal Flying Corps into the Royal Air Force, spent ten years as Chief of the Air Staff after the First World War. He remains widely admired to this day by the veterans of Bomber Command, and Robin Murray, who served as a front air gunner on Wellingtons, is typical in his reverence: 'Trenchard was virtually father of the Royal Air Force. He thought up the boy entrance scheme and virtually the whole of the training system, which was very hit and miss in the early days, but at least they were getting somewhere. He thought up the various volunteer schemes which meant that he'd got a nucleus of people he could call on, who were educated up to a certain standard.'

It was Trenchard who set up the RAF as an independent entity, the first time an air force had been created anywhere in the world with the intention of conducting an air war without reference or subordination to army or navy command. The RAF had quickly established a diversity of roles for itself, far beyond the scope of observing the enemy, which had been the primary aim of the airborne forces just four years previously. Defence against enemy aircraft was clearly one objective, but so too was the strategic bombing of Germany. In June 1918, Trenchard established the Independent Air Force, a sub-section of the RAF, with a remit to bomb Germany's industrial cities, and during 1918, 5,500 tons of bombs were dropped on the enemy, setting the precedent for the RAF as a bomber, as well as a fighter, force. In the years that followed the Armistice, Trenchard provided the RAF with a more permanent foundation and infrastructure than had been possible during the war. A training college for pilots was established at Cranwell, while technical colleges were set up at Halton, Cranwell and Flowerdown. One of the few politicians who encouraged him was Winston Churchill, Secretary of State for War and Air from 1919 to 1921, but as so often in the inter-war years, Churchill was something of a lone voice at Westminster. Trenchard may have been fêted for his role, and raised to the peerage in 1930 shortly after his retirement, but he was not supported in resources. The 1920s saw the RAF struggle to survive, short of men and equipment, and even though governments made commitments to improve the RAF's capability for home defence, investment didn't follow at the levels promised.

By the mid-1930s, however, it was becoming clear that such stagnation was no longer an option. Everyone knew that when the next war came it would come from the air, and the next war started to look less like a distant nightmare. The RAF was restructured in 1936 into four separate command units: Fighter Command, Bomber Command, Coastal Command and Training Command. While Fighter and Coastal Commands' roles would be essentially defensive, it would fall to Bomber Command to be an offensive unit. As politicians played the appeasement card publicly, not least to postpone conflict until the country had had time to prepare, the RAF set out on a massive expansion programme. New aircraft were introduced, including a new generation of medium bombers such as the Wellington, the

Hampden and the Whitley, and thousands more men were recruited. In the Air Ministry, Arthur Harris was a key advocate of the importance of going farther even than this, urging the development of heavy bombers, recognising that the medium bombers would not in the long term be up to the job.

Bombing, though, remained a shocking tactic. Stanley Baldwin, Britain's former (and future) Prime Minister, summed up the worst-case scenario during a House of Commons debate in November 1932: 'It is as well for the man in the street to realise that there is no power on earth that can protect him from being bombed. Whatever people may tell him, the bomber will always get through. The only defence is in offence, which means that you have to kill more women and children more quickly than the enemy if you want to save yourselves.'

This was the encapsulation of what most considered an ungentlemanly method of conducting warfare. The fear, though, persisted, indeed was growing. The world had already witnessed the Japanese bombing of Shanghai in 1932. Not long afterwards, and closer to home, the Spanish Civil War followed, during which the Nazi Condor Legion destroyed Guernica, a small town of 7,000 inhabitants in the Basque province of Vizcaya. In a three-hour raid in April 1937, explosive bombs and incendiaries destroyed the town, including many of its civilian population, who had been thronging its centre on market day. The assumption was that in a war against Hitler's Germany the indiscriminate bombing of British population centres would be part and parcel of a German war plan, just as it had been in the Great War. This time, though, the bombs would be delivered not by dirigibles, but by armadas of Heinkels and Dorniers. It was not yet anticipated that the British and their allies would reciprocate.

Indeed, exactly what Bomber Command's role might be was still not entirely clear. It was only with the drawing up of the Western Air Plans, agreed by the Air Ministry in 1937, that certain priorities emerged. For Bomber Command, this meant attacking the enemy air force, supporting the army by targeting communications behind the front line, and striking at the heart of wartime industrial production, particularly in the Ruhr area. Under Sir Edgar Ludlow-Hewitt, appointed commander-in-chief of Bomber Command in September 1937, it was the last of these priorities which would be most important, as senior RAF officers agreed that it was the only one likely to have any real success. A list of specific targets was soon drawn up, but both the British and French agreed that bombing civilians was out of the question.

As the Air Ministry considered its strategy in the event of the increasingly likely war against Germany, many of those who would fly with Bomber Command were blissfully unaware of the fate awaiting them. For them, flying was simply the most exciting thing about the age they lived in. The combination of the heroic adventures of First World War flying aces they read about in every comic, and the highly publicised advances in aeronautical technology, was irresistible. Arthur Smith, later a bomb aimer on Halifaxes, was one of the boys caught up by this enthusiasm.

When I was very young, must have been about four years old, I got really interested in trains, aeroplanes and steamrollers, which I used to call steamer-roller-puffers, and as I grew up and went to school, aeroplanes meant everything for me really. At the age of about fifteen, I started getting flight magazines every week, which I did for many, many years, and I used to draw aircraft if I got a chance. I'd go to the Handley Page aerodrome, which was near me. When the war came in 1939, I was still at school. I had another year or two to go but I knew exactly what I was going to do. I said to myself, Right, I'm going to learn to fly a Spitfire and shoot down Messerschmitts. So once I left school at the age of eighteen, I volunteered for the RAF, and started initial training to be a pilot.

Maurice Flower was similarly fascinated.

When I was about eleven, we moved to a little village and about twice a week this old aeroplane used to fly over the top. It used to intrigue me. It was a First World War biplane, and it turned out the pilot was a gentleman farmer, and he used to fly around his farms in Yorkshire and Northumberland. Later on, the celebrated pilot Alan Cobham and his flying circus came to a little village just near us. I went there and it was five shillings to fly in an Avro 504, and I had 4s 6d! I went to the lady and she said, 'You get in the five-bob queue!' That flight was about fifteen minutes and it was the thrill of a lifetime. Most people wouldn't have gone in an aeroplane at that time; my father never even drove a car. After that, I used to cycle to the RAF station at Usworth, near Sunderland, and sit with a friend outside the fence watching the old biplanes trundling up and down. We got to be quite well known there. One day, a flight sergeant came across and talked to us and he brought us a cup of tea from the NAAFI wagon and we were sort of regulars after that.

The great novelty of flying, and the new technology of flight, were encapsulated in Arthur Smith's imagination by the aircraft themselves. 'I should think today the aircraft look rickety and old fashioned, but of course we thought at that time that they were marvellous. We looked back to the First World War, which I read a lot about as a boy, and those planes were just it, the latest thing.'

It was clear to Smith which of the services he'd choose should he ever need to fight in a war.

The thing that appealed to me was to get into a Spitfire and fly like mad, shooting down Germans. I said to myself, Shooting down Messerschmitts; I didn't think I was shooting down a person, I was shooting down an aircraft. It didn't make an immediate impact that I might be killing someone. What did make an impact was that I wouldn't have volunteered to be a soldier because I thought I'd have to fight in the trenches with a bayonet, and I thought I could never have enough courage to charge an enemy with a bayonet.

The contrast between the bloody trench warfare the army had endured in the First World War and the gallantry of the flying aces was not lost on many young boys in the 1930s. For this generation, the spectre of the First World War had hung over their lives, casting a long and bloody shadow. Many of the boys who would later serve with Bomber Command remembered only too well the shattered, despondent expressions on the faces of their fathers when war was declared. Anything would be better than the blood-soaked quagmire of trench-war stalemate, and bombers promised to provide that deliverance. Robert Kee, later a pilot on Hampdens, was convinced as a young man that aerial warfare offered the promise of a shorter war. 'The main consideration in the 1930s was if there had to be war again, and it began to seem possible after 1936 when Hitler moved into the Rhineland, there mustn't be the casualties we had in the First World War. I think that's often forgotten, because my parents lived under the sense of horror of the casualties there had been among their friends and some of their relations.'

Like many of those who would fight on the front lines of the Second World War, Robin Murray had lost his father in the trenches of Flanders.

I don't remember my father at all as he was killed in 1916. He should never really have joined up. He had very bad eyesight but he joined up, I suppose with an excess of zeal, when they asked for sportsmen to join up to make the sportsmen battalions. They were going to man the home stations to allow the fit men to go to the front. But it didn't work out that way, he was just a number as far as the army was concerned and he was called up. He was in the Royal West Kent Regiment, and sent to the front. But without his glasses he couldn't see his hand in front of him. After the battle of the Somme he was reported missing. He has no known grave and he is one of the fifty thousand with no known grave on the memorial at the Menin Gate. He left behind my mother with three children to bring up.

Although Murray says he wasn't conscious of his father's experience influencing him, he acknowledges that it probably did subconsciously, and in 1938 he joined the Volunteer Reserve. 'I don't think there was any feeling of revenge, but at the back of my mind possibly that I should join up. One felt one ought to join up. But I can't imagine how my sisters must have felt when they got the letter saying I was shot down, having remembered the letter that my mother got, when my father was shot down.'

The RAF Volunteer Reserve had been established in July 1936 in response to the RAF's manpower shortage. In 1934, the RAF had only 30,000 men, with a further 11,000 reservists in the Auxiliary Air Force. It was clearly not going to be enough, and so a massive expansion programme was put in place, but this strained the RAF's capacity for recruitment and training, hence the introduction of the Volunteer Reserve. In three years, the scheme produced over 6,000 pilots, and many other airmen who would be crucial to Bomber Command's wartime strength. By 1939, the RAF had not only 118,000 regular members to call on, but 68,000 reservists as well.

It wasn't just a passion for flying, though, which helped the RAF boost its numbers. When John Holmes joined in 1935, his motives were very different.

> There was a massive depression in the country. There was very little work. I'd just finished my time as an apprentice motor engineer and my employer was not prepared to take me on as an improver, so I had to look around, and a friend of mine and I went down to Plymouth to join the navy, which we didn't do in the end. So the reason was purely economic. It looked like a good firm to belong to and it transpired that it was, except that they didn't tell us there was going to be a war.

It was only by chance that Holmes joined the RAF rather than the Royal Navy. His bid for a seafaring career came to an abrupt end with the compulsory dental examination. When it was discovered that he had had a filling, he was failed. The RAF was recruiting at the time, and was less rigorous in its recruitment criteria, so Holmes finished up an airman. By the start of the war, he would be serving as an observer, but in these early days he had no intention of becoming aircrew and started his life in the RAF training for the ground crew.

> I set off purely as a tradesman. I had no intentions of flying for quite some time and I realised promotion was so terribly slow in the pre-war air force. Getting from being an AC2 to an AC1 was done by examination, and then from AC1 to LAC by trade examination. It would take an LAC anything up to five years to get his corporal stripes, and so it didn't look as if I was going to get very far very fast. Then there was an opportunity to move, as by chance they were asking for observers, so I took the chance. But flying is something I never have liked. I didn't get that much of a thrill out of it but again economics were the motive. I got my sergeant's stripes on the strength of it very quickly.

Despite his love of aircraft and flying, Maurice Flower also initially joined as ground crew, in his case as a way of escaping grammar school. 'I was never happy at grammar school, but I was fifteen and my mother would never ever allow me to go into the air force or to leave home for that matter. The local vicar helped me apply for the aircraft apprenticeship at Holton and he fiddled it so that I sat the examination in his study, instead of having to go to Newcastle.'

Joining the RAF was also a way of avoiding an otherwise uncertain future.

> Up in Durham there were the mines and the Co-op where my father worked, and there wasn't much else. There was my grand-father's farm but that was well staffed. So there was no hope apart from the mines. My grandfather was an under-manager at the colliery and he said, 'I don't think you'll do for the mines at all, but I'll take you down.' So we went down to the bottom of the shaft and I said, 'You can take me back up again!' That's

as far as I ever went in mining, I couldn't understand anybody lying on their backs hacking away at a coal seam. The air force really was a way of changing my whole life. I was just interested in the aeroplanes and joined as a fitter to air frames as an apprentice. The apprenticeship was originally for three years but the war broke out and they reduced it to two. There were about two thousand of us and I did about a year at Holton and a year at Gosford.

Flower may have had little encouragement from his mother, but Richard Dyson's actively encouraged him to join up, which he did at the end of 1935.

I was very unsettled at home. My mother was more or less on her deathbed. My father had a piano business in Windsor, but it was the depression, and the wireless was coming in, and the piano trade was very badly affected. Lord Trenchard's expansion of the RAF was greatly advertised in the local press and my mother wrote for more information. The RAF offered an exciting career to young people with imagination and a flair to do daring things, and an ideal way to travel.

Working with the still relatively primitive technology of aircraft, John Holmes found that the role of ground staff was essential in the pre-war years, as it would be throughout the war. 'They couldn't fly without us. An aeroplane is a rather delicate thing. It's reduced in weight to the minimum so that everything is stretched to the limit, but there was a close examination of the aircraft every day. If you make a mistake somebody dies, it's as simple as that.'

In the pre-war era, the ground crew even got the opportunity to fly, something of a novelty for working-class men in an age when aircraft were still rare, and those who had the chance to fly them seemed to come from an elite club.

It was exciting and quite an experience. It looked interesting, and as I was deeply involved in keeping the things flying I thought it wouldn't be a bad idea to see what it feels like to take a ride or two. In those days it was a firm ruling in the RAF in any case that if you worked on an aircraft, you flew in it. The reason is obvious: if you haven't done a good job, you aren't going to fly in it if you can help it and that was a strict ruling. Either fitters or riggers, if you did a job of work on an aeroplane and every so often even if you didn't do a repair, your pilot would expect you to go and fly with him, just to instil confidence.

For Holmes, that first time in the air was a memorable occasion, his own role in the aircraft's safety implicit in his reaction. 'I was scared! I'd just put a wing on an aeroplane and I couldn't remember whether I'd put the split pins in. So I was scared. Taking off was a bit bumpy in those days, the old aeroplanes were not quite as smooth as the later heavily powered ones, and it was all very interesting but I was mainly concerned whether this particular wing was going to remain where I'd put it and as it did, it was a successful trip.'

Having completed his first flight, Holmes made quick progress as a member of the ground staff. The pre-war air force that he'd joined offered a regimented, but relaxed, existence.

We got up at 6.30 a.m., went to breakfast at 7.30, had a cere-monial parade of the whole station at 8.30. We went to work at nine, stopped at 10.30 for tea and buns, knocked off at twelve for lunch until two. Went back at two and worked until four and anybody in the air after four that we couldn't get down and get into the hangar and get the drip trays underneath was in dead trouble. Weekends they didn't fly at all. Night-times they didn't fly. We had two short weekends and one long weekend every month. The short weekend was Saturday lunchtime till Sunday midnight and the long weekend was Friday night till Monday morning. We had one weekend in every month that we had to remain on duty where we had a church parade and a kit inspection. We had twenty-eight days' leave a year, as well as three five-day breaks, almost like bank holidays, which added another fifteen days to your leave. We did do some night flying once at Netheravon and it was the biggest circus you've ever seen in your life. Nobody had done any night flying for years, we had no idea at all. This was in 1936/37 and they couldn't find the matches to light the goose-neck flares for a start! They were mainly concerned with whether they could get a vehicle to put the tea urn on for the airmen's midnight break, and the only illuminations the aircraft had were flares under the wings. If they wanted to use the flares for landing, they had to fire the flares but once they'd fired them they had to keep going and they had to taxi and taxi and taxi until they went out, otherwise they'd set fire to the wing. It was a circus, but a very enjoyable circus. I was having the time of my life.

There was, of course, a strict and complex hierarchy dictating behaviour and interaction between commissioned officers, non-commissioned officers and other ranks. John Holmes quickly discovered that officers commanded considerable respect.

You wouldn't lay hands on an officer, you wouldn't put your hand on his shoulder if you were talking to him. You would not touch an officer because he was wearing the King's uniform and you did not touch an officer. But we liked it that way because we all knew exactly where we stood. When I went to Upwood, which was my first posting as an observer of No. 63 Squadron, we lived in the sergeants' mess. If a corporal wanted to speak to a sergeant he went round the back, he did not go in the front door, it wasn't allowed. Even a warrant officer, if he required to speak to an officer, would go to the rear door, the domestic door, and be directed from there. It was extremely strict and in this day and age would be considered to be archaic but that's how discipline was bred and that's why men would do what they did. Some nights, I sat in my flight office and watched young aircrew go off, knowing full well that I'd be lucky if I saw 50 per cent of them back again. But they went, that was their job; they were asked to go and they went. And it all started from the old-fashioned way – an officer was an officer, an NCO was an NCO and an airman was an airman, that's the way it had to be.

Despite the apparent organisation, though, Holmes felt that the RAF was far from being prepared for the oncoming war, even given the progress that had been made in the 1930s. 'It was archaic. They were still living in the First World War in every way. They couldn't see any farther than formation flying and they hadn't made any provision for dealing with the German air force as far as I could see.'

By this stage, Holmes had got frustrated with his role in the ground crew and volunteered for aircrew. Unlike many airmen, however, it wasn't a yearning for flying which was instrumental in the decision.

It was a good life and I went flying simply because it was a well-paid, easy life compared with any other form of service life. You avoided most of the chores – guard commander, fire picket, things like that. It was comparatively a gentleman's life, keeping in mind that aircrew largely up to that point had been officers so if you were moved into the sergeants' mess, you started to lead a life which was slightly similar to the life of an officer, which consisted of largely doing nothing!

Holmes found his suspicions that the RAF was far from being prepared for the outbreak of war confirmed by his experience of training for aircrew.

The training didn't prepare us for war in any shape or form. We were still living in the dark ages of the end of the First World War, but the whole thing had become glamorised over the years and they'd forgotten the nasty bits. People didn't seem to have the vaguest notion at all. The civilian population hadn't got the faintest idea what they were in for and we thought it was a huge joke. We thought it was going to be fun, going to bomb things using real bombs.

The training was pretty limited.

When I first passed out as an observer and went on to the squadrons, we were restricted to ten hours' flying a month to save petrol. That was it! Night flying? I think in my logbook I did one trip in Battles at night. We were map reading still, navigation was in the crudest of forms. We'd got a speed calculator, which assisted with doing things on maps, but that was all. I went on an observers' course, but that was a joke. We were doing our navigation eight at a time in De Havilland DH-89As, cabinet machines. You couldn't see out of them so I don't know how you were supposed to navigate. We went down to do air bombing and air firing, but the weather wasn't very good so we didn't do much of that. We were only there a fortnight.

In the Volunteer Reserve, Robin Murray also found that the training offered was elementary, even by the summer of 1939, when the diplomatic situation had reached a critical stage.

I volunteered at the RAF Volunteer Reserve headquarters at Hove in 1938, after the time of Munich. I didn't do any real training. What we had to do before the war was to attend the RAF place in Hove once a fortnight for a couple of hours. But what can you learn in a couple of hours? Once a year you had to go to a camp for a fortnight and anybody you worked for had to let you go, they had to pay you your full pay for the fortnight, while you were away, and that was it. That was virtually all the training we were supposed to get. We did go to Shoreham Airport because all the RAF VR places had an aerodrome within easy reach. Ours was Shoreham Airport, which was only a very small, grass aerodrome, which just flew Tiger Moths and small aircraft from it.

It wasn't just the training which seemed inadequate. As the RAF prepared for a war that seemed increasingly likely, it was all too clear to John Holmes that their equipment was also going to be a problem. He recalls that the Handley Page Heyford, an aircraft that had first flown in 1930, was still serving with the RAF in 1939. It was incredible to him that anyone believed that this two-engined bomber was going to be up to the job.

> The Heyford was just a giant kite. It was completely open, no enclosed cockpits whatsoever. The pilot had a windshield; the front gunner was totally exposed from the waist upwards if using the gun. The mid-upper gunner was also exposed, they weren't in turrets. The Heyfords were slow, they were mostly out of date, they didn't carry a decent bomb load, they'd got no altitude. On the Heyford bomber, if you met a head wind of over 140 miles per hour, your ground speed was negative. In other words you weren't going anywhere. I don't think anybody would ever have convinced anybody that it would go into battle. The early bombers were completely useless. There was nothing in their favour. They had fixed undercarriages, for example. The air force was suffering from no money being spent on it, and the equipment was not up to it. We were outclassed all round.

At this stage, while political and military leaders were well aware of the growing possibility of another war against Germany, many young men like John Holmes were still oblivious to the threat. 'I wouldn't say there weren't any indications of a war, but I was twenty and you didn't think about that sort of thing at all, you didn't read about politics. I imagined that the government knew that a war was likely. They were expanding the RAF at a terrific rate so they must have been aware that something was brewing. But they didn't advertise that at the recruiting office.'

So when war was finally declared on 3 September 1939, it came as something of a shock to Holmes. 'We hadn't really thought about the war at all. We were enjoying ourselves. This was the whole tone of the air force in those days. We were an elite service, we were well looked after, we were provided with everything, we didn't work hard and we had a jolly good time and until the war broke out very few of us had even given it consideration.'

The first that he knew of this unexpected turn of events was just before the declaration of war when the order came through confining them to camp.

> I was at Abingdon and the first we knew of it was that all leave was stopped and that was about a fortnight before war broke out. We weren't allowed out of the camp, and that gave an indication that something was brewing, but we hadn't the vaguest notion of what it was likely to be: nobody had heard of an air striking force or anything like that. So we just sat it out, and then two days before the declaration of war, the squadron was due to take off the next morning to go to France and I was the junior observer, the very junior one at the bottom of the heap, and I hadn't got an aeroplane, I wasn't crewed up. So we saw the squadron off. They went off to France and we went back to our various messes and just sat around. We expected to fly over the next day with the ground crew.

Holmes discovered, however, that he would be going across to France more quickly than he'd anticipated.

> At about four o'clock in the afternoon I was sent for and went to see the flight commander and he said one of the aircraft had gone down in the Channel on the way over and that I was to crew up with Pilot Officer Rowan, who was a New Zealander, to take the spare aircraft over. So we went off the next morning. The first thing I did was ask, 'Can I have the necessary maps?', because navigation was largely done by map reading in those days. But the reply came, 'Oh, no, you can't have a map, there were only twelve maps and they were issued to the twelve aircraft and yours is at the bottom of the English Channel.' So I said that this posed a minor problem. He said don't worry about it, because you can formate on the Ensign there, which was a British Airways civilian aircraft taking the ground crew and the tool kits over. What he hadn't worked out was that the Ensign was flying at about 120 mph, and a Fairy Battle overheated at 120 mph. So instead of formating on him, we flew round and

round and round him all the way over. It must have looked rather funny from the ground! When we got there, we got on to the circuit expecting to land but nothing happened and the Ensign went round and round the circuit. We found out afterwards that the pilot was listening to Chamberlain's speech with his trailing aerial out, and he wouldn't land until Chamberlain had finished his speech. Then he wound in the aerial and landed and we followed.

The start of the war also saw a new posting for Robin Murray, but it would be a while before he would experience any active service. 'I was posted to Hamble at the outbreak of war, which was run by Air Service Training, and did a wireless course there. I then got posted to RAF Cranfield and six of us got lost in the system. Nobody knew anything about wireless operator/air gunners, there was no flying done from there and we just ended up doing various odd jobs for one of the sergeants there.'

While the outbreak of war had surprised John Holmes, others of his generation had been following political developments in Europe more closely. For Robert Kee, who would soon be training as a pilot, the outbreak of war was a welcome break from the policy of appeasement.

We'd been appalled at the way the British government simply played along with Hitler, as it seemed, giving him everything, the Munich agreement, giving him Czechoslovakia. Halifax, the Foreign Secretary, seemed to be almost sympathetic to him, and that was intolerable. I was very glad the war had broken out, I think all my generation were. The feeling of resentment by 1939 at what had been happening was quite considerable. I knew many people when I was at Oxford who joined the Communist Party.

Kee didn't hesitate to volunteer to do his war duty.

I actually joined up on the first day of the war. I had been in France the day before and came back and war was declared that morning. Of course, everyone expected bombs to start falling at once. We spent all that morning digging air-raid shelters furiously, thinking the bombs were going to come any moment, and then suddenly there was an alarm, nothing happened, it was some ordinary aeroplane. One of our planes had been mistaken wrongly, and nothing happened for nearly nine months.

So it would be a while before Kee was to get his chance to do his war duty. 'The first thing one did was just to sign up and be told, "You're on deferred service," which indeed I was for almost the next year.'

While Robert Kee waited to be called up, and thousands of other young British men who had already volunteered to fight for their country sat out the Phoney War, Bomber Command was immediately active. It was the start of a long campaign that would last almost six years, seeing innumerable developments along the way, but with an enduring commitment and dedication that spanned the war.

2

Overcoming the Obstacles

'Indiscriminate attacks on civilian populations as
such will never form part of our policy.'

John Slessor, Director of Plans at the Air Ministry,
7 September 1939

(top) Robin Murray *(middle, front row)* with fellow airmen at RAF Hamble, Christmas 1939.
(bottom) John Holmes *(fourth from left, middle row)* with colleagues at No. 57 Squadron.

It took just sixty-three minutes from the declaration of war for Bomber Command to launch its first wartime operational sortie. While most of the country, including the armed forces, waited nervously to see what was going to happen, a Blenheim reconnaissance bomber set out to photograph German warships. Its mission successfully accomplished, the three-man crew returned safely. One way or another, their colleagues would be flying and fighting until the very last day of hostilities.

As with so many other British pre-war preparations, this was not the outbreak of hostilities that had been planned for. Britain had declared war, but the country hadn't actually been attacked, nor had France, its closest political and geographical ally. Instead, both countries had gone to war over Poland, a *casus belli* nobody could have foreseen. The western allies were immediately distracted from the defensive war they had anticipated, and left to ponder what kind of offensive war they would be part of. Chamberlain had talked only a year previously about Czechoslovakia being 'a far-away country' full of 'people of whom we know nothing'. Now Britain and France were engaged in a war whose theatre was next door to that 'far-away country'. And if the Allies had been wrong-footed politically, they had become virtually impotent militarily. There was, for example, little Bomber Command could do to help Poland. The country was simply too far away for the medium and light bombers, like the Blenheims, Wellingtons, Whitleys and Handley Page Hampdens, the command was equipped with. The Western Air Plans were left looking pretty much defunct as an operational guide now that it appeared that the central axis for this war would be

45

eastern Europe, not Britain itself. Of course, it didn't stay like this for long.

At the start of the war, Bomber Command was divided into five operational groups, each equipped with different aircraft, and allocated different roles. As Poland was overrun by the mighty Blitzkrieg machine, President Roosevelt secured assurances from Britain and France that any target where civilians might be hit would be avoided, a commitment that in fact lasted for several months. Even Germany had agreed to follow it, although only on 18 September, once the invasion of Poland was more or less secured. This meant that Bomber Command was forced to steer clear of bombing any targets on German soil, instead concentrating on naval vessels in the North Sea. The only flights over Germany for the first months of the war would be to drop propaganda leaflets, and even these sorties were limited by the need to avoid flying over Holland or Belgium, at this time still both neutral countries.

While Bomber Command was active from the outset, its first few months of wartime duty were not marked by any great measure of success. Shipping patrols claimed the first casualties of Bomber Command's war, when five Blenheims were shot down by German anti-aircraft fire while attacking the battleship *Admiral Scheer* and the cruiser *Emden* in Wilhelmshaven harbour on 4 September, the second day of the war. Two Wellingtons were also lost on the first of many disastrous days for the command. In thirty sorties, seven aircraft had been lost. It was an early lesson in the danger of operating in daylight, when crews were simply too vulnerable to attacks by German fighters, a lesson the Germans would learn themselves during the Battle of Britain. Nevertheless, the shipping patrols continued. Targets such as the battleships *Scharnhorst* and *Gneisenau* were regularly sought, although rarely found, and even when they were hit, little damage was inflicted. At night, they would fly leaflet-dropping raids, ensuring the crews far greater safety against enemy fighters, but they were susceptible to poor weather. It was unlikely that these so-called 'nickel raids' were achieving any great propaganda coups, but they were invaluable for the training they provided. The experience young crews gained flying at night over occupied Europe would prove indispensable in the months to come.

While four of the Bomber Command groups embarked on regular shipping patrols, or dropping leaflets, 1 Group's ten squadrons of Fairey Battle light bombers had been sent out to France on 2 September, a forlorn, last-ditch attempt to shore up Allied defences against the imminent arrival of the Germans. Along with two squadrons of Blenheim twin-engine reconnaissance bombers, they formed the Advanced Striking Force, and it was as part of this group that John Holmes found himself on the continent. Like so many others, he too quickly discovered that Bomber Command was unprepared for the outbreak of conflict. 'At that time, the Air Ministry had not organised anything at all, unlike the later operations which were organised. We arrived in France and our field kitchens came six weeks later by sea from Liverpool!'

Holmes's squadron was involved in photographic reconnaissance sorties, cataloguing possible targets, and examining the Maginot Line, France's last line of fortified defence.

The only operations I had anything to do with were these photography efforts. We were shot at indiscriminately by both the Germans and the French, and you could tell the difference because when the shells burst, one was black and one was white. I've forgotten which is which now. We did get chased by a fighter on one occasion but my pilot was like me, a considerable coward, and he said, 'We'll go home,' which we did, and we went right down to about twenty feet. Fighters wouldn't attack you if they couldn't get under you, they wanted to get underneath the tail. They weren't aware of the fact that the gun was virtually useless at the back. So we hared for home on that occasion. We still had vague ideas about chivalry over the skies and all that nonsense and following First World War tactics. It was ridiculous, but it looked good in the papers. We had a lot of reporters come along one day, and we stuck them out in the middle of the aerodrome and did a low-level flight attack on them. They got a good picture, and wrote something about us attacking the enemy. Well, we weren't actually; just flying over our own aerodrome, over newspaper reporters!

In this period of 'Phoney War', eight months before the Wehrmacht launched their invasion of France, Holmes remembers the sense of inactivity that was characteristic of the time.

We sat around a lot. We were having a good time, but the aircrew had nothing to do, so were digging latrines. The object was to see who could dig the deepest, A flight or B flight. I think we got down to ten feet. We were going into Reims on days out and things like that. We were very lucky in No. 40 Squadron because our orderly sergeant had a French father, so we used to take him with us wherever we went. We were doing all right; plenty of French wine and ladies with kind hearts and all the benefits of life. We were sleeping in a barn on a bed which I made myself out of four-by-two and chicken wire; very comfortable. Our field kitchens still hadn't arrived and we were living on herrings and tomato sauce, which gets monotonous. So about half a dozen of the aircrew decided we would cook for ourselves. I built a field kitchen in the farmyard and we used to have grilled chops and chips, better than herrings in tomato sauce. Then we had a French territorial army unit move in to do the catering for us. We ate very well. One day we had steak and chips for the first time, and it was delicious. The French sergeant asked us if we'd enjoyed it, and we said, 'Yes, we're jolly lucky to have a chef like that.' He said, 'Well, he's not a chef, he's a wheelwright, but did you enjoy it?' Again, we said, 'Yes.' He said, 'Well, that was horse.' So that was the first time I ate horse.

As well as photographic reconnaissance, Holmes and his fellow airmen were sent on practice bombing raids. These didn't always go according to plan.

We were going to do some practice with 250-pound bombs. Now this was the first time any of us had ever dropped a 250-pound bomb. We'd dropped practice bombs but we'd never used a real bomb. We took off in a flight of three aircraft, because they were still obsessed with the idea of flying in formation, which they used to do in the First World War, and I was the third man because of my junior position. The flight leader went in and dropped a 250-pound bomb which didn't go off, and we were flying then at about 350 feet, which was very dodgy. The second one, the right-hand wing man, went in and dropped his bomb, and it didn't go off, and then I came lumbering along in the rear and dropped mine and all three went off and that was not funny. My pilot was a sergeant pilot called Scott and his language was something shocking. I pointed out to him it wasn't my fault!

Low-level flying was a continual feature of the early months of the war, but highly dangerous for the crews. 'At that height you could run into all sorts of obstructions. You'd think there was nothing there, look round and suddenly there's a church steeple. That happened all the time. Flying at about two or three hundred feet was ridiculously dangerous and almost certain to finish up a tragedy at some time. But when it came to attacking bridges, the Air Ministry expected the crews to do it.'

Despite the years of preparation for war, these early aircrews soon discovered just how pitifully inadequate their aircraft were. Their front-line aircraft, the Fairey Battle, was the worst. A single-engine aircraft, it had been developed as a small, light day-bomber from an official specification issued in 1933 to find a replacement for the biplanes then in service as bombers. In the autumn of 1939, they were the mainstay of the Advanced Striking Force, but as John Holmes recalls, these aircraft, whose very name did so little to raise confidence, were already completely outclassed. 'The Fairey Battle wasn't a bad aeroplane, it was simply developed and came into service too early and by the time it was needed, it was really obsolete. People were fully aware that they were obsolete, but we were young and stupid and we didn't think about these things, we were at the age when we'd do these silly things.'

The Battle's performance was seriously hindered by a number of fundamental design faults.

The Fairey Battle was a nice-looking aeroplane, it was fairly sleek, reasonably comfortable, looked a pretty good aeroplane. For anybody used to biplanes it was a vast improvement all round. It was comparatively roomy. The problem with it was that the bomb sight was situated mainly behind the radiator and as all aircraft radiators invariably leak and the oil cooler was included in the radiator, when you were using the bomb sight you were getting a liberal amount of leaky hot glycol and a certain amount of engine oil and it used to get inside your helmet and into your hair and you needed a shower every time you landed.

The Battle's design problems were not helped by the addition of a third crew member, which added weight to the aircraft; nor by its notoriously unreliable engine. The trouble was that the RAF had little else to offer.

They were inclined to be temperamental. They were under-powered, as a lot of the RAF's aircraft were. With the aircraft that Pilot Officer Rowan and I took across, we were flying on one magneto [a small dynamo] anyway. When we ran the aircraft up, we had a magneto drop of about 250, which would normally have rendered the aircraft unserviceable. But they said, 'No, there's a war on, you've got to go over, it doesn't matter about having only one magneto as long as you've got something.' So we were only getting about two-thirds of the power of the engine anyway, and these Battles were fairly elderly by then. So we weren't a bit surprised that one had gone down. Anything that a Battle did didn't surprise you very much.

Many senior RAF commanders were well aware of the Fairey Battle's shortcomings, but despite their pleas production continued right up until October 1940. By then 2,200 of the aeroplanes had been produced, despite proving such easy fare for German fighters, which inflicted grievous losses during the Battle of France. The remaining aircraft were relegated to training units, and it was while training in South Africa that Tom Wingham encountered the aircraft.

They were used for bombing and gunnery practice, and even for that they were more or less inadequate. I remember one day, for instance, it took us three take-offs before we could go on an exercise, because the first and second times the aircraft was unserviceable when we got it in the air and had to land. They were a smelly aircraft too, and you had to use a voice tube to speak to the pilot and give him directions. So you were holding that tube to your mouth while you were trying to operate a bomb sight at the same time, and you were stuck in the fuselage with a perspex panel to look through, which was often dirty. So it wasn't a particularly good aircraft for navigators and bomb aimers to fly in!

It wasn't just the Fairey Battle which caused problems. Robert Kee flew his operations on Hampdens, a real stalwart of Bomber Command's early years. 'The Hampden was almost obsolescent. It was old fashioned, but a delightful aeroplane to fly, because you had a proper pilot's position, like a fighter pilot almost, as if the wings were yours. You really felt you were flying them.'

Kee was second pilot, a position that would later disappear, for many of his operations.

On Hampdens, you needed to be a good navigator because the second pilot was the navigator. I remember doing a special course for about six weeks, learning how to navigate. As second pilot, everything in a Hampden was very cramped. The second pilot/navigator was down in the nose. There was very little room indeed, just enough to do a few sums, because that was the only way of navigating, occasionally asking one of the gunners to drop a float to see what the wind was.

The Handley Page Hampden, a twin-engine medium bomber, made its maiden flight in 1936, and was fully operational only by 1939. That it was one of the newer aircraft available didn't compensate for its failings. It had a cramped interior, and its shape led to it being dubbed the 'Flying Panhandle'. More seriously, it suffered from poor manoeuvrability and its defensive firepower made it particularly vulnerable in daylight raids. The Luftwaffe's Messerschmitt Me-110s quickly learned how best to dispose of the Hampdens, by flying into their enormous blind spot, inaccessible to the gunners, and picking them off at will. The 'Flying Panhandle' soon acquired the more sinister and inevitable nickname of the 'Flying Coffin'. The Hampdens would be relegated to mine-laying operations, known to the crews as 'gardening ops', and by September 1942 they had been withdrawn from front-line service altogether.

For those who'd been in the RAF from the mid-1930s, aircraft such as the Fairey Battle and the Handley Page Hampden had seemed comparatively modern. They had represented a giant technological leap forward from the biplanes produced in the early 1930s. But up against the Luftwaffe, their confidence, and their aircraft, were soon in shreds. Bomber Command's aircrews found to their considerable cost that there was simply no contest. Even the Armstrong Whitworth Whitley, the RAF's first medium bomber, which could carry an impressive 7,000-pound bomb load, had major drawbacks. It had a better range than most of the other early aircraft, but as John Holmes recalls, the Whitleys were 'as slow as a funeral'. They were also particularly susceptible to problems of ice. Icy conditions were a frequent problem for crews, as Arthur Smith explains.

What happened in a cloud was that the water vapour in the cloud hits your aircraft, and the conditions in the cloud are such that it freezes where it hits. So you get ice building up on the leading edges of the aircraft. The worst place is the leading edge of the two wings, and it builds up and builds up, and on the propellers, until it breaks off. When it breaks off, a lot of it hits the side of the fuselage, just as if you're being fired at, for instance. And you can hear it, it's frightening.

For John Holmes, one of the early aircraft did stand out: the Bristol Blenheim.

It was like getting off a bicycle and getting into a taxi. It was luxurious. There was a chart table in the nose; the bomb sight was virtually enclosed; your normal seat was a comfortable padded seat alongside the pilot; and it was virtually draught proof, it wasn't a bit cold. It was considerably faster than the Battle and it felt altogether more like a big aeroplane. We started off on Mark Is, which were the ones with the short nose, and they were rather inclined to explode on landing.

The problems with the Mark Is were quickly rectified, and by 1939 the much improved Mark IV version of this medium bomber was being introduced. Yet even as the aircraft started to improve, the rest of Bomber Command's equipment was still fairly basic, as Robin Murray discovered. 'The navigational and bomb-aiming equipment was almost useless. When I think of the bomb-aiming equipment, it was almost a bit of wire. It was very elementary. It wasn't until later that all the modern stuff was beginning to come in.'

For John Holmes, another key restriction on the crews' ability was the limitations on the guns. 'I'd got a rear gun that would only fire one shot at a time. It was so worn it wouldn't recoil and reload itself. So you fired a round then you cocked it and fired another round. In an aircraft moving at 140 mph, facing an enemy aircraft with about four guns in the front firing a thousand a minute, you didn't stand very much of a chance firing one shot at a time.'

For Holmes, the war was proving to be very different from the image he and most of his generation had had of dashing flying aces. 'We had visions of doing a Biggles thing, dashing about the sky and winning medals and killing everybody for miles around, which just didn't happen.'

Holmes would be fortunate. He would be spared the reality of war that many of 1 Group would experience in France the following year, having returned to Britain at the beginning of December 1939. For him, being on the front line had been a big adventure, the Phoney War a merciful escape from real enemy action.

> We were larking about. We were enjoying ourselves; we were young men, just twenty, twenty-one years old. We were having the time of our lives. I was getting 850 francs a fortnight and sending an allowance home to my mother. At home, we'd been used to paying a pound a month in the sergeants' mess for extra luxuries. So we tried to pay the French sergeant the amalgamated collection and he had the fright of his life, he'd never seen so much money. So we were doing very nicely.

The larking about of the Phoney War was not to last. On 9 April 1940, the Blitzkrieg forces arrived in Norway and Denmark, the beginning of a devastating assault on western Europe. Britain and France declared support for the two nations, and Bomber Command crews were sent out to help, but there was little they could do and both countries were quickly overrun. From 10 May, the Wehrmacht's invasion of Belgium, Holland and France got under way, and with Italy's entry into the war the Axis powers must have seemed invincible.

Bomber Command was engaged throughout the Battle of France, their objective to attack bridges, railway lines, communications systems. Anything to get in the way of Blitzkrieg. It was a miserable experience for the crews, as John Holmes realised.

> The crews were just being decimated; they were bringing back what was left of them and then quite a few of them got caught

when the Germans advanced. They were mostly occupied in bombing bridges, and really they just didn't stand a chance. They were being knocked down by ground fire, they were being knocked down by air fire. I never went on one of the trips so I don't really know what happened but I can imagine. The aircraft were too slow and they wouldn't be able to get out of the way at all. Fighters would knock them off for a pastime and the losses were colossal.

Wolfgang Falck, who would be instrumental in the development of the Luftwaffe's night fighter force, was surprised at the bombers' lack of success.

We were surprised that on a clear day they didn't fly in a closed group. The majority of the British flew in open formation and we were able to penetrate very easily and attack them from behind without being shot at by the others. But they learned from their mistake and then flew in close combination and they were more efficient by both day and night. I think the other major handicap of the RAF was that the aeroplanes were old. The main weapon was the Wellington. They were lightweight aeroplanes made out of plywood and canvas. They caught fire very easily.

All too soon, Bomber Command's casualty rates had shot sky high. Operations were still small-scale compared to what was to follow in the latter years of the war. Less than a third of the available aircraft would be dispatched at any one time, and it was often just twenty or thirty aircraft flying on an individual raid, and frequently far fewer than that. Even though the Hampden and Wellington crews had been taken off daylight raids in April, leaving only the Blenheims as a daytime bombing force, it was still operations during the day which were causing the highest casualties. In May and June 1940, RAF Blenheims had a loss rate of 5.7 per cent. While the night raid figures were considerably better, with a loss rate of 1.5 per cent, these figures disguise the very serious impact on the command's front-line strength. In the six short weeks it took France to fall, the command lost 145 aircraft, about half of what they had available. The losses among aircrew, too, were sobering, and on an unprecedented scale. John Holmes noticed that aircrew messes all over Bomber Command were being brutally forced to discard some hallowed rituals. 'We started the old First World War thing of leaving people's places at the dining-room table. The commanding officer had to step in and stop it because there were people sitting at one end of the table with eight spaces in between them and the next person.'

It wasn't just in the air that the losses were apparent. Holmes had now returned to work on a ground crew, and witnessing the loss among his colleagues had become a daily event.

The foyer of the sergeants' mess was stacked from floor to ceiling with the kit of people that had come in, dropped their kit, reported to the flights, and been told to get their flying kit straight away and get into the air. We were sending off aircraft which hadn't got any squadron markings on them because they hadn't had time to put them on, and they weren't coming back. It was heartbreaking but you had to get a hold of yourself mentally and forget all that because you'd got a job to do, it was an exacting job and you couldn't be soft hearted.

As those airmen who'd had the benefit of years of pre-war training were lost, increasingly the faces in the squadrons were getting younger and younger, and the atmosphere in the mess was slowly darkening as the losses mounted up.

As soon as they were eighteen they were eligible for manned service. There were aircrew flying at eighteen. We were drinking brandy for breakfast in the sergeants' mess, you know. Half of us probably wouldn't have gone in the air if we'd been cold sober. I wouldn't. Never been so scared in all my life. If anybody says that they weren't, I would be very doubtful about it. The war changed everything. Old values went; old institutions went. Wartime conditions meant adapting to a new way of life almost entirely. I'd been in the service for nearly five years and it was not easy at all.

Holmes was grateful that the authorities seemed eager to retain his services on the ground, rather than sending him back into the air. 'They were more intent on getting me back on the ground than they were in getting me in the air. They'd got or were preparing plenty of aircrew but experienced junior ground NCOs were pretty scarce in those days. So that is one of the reasons why I didn't fly again and I'm duly grateful for it because I wouldn't be here now if I had done.'

During the Battle of France, one event played a fundamental role in changing bombing policy. On 14 May, the Luftwaffe switched from its Blitzkrieg strategy to direct terror bombing when it launched a savage attack on Rotterdam. The uneasy truce, encouraged by a fearful President Roosevelt to help protect civilian populations from attack by bombers, was in tatters. The next day the British War Cabinet took the momentous, retaliatory decision to allow Bomber Command to cross the Rhine and move its campaign into Germany itself. No longer would attacks on the Reich be restricted to dropping leaflets. On 15 May, a force of 108 aircraft – the first time a raid had ever been mounted with more than a hundred bombers – was sent to attack industrial targets inside Germany.

A key proponent of this intensification of the bombing was the ever belligerent Winston Churchill, who had arrived at 10 Downing Street just days earlier, replacing Neville Chamberlain, who had never been an enthusiastic advocate of bombing. Churchill had no such reservations, only too aware of what kind of battle lay ahead, and the overwhelming importance of winning it, whatever it took. In any case, as he knew just as well, the British position was too perilous to allow him the luxury of qualms about bombing, even if he had had them. Attacking Germany directly was therefore added to the growing list of priorities for the new chief of Bomber Command, Air Marshal Sir Charles Portal, who took over from Ludlow-Hewitt in April. He could now plan for a strategic bombing campaign against Germany with Churchill's full support.

By the end of June, however, the situation was growing ever more desperate. Ricky Dyson had also been sent out to France in 1939 to carry out photographic reconnaissance work. He was still there when the Battle of France started, working as ground staff with No. 59 Squadron.

We were stationed near Amiens at a village called Poix. The aerodrome was on a hill, we had French aircraft and Blenheims, taking photographs of the coast, and dropped one or two bombs. When the Germans went through the Low Countries, I was in Amiens at the time. We had people coming around the cinemas telling us to get back to the camp, where we were living above the cows in the barn. We were told that we were going to move, they didn't say where, and eventually we ended up at Arras. We heard the German guns firing across a wood, and then the order for the 'scorched earth policy' came. Everybody had to burn everything that they weren't wearing. Every unserviceable vehicle had to be burnt, and we spent the day with bonfires. We were told that the ground staff had to be independent and make their own way to a foreign port. I couldn't drive a tractor so I went on a tractor with somebody else but it ran out of petrol so we joined the refugees on the roads. We walked from Arras to Boulogne. It took us a day and a half, and I spent my twenty-second birthday in a warehouse in Boulogne.

By now, the Blitzkrieg machine had caught up with the evacuating British forces. 'On the way, the Germans strafed us with Stuka dive-bombers. They came down in their tens and strafed the roads. Women and children and babies all got shot up. We went in the ditches and we tried to do what we could but it was one of the most horrific experiences I had. There were not only women and children screaming, but horses were being strafed and left dying on the road screaming in pain.'

Dyson was soon part of the hurried evacuation of the British Expeditionary Force. 'I was taken off on a paddle steamer. We were packed in so close like sardines and the sea was rough and people were vomiting all over the place. Two people vomited all over my shoulder! We landed at Dover and these Women's Voluntary Service ladies were on the quayside, waiting with cups of tea.'

It had been a devastating blow for the western allies, and some blamed the RAF for not doing more to prevent the disaster, as Peter Baker discovered. 'I remember walking through Victoria Station shortly after I joined the RAF just after Dunkirk. I was booed by the army. I think they felt that the air force had rather let them down over Dunkirk, although the air force was fighting behind the lines.'

Of course, the credit for what happened next is deservedly given to Fighter Command. Their Battle of Britain triumph in the summer and autumn of 1940 prevented Britain from becoming yet another Nazi conquest. Day after day, the Spitfire and Hurricane pilots fought for the skies of southern Britain, battling to keep the vital air superiority that would prevent Operation Sealion, Hitler's invasion plan for Britain. Victory in late October 1940 didn't itself win the war, but Fighter Command's success ensured that for Britain, and indeed the now overrun countries of western Europe, there was at least still a war there to win. By the end of October, the threat of an invasion was effectively over, the Luftwaffe forced into a night bombing strategy that would last for months. The Blitz would be the spur for many young men like Arthur Smith to volunteer for the RAF – and it was also, of course, a grim premonition of the kind of war they would be asked to engage in. 'They were bombing our cities while I was finishing at school. I lived in St Albans and I remember coming back from church one night when it was dark and seeing the glow from the docks' fires, even in St Albans.'

Jim Rogers also witnessed the Blitz for himself.

I was born in the East End of London. The first big raid took place on a Saturday afternoon, and the bombers came up from the river, following the Thames along the dock area. I lived by the West India Docks. People were running and crying through the night. I went through the bombing up to November and after seeing that, and being rather patriotic, I decided that we should do something about it. I was nineteen at the time and knew that I'd probably be called up anyway, so I went into the RAF.

Despite his being relatively young, the Blitz made Leonard Miller determined to join the war effort in whatever way he could.

I was an engineer apprentice in the London docks and we were bombed to pieces down there. I remember going out on a lifeboat to go across to Dunkirk. I got as far as Gravesend and the navy stopped us as we were too young to go! The company that I worked for wanted us all back to get on with the work! One day, in East Ham where I was born, my friend and I were standing on a corner of a road when a two-thousand-pound parachute bomb came down and blew us right across the road. It blew about four houses down. We went straight away to help dig the people out. Above the trees was another bomb that was swinging on its cords above our heads.

It wasn't just London. The Blitz hit cities around the country, causing devastation night after night. Jack Eveleigh was living in Dartmouth in 1940. 'We'd seen some bombing even in this area. In fact, some bombs were dropped right behind the house that I was living in. It didn't do a lot of damage, brought down a ceiling and made a couple of craters in the field, but otherwise we were fairly lucky to get away with it. So I had no illusions about war, I knew it wasn't a particularly pleasant sort of occupation.'

If the Blitz would encourage many young civilians to volunteer for the RAF, the bombing of RAF stations had also been a spur to those who were already serving. Having returned from France, Ricky Dyson rejoined No. 59 Squadron, and was based at Thorney Island during the Battle of Britain.

> The air-raid alert went and we went to the shelters, but of course like everybody we just stood and watched what was happening. One terrible time was when a stick of bombs hit a hangar and the massive hangar doors came down on top of an airman who was running to the shelters. That was a great shock to us all. The bombs destroyed personnel and lorries and made dirty great holes in the aerodrome itself. There were no concrete runways in those days, so it was mainly grass. The administration buildings were often hit, and so there were casualties. This was obviously hushed up at the time. But they did quite a lot of damage to the airfields, especially around the coast.

The Battle of Britain and the Blitz offered a direct continuity with the terrible memories of those early Zeppelin raids of the Great War, proof that the prophecies of future aerial Armageddon had been correct. They shattered any sense that this would be a conflict fought out of sight of the British mainland, away from its citizens. This was a war that they were able to watch, a war that had been brought to Britain itself. Some had been personally affected. One young office boy working in his local town hall in 1940 came home to find his home ruined, his mother sitting on the front steps surrounded by rubble. For him, it was a short step from that moment to volunteering to join the RAF, in which he completed a tour of operations as a pilot. But it would also prove a powerful lesson to the man who would eventually take the war to Germany, Arthur Harris. The raid that wiped out central Coventry, and with it a whole range of industrial capacity in the surrounding Midlands, had helped convince him that this was the way to wage a bomber war; that it wasn't about hitting individual factories, an impossible feat anyway, but about destroying a nation's workforce and their ability to keep their factories running. And around Harris, the cities of Britain would see a hardening in attitude towards the use of bombers, at first as simple retaliation, but later as a weapon commensurate with the threat posed by Nazi brutality. Step by step, the war of the bombers was coming closer and its savagery increasing.

All through that 'Spitfire Summer', Bomber Command was busy behind the scenes. A series of new directives was issued with raids on German industrial targets now the key priority for the bomber crews, and oil refineries the highest priority of all. Communications systems would be attacked, forests burnt and crops destroyed. Sorties to the Luftwaffe's airfields and German aircraft factories were designed to cripple the forces responsible for the Blitz, which was devastating so many British cities. Most significantly, Bomber Command attacked and destroyed many of the invasion barges that were lined up along the European coast, lying ready for the moment when German aerial supremacy was achieved and the land invasion could start. John Holmes was involved in this part of the campaign. 'It was just a river mouth with jetties all along both sides with buildings and cranes and what have you. But the main target was rows and rows of barges moored side by side, I should think six deep, right up the river as far as you could see. We went for the first ones that we came to. I don't know whether we hit them or not but we were so damned low I don't see how we could have missed them.'

The bombing raids were now getting bigger. Although sorties of more than a hundred aircraft were carried out only rarely, groups of forty or fifty aircraft were being sent out more frequently to the same target. It was more typical, though, for the command to send out much smaller numbers of aircraft to numerous different targets. The resources were being too thinly spread, and Portal knew it, urging the command to concentrate on fewer, heavier attacks. The problem wasn't that the crews were coming up against German night fighters. The Luftwaffe had only forty of them, mostly Messerschmitt Me-110s. These twin-engine fighters, designed for both attack and defence roles, had been nicknamed '*Der Zerstörer*' ('the Destroyer'), but without the radar devices they would receive later in the war they could only make limited headway against British bombers. Searchlights were no use for them either; any German fighter stupid enough to close in on an illuminated bomber would risk being riddled by his own side's Flak.

Bomber Command's *real* problem remained navigational accuracy. With no technical aids yet available, crews were forced to rely on manual navigation to get to the target and back – as often as not little more than educated guesswork. Hard enough on a moonlit night when you could at least make out key features on the ground, it was nigh impossible on moonless nights, and navigators were forced to use 'dead reckoning', the theoretical course of the aircraft based on forecast winds, as Tom Wingham explains.

> With dead reckoning, basically you start off from a point and you know we won't follow exactly the course we are aiming for because we'll be blown to one side by the wind. So we work out exactly where we will be if the wind continues exactly as it is at the time we start. Unfortunately it doesn't work out that way. Winds tend to change and so you also take into account what the forecasted winds are going to do on your journey.

'Dead reckoning' was never a particularly reliable method, and the effective German blackouts of towns and cities ensured that crews had little opportunity to confirm that they had in fact reached the target. The increasingly dense Flak and searchlights made what cities they could make out highly hazardous places to fly anywhere near. This forced crews to rely on a technique even more hit and miss than 'dead reckoning'. For Robin Murray, as for many other airmen, the only recourse was to 'bomb on ETA', estimated time of arrival.

> We frequently bombed on estimated time of arrival, in other words it was estimated that you were going to fly at, let's say, 112 mph, which was about the maximum speed for a Wellington

with a full bomb load, so it would take you x number of minutes to get to your target. The wind was in such a direction so that would blow you off course to a certain degree, so that was taken into consideration. So they'd say, 'Your estimated time of arrival is 1200 hours.' So at 1200 you bombed. You couldn't see anything, you didn't know where you were in relation to the place you were supposed to bomb, but that was the estimated time of arrival, so that's the time you bombed.

Robert Kee was only too aware of the inaccuracy of his crew's bombing when they relied on ETA.

We were pretty inaccurate most of the time. Over and over again, one bombed on ETA, and you couldn't see anything. Once I remember bombing Hamburg and we came quite low. I could definitely see the bomb went off in Hamburg, which was – it's an awful thing to say – a pleasant surprise, because so often one had simply bombed wondering exactly where we were. Had it gone into the sea, or had it just gone into a field? I think very often it just went into fields. At that time, the records of the success of bombing showed that very, very few aircraft actually achieved their target.

It was as hopeless as it sounds. Some aircraft were by now carrying bombing cameras, which were used to photograph the ground at the moment the bombs exploded, to record the enormous damage supposedly being inflicted. All that studies of these photographs actually showed was the stupendous inaccuracy of the bombers, often miles off target, though the RAF was slow to draw the right conclusions from them. German municipal records from some of the targeted cities have since shown how little damage they were suffering, even from apparently major raids. Even when the target was reached, the inaccuracy of the bombing often meant that the civilians of the town were affected more than the military or industrial installation that was the target. It wasn't just German civilians who were affected either.

Like many airmen, Robin Murray was sent on raids to Nazi military targets across occupied Europe. 'It was very sad when we bombed parts of France, for instance Brest, Dunkirk, Boulogne. It was very sad that an awful lot of French people – innocent French people – died, but of course you couldn't just bomb the docks. Bombs could fall anywhere, and an awful lot of perfectly good French people died through it, which was sad, but unfortunately war is not a selective occupation.'

At the time, though, Murray gave little thought to the effectiveness of the bombing. 'As I remember, you never had any sort of sense of feeling for the people on the ground. Thinking we've probably killed twenty or a hundred or two hundred people didn't strike you at all. That was what your job was, and you did it and came back and had a couple of pints and that was your lot.'

Flying in Wellingtons, Murray was part of a five-man crew, but in these early days of the war most bomber crews were smaller even than this. The seven-man crews that were typical would become standard only with the heavy bombers later in the war. While serving as aircrew, John Holmes was often part of a three-man crew. 'On a Fairey Battle the crew would have been two or three depending on what the aircraft was doing: the pilot, an observer and sometimes a gunner. For most of the flying I did in Battles, I didn't have a gunner with me at all. You were expected to do the lot.'

In his crew, Holmes held the key position of observer.

The observers in my day were everything after the pilots themselves. You had to be able to work the radios, use a Morse lamp, fire the rear gun or guns, do the bomb aiming and the navigation. In your spare time you could just have a look round! In the very early days, long before the war, there was only one observer per squadron and he flew with the commanding officer, as they always flew in formation everywhere, and the rest of the squadron didn't navigate. In the two-seater aircraft, the observers had dropped the bombs by hand and fired the rear guns, and navigation had always been done by the pilot. Then they decided that with the introduction of the faster aircraft like Battles and Blenheims, they needed a navigation expert. So really the observers tended to be navigator/bomb aimers. Then when we went on to Blenheims they decided that the observer should have enough flying ability to land the aircraft with the wheels up on soft ground if the pilot was either killed or incapacitated. So we used to do landing practice on clouds. We'd go up and find a nice thick cloud and then sit in the pilot's lap because there was no other way of doing it, there weren't any dual controls.

As the aircraft got bigger, the role of observer would be split into the two distinct functions of navigator and bomb aimer, and many of the airmen who were training as observers at this time would specialise in one of the roles before starting their tour of operations. Another specialised role that quickly emerged was that of wireless operator. Wireless operators initially trained as gunners as well, but usually found themselves cocooned away with their equipment, one step removed from what was going on immediately around them. This suited Fred Stearn well.

As far as I was concerned, I was in my own little place, and I didn't see out. I was sitting on my radio in case there was a message coming through from base. So we had a few prangs but I couldn't see what was happening. The poor pilot and bomb aimer, lying flat out, must have seen it all and been devastated, and of course the mid-upper and rear gunners saw it all. But as far as I was concerned, I didn't see it, so I wasn't frightened. I was cushioned from the action.

In Stearn's short but memorable operational flying career, this is something he was extremely grateful for. 'It took off the fear. The wireless operator's section was the warmest place in the aircraft; we had it good! I felt secure, on the set trying to see that there were no messages coming in from base. What went on didn't worry me until Joe said, "We're turning out."'

By the autumn of 1940, it was clear that Britain faced a long war. When Portal became Chief of the Air Staff in October, he was replaced as head of Bomber Command by Air Marshal Sir Richard Peirse. The new commander-in-chief soon had in his hands a detailed directive of German targets his bombers would have to concentrate on, including oil, industry and the railways, combining this with mine-laying operations in the North Sea, and having to maintain pressure on the Channel ports to prevent any new invasion attempt. It was a long list which would stretch Bomber Command beyond its limits. With many aircraft lost, or being taken off front-line duties, Peirse had limited resources to call on, and over the winter months operations had to be reduced in scale considerably. His strategy was to concentrate his forces on fewer targets to increase the impact of individual raids.

Area bombing was not part of official policy at this stage, but surreptitiously and inexorably in 1940 it was entering the canon of aerial strategy. On the night of 24 August, the Luftwaffe had dropped bombs on central London, which was seen by both the British, and by Hitler, as an inexcusable deviation from attacking military targets, especially airfields and aircraft factories. The Luftwaffe bombers were at this early stage told, from the highest level, that civilian targets were off limits. In the space of a few days, however, all this would change. In fact, those first German bombs hadn't been intended for the city at all, they had simply been dropped there accidentally by an inaccurate German bomber. The following day Hermann Goering, Reichmarschall of the Luftwaffe, was quick to issue a telegram to all German bomber units demanding the names of the pilots whose crews had broached this important protocol. The British War Cabinet, however, took matters into their own hands, ordering a retaliatory and audacious raid on Berlin. The stakes had just got very, very high indeed. It wasn't a particularly successful sortie as the German capital was covered in heavy cloud. The only serious damage within the city was sustained by a summer-house, and most of the bombs fell on farmland around the metropolis. But the provocation provided by these, and subsequent raids on Hitler's capital, proved even more incendiary than the bombs. More damage was done on 23 September when 129 bombers were sent to eighteen different targets in Berlin, one of the few occasions when such a concentrated bombing force was used in this period. The real victim of these raids was German restraint; Hitler, and the humiliated Goering, abandoned their earlier inhibitions. Now British cities would have meted out to them the ruthless destruction that had been the fate of Warsaw and Rotterdam before them. A terrible and irreversible tit-for-tat had been set in motion. The Blitz was soon at its height, Coventry and Southampton sustaining terrible damage. Bomber Command was by now mustering forces of over two hundred aircraft, though they achieved nothing like the devastation visited on Britain by German bombers, which only had to fly from bases in France, rather than make round trips of over 1,000 miles.

Among young pilots like Robert Kee the chance to bomb the enemy was relished. Fighter Command had won the Battle of Britain; now Bomber Command would have its chance to shine. 'There was a feeling, "I wish we could bomb Berlin." I did go to bomb Berlin twice and I think there was pleasure in the thought that we were reciprocating after the bombing of places like Coventry and London. I remember seeing the bombing of Coventry from an airfield where I was learning to fly twin-engine aeroplanes and there was a feeling of getting our own back a bit.'

In Germany, of course, the bombing had the same effect. Peter Spoden joined the Luftwaffe for the same reason that so many joined the RAF. 'I had been a glider pilot in the Hitler Youth and was always interested in flying. In 1940 the first bombs fell on Essen, where my family lived. Suddenly we had war at home. We saw people we knew being killed, and of course that affected me much more than what had happened in other areas. I wanted very badly to join the fighter pilots. When I got my wings, I was very proud.'

So the stage was now set. What had seemed to define the early bombing war was a paralysing awareness of all the obstacles that would need to be overcome. While the crude potency of mass bombing was clear enough, as city after city found itself pulverised for nights on end, there was no doubt that the road ahead would be long, and fraught with difficulties. The aircraft were nowhere near up to the job. Navigation was a game of blind man's buff. And the bomber crews could not yet match what they had in courage with experience. The only answer would be to overhaul Bomber Command, and start to build one of the largest, most expensive and overwhelmingly ambitious war machines that the world had ever seen. It would require a system of mass production at one end, churning out thousands of the world's biggest and most complicated new aircraft models, a training programme of unprecedented scale and thoroughness to equip the bombers with the crews that would be capable of executing these missions, and a strategy that would translate all this high explosive into victory. In the end, the machine would be built, and it would attain a scale and a momentum all its own. In many ways this achievement would become Bomber Command's greatest triumph, but also its greatest tragedy.

3

The Volunteers

'Coming to this Theatre shortly: "Target For Tonight".
The film that tells you about the service which needs you.
Join the RAF, or the WAAF.'

RAF recruitment poster, 1941

(top) Leonard Miller *(right)* at the controls of an Airspeed Oxford during his training.
(bottom) Maurice Flower *(second from right, front row)* with his crew. His navigator is top row, second from right.

From the mid-1930s it had been clear that the RAF would need considerable operational manpower in the event of a war. Yet even the massive expansion of the air force during that decade was not going to be enough. With thousands of aircrew already lost, and a prolonged war in sight, the recruitment and training of airmen were essential throughout the war, and by the early 1940s hundreds of thousands more men across the world were in training to join Bomber Command. By the climax of the war, the RAF had developed one of the most sophisticated, complex and effective training programmes of any military organisation.

One thing that unites all the airmen of Bomber Command is that they *volunteered* to join the RAF. For Britain's young men, war service was not optional, but being in the RAF was. The Military Training Act had been passed in May 1939, stipulating that men aged between twenty and twenty-two could expect to be called up for six months' military training. That was only a start. On 3 September 1939, under the National Service Act, conscription was taken much further, with all men aged between eighteen and forty becoming legally liable for call-up. Certain parts of the services retained special status, however, and you could still only join the RAF if you volunteered. The Air Ministry continued to use the RAF Volunteer Reserve, the body that had been so crucial in the manpower expansion of the 1930s, as the principal point of entry for airmen throughout the war, and by its end the vast majority of Bomber Command's men could wear the RAFVR badge with pride. Not that there was a shortage of volunteers. The RAF's glamorous image and synergy with the very latest in technological developments ensured widespread appeal. Many of those falling into the conscription age bracket, including Robin Murray, made sure they put themselves forward for the RAF before they got called up into another service. 'I thought it would be better to go into something that I wanted to do, rather than get posted into anything – maybe even go to sea, which I would have absolutely hated.'

Similarly, Bill Burke had no hesitation in applying to join the RAF in 1942. 'When I turned eighteen years of age, it was a matter of going into the services. I didn't fancy going into the navy, the thought of being perpetually seasick didn't appeal to me at all. My father's stories of the fighting conditions at Passchendaele and on the Somme set me against the army. So if I had to go into a service, I thought the RAF would be best and I would emulate the knights of the air from the First World War.'

For Burke, there was another important reason for joining the RAF.

> At that time, there was only one part of the armed services at our disposal to carry the war into the heartland of Germany. We'd been faced with the retreat from the continent but at least Bomber Command was striking against the Germans. If it hadn't been for Bomber Command, the German population wouldn't have really known there was a war on, except by basking in the victories they'd secured against so many other nations.

The RAF also had an obvious appeal for Alan Bryett. 'Joining the RAF seemed the most exciting thing to do. I had no connections with the navy and I didn't particularly want to go into the army. If you went into the RAF, with a bit of luck you were going to be at the sharp end of the action reasonably quickly, with quite good rewards and quite a good life while you were training.'

Some airmen couldn't join up quickly enough. Harold Boal, known throughout his life as 'Adge', was trying to get in long before he'd reached the minimum entry age.

I'd wanted to fly since I was a little lad. I used to get into trouble at school because I was pretending to be an air gunner shooting aeroplanes down, and I had models of aeroplanes and gliders. When I was thirteen or fourteen, I thought the next stage was to try and get a job working with aeroplanes. I went to a flying school just outside Derby but was turned down because I lived about sixteen miles away from the airfield and they said it was too far to bike. By then, we all knew the war was coming. When I was sixteen, they started to recruit for the air force. I went down with a friend to the recruiting office and joined up. That lasted for about ten minutes. They asked when we were born. I gave them a date, got a thick ear for my trouble and was told to come back in about nine months' time.

Men were still being drawn to the RAF for the same reasons their predecessors had been in the pre-war decade. The novelty of flying, the image of the RAF and a desire to avoid the quagmire of the trenches were all powerful incentives to join the youngest of the three armed services. Now, though, there was an important new factor that made the RAF the most appealing of the services for thousands of men becoming legally liable for call-up. For Alan Bryett, like so many other airmen of his generation, the legacy of the Battle of Britain ensured that the RAF was *the* service to be associated with. 'I saw the RAF as the saviours of Britain after the Battle of Britain. The RAF were absolutely the tops in 1940 because they had saved us, so it was quite exciting to be going into a branch of the services held in such good esteem and well regarded by everyone.'

The RAF's success in the Battle of Britain, and the signal that it sent out to the world that Britain was still very much in the war, also greatly encouraged those who had already volunteered, including Robert Kee. 'At university I'd known people who were in the university air squadrons, and that was rather a smart thing to be. It was fairly gallant, and within a few months of me joining the RAF, the Battle of Britain was on, and that got me thinking fighter pilots were wonderful. I was attracted to life in the RAF, because I thought that I'd get something out of the war at least, which would be learning to fly.'

Peter Baker had also joined the RAF before the summer of 1940, but the desperate straits that Britain was now in had become all too evident.

> I was very influenced by the fact that I was stationed at Mildenhall in Suffolk during the Blitz and I could see London burning. I felt that I had to do the same to the Germans. Later on when I was bombing Germany and looking down, seeing targets burning, it gave me no qualms at all. They had bombed London, Coventry, Manchester, Liverpool; in Holland they had devastated and flattened towns and we were retaliating. I was very proud to be in Bomber Command because we were able to give something back. It's not easy to put over the spirit in the country at the time. We really were up against it, particularly after Dunkirk, and I think that even as a young man I realised that unless we won the war it was probably the end of civilisation, it was certainly the end of the British. We had to win and this was the part we were playing.

Like many of the volunteers before they started training, Robert Kee had harboured ambitions of becoming a fighter pilot. 'A fighter pilot was someone who was very quick, brave. While doing my early training on the aerodrome at Fairoaks in Sussex, we saw several flights of German aircraft coming over, being attacked by our own fighter planes, and one or two of them shot down, and that made one feel full of admiration for fighter pilots. I rather wanted to be one myself at that stage, and hoped I'd be selected as such.'

Kee's veneration of the RAF's fighter boys was only heightened during his own training. 'There were a lot of fighter pilots in class with us on my navigation course and one would hear them talking among themselves about the sort of things that had happened to them, and one felt full of admiration.'

Being in the RAF was a matter of considerable pride, but not just for those flying Spitfires and Hurricanes. The airmen of Bomber Command already had their own distinct reputation, and for Alan Bryett it was an alluring one. 'The image of the Bomber Boys was of a family of fellows who got together in crews of five, six or seven. You worked very closely together and they were your brothers. You trained with them, you drank with them, you had leave with them. You were essentially a little family unit.'

For Fred Stearn, getting accepted into the RAF was a matter of honour.

> The air force meant the Battle of Britain and flying on your own airfield. You go back there day after day, night after night. Everyone was a volunteer and I thought that was for me. It's a gut feeling; nobody had done much flying. Once you were accepted, you're with the elite because you had to be pretty good. They considered you to be the cream of the nation. It was the proudest moment of my life to be accepted for aircrew.

It was a good job that so many young men wanted to join the RAF. As aircraft production increased rapidly, the pressure was on to maintain the momentum of recruitment into the force to ensure there would be enough trained crews to fly the machines. At the start of the war, Bomber Command had just a few hundred aircraft; by the end it could boast nearly 2,500. Recruitment posters were displayed around the country, and in cinemas the 1941 documentary film *Target for Tonight* was shown to encourage the potential volunteers. The image of heroic airmen presented certainly captured the imagination of Harold Nash, who'd already served in the Home Guard.

> There used to be posters on the walls, 'You too can fly with the RAF', with a picture of a young man, clean looking, the aeroplane behind him and a vista of fields and hedges and trees. I came from a very humble background, my father was a postman, but

'You too can fly with the RAF' meant me as well. I can remember going to Elmdon airfield, now Birmingham Airport, and walking round the edge and seeing some RAF aeroplanes that were stationed there, and I got that thrill. When I was walking on the Malvern Hills once, an aeroplane flew over low and I thought I shall be in one of them one day! My great fear was that the war would finish before I could get into it, so I joined not long after my eighteenth birthday. I had a foolish picture in my mind of myself in the *Birmingham Mail*, looking rather intelligent in the distance as 'Birmingham's war hero, VC'. It shows how stupid you are when you're young! When I got to the Operational Training Unit, somewhere up in Yorkshire, I suddenly thought, I might get killed, and the whole of the glory, all these childish fantasies, disappeared.

Not all aircrew were eighteen when they volunteered, but a large number were, and their extreme youth remains compelling when you consider the demands that would shortly be made on them. Many volunteered as soon as they were old enough to do so, a few succeeded in sneaking in early, all anxious to do their bit for the war effort. The average age of the aircrew in Bomber Command was just twenty-two. Ron Pitt would celebrate his twenty-first birthday on an operation over Le Mans. Some airmen had completed a tour of duty, or been shot down and spent time as a prisoner of war, and were still only nineteen when the war ended. Many airmen celebrated their nineteenth, twentieth and twenty-first birthdays in POW camps deep in the Reich. There were older airmen, though. Ron Pitt was in a crew with a rear air gunner who was thirty when they were flying on operations, and the crew's flight engineer was even older than that. Dennis James Chapman, always known as Jim, was older than most gunners at twenty-four. He was part of an older-than-average crew, quickly nicknamed the 'Chelsea Pensioners' in their squadron. As the only teenager, the crew's flight engineer was conspicuous. The average age of the crew was still only about twenty-eight. John Whiteley was also older than average when he volunteered, having already seen active service before joining the RAF. Once again, the legacy of the fighter pilots in 1940 was an important influence.

> My service career started in 1939. My brother had just joined the Territorial Army, and we knew that war was likely to break out, so I thought I'd do the same. I joined the TA in March 1939 and started my training as a soldier in an anti-aircraft unit. I was first attracted to join the RAF just after the Battle of Britain. I was rather despondent with the army and I couldn't leave it soon enough. There was a notice saying that they were looking for recruits to join the air force to be trained as pilots, navigators and bomb aimers. I'd never flown in my life before, never been very close to an aeroplane, but I thought I'd have a go. So I put my name forward and was eventually accepted in May 1941. I went through a pretty strict medical examination and was asked a lot of questions before being accepted for training as a pilot.

Volunteering for aircrew was one of the few ways of getting into active service for those in reserved occupations. This was the main reason why Jim Chapman finished up as a rear air gunner in Bomber Command.

> When the war started, I was in the army because I was mobilised with the territorials. At the end of 1939, the factory that had employed me applied for me to come back. I was an AID [Aeronautical Inspection Directorate] inspector and the factory was making arms for the air force. It happened to other people as well and I was instructed to hand my uniform in and to report the next morning at 0800 hours to the factory. I protested as best one could, but was told no, I would have to report to the factory at 0800 for work, or failing that I would find two soldiers at my door wearing red caps. So I went back.

Chapman's return to his factory job seemed to mean the end of his service career, but he was eager to get back to the services.

Chaps were being called up, going into the air force, the army, the navy, and I was still there. This got to me. It bothered me what people would think. Friends had known me soldiering in peacetime, and I could imagine them saying, 'Now there's a war on, he's come out, hasn't he!' I decided to make official enquiries at the Ministry of Labour. The chap at the ministry sympathised with me. He told me the only way I could go back into the army was to join the tank corps. I asked about the other two services. I could go into the navy, but it would have to be in submarines, or the RAF as aircrew. I'd never thought about being aircrew, I'd never been interested in flying. However, if that got me out of the factory and got my self-respect back, I decided so be it, so I volunteered for aircrew.

There would usually be a delay between volunteering and actually being called up, which meant several more frustrating months spent in civilian life. Only then would the marathon training start. It must have seemed like an endless tour of different flying schools, each with its own acronym: ITW, OTU, HCU. It took two years for a pilot to emerge from this system ready to join an operational squadron, the longest spell of training that anyone fighting in the Second World War would receive, and perhaps the most technically challenging. It's worth remembering that in today's civilian aviation industry pilots need ten years of flying before they can expect to take command; in the Second World War young pilots were doing so straight after training. For gunners, it was somewhat less thorough, just thirteen weeks, meaning that the youngest volunteers were still only eighteen when they started flying operational sorties.

It wasn't just Britain's young men who were volunteering. Thousands from across the British Empire were also putting themselves forward. The contribution they made to Bomber Command was no token gesture but accounted for a very considerable section of the force. It is noticeable just how many veterans, including several of those featured in this book, recall being in crews that included several different nationalities. Although he's British, Maurice Flower's crew, for example, was predominantly Canadian.

> Percy, my navigator, was a Cree Indian. I don't know whether he was a full Cree but you can see on a photograph that he looked like an Indian with jet-black hair. He taught himself to speak English from a Sears Roebuck catalogue, and taught himself right through university and got a degree. He was a fantastic navigator. We used to go up in the woods around Norfolk, and he could walk up to a wild rabbit and pick it up off the floor and stroke it and then he'd put it down and let it go and it would sit and look at him. I don't know whether he hypnotised them or what he did but he had this knack.

Adge Boal was also in a crew drawn from across the Empire. He welcomed the opportunity to get to know people from other countries. 'We had two New Zealanders and an Australian. They were more interesting to be with than our own people; we knew our own people, you knew the life they'd had in the past. The Australians, New Zealanders and Canadians had a different life, and a different attitude to life.'

Boal's Australian crew mate was Ron Pitt. Born and brought up in Tasmania, Pitt volunteered for aircrew and would be the crew's mid-upper gunner.

> It appealed to me after hearing the exploits of 'The Few'. There was the adventure and we're very patriotic in Australia. A lot of our parents were of English stock and they spoke about England as being 'home' and the 'old country', so we were looking forward to it. I did enough training in Australia to get my gunner's wing and stripes. It was very basic: when I look at my logbook, I see we fired about twelve hundred rounds! Of course, we had more training when we got to the UK. There were about three hundred of us on the ship coming over. We took off from Port Adelaide, crossed the Pacific, went through

Panama and landed six weeks later in Southampton. We were about a third gunners, a third pilots and the rest were wireless operators.

Whole squadrons were dedicated to those who'd come from overseas to take on the Nazis. No. 44 Squadron, for example, was renamed 'No. 44 (Rhodesia) Squadron' in September 1941 in recognition of the country's contribution to the war effort. About a quarter of the squadron's personnel were themselves Rhodesian, and the squadron badge was changed to include an African elephant. Of all the countries of the Empire contributing to Bomber Command, Canada was the most significant, with fifteen Royal Canadian Air Force squadrons, enough to form the RCAF's own group, 6 Group. The Royal Australian Air Force had eight squadrons of its own, including No. 460, which is believed to have dropped the greatest tonnage of bombs of all Bomber Command's squadrons, releasing around 24,000 tons during the war. No. 75 Squadron, a Royal New Zealand Air Force unit, had been the first Commonwealth squadron to be formed in Bomber Command. Another RNZAF squadron, No. 487, was formed in August 1942 as a light day-bomber squadron. It experienced one particularly terrible operation in May 1943 when ten out of eleven aircraft were shot down on a raid on Amsterdam.

Beyond the Empire, Bomber Command was joined by many other volunteers from around the world. Among those most eager to join the cause were those who came from the now occupied countries of Europe. No. 305 Squadron was one of four squadrons of Polish airmen, logging 1,117 sorties with Bomber Command between April 1941 and August 1943 before being absorbed into the Second Tactical Air Force. The members of No. 311 Squadron were former Czech Air Force personnel who had served in France before escaping to Britain at the time of the fall of France. The squadron was active with Bomber Command, and later Coastal Command, although like several Coastal Command squadrons it was called into service for the Thousand Bomber Raids in 1942. Members of the French Air Force themselves formed two heavy-bomber squadrons. Roy Finch found himself training alongside a French airman who'd joined the RAF after the fall of France. In the multinational force that the RAF was becoming, misunderstandings could sometimes arise.

This French fellow didn't speak a word of English. French was my best subject at school, and I was the only one able to converse with him. He said to me one day, 'What do you do in the evenings, in the squadron?' I wanted to tell him, 'We go into town and find a public house.' With my schoolboy French, I was thinking, how the hell do you say public house? The house was '*maison*', no problem, and public '*publique*', so I told him we'd go to a '*maison publique*'. He asked what sort of girls were they, what were the women like? I said, 'You don't very often see them, in pubs, and if they're there at all, they're always with a man.' 'A brothel with no women?' was his reply!

In the early days of the war, airmen such as Robin Murray found that the training process was somewhat haphazard.

We were eventually trained to be wireless operator/air gunners, so we did a wireless course at Hamble, then we went to Cranwell and did another wireless course. We did a gun air course at Dumfries in Scotland and there we were posted to squadrons. I was posted from Dumfries to Bicester to a Blenheim squadron but the only trouble was the Blenheim squadron had been posted to the Far East, so I never joined them! So I got posted to RAF Honnington. The same afternoon when we arrived there, a German aircraft had flown across in front of the blind approach training flight aircraft and dropped a series of bombs which damaged one of the hangars and there was nobody in the aircraft who could fire at it, so it just got away. We were then transferred to the blind approach training flight and that was one of those boring jobs doing continual circuits and bumps as they called them. We did that for about six weeks and got posted to RAF Stradishall in No. 214 Squadron. Two of us were spare gunners. Normally you went to an operational training unit and got crewed up, so that the whole crew got posted as a crew, to a squadron, but we were two spares so if an air gunner was taken ill, we took their place.

Roy Finch, also training at the very beginning of the war, recalls being prepared for night flying through blind flying exercises on Avro Ansons.

They'd put a hood over you so all you could see were the instruments. Then in order to get your wings, you had to do a qualifying cross-country flight. I was flying from an aerodrome near Grantham, and the inevitable happened. I got completely and utterly lost, and then suddenly I saw down below me the Wash, which was quite distinctive from the air. By following railways and roads, I managed to find my way back to Grantham. After I landed, my instructor took a look at my log. 'The Wash?' he asked. 'You can't put that down!' I said, 'Well, sir, that's where I got the fix, I got lost.' He replied, 'The squadron leader won't pass you on that. Get a fresh sheet out, and I'll dictate. You write.' So he dictated and I wrote. At the end, he took a look and said, 'That's better, you've passed!'

With that incident behind him, Finch continued his training and went on to get his wings. 'I was so proud. We had a passing-out parade, and the wings were handed out. But the ones they issued were a bit cheap and nasty, so most of us went out and bought these padded ones and sewed those on.'

Robin Murray would find that learning on the job would be as crucial for his crew as the formal training.

I was very lucky because the crew were very good. They all knew their job and we'd been well trained, as far as they were able to at the time. They had the regulars and then we'd be a second line of defence, so our training was rather elementary because under normal circumstances it took several years to train a pilot, for instance. They were doing it in months in those days and cutting it down to the bare necessities for air gunners and wireless operators as well. Once you were operational, you had to learn an awful lot while you were going along.

Robert Kee recalls a lot of 'square-bashing' during his initial training.

I was called up in 1940, when the Battle of France was raging, and going badly. It was clear the French were being beaten. The first phase was elementary training, which was ridiculous because all we did was to learn how to fall in properly, eyes right, march, etc., and the people who were doing that were senior non-commissioned officers, who knew the cadets were going to be officers so they had a very tempered, slight respect for us, and at the same time they rather enjoyed making us obey their orders.

Jim Rogers found that in the confusion of the Blitz his training as a Bomber Command wireless operator was somewhat delayed.

When I first joined, I was sent for four weeks of what we called 'square-bashing' at Blackpool and then I was posted to what was supposedly No. 219 Squadron at Catterick. When we got there, this squadron had left three months previously so we passed on to Tangmere, which was a fighter aerodrome. The same thing happened, the squadron had gone to convert to Blenheims. The commanding officer couldn't do much with us, but as Tangmere was getting a lot of very severe attacks, we spent four months filling bomb craters before we started wireless training! We used to lie out on the aerodrome and as soon as the raid was over, dash up with shovels and spades and fill in the bomb craters to enable our own fighters to land or take off.

To Kee, the RAF still seemed a rather eccentric body at this stage.

One morning I remember they said, 'Fall in as usual, sirs, fall in,' and the sirs fell in. 'Now eyes right, come on, attention! Now I've got something to tell all you sirs. You're all going to be Frenchmen from now on, because Mr Churchill's decided to stop the French asking for an armistice by allowing them to become British too. Right turn, quick march,' and that was it. We used to march through Hastings day after day, very correctly, singing not patriotic songs but slightly lewd ones, because all the secretaries in offices used to come to the windows and watch us pass. And that was the first phase of our training.

Roy Finch had also had an early lesson in the peculiar world of the RAF.

When I first joined up, we all had to present ourselves at RAF Cardington. We were all formed up into squads of fifty men, and six of us were Under Training pilots. There was a little corporal in charge who said, 'I'm sorry, but all the billets are full, you'll have to sleep in the Nobel tents.' So one of our six, who was well over six foot tall, said, 'Corporal, excuse me, but do you realise that some of us are UT pilots?' The little corporal replied, 'I'm sorry, but I've got no alternative, you'll have to sleep in the Nobel tents.' That's where we slept. The next morning, he got us all on parade, still in civvies, and he went up to this fellow and looked up at him and said, 'Excuse me, did you say yesterday you were UT pilots?' 'Yes, Corporal, I did,' came the reply. 'Put that pilot on cookhouse fatigue!' That was the first lesson we learned in the RAF: do as you're told and keep your mouth shut.

The training was undoubtedly limited in those early days. Roy Finch quickly discovered how poorly trained the airmen were for the realities of going into combat.

The training wasn't long enough, and subsequently they lengthened it somewhat. It had been a question of getting people trained as fast as they could, we were desperate. But we just hadn't

got sufficient knowledge about navigation and the wireless operators hadn't had enough training. I think had we had more training, more of us would have survived. We didn't do dinghy drills,
which would have been helpful. The nearest I got to firing a gun
– and as second pilot you had to take over from anybody else
if necessary – was sitting in the rear gun turret. It was just
moving around, in a hangar, in a sort of a 180-degree circle.

By the middle of the war, however, the RAF had produced a
vast infrastructure for training, and getting volunteers ready for
operational duties had become a major organisational feat. With
the introduction of the heavy bombers, there were crews of seven
to find, with a variety of trades and skills that all required
specialist tuition: pilot, navigator, bomb aimer, flight engineer,
wireless operator, mid-upper gunner and rear air gunner. The
role of second pilot that had been considered essential in the early
Wellington crews had quickly disappeared, the losses sustained in
the early part of the war making it simply too costly to lose two
trained pilots every time an aircraft was lost.

The volunteers quickly found themselves dispersed around
Britain and the Empire to be turned into fully fledged aircrew.
The Empire Air Training Scheme had 153 flying schools in
Britain, as well as 180 overseas, mainly in Canada, Australia,
South Africa, southern Rhodesia, India and New Zealand.
Recruits from around the Empire would do much of their training
in these schools, but many British volunteers were also sent
abroad, where good weather and safety from enemy action
allowed training to be unhindered. Yet even travelling so far
across the Empire was a big adventure for most of the volunteers.
Tom Wingham was sent to South Africa to train as an observer.

The first thing I remember is the six-week journey it took us to
get out there! We left on a dull November day, Armistice Day
in fact, from the Clyde. We were on a twenty-thousand-ton liner
with around five hundred trainee aircrew on board, but also
about two thousand troops going to the Middle East. We were

only trainees who'd been in the air force a short time, but we were given a Bren gun, which we'd never seen before, and posted as lookouts for enemy air attack. It was a bit cold going across the Bay of Biscay! Eventually, we arrived in South Africa and spent three weeks in Durban over Christmas and New Year, which was great fun. To see the plentiful food, lights on, warm sunshine was great! For somebody who had been brought up in the East End of London, it was a different world completely. We used to spend the weekends surfing on the coast and the girls were plentiful, all looking after us, taking us home and entertaining us.

Dennis Wiltshire was delighted to be sent to Canada. Having originally joined the Volunteer Reserve in March 1939, he was sent overseas in 1942.

Things were pretty grim in Britain. No street lighting, very limited car lighting, very limited lighting altogether except when the searchlights were on. When we left it was complete blackout. We had five or six days on board ship crossing over to Canada, able to have some lighting, but that was quickly subdued after we found we were being followed by a submarine, so we had to dodge that for nearly two days. When we arrived in Canada, it was literally a different world. We were completely awestruck by seeing all these lights after so long in the blackout. The food was just incomparable to what we were eating at home. Not so much the quality but the quantity. No one I knew had ever been to the American continent at all and it was quite an eye-opener.

Hal Croxson remembers a warm welcome for the thousands of trainee airmen arriving in Canada. 'We were well into rationing in Britain and you didn't see much fruit or anything of that nature, but when we got across to Canada the first thing we were met with were the Women's Voluntary Service ladies. They came walking through the train handing us oranges, apples and fruit that we'd never even seen before. We were in heaven, and for the fifteen months I was over there in training, it was like living in Utopia.'

While the North American weather was on the whole preferable to what the aircrews experienced in Britain, Wiltshire certainly hadn't been prepared for Canada's winters.

The weather was extremely harsh. Where we were stationed, we had the coldest winter there for over sixty years and that was giving us a reading of sixty below zero. We couldn't work on the aircraft outside; all maintenance and repairs had to be done in the hangar. There were no problems until we came to the end of our first period of servicing. They turned the heat off in the hangars and opened the doors. Every piece of glass in the hangar doors went. They were there for weeks afterwards repairing the hangar doors. We had to make final adjustments to the aircraft outside, and boy, was it extremely cold! As far as the snow was concerned, we had rollers constantly being pulled up and down the main runways and tarmacs being pulled by trailers to compress the snow.

Of the 300,000 men who trained as RAF aircrew during the war, 220,000 of them would have undertaken at least some of their training overseas. Around 125,000 of them went on operational duties with Bomber Command, many of the rest seeing action with Fighter or Coastal Command, or themselves becoming instructors. There were of course several thousand who never in the end saw any action, their long training courses cut short by the conclusion of the war.

Although the USA didn't enter the war until Pearl Harbor, and was officially neutral up until that point, there were many tacit signs of America's sympathy for Britain and her allies. Under the Arnold Scheme, trainee RAF airmen were allowed to train alongside their US Air Force counterparts even before America entered the war, and altogether 14,000 British aircrew would be trained at bases in the USA during the course of the war. Once America had officially entered the war in December

1941, the possibilities for cooperation greatly widened. No doubt the new alliance between Britain and America helped foster a particularly convivial atmosphere at Christmas parties for those British airmen training in the United States at the time. Stephen Nolan, who had served with the Coldstream Guards and had been evacuated from Dunkirk before joining the Volunteer Reserve in September 1941, had recently been sent out to Florida to train as a pilot. He was one of several British airmen featured in a full-page feature in the *Fort Lauderdale Daily News*, which proudly reported that Lauderdale had 'played host to young men in Uncle Sam's service and to Britishers as well' over the Christmas holidays. A large contingent was expected at the New Year's Eve dance, and a New Year's Day breakfast.

Most volunteers from Britain started their RAF careers in north-west London, the first posting being to the Aircrew Reception Centre at Lord's cricket ground in St John's Wood. Crews were billeted in flats along the edge of Regent's Park, and fed in the canteen of London Zoo. A few months of square-bashing were usually involved. Those volunteers hoping to train as pilots then started on the PNB scheme, which trained up pilots, navigators and bomb aimers. Most of those who finished up as navigators and bomb aimers had originally aspired to be pilots as well, but had fallen at one of the many hurdles designed to weed out those who didn't demonstrate the high standards required for the job of skippering a bomber. At Grading School, would-be pilots were quickly streamed through a series of aptitude and flying tests, and it's fair to say that there were few second chances for those who didn't immediately shine. This was the first occasion on which the least successful were 'washed out' of pilot training altogether, and sent off to train in another capacity; but those left behind still had no guarantee of becoming pilots either. Alan Bryett was determined that he wasn't going to be washed out.

I most definitely wanted to become a pilot, and joined up as a trainee pilot. The only real question was whether you were going to be a trainee bomber pilot or a trainee fighter pilot. One didn't realise which until you began to get into your training and you could begin to see the mavericks who were going to be the fighter chaps and the more steady sort of chaps who were going to be the bomber chaps. So you could see these two classes of pilot at this stage, and you weren't quite sure yourself which you were going to be.

As Bryett explains, the difference between being a bomber pilot and a fighter pilot was marked. 'Bomber pilots have got to be steady, got to be patient. They've got to be tolerant and have got to do a pretty boring job. There will be moments of action, but only moments in what would probably be several hours of pretty boring flying which you've got to be prepared for.'

Robert Kee found that he was better suited to the temperament required of a bomber pilot. 'I think that they were a rather slower lot. As part of the initial training one was learning to fly very elementary planes like Tiger Moths but at the same time, one was being sorted out as to whether one would be a better fighter pilot or a better bomber pilot, and half the people there with me in the first initial training operation became fighter pilots, but I was selected as a bomber pilot, being a slower person.'

Despite the prospect of some 'pretty boring flying', Bryett's enthusiasm for becoming a pilot was undiminished. He also looked forward to the higher status that he perceived pilots enjoying within the RAF.

If you were a pilot you had far more chance of being commissioned, there was no doubt about that. The greatest number of commissions were given to pilots because they were the good all-rounders and the leaders of aircrew. With that rank went money, and in the long term if you survived a tour, your future in the RAF was going to be far greater. At that stage the RAF was very much a pilot's air force. If you were going to move on to the greater echelons of the service, and even stay in the RAF in the long term, it was the pilots who were going to lead the RAF, certainly not the air gunners.

All aircrew, including those who'd been allocated places on the PNB scheme, were sent to an Initial Training Wing (ITW), where they'd stay for approximately twelve weeks. Here, they attended classes in a variety of subjects including armaments, aircraft recognition, hygiene, mathematics, basic meteorology and LDAO (Law, Discipline, Administration and Organisation in the Air Force), all designed to give the students the solid theoretical grounding that was essential for aircrew. There were also physical training sessions involving PT, parade drill, route marches and parachute training, and drill on anti-gas procedures. Even at this stage, there was some basic specialist tuition for the different crew positions. Pilots would have classes in aerodynamics, airmanship and the principles of flying; navigators would learn basic map reading; bomb aimers basic bombing procedures; wireless operators would become familiar with basic Morse code. Aircraft recognition exercises were an important part of the training for all aircrew. Although no one talked about 'friendly fire' at the time, everyone was aware of the danger of shooting down the wrong aircraft. It was particularly important for gunners such as Jack Eveleigh to be able to identify aircraft correctly.

Aircraft recognition was almost always inside a lecture room where model aircraft would be suspended from the ceiling. The instructor would point at an aircraft and you would say 'Junkers 88' or 'Messerschmitt 109E' or whatever. That was one way of doing it. The other was to have actual photographs flashed up on to a screen, and sometimes they would obscure the main body of the aircraft and perhaps just show you a portion of the tail or the wing. If you were any good, you would be able to recognise them. It was just a matter of practice, practice, practice all the time and being keen and wanting to learn how to recognise aircraft.

In an age when flying was still such a novelty, getting into the air for the first time was a momentous occasion for any trainee. Jim Rogers, who'd volunteered for the RAF in July 1940, was certainly not alone in finding it a disconcerting experience.

> The aircraft we were in at the time, a De Havilland Dragon Rapide, was an old type of aircraft with a lot of dope on the wings. With the smell of dope and the confined atmosphere, and being so hot inside, I just felt physically sick. We used to carry a Peak Frean's biscuit tin, and once somebody started being sick, he finished up passing the tin round because everybody was being sick! Invariably we flew over Wales during training, where it's very hilly and we weren't at a great height, so it caused a lot of up and down sensations. But I did overcome it in the end. I'd made up my mind I wanted to be in Bomber Command, so I had to sort of get over it.

For Leonard Miller, who had wanted to fly ever since he was a small boy, the chance to train as a pilot was a dream come true. 'It was wonderful, like being an angel flying! I was in Canada at the time, out on the prairies, and you were free.'

Tom Wingham immediately felt at home in the air. 'I just felt that I belonged there. Quite a number of my friends suffered from air sickness, but I never did. I just felt comfortable the whole time. It was something I had been looking forward to since I'd been a boy. It was great to see the ground disappear!'

Having got through Grading School, the next stage for those training as pilots was Elementary Flying School. It was at this moment that many would now be sent abroad on the Empire Training Scheme, although there were also flying schools in Britain. Overseas, they could take full advantage of the more predictable weather, allowing the pilots to fly on far more days of the year than could ever be possible in Britain. The rigorous selection procedures that had already seen some candidates washed out at Grading School continued during the initial lessons on Tiger Moths, as pupils would learn about flying instruments, and daytime and night-time flying practices. It was usually on Tiger Moths that pilots would fly solo for the first time. Ground classes continued, with further tuition in aircraft recognition, navigation, instrument flying (without sight of the ground or landscape), the theory of flight, airmanship and engines. Pilots were also taught to strip and reassemble their guns, and given practice on firing ranges, crucial skills for those pilots destined for fighter aircraft where they'd be one-man crews. By early 1942, Alan Bryett had made it through to Elementary Flying School.

I did my initial training at Paignton in Devon. That lasted three months. I then went to Perth Flying Training School training on Tiger Moths, with the instructor and one trainee pilot. The training pilot had about a dozen pupils and he explained to you that you were going to be given fifteen hours of instruction and at the end of fifteen hours you should have enough confidence to take the aeroplane up, fly her to a thousand feet, do about a mile square round the aerodrome and land. If you could do that to satisfaction, you would stay on pilot training.

For Bryett, though, the dream of becoming an RAF pilot would end abruptly in Perth.

I did my fifteen hours and it was perfectly obvious to me I was not going to be a pilot. The main problem was that I was nineteen and had never driven a car. Most people didn't have cars in those days but many of those fellows who became pilots had driven cars and they could understand an aeroplane relatively easily. I couldn't coordinate my hands sufficiently well with the actual physical motion of the aircraft, and it was quite clear to me that in each part of the training I was taking a good deal longer than most. So at the end of fifteen hours I was nowhere near going up and soloing, and I think I did twenty-one hours in the end. I won't repeat what the instructor said to me, but it was blunt!

Bryett was no longer a trainee pilot, but it certainly wasn't the end of his RAF career. Aircrew were badly needed, and every volunteer would have his part to play.

> I was disappointed but it was the right decision and I was then taken off pilot training and sent to Heaton Park, where they reclassified the fellows who had failed as pilots. They had a certain number of tests and you might become a navigator or an air bomber – at that time the new category of air bomber was coming in. After two or three weeks, I was told I was becoming an air bomber and it was a disappointment in a way, but it was pointed out that the air bomber was a key person in the aeroplane. In other words the aeroplane was quite useless if you got to the target and then the air bomber made a mess of it in the last two minutes. So your morale was built up in that way and I happily went to the bombing and gunnery school which was at Wigtown, on the west coast of Scotland.

Bryett was just one of thousands of trainees who discovered that becoming a pilot was simply not for them. Arthur Smith also successfully made it through Grading School to get his chance to learn to fly and solo for the first time. He was already having misgivings about his suitability for becoming a pilot. 'My first solo flight came really as part of my duty. I don't remember being excited as such, I remember being apprehensive and surprised that I was the one person in this aeroplane, taking off on my own. But I realised I had to do it, and I hadn't made up my mind what I was going to do about my feelings at that precise time, so I went ahead assuming that I was still going to be a pilot.

Having soloed, Smith was sent to Canada, where his misgiving became more serious.

> I was trained as a pilot initially and I went on to Tiger Moths in this country, at Woking Flying School. I think it was after seven and a quarter hours that I went solo, and after a few more

bits of instruction I was sent over to Canada. I was continuing my training to be a pilot in Tiger Moths over there, and it took me quite a long time to go solo again. When I did go solo, I had a bit of a scare because I took off and when I turned on to the cross-wind leg, I inadvertently got into a sideslip, which is actually a controlled way of losing height quickly. But it wasn't controlled with me, I just got into it by mistake. I panicked, and thought I can't get out of this, I don't know what to do, and I very distinctly saw the conifer trees coming up at me. I must have done the right thing with my feet and hands and on the joystick, because I got out of it, but that was the first inkling I got that I probably wasn't fit to be a pilot.

So despite having soloed successfully in Britain, Smith had to address his unease. 'No one saw it happening, I certainly didn't tell anybody. I didn't even write it in my diary. Eventually, when I knew I had to do aerobatics on my own, I said that I didn't want to be a pilot any more. I asked to be remustered. Luckily they were quite good when this happened, and I wasn't the first person, but my instructor was very surprised because outwardly I seemed to be getting on well.'

Like Alan Bryett, Arthur Smith had realised that his dream of becoming an RAF pilot was not going to be realised, and he was remustered as a bomb aimer. 'In my case it was really a fear of being in control of something that I didn't feel in control of. I didn't have the confidence to be flying as the pilot of a crew or on my own. I realised that I just didn't have the courage to be in charge of an aeroplane, but of course I didn't see that at all until I started flying.'

John Whiteley had a happier experience. He quickly took to flying, inspired by a Battle of Britain pilot who became his first flying instructor at Elementary Flying School.

I had done eight and a half hours flying with him, doing circuits and landings and stalling and spinning, when he said, 'I'm putting you up for a test with one of the flying instructors.' The

examiner said, 'All right, take off and do a circuit and landing.'
So I did a couple, including an overshoot, and then he said, 'I'm
getting out now, all I want you to do is take off, circuit and
landing.' I took off, climbed up to eight hundred feet and did
the circuit. Fortunately at the time it was a tea break so there
weren't very many aeroplanes in the circuit or on the ground
and I came in and landed. I was the second of fifty potential
pilots on my course to go solo, and I never looked back!

Robert Kee also took to flying and was soon on his way to
becoming a fully trained bomber pilot. 'The first time I was
airborne was absolutely delightful. Going solo was the most
wonderful feeling, to take a Tiger Moth off by oneself. I did that
and thoroughly enjoyed it. It was like being a bird.'

Before he went solo, Kee did have one experience that might
easily have unnerved many trainee pilots.

> Before anyone went solo, a senior officer had to go round sitting
> beside you to see that you could do it properly. The day I went,
> the group captain in charge of the station came with me. I was
> doing all right, and just turning to come back to prepare to
> land when a German bomber came flying past the aircraft and
> hit the ground with an explosion. The group captain said, 'I
> think after that you're better to go round once more, in case
> that's worried you at all.'

Kee duly went round again, and passed the test. It was after
this that he and his fellow trainee pilots were streamed into
fighter and bomber pilot groups. 'I'd been hoping to be a fighter
pilot but there was a psychiatric test. The psychiatrist fellow
talked to you, and there was a mechanical way of testing the
speed of one's reactions, and it was fairly clear to me that my
reactions weren't fast enough, and sure enough, shortly afterwards, I was told I was going to be a bomber pilot.'

Nonetheless, Kee was delighted to have been passed as a pilot.
'When I got my wings, I was very pleased. That made one a

proper pilot, a proper RAF man. My mother was very pleased too.'

Those pilots who made it through Elementary Flying School successfully moved on to Service Flying School, where they progressed on to flying dual-engine aircraft, such as the Avro Anson and the Airspeed Oxford, or, for those training in the USA, the Beech 18. On these aircraft the pilots would learn to handle more complex instruments, more complicated manoeuvres and more powerful engines. John Whiteley learned how to fly a twin-engine aircraft on an Airspeed Oxford.

The Oxford was a nice aeroplane to fly but it felt a bit unusual. With the Tiger Moth, there was a blind spot and, to avoid it, you had to swing the nose from side to side. But with the Oxford, you could see over the front and to keep it straight you had to do it on your engine revolutions. It was a little bit tricky to begin with but it soon became second nature, and the Oxford had a pneumatic braking system which helped. You did have to practise keeping the aeroplane straight on take-off. The Oxford would swing to the left, so you opened up the throttles to give slightly more power on the left engine. This kept the aeroplane straight until you got rudder control, and you could then push the throttles forward to get full power for take-off. This could be a problem because in correcting the aeroplane swinging to the left, you probably gave it too much power and then it would swing to the right and you could land yourself in all sorts of trouble.

Having mastered the basics of flying the Oxford, Whiteley was able to move on to learning some of the more complicated manoeuvres that would be essential for operational flying over enemy territory.

We used to practise corkscrewing. You were told that there was an enemy night fighter, probably half a mile back up on the port side, coming in. At about five hundred yards, you're being controlled by the gunner, and he'd say, 'Corkscrew port, go!'

and you put the thing into a dive and follow the corkscrew round. You hoped by this manoeuvre you could outwit the German night fighter. It was quite a violent manoeuvre and the Lancaster's controls weren't power assisted like the modern aircraft. It really was hard work with a full bomb load and you lost a lot of height so once you'd lost the German night fighter, you had to start climbing up again!

As the pilots became more competent in the air, they continued to learn on the ground too, leaving Service Flying School with a comprehensive understanding of navigation, reconnaissance and armaments. Now those who'd been flying overseas returned to Britain, but they quickly discovered that they would need to acclimatise to very different flying conditions from those they'd become accustomed to in North America or southern Africa. The clear skies of the Empire Air Training Scheme would be replaced by the cloud, rain and fog of northern Europe, along with complete blackouts on the ground. Aware of the very significant dangers that these different conditions posed, from 1942 the RAF introduced Advanced Flying Units for pilots returning to the UK to help them adjust to flying over Britain.

For those who hadn't made it as pilots, becoming a navigator was one of two alternative trades to be transferred to. The continued development of navigational aids throughout the war had made an already difficult job even more complex, and vindicated the decision to split the role of the old 'observer' into those of bomb aimer and navigator. Having been washed out of pilot training, Bill Burke started his career as a navigator. He considers it fortunate that he did his training in Northern Ireland. 'If I hadn't trained in Northern Ireland, I'd never have flown operationally because it was a long period of time for people to go to Canada to be trained and come back again. My initial flying training was over the Irish Sea up to Scotland. That was flying Avro Ansons.'

Peter Baker, who had wanted to fly ever since he was a boy,

also trained as a navigator in the UK. 'We had a lot of lectures and navigational exercises on the ground before we took to the air. The first time I flew was in a Fokker, which was of course a Dutch aeroplane, known as the "Flying Classroom", at Prestwick. It held thirty or forty people and most of us were busy being sick rather than learning navigation!'

After Initial Training Wing, or being washed out of pilot training at a later stage, navigators were sent to Air Observer School, where they trained in map reading, armaments, guns, turrets, astro and practical navigation, Morse code, aerial photography, instrument and radio direction-finding, compasses, radar, meteorology, maps and charts, reconnaissance and practical navigation. In the air, the trainee navigators would get their first taste of navigation through dead reckoning, calculating the aircraft's position without any external aids. Before the introduction of navigational aids such as *Gee* and H2S in 1942, dead reckoning had been the most common method employed by observers and navigators on operational flying. Navigators would chart their position with the help of navigation computers, which were complex slide rules, using graphs and direction-finding radios. For Bill Burke, there was a steep learning curve to becoming an operational navigator. 'It was very easy to get lost and I certainly succumbed on more than one occasion. The problem was that in the initial flying over the Irish Sea, there really is no means of identifying where you are. It was only when you reached the turning point on a coastline or an island that you could get a real identification of where you were. So I did get lost, fortunately never to the point where I didn't get back in the end.'

The alternative to becoming a navigator was being sent to Bombing and Gunnery School to train as a bomb aimer. In some cases, this was third choice for trainees washed out of both pilot and navigator courses, but more often airmen went straight from being trainee pilots to trainee bomb aimers, and it was frequently a case of getting the numbers right to ensure that there would be enough trained aircrew within each discipline.

After failing as a pilot, Alan Bryett went through a selection process to decide whether he would become a navigator or a bomb aimer. 'They asked you a series of questions and you spent an hour doing a small reclassifying exam. I think it was very largely down to the numbers required – if the losses had been great at the sharp end, they might want a lot of navigators or a number of bomb aimers. The one thing that was quite clear was that if you were not suited to being a navigator or an air bomber, you would finish up an air gunner.'

At the time, the prospect of becoming a bomb aimer was promising, and Bryett believed he could still pursue a successful RAF career.

I was not unduly worried. An air bomber was a new category and there were going to be some commissions offered. There was a feeling amongst some fellows that having been failed as a pilot they were no good. I didn't look on it like that at all and I think the RAF's morale-boosting qualities were very good. It was made perfectly clear once you got to bombing and gunnery school that you were going to be doing a very important job and this new category was coming in because it was such an important job. That was played up and I didn't feel inferior in any way, in fact I felt rather important that I'd been picked for that job!

At Bombing and Gunnery School, the trainees attended lectures on bombs, bombing theory and pistols, as well as going on practical courses on range firing on the ground, and firing from mounted machine guns. Bryett also recalls some of the practical exercises involved, such as learning to find the target.

You went into a room with a gallery and you laid on your tummy and you looked over the edge of the gallery where you could see a detailed map of the whole of the British Isles which was moving ahead on the ground. First of all you were just told to make your way from one place to another and you map-read your way along. Sometimes you would have a navigator with you and he would help you with regard to the course. It was very useful and saved hours and hours of flying time. Of course, when it came to night flying you had to be in the air but in the elementary stages, hours and hours were spent on that training and it was very valuable.

Bryett recalls that a typical exercise might involve being asked to 'fly' towards Oxford, and bomb one of the colleges in the university. 'After a while you had tests and a more complicated route to fly. It might be to go from Reading up to Leeds and bomb the town hall in Leeds, and you were marked on this skill.'

It was crucial that a successful bomb aimer should be able to judge when to drop the bomb accurately. 'On the simulator training you got to the destination and pressed a button which stopped the map going along and then you said, "Right, there is the point, that's where I'm going to drop it."'

From these static exercises, Bryett progressed to air-to-ground bombing runs. Flying over the bombing ranges of the Yorkshire Moors, the trainee bomb aimers dropped 25-pound smoke bombs over practice targets. These dummy bombing runs, usually in Ansons, Whitleys or Fairey Battles, were primitive experiences compared to the real bombing runs the trainees would be taking part in just months later.

At bombing school we flew Ansons, which were a small aircraft that had a pilot and four trainees. It had a fixed undercarriage, I remember you had to wind the undercarriage up, it was a very old-fashioned aeroplane. One of the four fellows would be the navigator and he would get you there. In most cases to start with we were bombing by day and that was really a piece of cake because when you got within two miles you could see the area where the target was. The navigator would have given you the wind, and so on the bomb sight you would set the wind. You were given half a dozen smoke bombs and told to fly to the bombing area, and you would make five bombing runs over the target. It was quite tedious because there were four trainees and you each had to drop one or two bombs and it took some time to get positioned.

These practice bombing runs were essential for developing the bomb aimer's accuracy, and for learning to use bomb sights.

To start with, it's quite difficult to position yourself, you'd be maybe fifty yards to the left or right and have to go round again. By the time you got on ops you'd conquered that because you weren't very popular if you had to go round again. In training, you were expected to get reasonably close, maybe within fifty yards or a hundred yards to start with, and of course every now and again you would have luck and get a bull's-eye. The difficulty came when you were flying from a greater height. From a thousand feet was fine but towards the end when they were really getting you to be accurate, you were flying from nearer five thousand feet, when with a slight mistake you'd be quite a long way out. If you were flying at a thousand feet you would hope to get within fifty or a hundred yards. If you were flying higher, within two, three or four hundred yards was reasonably good.

The progress of the bomb aimers would be carefully monitored.

Some of the targets were at sea. I remember one in the bay at Weston-super-Mare, which was floating in the sea, and there were RAF chaps on the ground marking exactly where you were. If you hit the target you could usually see you'd hit it, because the smoke went up, but if you were reasonably close they would explain to you how good you were, and you were being assessed on bombing accuracy throughout the whole of the training at bombing school. One of the most thankless jobs from the RAF's point of view was the chap who was on the ground plotting these fellows who were going over hour after hour. By the time you got back to the aerodrome, he would have phoned through, and you would go into the flight hut and they would tell you how good you were. You weren't very good to begin with but towards the end you got fairly accurate.

For those volunteers who weren't allocated to the PNB scheme, training as either wireless operators or air gunners beckoned. Fred Stearn was determined to succeed as a wireless operator. 'I worked a lot harder when I went into the RAF than I did at school. My father was in the trenches in the First World War. He was a sergeant, a machine gunner. I was determined that I would go home and show him that I got my stripes.'

After ITW, Stearn was sent to Wireless School in April 1943, from where he passed out in December. At Wireless School, the trainee operators would be taught radio and electrical theory, as well as being tutored in practical theory on wireless equipment so they could not only use it to transmit messages but also service a wireless set in the event of mechanical failure, or damage from a Flak attack. For Stearn, the technology involved was not particularly complicated. 'There were about ten valves in the set and you could actually run it on three volts, using all these other leads. You had different coils in case it didn't work. On the first trip, the intercom went a bit wrong and I was lucky to find a loose lead. Normally if the radio set got shot up, there wasn't really much that you could do about it.'

Morse code was essential for wireless operators, and at Wireless School the trainees practised until they could transmit at a rate of twelve words per minute. As well as Morse itself, wireless operators needed to be proficient in using 'Q codes'. These three-letter codes, so called as each one begins with the letter 'Q', were used to transmit radio signals between aircraft and air traffic control in Morse and acted as a shorthand for what would otherwise be rather long and unwieldy messages. 'QBZ', for example, was short for 'Report your flying conditions in relation to clouds', while 'QFO' could be used by a crew to ask whether they could land immediately. These codes would need to be memorised so that wireless operators could use them on operations. Fred Stearn spent a lot of his time at Wireless School learning the various Q codes. 'In the air, I had to practise contacting all different stations to get QDMs, which was the magnetic heading for the aircraft to steer towards its destination, which we'd need to use in the event of getting lost. I had to listen out every half an hour because there'd come a message from base to say come back to base or abort the exercise.'

The learning of Morse code and Q codes could be fairly relentless for trainee wireless operators, as Jim Rogers found when he finally started his training after filling in the bomb craters at Tangmere.

My initial wireless training was at Blackpool, in the old tram sheds which had been converted to training schools. We were almost continually reading Morse code and trying to get up to speed, and learning the meaning of QDMs. You had to be proficient by the time you finished and I think a few people went rather berserk with the continual 'Dit dot, dit dot' on those long days in the tram sheds. I found myself going around looking at signs on buses, reading them in Morse. It was totally integrated into you.

As well as learning to use the radio equipment, the trainees at Wireless School would undergo other practical tuition, such as parachute training, before moving on to Signals School, where their theoretical training was consolidated with more practical exercises, and Advanced Flying Unit, where their skills were honed further. By now, Morse code was being sent and received at eighteen words per minute, and this was the opportunity to get experience of using the equipment in the air. Whereas earlier in the war wireless operators and gunners trained together, by the time Fred Stearn was at Wireless School the two disciplines had been separated. 'You were a wireless operator or you did training for gunnery and you got sparks. We were getting so many of these new radar installations in the aircraft that the wireless operator had to use that they dropped the training for air gunner.'

So from 1942, the only volunteers who went to both wireless and gunnery schools were those who started as wireless operators but couldn't pick up the Morse code quickly enough. They remustered and joined those who'd volunteered to be gunners from the outset at Bombing and Gunnery School following their time at ITW. Here they would be taught how to fire guns while flying, handling Lewis guns, Vickers gas-operated guns and Browning machine guns. As they learned to use the guns, they flew mainly on Bristol Blenheims and Boulton Paul Defiants. The Defiant was a largely obsolete fighter aircraft relegated to training use, the Luftwaffe having quickly realised how easily it could exploit its main shortcoming, namely that it had no forward-firing armament, making it extremely vulnerable to attack from the front. Trainee gunners would progress from air-to-ground firing to air-to-air exercises, simulating attacks on fighters using drogues towed along by another aircraft. Back on the ground, gunners were given a comprehensive education in the theory of gunnery, taught how to strip the weapons down and load them (in some cases blindfolded), and they were introduced to electrical, hydraulic and pneumatic gun turrets. Having arrived from Tasmania, Ron Pitt continued his gunnery training in Britain.

We had to know the mechanism thoroughly. I was in the artillery for a while in the National Service so I knew a bit about the bigger guns, and at school I was in the Cadet Corp, so I grew up with them. We had training with cameras to improve our accuracy and that was helpful as they analysed the results and gave you marks. We'd fire at drogues, towed by another aircraft, and then we'd have firing on the ground too, into a sandpit, and that was our general training. I think the Australians mixed in pretty well. We had a reputation for being good at shooting kangaroos, but a lot of us had never seen a kangaroo except in the zoo! I felt quite at home with the Browning .303s. You had a sense of power when you got behind those. We didn't really have sufficient training to meet the experienced pilots of the Luftwaffe, but I did feel confident at the time. Most of our instructors had been on a tour of operations themselves and we held them in very high regard.

Clay pigeon shooting was one of the techniques used to help train Jack Eveleigh as a rear air gunner.

We started clay pigeon shooting when we were at ITW, which was at Bridlington in Yorkshire. We used to shoot the clays up on the front of the esplanade and I was pretty good at that. We put a bob each into the kitty and usually I managed to make a few bob. I liked clay pigeon shooting. It showed you the reaction of going through the target. Most of the boys had never handled a shotgun, but I was a country boy and I had used one, so I had a little bit of an advantage there.

Eveleigh also practised firing at pop-up targets. 'At the butts, which is the target end of the range, the men would be in a trench so that you weren't going to shoot their heads off, and they would have a target on the end of a pole which they would just pop up. You would be firing at them for a limited time, and when they brought the target down, they'd count up how many holes you'd made.'

The way airmen were allotted their crew positions was often fairly arbitary. Having started training initially as a pilot, Hal Croxson finished up as gunner. The switch in roles had come for him while he'd been training in the USA on the Arnold Scheme.

I had over a hundred hours of flying, most of it solo, down in Georgia, and felt I was doing pretty well. But I went into hospital for two and a half weeks with some strange complaint that nobody knew anything about. By the time I came out, I'd lost my position in the training scheme and could not join up with any other course that was coming through. So they shipped me to Toronto, and I was idle there for about three months, protesting that I wanted to continue my pilot training. They kept telling me there was no place, and eventually they said to me I could be a navigator or a bomb aimer. I said, 'I don't want to fight my war with pencils and rulers, I want to fight them.' That's youth for you! I said, 'Put me in a tail turret and give me four guns and I'll fight it that way.' Of course, it ranks as pure stupidity but at the time I had that feeling that I just had to do something involving action.

Croxson found the training he now underwent as a gunner relatively straightforward.

When you've been doing the training of a pilot with seven subjects, and you must pass in all of them, to go and be trained as a gunner was simple, just thirteen weeks. You'd do a little bit of flying in an aircraft where you had a gun on a pivot, looking out of the back of the aircraft, and you shot at drogues which were towed by other aircraft. You had to get so many hits in a drogue every time you went up and it was a very low percentage. I think we used to be allowed to fire a hundred rounds and out of that, if you had a five or six per cent hit rate, you passed.

That pass rate may see extraordinarily low, but during the training achieving accuracy was not easy. 'The type of gun we were firing with was a 1914 model, a Lewis gun, and the aircraft that was towing the drogue was a few hundred yards away. Bearing in mind that the gun would have a terrific sort of spray shot, rather than a very controlled action, and you had the rattle of it and the shake of it in an aircraft that's moving anyway, it was a bit haphazard as to whether you could hit anything.'

Officially there was no class distinction between the different crew positions; indeed, many veterans recall how the camaraderie within a crew blew apart the class divisions that were part and parcel of British society in the 1940s. Nevertheless, class does seem to have played a part in selection. Pilots, and consequently navigators and bomb aimers, were largely drawn from the universities and public and grammar schools. Many of those who volunteered to train as gunners instinctively felt that their poorer educations would prevent their selection to the other positions, and subsequently volunteered immediately as gunners, never believing an officer's role to be within their grasp. Rear air gunner Jim Chapman certainly sensed a distinction between the different crew positions. 'We were what one would call "ordinary". Pilots are not ordinary, they are the supermen. The bomb aimer was a cut above the gunner. The bomb aimers and navigators were like schoolmasters.'

Even when he was offered entry into the first stage of the RAF elite, Fred Stearn turned down the opportunity. 'After I'd only been in nine months I got a commission, which was the greatest surprise of my life. I couldn't accept it because I was a working-class man and most of the officers in the mess had a high-class education.'

The experience of working together as a crew, however, meant that such preconceptions quickly became redundant for Chapman. 'Where class is concerned, Bomber Command helped dispel class, it faded out. You're in a crew with people from all walks of life. If you were to succeed and live, let alone hit your targets, you do your duties successfully and class never came into it.'

Once trainee aircrew had completed their initial training, they were sent to Operational Training Units. Here, individuals would come together as a crew for the first time. Crew selection was not the organised, regimental process you might expect from the RAF, however. Instead, the usual routine was for anything up to a hundred trainees of each position to be left in a hangar, and instructed to form themselves into five-man crews. For Fred Stearn, the process was on a smaller scale than some airmen experienced, but no less haphazard. 'We were thrown into a room and there were twelve pilots, twelve bomb aimers and twelve navigators, twelve wireless operators and twelve mid-upper gunners. You milled around the room until the pilot comes and says to you, "Oh, you're not a bad old wireless operator.

Would you like to join my crew?" And you'd probably say no, because you didn't like him. It was as simple as that – it was love, or not, at first sight!'

Like many airmen, Stearn had already started to crew up before the order to do so came through. 'Just before, in the mess, the navigator and I got together. We'd gelled and we said we'll form our own crew and find a pilot. Fortunately we did, we found this Australian and he saw us, and he says, "I'm looking for a wireless operator and navigator. You look intelligent." I knew that I'd picked the right chap. It's a gut feeling, and it is a momentous decision in your life. Pick the wrong pilot and you might get the chop.'

Inevitably, some airmen had more problems selecting the right crew than others. While gunner Jack Eveleigh was at OTU, he and his fellow trainees were told in the usual way to sort themselves into crews. He quickly joined up with another gunner he'd been friendly with at gunnery school.

> We went out to look around for the most likely pilot. The other gunner asked if I'd got anybody in mind, and pointed out an Australian who he reckoned looked OK. So we went down and found this Australian. We were walking down a gravel path and we fell in either side of him. 'Do you want a couple of gunners?' He looked at us, and replied, 'I'm a rotten pilot.' We answered, 'We're not much good as gunners anyway!' He said, 'Oh well, we don't want to spoil anybody else's crew, so you're in.'

Eveleigh's new pilot already had a bomb aimer and a wireless operator, but still needed a navigator, and he was eager to get a good one.

> The pilot told us, 'I can fly the ruddy machine, you can probably do some gunnery but we want a man who is going to take us there and, more importantly, get us back home.' So we went out that evening and tried everywhere, but most of the blokes were spoken for already. Eventually, I came across two navigators

talking and one was saying to the other that he hadn't got a crew yet. I asked if he was any good, and the other navigator said that he'd come top of the class but he didn't speak much. I asked which hut and went back to see the new skipper, told him the hut number and told him to go and get this navigator quick. It's true that he never said two words if one was enough, but he knew his stuff and I'm still in contact with him.

Now united as a crew for the first time, the pilot, navigator, wireless operator, bomb aimer and gunner started flying together at OTU, usually in Whitleys, Stirlings and Wellingtons. Sometimes they'd even be sent on 'nickel raids'. This was a chance for the crew to learn to work together, a crucial stage for Fred Stearn. 'Before you got to OTU, you were basically training for your own qualification, but once you got to OTU, that was the point that you crewed up and had the chance to prove yourself.'

Alan Bryett agrees that this opportunity to develop the crew's sense of teamwork was pivotal.

You've got to trust each other. No. 158 Squadron's emblem was a chain with seven links in the chain and those links were joined together. There were seven crew members in a Halifax and as long as those links were standing together, you held together. You had to have great confidence and you had to know them well and you had to reassure them. The rear gunner – the 'tail-end Charlie' – was out on a limb, right at the end of the aircraft, sitting by himself. The rest of the crew had a little understanding, and this was quite common, that about every ten minutes one of us would speak through the intercom, 'Hello, Mac, how you going, everything all right?' so that Mac wouldn't feel that he was left out of it. Little things of that sort were important.

As the crew's captain, the pilot was the key figure in creating the bond within the crew.

The pilot, who was a flight lieutenant, was a very experienced fellow. He hadn't done more ops than us but he was more experienced in flying and it was a morale-boosting exercise for all of us, but the important thing was to feel confident that everyone was doing his job well. We'd worked together for many months, in all sorts of operations. One of our engines had failed when we'd been on a Wellington at OTU, and we crash-landed in Yorkshire. We'd all got through that all right and we were confident with each other.

If the crew didn't quite gel, it was possible to change crew members, an opportunity which Stearn and his new crew mates took advantage of. 'The bomb aimer wasn't too good and the crew decided that he was not as good as the rest of us and so we as a crew went to the commander and said we weren't happy and we'd like to get him changed.'

Jim Chapman also changed crew.

I didn't really get on with the captain. I was happy enough that they had chosen me, but when it came to flying I hoped I would never have to go on ops with this chap. Without being funny about it, he stammered. He couldn't get words out and he was the captain. I visualised having to bale out and by the time he'd got the words 'Bale out' out, I'd be down in the drink! A bit of a fracas led him to dispense with my services. One day, I walked into the mess wearing my hat. This was the sergeants' mess and that was considered a crime. The captain strongly disapproved, and being young my attitude was 'Well, mate, if you don't want me, I can do without you!' I was glad to be shot of him, and it wasn't long before I got another crew.

The OTU syllabus was complicated, marking the biggest leap from training to being prepared for operational flying. There were lessons, and examinations, in parachuting, dinghy drills, aircraft layout, fuel systems, low-level flying, dummy bombing raids, and gunnery practice out at sea. Then there was just one more step for a crew before they were sent on operations. At Heavy Conversion Units, crews progressed to the heavy bombers,

Halifaxes and Lancasters, that they needed to become accustomed to for operational flying. Their competence would be improved on circuits and landings, overshoots, landing with just three engines and in cross-wind landings, dealing with a variety of other emergency scenarios, and in night flying. Maurice Flower even remembers mock fighter attacks. 'We called it fighter affiliation. You'd fly along and they'd attack you from any direction. It would just come out of the blue, a mock attack, and the gunners would pretend to fire back but they didn't have ammunition.'

At HCUs, the crews were also joined by a second gunner if they'd acquired only one at OTU, and a flight engineer, completing the seven-man crews used on heavy bombers. Flight engineers were selected from former ground crew members who, despite witnessing the terrible losses sustained by the aircrews for themselves, volunteered to become aircrew, taking their skills into the dangerous night-time skies. Their job in the air was to ensure the aircraft could get back on the fuel available and to fix any mechanical problems. On longer sorties to distant targets such as Berlin, the fuel allocation was tight, so controlling fuel consumption was crucial if the crew were to make it back to their stations. Flight engineers were also trained by their pilots to be competent in rudimentary flying skills so they could take over the controls in case of emergencies. Rarely, though, did this go farther than flying the aircraft in a straight line, and few flight engineers would have had prior experience of landing. It took nine months to train as a flight engineer, and there was only one school to go to, at St Athan. Here, the trainees would become experts at manipulating the undercarriage, flaps, intercom systems, engine and pitch levers, leaking pipes, and the wiring. Maurice Flower would become a flight engineer after serving as a member of the ground staff at a flying school in South Africa.

I was on the Empire Training Scheme at RAF Bloemfontein. The pilots came to us for the second stage of their training, and they used to do air-to-air firing and ground firing and use twenty-five-pound practice bombs. They were flying on faster aeroplanes, having trained in a Tiger Moth already. We had Miles Masters and Havards from America. I never really liked the Havard. It had a direct-drive propeller, there wasn't a gearbox between the engine and the propeller, and the noise was appalling. The Bishop of Bloemfontein complained to our commanding officer about the noise on Sundays of our aeroplanes flying around. The CO wrote a letter back saying, 'I apologise for the noise, but if you will stop the war, I will stop flying on Sundays!' We didn't hear another word about it. I much preferred the Masters. They were wooden aeroplanes, with a gull wing and radial engine, but they were nice aeroplanes and quite quick. They were designed as a fighter but ended up as a two-seater trainer.

Although Flower enjoyed the work, he became jaded with the life in South Africa, knowing that the real war was being fought elsewhere. 'It was like being in a peacetime air force. There was no thrill in it at all! We couldn't get spares, and although we had good food, lots of entertainment and every amenity that you'd think of, even electric lights at night, it got a bit boring. One day I saw that they wanted volunteers for aircrew, especially flight engineers. So I volunteered and came home with about half a dozen others.'

Flower discovered that as a trained and experienced ground engineer he would be expected to adapt quickly to his new role. 'We didn't have any air experience. We were already fitters and were expected to know everything about every aeroplane. In the air force when you were posted to a new station, you may have come from fighters on to a bomber station but you were expected to know everything about bombers on day one and just start work!'

By the time they emerged from Heavy Conversion Units, the crews had been flying together for some time. They'd been trained in their own disciplines, and learned the importance of teamwork, and it was time to put all that into practice. The only other school that might be required would be a Lancaster Finishing School, where pilots and flight engineers destined for Lancaster squadrons might be sent on a short course to be given fourteen days of Lancaster flying if their HCUs hadn't been equipped with these aircraft.

Throughout their training, aircrews had also been schooled in emergency situations and preparing for crash landings. In the early days, escape drills were largely dependent on the diligence of the pilot. Robin Murray was fortunate to have a conscientious captain. 'We had escape drills. It was up to the skipper of each aircraft to do these escape drills and go through all the motions. You wouldn't actually get out of the aircraft because you were too high up! But you'd go through all the drill. We did that regularly, but it depended a lot on the skipper.'

He was also sent on dinghy drills. 'They had a sort of mobile pond on the aerodrome and they had this dinghy in it. You'd take it in turns to get into this dinghy and go through the drill and then get out on to the side, but of course you were stationary! When you were out at sea with the waves you were bobbing about a bit so it wasn't quite as simple as it appeared on dry land, but it gave you the idea.'

By the time Maurice Flower was training as a flight engineer, such drills had become more formal. He remembers doing dinghy drills at St Athan.

You got dressed in flying suits with all the clobber on, including flying boots. They put an eight-man dinghy into the swimming pool upside down and turned all the lights out. You had to jump into the water, turn the dinghy the right way up and get into the dinghy. I couldn't swim, not one stroke, so somebody held me up. I remember this big fellow turned the dinghy over the wrong way. It had a gas cylinder on the side which inflated it and the dinghy came over and hit me on the head. I went under and I don't remember another thing until I ended up in the dinghy. So somebody must have put me in the dinghy! That was the kind of training we had, a bit haywire but good fun.

Flower was not the only airman who couldn't swim, as Jack Eveleigh discovered when he came to do dinghy drill while based at St John's Wood.

We did our dinghy training in Seymour Baths in London. You had to be able to swim fully clothed for two lengths of the bath. You would be lined up at the end, and about four NCOs with lists of names called each of us in turn to step forward, jump in, swim one length and back again, and at the end of that you'd be crossed off the list. Several of my friends couldn't swim, and a couple of the fellows came to me and said, 'Jack, you can swim. Can you swim for me?' I said OK and I'd go to the end of each queue and give another name. I think I swam about five times, and I was kept going with cigarettes for some days afterwards!

As well as dinghy drills, there was basic instruction for the aircrews in parachute jumping. Harold Nash also remembers being taken on evasion practice.

We were taken out in coaches with the windows boarded up. You sat in the coach, about twenty of us, and it would roll off through the country. You had no idea where you were going, and they dropped you in the middle of nowhere. We had to find our way back to the airport. The signposts were removed, but when you came to a village you could ask where places were, although not the airport. So gradually you'd get back that way, and you had to evade the soldiers who were out looking for you. It was great fun, and when I was shot down, and trying to get to Holland, it came in very useful.

Nash was also prepared for coping with a reduced oxygen supply in an emergency.

We went into an oxygen chamber, and they gave you a piece of paper and a pen and you started to write. You kept writing until you were asked to come out. You didn't feel much difference at all, but they had been reducing the oxygen supply and when the air came back in again and you looked at your writing, you saw that the latter part of the writing had grown. Big, squiggly, unrecognisable letters due to the lack of oxygen. I also remember being put in a simulator and being swirled round to demonstrate the G factor. That was important. I nearly fainted once.

As well as drills, Robin Murray was given first-hand advice. 'We had one or two people who had landed in France and got home and they gave talks about it. When I was at Honnington, we had a crew from No. 9 Squadron that came down. Two of them had walked right across Spain and got home through Gibraltar.'

The training process had itself produced a shocking number of casualties. During the course of the war, a total of 5,327 airmen were killed during training, accounting for approximately 10 per cent of all Bomber Command's losses. A further 3,113 were injured. Arthur Smith witnessed a number of accidents while he was training.

I remember one accident at the air navigation school in Canada. We had a night flight, involving several aircraft in very bad weather, and we got into a terrific snowstorm. It was absolutely blind flying, very frightening because you're sitting in the aircraft and you see snow absolutely dashing against the windscreen, and you feel as if you're manoeuvring and of course you aren't. When we got back, we heard that our flight leader hadn't returned, having crashed in the storm. If you were on a station for a month or two, this sort of thing might happen once or twice. You took it as part of what was just going to happen, and unless it was your particular friend, it was just a loss. I don't remember worrying too much about it, as long as I didn't crash.

Alan Bryett recalls that the poor flying conditions in Britain were the main cause of crashes in training units.

There were a tremendous number of accidents, far more than most people ever realised. Trainees were being killed when I was at the bombing school in Wigtown, nearly always with night flying. On the eastern side of the Pennines were all the operational aerodromes, on the western side were all the training aerodromes. On the western side, you had the mountains of Wales and Scotland and at night-time you were going out on cross-country trips flying across to Northern Ireland and aeroplanes were getting lost. They would come down low to try and see where they were, because if you came down low you could see the flashing beacons.

These flashing beacons were placed all over the British Isles, each one flashing two letters in Morse code to indicate their position, an invaluable aid for crews that had got lost, but also potentially lethal. 'People would come down low in order to see where they were and crash in the mountains. It was a real hazard.' While he was based up at RAF Kinloss in Scotland, Maurice Flower witnessed a number of accidents.

We lost a Whitley up in the mountains in the Highlands and we went to look for it. It just flew into the side of the mountain. The pilot lost an engine and he just couldn't maintain height on one engine. While we were searching, we found a Sopwith Camel from the First World War, with the skeleton of a man still sitting in the cockpit. They traced him and he was a naval sub-lieutenant. He'd been there since 1914/18 and nobody had ever walked past that spot.

As Flower discovered, the accident rate in training wasn't helped by the fact that the training units were often using the older aircraft taken off front-line duty.

The Whitleys, especially, dropped at an alarming frequency. We saw quite a lot of crashes at Kinloss. The Whitley was a huge aeroplane. It only had two engines and was very slow. The high mountains and horrible engines in these old aeroplanes were not a good combination. The engines used to leak oil all over the wheels and whenever they came to a stop you had to dash out and put covers over the tyres because the tyres would rot with the hot oil dropping on them. Really they were just a menace.

It wasn't just natural hazards which threatened trainee crews. As Fred Stearn recalls, there was also the danger of enemy attack, before the crews even got as far as operational squadrons. 'It was dangerous when you were training because the German fighters used to infiltrate and wait for you to go on the actual flare path when you were training and they killed quite a few then. But I had no fear. You just didn't, you were so young. It was an experience and once you'd volunteered you made sure that you never let them down. It wasn't going to happen to you.'

Although training overseas in the Empire Training Scheme offered some protection from such accidents, the trainee aircrews were still vulnerable. Quite simply, wartime flying was a dangerous activity, even without the enemy's involvement. For the crews that made it through, though, the end of training meant the end of the waiting. Arthur Smith was excited by the knowledge that he could finally go on operations. 'It was with a certain amount of satisfaction that I went on to my bomber squadron. I'd crewed up and we were a very close crew, and we were glad to get on with the job. We looked forward, I think, to our first flight over enemy territory, and at that time, of course, you had no idea what it was going to be like.'

Despite having volunteered to join Bomber Command, Arthur Smith had in fact given little thought to what he was about to be asked to do. 'I don't remember thinking ahead, about what I was going to do, what it was going to be like, what I was going to feel about it. I just looked at one day at a time, except that when I initially volunteered to be a pilot in the RAF, I thought it was going to be quite exciting and just the thing I wanted to do.'

Like Smith, Fred Stearn was largely ignorant about the high loss rates on Bomber Command's squadrons. 'On operational training, morale was very high. We certainly weren't aware of the casualties. We knew the casualty rate for training when we were on OTU, and we read about losses on Bomber Command, but the losses were a great deal more than we had realised.'

Having been through a rigorous training process, the volunteers were distributed across Bomber Command's squadrons. Still young and carefree, they were largely oblivious to what lay ahead. Now, though, it was time to face the enemy.

4

Target for Tonight

'The fighters are our salvation, but the bombers alone provide the means of victory.'

Winston Churchill, September 1940

Sandy Mcilroy   Bert Chandler   Eric Read   Len Petty   Adge Boal   Freddy Parkin   Ronny Pitt
RAFVR   RAFVR   RAFVR   RNZAF   RAFVR   RNZAF   RAAF

Rear Gunner   Engineer   Navigator   Pilot   W/op/AG   Bomb Aimer   Mid Upper Gunner

514 SQUADRON JANUARY - JULY 1944

(top) Adge Boal *(third from right)* with his second crew, including
Ron Pitt *(far right)*.
(bottom) Bomber Command airmen from Peter Baker's squadron
relax in the mess.

The supply of new crews coming on to Bomber Command's squadrons at the start of 1941 gave fresh hope to a command that had been feeling rather beleaguered in the aftermath of the Battle of Britain. Yet as Fighter Command basked in its glory, and Britain's cities sat out the Blitz, it seemed entirely right to look to the bombers to deliver some good news. No military action was possible in western Europe after all, and the prospect of a fresh invasion attempt had been deferred until at least the next summer, and only then if the Luftwaffe could win a rematch of the Battle of Britain. Bomber Command had continued the war throughout the autumn of 1940, but its activities were on the whole low-key, allowing the number of experienced crews to increase across the squadrons. This had the positive knock-on effect of giving the new arrivals time to acclimatise to operational life and gain plenty of practice on the relatively easy 'freshmen' targets. The scene was set, it seemed, for Bomber Command to take the war to Germany in the new year, a lone force keeping the western front active.

The year 1941 would not prove, however, to be the vintage one for Bomber Command that its leadership hoped for. While there would be important breakthroughs in the war during the year, they weren't going to come from the bomber boys. As commander-in-chief, Sir Richard Peirse was issued one new directive after another; the command's foothold appeared to be eroding. First, in January, came the directive to concentrate on the destruction of Germany's synthetic oil plants; that was now to be Bomber Command's 'sole primary aim'. This was a clear brief against Peirse's preferred strategy of concentrating his available forces on large raids once a month to take advantage of the new moon. Yet just as he had seemed to be making some impact, the Air Ministry was telling him to concentrate on oil targets. Such attacks, however, were mountable only in the clearest possible conditions, and the early months of 1941 brought a run of particularly poor weather. The oil offensive was continually hampered, many aircraft were forced to turn back and a high number of crashes on airfields within Britain followed as the descending fog made safe landing impossible. More often than not, Peirse had little choice but to suspend the oil directive in favour of less important targets, but chosen so there was at least some chance of bombing something. Cologne, which had the dual advantages of being within a relatively short range of Bomber Command's airfields, and outside the main concentration of Flak and searchlights in the Ruhr area, was attacked time and again in those months.

Then, in March, came another directive – this time to counter the threat to British shipping convoys in the North Atlantic from U-boat attacks. In some senses, it was a welcome relief from a failing strategy, and a distraction from the unwelcome truth that Bomber Command simply didn't have the ability to carry out an effective campaign against Germany's synthetic oil production. This new job for the bombers was of the utmost importance, the order to change policy coming directly from the Prime Minister.

Churchill had been appalled at the loss of nearly nine hundred British, Allied and neutral ships between June 1940 and March 1941. With many of the ships carrying vital supplies, Britain's island status had never seemed to count against a nation as much as it did now. So Bomber Command would spend the next four months engaged in attacking not only German shipping (and those old adversaries the *Scharnhorst* and the *Gneisenau* were still roaming the high seas), but also the industrial sites that were making Germany's control over the oceans possible. So high on the list of targets were the U-boat shipbuilding yards at Kiel, Hamburg, Bremen and Vegesack; the marine diesel-engine factories at Mannheim and Augsburg; aircraft factories at Dessau and Bremen; U-boat bases at Bordeaux, Lorient and St-Nazaire; and the airfields from which the Focke-Wulf Kondor aircraft were making their devastating attacks on British shipping.

While Bomber Command's list of targets was unquestionably directed to legitimate military ends, there was another important provision in the directive which ordered Bomber Command to concentrate its forces on the threat to the shipping convoys. It was specified that 'Priority of selection should be given to those [targets] in Germany which lie in congested areas where the greatest moral [*sic*] effect is likely to result.' This dictate wasn't necessarily carried through to the crews' briefings: Roy Finch distinctly recalls being given very firm instructions to keep well away from any civilian areas when he was flying operations in November 1941. Such directions were becoming rarer, though. The March directive is the first endorsement of a policy of area bombing, a deliberate assault on Germany's civilian population. It was Portal's policy, although certainly condoned by many other officials, and it was derived from the simple fact that accurate bombing of specific targets that would help the battle in the Atlantic was at best going to be possible only for around eight or nine of the most moonlit nights in each month. So while industrial targets would be cited in battle orders, the crews would in effect be deployed in area bombing of the chosen towns and cities. The civilian deaths in Germany started to increase.

In July 1941, there was another change in policy. Following Hitler's invasion of Russia, the threat in the Atlantic receded, and Bomber Command was once again to concentrate its efforts on Germany. There was continued confidence that the bombing campaign could force a dramatic change in the morale of the German population. There was little evidence so far that any such change was taking place, and indeed there was no real sign of bombing affecting civilian morale even when the tonnage dropped was at its heaviest. Again, area bombing was based around the strategic campaign. Railway installations in the Ruhr region, the key mode of transport for the heart of German industry, were a priority – on dark nights the relatively well-defended cities of the Rhine, such as Cologne, Dusseldorf and Duisberg; more distant cities if poor weather made these targets unattainable, with Hamburg, Frankfurt and Stuttgart among those hit most frequently.

As the strategy evolved, so did the equipment. During 1941, the Vickers Wellington, which had been part of Bomber Command's fleet since the beginning of the war, began to dominate. On some raids, more than half the crews dispatched were in Wellingtons; 'Wimpys', as they were affectionately known to their crews, would make up half the forces taken on the Thousand Bomber Raids the following year. A twin-engine medium bomber, the Wellington had been almost a quantum leap forward for Bomber Command when it was first introduced in terms of its construction, bomb load and armament. With a flying ceiling of 15,000 feet and a maximum speed of 245 mph, it would of course be far outclassed by the heavy bombers that were about to be introduced, but it had been the linchpin of Bomber Command's war effort for the first few years. Robin Murray flew his operations in the Wimpy.

What always struck me about a Wellington, as soon as you got into it, was the smell of the dope, and as soon as it started to move you got this sort of flapping noise. But it was a very comfortable aircraft to fly in. You somehow felt safe in it, even though on the front turret you just sat on a little seat and you had your stuff in front of you. It was an aircraft that took an enormous amount of punishment and came back. A wonderful aircraft, very forgiving.

Murray's role was as front gunner. 'I had four Browning machine guns in the front turret. They were power operated and very efficient because they were tuned to fight at about two hundred yards. So that was your firing zone; you realised how far an aircraft was away from experience.'

As a second pilot, Roy Finch flew his operations in Wellingtons, and it was an aircraft for which he felt a special affinity.

I liked the Wellington very much, it was fairly docile, comfortable, and in the days before the Lancaster, it was a big aeroplane. We knew we'd got the best bomber in the world! You climbed up a ladder under the nose at the front to get into the cockpit. For the time, it had a very big dashboard, with all sorts of instruments, and you continually had your eyes flickering from that on to the sky above or ground below, and dead ahead. The noise was pretty horrendous, like a lot of old tin cans rattling, but it felt great to be flying a Wellington.

By the time Ron Pitt was on operations, the Wellington, very much an aircraft of its time, was seen as outdated, but it continued to be a mainstay of the fleet of aircraft used in training. 'Towards the end, the Wimpys were pretty unreliable, and there were a lot of crashes at OTUs. They had a pretty bad name for that reason and quite a few people were killed on them at OTUs.'

For Pitt and his contemporaries, the Wimpy became the subject of one of the many Bomber Boys' songs.

> Ops in the Wimpy, ops in the Wimpy,
> Who'll come on ops in a Wimpy with me?
> And he sang as he pranged that Wimpy on the flare path,
> Who'll come on ops in a Wimpy?
> And his ghost can be heard as he pranged on the flare path,
> Who'll come on ops in a Wimpy with me?

The Wimpy would remain an important part of Bomber Command's operational fleet for some time to come, but by 1941 a new generation of heavy bombers was also being introduced. The Manchesters, Stirlings and Halifaxes were still few in number and their real impact would come later, but they were indicative of a growth in the scale of Bomber Command's ambition that would bear fruit in the latter part of the war.

The Short Stirling was the first four-engine bomber to join the

RAF. On paper it seems an impressive beast: a flying ceiling of 17,500 feet, and the potential to carry a 14,000-pound bomb load. The Wellington had been considered impressive with a bomb load of just 4,500 pounds. The Stirling would not, however, be as successful as had been hoped. Its design was hindered by a requirement to have a wingspan not in excess of 100 feet, simply because anything wider wouldn't fit into the RAF's hangars, many of which dated from pre-war days when such mighty aircraft were beyond the imagination of all but a few in the RAF. This greatly affected the Stirling's performance, as did problems with the undercarriage. Its four Bristol Taurus engines were somewhat underpowered, and in practice the Stirling's bomb load was reduced to just 3,500 pounds for long-range targets. When Bomber Command raided Milan and Turin to help bring the war in Italy to an end, the Short Stirling lived up to its name, struggling to climb over the Alps. Few airmen were envious of those flying in Stirlings. Lancaster navigator Bill Burke remembers cheers going up in the briefing rooms if it was announced that Stirling squadrons would be flying on the operation; it made the Lancasters that bit safer.

> It wasn't a case of gloating, just regarding yourself as fortunate. The Stirlings didn't have the height of the Halifax; the Halifax didn't have the height of the Lancaster. You felt sorry for those poor sods down there, because somebody dropping a bomb on you was a very real danger for the Stirlings. They would aim to get the Stirlings onto the target at a different time to the Halifaxes and Lancasters, but there were occasions when it didn't work out as planned.

The Stirling would endure heavy losses in its relatively short operational career, and long before the war ended it had been relegated to join the remaining Wellingtons in the RAF's training units.

Having completed their training, it was usually with a sense of nervous excitement that the airmen made their way to their new squadrons, ready to play their part in the defeat of Nazi Germany. In 1941 Robert Kee was posted to No. 44 Squadron, one of several squadrons then based at RAF Waddington in Lincolnshire.

Looking at my diary of the time, I can see I felt rather ill at ease with the other people there because I was the only new person at the time, so felt very much like a new boy. But once one got going, one was part of them. People sometimes say, 'Oh, weren't you feeling fear all the time of what might happen?' and the answer really is no, because one was leading a fairly normal life most of the week. One would be going into Lincoln, to pubs, the cinema, that sort of thing, with other people, and coming back, and perhaps there were no operations for you that week. But people you'd been going to the cinema with sometimes weren't there any more. Somehow one took that for granted. I mean, if you've been in battle in the trenches in the First World War, the blood was all around you, and the fear was all around you, but it wasn't around us. We had a perfectly normal everyday life for three days, and on the fourth night you'd go off and face the Flak, over Germany, and if you were lucky, come back again.

When he arrived fresh from his training in September 1944 as a new member of No. 619 Squadron at Strubby in Lincolnshire, Lancaster pilot John Whiteley quickly felt at home. 'I felt very insignificant because I was then mixing with crew who had been flying over Germany and bombing Germany. But you were made most welcome by the squadron commander and all the other people in the mess. I was made to feel a part of No. 619 Squadron.'

There was a particular solidarity among the aircrews who'd come from overseas to join Bomber Command. Ron Pitt felt it when he arrived on No. 514 Squadron, and it eased his nerves. 'One thing that helped me when we arrived on the squadron was an Aussie gunner who had done a few trips. We went into the sleeping billet and he said, "Great to see you, Aussie!" We shook hands and that gave me confidence. Often when crews had arrived at squadrons, the ones that had done a few trips were a bit offhand towards the sprogs coming in, but he was so welcoming and it helped considerably.'

Sometimes, however, those experienced crews were most conspicuous by their absence. It was something that immediately struck Alan Bryett when in 1943 he arrived as a new member of No. 158 Squadron at RAF Lissett, near Bridlington in Yorkshire.

When you arrived on the operational station, there weren't that great a number of veterans because people were not doing all that number of trips before they were shot down. There would be a certain amount of celebration if someone had completed a tour of thirty ops. Maybe four nights in a week we were losing one or two aeroplanes – altogether we had thirty operational planes. People were arriving each day because planes had been lost the night before. So you didn't have a great number of veterans to talk to.

Despite this, Bryett remembers that morale was still strong among the new crews. 'There was a very high sense of morale. We are here, it's what we've been trained to do, it's all going to be all right with us because we're going to do all the right things, we're not going to take any risks, and the time has now come. It was a time of great excitement really that you were going to do the job that you'd been trained for.'

Fred Stearn was similarly eager to go on operations. 'At any time I could have stopped, I'd have been grounded and taken away, but you had that option. But I didn't, I'd volunteered and I'd done the training. When you get on to the squadron you change from being youths to men and you've got to prove yourself. You rely on each other because your life will depend on any one of the crew.'

Crews could potentially find themselves on operations every three days. For most of the war, a tour consisted of thirty operations. Technically speaking, although the aircrew had entered the RAF as volunteers, having made that step they were bound by military law to carry out whatever orders they were issued with. There was certainly no sense of choosing which operations you might take part in. The Air Ministry was quick to recognise, however, that wartime flying would take its toll on any aircrew, and by the end of 1940 had decided that a tour of operational duty would comprise 200 hours of operational flying. Following at least a six-month break, a second tour would be expected, although a third would be optional. Under the influence of Arthur Harris, the definition of a tour of duty was amended, with thirty sorties the standard for a first tour, and twenty for the second. The Pathfinder Force would be expected to complete forty-five sorties. The numbers of airmen available meant that the pressure to complete a second tour was reduced by the end of the war, but many airmen volunteered anyway. It would take most crews around six months to complete their first tour, as many nights on operational duty would never see a take-off, the sortie cancelled owing to poor weather. Sometimes crews got as far as the aircraft before the raid was called off.

Although crews flying at night wouldn't normally take off until around eight o'clock in the evening, preparing for an operational sortie required detailed planning over the course of the day. The crews would be gathered together for a series of briefings, as well as spending time checking the relevant parts of their aircraft. For Maurice Flower, a day on operations soon had an established routine.

In the morning you would have briefings but you wouldn't know the target at this stage. It was on the board but covered up. After the briefings, I used to go out to the aeroplane and walk round it, inside and outside, checking it thoroughly. I'd make sure the tanks were full; you'd have a fuel load according to the length of your trip with a bit of spare for getting back. In the afternoon, we used to go and have a shower and put clean underwear on. If you got a bullet hole you wanted a clean vest for it to go through to stop any nasty stuff getting into your wounds. So clean clothes and then we used to go for the final briefing and have a pre-op meal, which was usually bacon and eggs.

An operational day had a similar pattern for Hal Croxson.

We wouldn't have been on operations the night before because that never happened in my experience. We'd get up and go to the mess for breakfast between eight and nine. Then each of us would go to our own departments. I would go to the Gunnery Office and see the battle order. If our crew was on the battle order, we had quite a busy morning. The first thing you've got to do is an inspection of your own particular part of the aircraft, in my case the tail turret. Then we'd all come back together by lunchtime. We'd go and have lunch in the mess and then probably go for a sleep.

Not everyone could get to sleep. Many found themselves lying on their beds in the Nissen hut, staring at the ceiling, just waiting for the time to pass. The huts made for pretty inhospitable accommodation – bare, corrugated iron walls; humid air causing water to drop down from the inside of the ceiling, one coke stove in the middle of the hut for heating, even in the middle of what were often bitterly cold winters where the bomber squadrons were based in Yorkshire, Lincolnshire and East Anglia. From the moment he knew he was going to be on operations until the moment of take-off, the anxiety gradually increased for navigator Bill Burke.

The tension builds up on the day as it does in Ravel's *Bolero*. You get up in the morning and have breakfast and wander down to the flight offices to see whether you are going to fly that night. If you were not going to fly that night there was an immediate sense of relief, I'm not going to dice with death, I'm down at the local pub or into the local town chasing girls. If you are flying, the automatic reaction is 'Is this going to be the trip when I buy it?' There's tremendous security about the target, but you tried to find out how the aircraft were being loaded. If they had a heavy load of fuel and a light load of bombs you knew you were going deep into the German heartland. That implied high risks so your feelings went up a notch. Sometimes, of course, the briefing for the night's target was very late. It was really determined by the time which you were going to be on target.

The final briefing would normally be at the end of the afternoon, typically around four or five o'clock. 'You went into the briefing room, and when everybody was assembled, the doors were closed. Service police were guarding the doors. They pulled back the curtain and that's when for the first time you saw where you were going.'

Red tape would be used to indicate the route the crews were to follow. The briefing room itself was always very closely secured; guards on the door, windows all blacked out, sealed inside and out. With twenty or so aircraft going out from the squadron, Hal Croxson would normally be one of around a hundred and fifty aircrew waiting for the target to be revealed.

As you walk in, there's a massive map on the entire end wall of the building, which is covered in curtains. The squadron commander came out, and the curtains would be opened. You'd hear a groan if it was going to be a long trip. Once the squadron commander had given you what you might call his 'chatter', he'd hand over to an intelligence officer who would fill you in on a lot of the detail. Then there'd be the met officer, who would tell you exactly what the weather was not going to be – if you follow me! Then you might have a visitor from Air Control for a final word.

The swish of the curtain being swept back to reveal the target for that night was the moment of real dread for Maurice Flower. 'The worst moment was when they pulled the string and pulled the curtain back and you saw where the target was. You'd think, Oh blimey, not that one again, I was shot to hell the last time we went there. It was really terrifying, that moment.'

There was a certain kind of hierarchy to the different targets, with crews well aware of the dangers each imposed. 'There were no good targets. We did quite a few French targets which we always termed as "easy" ones. The Ruhr wasn't terribly popular, a bit of a hellhole really. It was probably the worst area. It was heavily defended and they used to stick the searchlights upright and it was like flying into light. They could pinpoint you against the clouds and you didn't stand much chance either way.'

The final briefing was an important opportunity for the crews to understand the true nature of that night's operation, as Alan Bryett explains. 'It was a time when you learned as much as you could and you asked as many questions as possible. People asked all sorts of questions and you were told what the timing was going to be. There was a great feast of knowledge. The station commander had got everything at his detail but then he said, "Now ask questions, we've got quarter of an hour, ask what questions you like."'

By the middle of the war, crews were routinely briefed to attack a single target, but in the early years of the war Robert Kee was briefed on several targets.

> We were in Four Group, and the operations for the whole group would be read out to us. The main target would usually be an armament factory, or harbour installations, really obvious good targets. There'd also probably be a secondary target, something like a railway station that was quite clear and easy to find, although it never was, and in recognition of that fact these instructions always ended with the same thing, 'After that, anything that opens and shuts in Germany', and everyone always cheered.

In the days before area bombing was endorsed – indeed, became policy – this last instruction was a nod to the problems of accuracy that were plaguing Bomber Command. It was also an acknowledgement that the bombing wouldn't affect just military targets but civilians too. For airmen like Kee, though, it wasn't something that he was aware of worrying about unduly.

I remember when we came back from Hamm, we flew very low and fired a lot of machine guns at odd targets that were in our way, and they weren't proper military targets. When I've said that to my children, they say, 'Weren't you absolutely appalled?' The awful thing is, no, I am rather appalled when I think about it now, but the spirit of the war was that the Germans had been doing so well in the war, one felt one was getting one's own back. I don't think very many people in the RAF during the Second World War would have said they thought it was a bad thing if they killed civilians. Yes, one would have preferred it if one was only hitting military targets all the time, but it was very difficult to do, certainly in that early phase.

Many veterans, including Alan Bryett, recall that it was the time after briefing that was the worst, hanging around waiting for the sortie to begin.

I can't say you felt fear. You felt apprehension. I felt fear when we were being shot down, of course, I felt terrible fear, but on the actual operations we were all so busy, we all knew our job. We all had confidence in the other person that he would do his job well and you went off quite confidently into what you knew was a fair bit of danger, but with a bit of luck we'd done six operations all right and we'd done that quite happily and not been attacked or anything. So this one was going to be all right and we'd be back from Berlin.

For Bryett, this period of waiting was a time for the crew to reassure each other.

Depending on the length of the trip, take-off would probably be around seven o'clock. You had a meal before you went and you got yourself ready. It was just general apprehension really, just waiting for the moment and getting everything ready and steady. You'd have a quiet talk amongst yourselves and the pilot would brief you. The pilot was not only the pilot of the aeroplane; he was the coordinator of six other fellows who were all busy doing their own job. You knew each other very well, as friends. You'd been on leave together, you'd drunk together, you were a little close family and you couldn't wait for the couple of hours to go to be off.

However much these young men tried to jolly themselves along, the atmosphere must have been electric as the crews gathered together at the end of the afternoon for their pre-flight meal, that sense of trepidation permeating the mess. Dozens of crews all gathered together, knowing the target and what was required, but not knowing whether they'd ever eat in that mess again. The standard fare to see the crew on the way was bacon and egg, a real treat during wartime rationing. Maurice Flower remembers that the pre-flight meals given to the aircrews could be a mixed blessing. 'They started off giving us chips on pre-flight meals but at twenty-two thousand feet they don't work too well on the stomach! The smell used to be a bit obnoxious in the aeroplane, so we asked them, "Please, no more chips on pre-op meals!" So we used to make do with bacon and egg – the poor civilians never got bacon and eggs.'

Chips weren't the only less desirable part of an operational meal. Tom Wingham's squadron were given beans, which were even less helpful several hours later, flying over Germany. Having been fed, there was nothing for it but to face the music. The crews made their way from the mess towards the aircraft. 'We'd be picked up and go to the parachute section and pick up all our flying kit. The wagon would take you out to where the aircraft was sitting and I'd have another walk round it and check with the ground crew anything that they'd found. Then a final cigarette, get in and go.'

As Hal Croxson climbed into his rear turret on each of his operations, the sudden quiet after the build-up of the day was eerie.

We all chatted amongst ourselves, bags of banter going on, lots of jokes, rude comments on what you were doing last night. It was a protective attitude. You're kept in that frame of mind until you get out to the aircraft and then when you finally get into your turret on your own, that could be the worst moment. But I never ever experienced any actual fear of what I was going into. I knew I was going into it, and I was going in to do my best. Once you got in there, you checked your equipment through again, having done the inspection in the morning. You called through on the intercom to your skipper to say, 'We're OK in the tail.'

These last moments before take-off were understandably a nervous time. They may not have admitted it, but the aircrew were edgy as they waited to set off on the sortie. Sometimes, tensions rose to the surface. Robert Kee flew with a gunner who always used to wish people good luck before an operation, until one night somebody snapped at him, 'Oh, for goodness sakes, stop saying good luck, not in the truck going out to the aircraft, just forget about that.' When he arrived on his squadron, Maurice Flower was quick to notice the superstitious rituals that some airmen performed before taking off. 'Everybody used to have a pee on the tail wheel. We considered that lucky but all it did really was rot the tail wheel! Some people did certain things religiously, like walking round the aeroplane three times or something of that kind, but I don't remember anybody in our crew being superstitious as such.'

The pee on the tail wheel was a gesture in squadrons across the country. It was one last bonding moment for the crews. When the ground crew put paid to the tradition, Bill Burke noticed that other rituals took its place. 'Some crews would form a line and walk round the aircraft and that would bring them good luck.'

Privately, many airmen had their rituals as well. It was

common to carry items given to them by their families. Lucky scarves were in abundance, often a gift from a sweetheart. Maurice Flower had a lucky mascot, an item he still has sixty years later. 'I carried this little toy Scottie terrier my mother gave me. I took it with me on every trip, I suppose because it was something my mother had given me, and it survived the same as I did.'

Bill Burke also carried a lucky charm, something that again is still a treasured possession.

> I had a little wooden doll given to me by my maternal grand-mother when I set off for war. She said to me, 'Here is a lucky charm which you can carry with you when you go into battle,' and I did. Every operation I flew on, I took this with me, and it saw me right in the end. I also had a little enamelled lapel pin of Doodles, the Blackpool circus crown, and in a mistaken moment I gave it to a girlfriend. I couldn't get it back and I felt its loss very severely!

Peter Baker never flew without his lucky charms. 'I never flew without my lucky scarf which was given to me by a girlfriend before I started flying. I always had a picture of my pin-up girl at the time in my navigation bag. I think it came out of *Tatler* magazine and I thought she was very scantily dressed, but she was a morale-booster. I don't think she would be considered to be scantily dressed nowadays!'

Many of those who'd trained abroad brought lucky charms back with them from the outposts of the Empire; Tom Wingham brought a charm back from South Africa. In Adge Boal's crew, there was the usual scattering of 'anti-chop' scarves as they were known, in his case his old Boy Scout neckerchief, and he carried a little black cat mascot. Later a photograph of a girl he'd met was added to the collection. They didn't do a thirteenth operation; instead it was numbered 12A. The first raid was successful, so thereafter the crew ensured that they wore exactly the same clothes for every raid, the same anti-chop scarves, the same

mascots. Such routines were common enough, but the super-
stition in Boal's crew went a stage further.

My pilot spent half his tour as a flight sergeant, but was promoted, got a commission and met a young WAAF girl who
was an officer in the mess as well. He started to date her but we
discovered that every date this girl had had got the chop. So we
threatened him, 'You've got to stop seeing this girl, end of story,
otherwise we're out.' He stopped seeing this girl because we were
completely sure that she was a jinx. I don't know whether this
poor girl ever managed to get any more boyfriends after that!

The extraordinary camaraderie within crews is almost universally recalled by the airmen. Crews would generally stay together
for a tour of operations, and a brother-like bond would develop
between the men. The importance of the camaraderie was clear
to Arthur Smith.

If you didn't know your crew members well and get on together
well, you wouldn't make a good group to operate a bomber
aircraft. If you had someone that didn't fit, you said so and
someone else was put in your crew, but once you amalgamated,
the comradeship and the discipline was everything. You did
exactly what you were supposed to do, the pilot was in charge.
What he said went, and if you had a good pilot, which we did,
discipline was excellent, there was no chattering around on an
operation like you see on the films.

This camaraderie endured, despite the hierarchical nature of
the RAF, which, as Robert Kee discovered, divided up the crews.

There was a division, of course, between the officers' mess and
the sergeants' mess. The gunners were often sergeants, so you
saw less of them. In the officers' mess you played a lot of shove
ha'penny, and that sort of thing. Sometimes people came to
lecture to you. I had friends and we'd go into Lincoln every
night, seeing girls there whom we very much liked being part of

the air force, which they were really. They used to speak the same language as we would, the girls in Lincoln pubs.

For those who were commissioned officers, a booklet entitled *Customs of the Service* was issued with advice on every possible matter of etiquette for the newly commissioned officer, from the wearing of formal dress to the correct size of visiting card. Appropriate behaviour in relation to non-commissioned officers was explained in detail. If invited to a dance in the sergeants' mess, for example, officers should never stay more than an hour. Offering to buy your sergeant host a drink was an 'unforgivable blunder'. Back in their own mess, officers were advised that dressing gowns and slippers shouldn't be worn in certain rooms, that nothing was more deplorable than addressing the commanding officer as 'old boy', and that 'talking shop' should be avoided in the mess where possible.

Like most airmen, Maurice Flower spent most of his spare time with his own crew, even when they weren't on operational duty.

I was closer to my crew than I was with my own brother and sisters. You relied so much on each other. You flew as a team and this extended to your private life. Outside the aeroplane, you'd do things together, help each other out. You'd get the odd brawl in a pub but the crews would always stand back to back and help each other. We used to get seven days' leave every six weeks, and one time I went home and all the Canadians went with me, mainly because I said we have an ice rink in Durham. So we went skating in this ice rink, which had a canvas roof, like a circus tent with big poles supporting the roof. I really couldn't skate but I could stand upright and I was on the end of the stream. All seven of us did this big whirling circle with me on the far end. I must have been doing about fifty-five miles an hour and I hit one of these poles and the whole roof came down. That was the end of our skating!

The hospitality Maurice Flower showed to his crew members who'd come from overseas was typical. Australian airman Ron Pitt was well looked after by his crew too. One of his fellow crew members, wireless operator Adge Boal, remains one of his closest friends. 'As a crew we worked well together and we were friendly on the ground too. Flying with Adge, we were all quite comfortable with the job he did. He was conscientious and didn't panic at all. Two or three of us visited his home when we were on leave and got on well with him. Our rear gunner came from Inverness, and they made us most welcome up there at his home too.'

Pitt and Boal would go out together regularly in Cambridge with the rest of their crew, or farther afield when they had longer periods of leave. 'I remember going to the films in Cambridge and one time the newsreel showed a raid that we were on the night before. In those days it was a real fluke to see that on film. We'd always go on leave together and go down to London when we had the chance. There were a couple of pubs we patronised where the proprietor and the barmaid welcomed us as friends.'

Whenever he had the chance, Leonard Miller would take his crew home to London. 'We used to pile in my car and we all went down to London. Some of them came from London, but if they didn't have anywhere to sleep, they'd come and sleep at my house. I made them all swear not to say we were on operations, because my mother used to worry like hell!'

Miller wasn't alone in keeping the exact nature of what he was doing quiet from his mother. Some aircrew kept up the pretence that they were still in training throughout their operational careers. In Ricky Dyson's crew, the camaraderie was so strong that even dates were shared. 'You welded your life around that particular bunch of blokes. If one had a date you got to share the date! I remember taking a girl out and the whole crew came with me to the pictures. That was the atmosphere.'

There was a strange juxtaposition in the lives of the aircrew. On the one hand, they were risking their lives, and in many cases losing them, on a regular basis. On the other, many would admit it was an idyllic existence for much of the time. Peter Baker enjoyed his time in Bomber Command, and was aware of the advantage he had over those in the forces sent overseas.

We were lucky because we were based in this country. We were at home every night, we slept in sheets, we were reasonably well fed. We could go for walks in the country. We went down to the pubs, we had our girlfriends or sweethearts. It was extraordinary to think that people might have been walking along a country lane enjoying a pint in a pub, and a few hours later either dead or floating down over Germany on a parachute.

Maurice Flower and his crew were quick to cultivate useful local contacts.

At Foulsham, our crew met a farmer called Old Jim, and we used to get twelve-bore shotgun ammunition and go clay pigeon shooting with him. We always used to manage to get the odd box of cartridges and of course Old Jim couldn't get cartridges, although he had the twelve-bore shotguns. The farmland hadn't been shot over since the war had broken out, so it was just alive with pheasants and partridges, and we'd shoot half a dozen pheasant or partridge, and an old lady who lived in the next village used to cook them and we'd take them back to the mess and have pheasant for supper.

The crews became well known in the villages that surrounded their stations, and Flower and his crew were treated as heroes by the local community. As the airmen always wore their uniform off duty, they were easy to identify.

In the village in Foulsham, we used to go to a pub called the Unicorn and it was just like a little house really. We used to go in the back room and the old landlady had a son in the navy and we always used to ask about her son. She would make us batch cakes with raw onion and cheese in. Whenever there was cause for any celebration, like when we finished our tour, she'd put a barrel of beer up. We'd stay there until we'd drunk it, eight of us, along with two or three WAAFs. One night we took a candle and we smoked all our names on the ceiling.

Many years later, Flower returned to the pub and found the names of his crew were still smoked on the ceiling, even though the pub had long since been converted into a private house. Many other crews smoked their names on the ceilings of a local pub. Peter Baker and his crew wrote their names in smoke on the ceiling of their Nissen hut. 'We were hoisted up on a human chain to do it. Usually we'd had a few drinks and we had a big fireplace in the Nissen hut. Footprints came out of the fireplace, the Nissen huts were semicircular, and the footprints went right up across the ceiling and disappeared out of the window. We did stupid things, but we were young and it was good fun.'

While crews had their own favourite haunts, there were certain places that attracted a wider following. For those airmen based in the area around York, there was one place where all the crews could be found. Alan Bryett was often among them. 'In York there's a famous tearoom called Betty's Tea Rooms. During the war the basement was a bar and all the aircrew from 4 Group used to go and drink in the bar and all the WAAFs were there.'

It was in Betty's that Bryett became aware of just how high Bomber Command's casualties really were.

We knew the casualties were bad, but we had no idea of their extent. There was no list put up on the board, you just kept your ear to the ground. So while we knew the losses were quite bad, it was only after the war, when the lists began to be published, that we realised. During the war, the only way to find out about casualties was unofficially. We were stationed at Bridlington and for leave or a day or two off, you would go into Betty's in York. When you got there, you met friends of yours who had been bomb aimers training with you on the west coast of Scotland and you began to talk and you got an idea there that the casualties were quite great because there were people from all the twenty squadrons on the group there.

The airmen knew, of course, about the losses from their own squadrons. What was shocking was the realisation that they were far from unique. Their squadron hadn't simply had a bit of bad luck, the appalling losses were endemic throughout Bomber Command.

Not all airmen flew with a regular crew. There were occasions when airmen would fly with 'scratch crews', or join another existing crew if one of their members had completed his tour, or was unwell. Many veterans recall occasions when an otherwise unremarkable illness saved their lives. Taken off operations on medical orders, they watched the rest of the crew go off without them, a spare making up the numbers, not to return.

Robin Murray flew as a 'spare' throughout his operational career, but the camaraderie between airmen was still important for him, even if it wasn't centred around a single crew.

It was definitely there, but it's difficult to explain it. You got on well together, you trusted one another but you also had your own life, your own friends outside the crews on the squadron. You didn't always go about together. Some did, but in my case, being a spare gunner, I had people all over who I knew and went drinking with. The fact that the crews trusted one another was important. They realised that everyone had his job to do and they could do it properly and they could be trusted to do it. If there was one person in the crew who didn't know what he was doing or didn't do it at the right time, it mucked up everything. In a crew, it was almost as if you were one person. You had to know what you were doing and do it at the right time. You can't explain to anybody that wasn't aircrew the togetherness that there is. You could be a dustman or a duke, it didn't make any difference.

Whether socialising as a crew or with other members of the squadron, the airmen of Bomber Command worked hard, and they played hard. These were young men, some still teenagers, who knew they were going on dangerous operations, as Murray explains. 'At the back of your mind you knew it could be your last day. An awful lot of people never even saw operations: there were terrific losses in training. Flying was a dangerous occupation in those days. You knew all right the aircraft were very well maintained by the ground crew but they had so much to do, there could be times when they forgot things.'

No wonder Maurice Flower can remember some nights in the mess when the airmen made sure they enjoyed themselves.

We had big dormer tables in the mess and we put two or three tables end to end and we'd all sit round with a pint and sing songs. The bloke on the end used to have to get up on the table and run the whole length without kicking anybody's beer over and come back and sit down and drink his pint and then it was immediately filled up and then the next bloke would do the same. By the time you'd got to the second table you didn't give a damn who was on the table or where they were going!

Bill Burke was also familiar with some fairly boisterous entertainment that formed part and parcel of squadron life.

The games we played in the mess were really quite remarkable in their own right, such as Follow My Leader, where somebody would set off with a line of people behind him and you'd go under tables, in and out of windows, in and out of buildings and putting footsteps on the ceiling. One of the most popular games was where we formed a short line facing a wall and then we all vaulted on top of it until it collapsed. People ask, 'Action like that in an officers' mess? Didn't the senior officers stop it?' but they didn't because they were aircrew and they were joining in. They'd take off their jackets so there were no signs of rank and they played the game with us.

There were many Bomber Boy songs to be heard in the squadron messes, including this one, which Ron Pitt remembers to this day.

If those guns could only fire,
If those bombs could only fall,
But it's only a beautiful picture hanging on the guardroom
wall.

Another favourite song was a light-hearted jibe at his own squadron, No. 514.

Oh, where are those airmen of 514?
Boozing, all boozing
Where are those airmen when Jerry's about?
Boozing, jolly well boozing

They sit in the hangars, they sing in their shower,
They talk about things they know nothing about
Where are those airmen when Jerry's about?
Boozing, ruddy well boozing

We have the engineer
Who is always out on the beer
And when he awakes in the morning
His actions are mighty queer

He goes to bed with his dong
The dirty old rotten old song
You can tell by the rings round his eyeballs
He's up to no blinking good!

Oh, where are those airmen, etc.

Several songs featured a verse for each member of a crew. Tom Wingham's crew sang an adaptation of 'Sweet Violets'.

Dave Hewlett's a bit of a pilot
And up in the clouds he doth flit,
And sometimes he lands on the tarmac
But more often he lands in the . . .
Sweet violets
Sweeter than all the roses

Covered all over from head to foot
Covered all over in sewer

Riley was our rear gunner
He really doth think he is
He says he can shoot fifty holes in a drogue
But we know his shooting is . . .
Sweet violets, etc.

Our engineer is Joseph
And levers he pulls like a tit
But when we're all over the target
He yells for God's sake get out of this . . .
Sweet violets, etc.

Now Wingham is Hewlett's bomb aimer
And up in the nose doth sit
But the day that he says he saw a target
We'll all know his shooting is . . .
Sweet violets, etc.

A blind eye was turned to the antics of the bomber boys. There was undoubtedly a degree of recklessness which was tolerated because those in command knew only too well that some of the boys in the ballroom on a Saturday night weren't going to be there the following week. No one liked to think it might happen to them, but that possibility was present in everyone's subconscious. A few wild parties would at least help them to keep going. Having been allocated to a squadron in 6 Group, Jim Rogers found himself socialising with a large number of Canadian aircrew.

The Canadians were quite a wild bunch, although I've seen some of them in tears from homesickness. We would invariably have a dance in the sergeants' mess. We invited girls from York and it usually finished up with a punch-up! They'd all been drinking and a lot of the furniture would be broken. We'd have to go into Leeds and buy new furniture on the Monday! A lot of us lived in Beningbrough Hall, a country mansion about three and a half miles from the actual camp. A coach would take us to the camp and take us home at night. We had a few wild parties there too! They were a bit lenient with us regarding discipline, they'd overlook things realising that we were on tenterhooks quite a lot of the time.

Rogers remembers singing 'Salome' in the confines of Beningbrough, one of the ruder bomber songs.

Salome, Salome, who would see Salome?
Standing there with her breasts all bare
Every little wrinkle made you blink and stare
She swings it, she flings it around her, right up her bloody chute!

When histories of air wars are written, it is the aircraft and the aircrews which draw most attention, but no air war would be possible without the considerable work of the ground staff. Without them, no aircraft would ever get into the air, and never was that more the case than during Bomber Command's campaign. Following his experience as an observer in France during the Phoney War, John Holmes had returned to Britain, where he would spend the rest of the war as a senior member of the ground staff. The luxuries of peacetime had disappeared, but nevertheless Holmes enjoyed much of his work.

It was sheer hard work. Craning, lifting, lugging about, getting the things up on trolleys. The flight commander would come along and say, 'How long are you going to be getting this runway clear?' I'd say, 'Well, six hours, sir,' and he'd say, 'Make it four, Flight Sergeant.' I would call it an enjoyable hell on earth. You get completely sold on it; you take an enormous pride in your work and in peacetime it's a doddle, it is just pleasure to me because I am an engineer by nature. In wartime it's that pleasure overlaid with frost, rain, mud, pressure.

In the early part of the war, when the RAF's facilities were yet to catch up with the force's rapid expansion, the ground crew were often housed in primitive conditions. Long before he became a flight engineer, Maurice Flower's first posting as apprentice ground crew had been to RAF Kinloss.

There were no huts on the camp at all, so although we ate on the station, we were billeted three miles from the airfield, and we had to walk out every morning. There were three hundred of us in a distillery barn, some upstairs and some downstairs. Downstairs was a concrete floor, upstairs was a wooden floor, and when they walked around, all the dust came down from between the floorboards. It had been a grain store originally and we had three cold-water taps outside and that was the total toilet facilities. There was a stream to pee in and if you wanted a number two, you waited until you went to work and you could use a toilet on the airfield! It was really primitive and in the winter it was just awful. You got a lot of snow in winter, like a three-foot blanket, and you had to walk through this blanket to get to work. You were wet up to your knees until you dried out around about one o'clock in the afternoon. We were modifying Spitfires from Mark Is, taking the manual undercarriage pumps out and putting in hydraulic pumps. We worked round the clock, twenty-five hours a day doing this kind of work.

Having also worked as ground crew before becoming a rear air gunner, Ricky Dyson was only too aware of the working conditions the ground staff endured, even later in the war. 'It was always very cold. They never put airfields in places that were without wind, rain or snow. We had some very hard winters but the ground crews did a magnificent job in all weathers. The aircraft weren't always maintained in the hangars; they were sometimes outside under canvas tents. My admiration has always been for those fitters, riveters and armourers, who did such a magnificent job on our behalf.'

Considering the conditions on even the best stations, the dedication of the ground crews was extraordinary. John Holmes oversaw a team of ground staff.

Nobody ever mentions some of the lads that I had working with me, heroes up to their ankles in mud in all sorts of temperatures. There weren't any limits to what they would do if you handled them properly. At Winthorpe we were clearing snow from the main runway for five days, the same blokes for five days. I'd let them off for an hour for a sleep and a meal, but then back on the snow clearing again. You'd get a Lancaster stuck in three feet of mud and somebody had to go and dig a trench from the wheels in mud, freezing cold, pitch black, by torchlight. It was a very devil of a job, and a lot of them had really no great prospects of promotion. There was nothing that I ever had to ask that they wouldn't do. Picking up crashes is not funny, but they would do it. All sorts, men from all walks of life, all ages from twenty up to their forties. Some men had been professional men.

Holmes felt considerable responsibility for the aircraft he maintained.

The aircrew would come into my flight office and sign the Form 700, which is the big final form before an aircraft can fly, which all the tradesmen sign, and they would accept my word that the aircraft was fit to fly. Now that's considerably something because you could easily be sending seven men to their deaths. It only needed a slight slip and we're all human. So I've sat and worried some nights for a very, very long time.

With bomber crews flying throughout the winter months, often in appalling weather, it fell to the ground crews to work around the clock in terrible conditions. Holmes remembers having to revive one of his colleagues who'd fallen off the wing of an aircraft. In the intense cold of a frosty night, the colleague was refuelling an aircraft when his body temperature fell dangerously low, and he simply fell off. This, though, was certainly not the worst situation faced by the ground crews. It regularly fell to them to deal with the wreckages of aircraft that crashed in Britain, and to rescue the aircrew inside. Like ground crew across Bomber Command stations, John Holmes had to deal with many crashes. One incident stands out in his memory more than most.

The first thing always in a crash is fire. And there wasn't much that my lads could do about fire. That rested with the fire crews. Once the fire was out you start looking for bodies or parts of bodies. We had a Wellington crash in a field where the ground was semi-marshy, and it crashed in the middle of a beet field. We went across to collect it, pick it up and found that nothing would stand. The ground wouldn't support the cranes, it wouldn't support anything.

It was clear that it wasn't going to be possible to get the Wellington out of the field; the local farmer estimated it would sink out of sight within just a fortnight. More importantly, it wasn't going to be possible to get the bodies of all the aircrew out either.

There was a crew of five, and we had only got four bodies, the other one was out of reach. So we made five bodies out of four. Now this is gruesome, I know, but the fifth man had a family and children. He would have been put down as missing, his wife wouldn't have got her allowances; there would have been endless delays, so we buried five bodies. It's not the sort of job that you look for or want but it's a job that has to be done.

The ground staff got to know their aircraft, and their aircrews, well, which made it even harder when they realised they weren't going to come back. 'If you let it get to you, it could have wrecked you. You just had to create a shell around yourself. They went off, you had a joke with them when they went and the next day they hadn't come back.'

Like many ground crew, Holmes felt he was waving off his aircraft, and his crew.

It was very much a proprietary air. On the operational units the same crew would use the same aircraft all the time and the same ground crew, and the aircrew were fully aware that they relied for their lives on the skill of the ground crew and the ground crew were intelligent men and they knew where these boys were going and the chances of coming back. And they got to be very, very friendly. The word went around that if I got some possession of an aircrew, he would come back. So they used to leave me wristwatches, wallets, pens, signet rings and I had to go and buy a large cash box to put all this stuff in. I was never left with anything, it all went back where it came from. But I used to feel desperate when one aircraft hadn't come back, and there were two signet rings and a wristwatch in the tin. Not nice, not nice. You couldn't let yourself react to it because the next day you would be hard at it again.

The aircrew veterans retain great respect for their ground staff colleagues to this day. Hal Croxson sums up the attitude of thousands of his fellow former airmen.

The ground crew were our lifeline. They kept us flying and kept the aircraft in a condition that would see us through. They nursed that aircraft sometimes, because it would come back from one operation and they'd be patching it up ready for the next one and it would all be in good nick before we used it. They were a super bunch. They knew what we were doing and when you'd come back with holes through your aircraft and the turret shattered, they knew what we were going through and they supported us to the end.

Leonard Miller is also full of praise for the work of the ground staff. 'You had a lot of faith in your ground crew. They did an awful lot for us. Being an engineer in civilian life, I used to go down to dispersal and we'd talk about engines and pressures and temperatures and superchargers. I think they were quite gratified that I knew something and didn't walk by with my nose in the air.'

Another group of people who were key to the running of Bomber Command's stations were the members of the Women's Auxiliary Air Force. At the outbreak of the war, there were already 1,700 members of the WAAF, but with the requirement from the end of 1941 for single women aged between twenty and thirty to do some kind of war service, the numbers quickly grew. By 1943, 180,000 WAAFs were engaged in a variety of support services, some essential in the logistics of running an RAF station, others directly linked to the bombing operations. From catering to cracking codes and ciphers, WAAFs were to be found doing their duty in just about every aspect of Bomber Command's work. They worked in the meteorology units, security and operations rooms, ran telephone exchanges and sent telegraphs. It was the reassuring voices of the WAAFs which the crews heard over their wireless sets as they returned to their stations, and it was often the WAAFs who were the intelligence officers debriefing the crews after each raid. Some WAAFs even flew aircraft – not on operations, of course, but they were part of the team delivering them from the factories to the stations, one of those essential but easily overlooked wartime jobs. Some WAAFs flew more than two hundred aircraft in the course of the war. Few WAAFs can claim quite such a glamorous occupation, but what they all had in common was that they were doing a job without which the command could never have operated. The extraordinary dedication of the WAAFs, and the sometimes unpleasant jobs they faced, was brought home to Maurice Flower on one particular occasion during the war.

One Sunday afternoon we were going for an air test and we taxied up to the end of the runway. On the right-hand side of us was the four-thousand-pound bomb dump. They were like fifty-gallon drums, all stacked up. We'd just been given the go-ahead for take-off, the runway was clear and it was a beautiful sunny day. There was a squadron of Liberators going on a raid, and some Fortresses coming back. There was one cloud over our airfield and the Liberators flew into this cloud and one of them collided with a Fortress, and all the Liberator's bombs dropped all round us. One hit the four-thousand-pound bomb dump on our right-hand side. I wasn't scared; I was just fascinated to watch this four-thousand-pound bomb. It rolled in from behind the starboard wing, rolled through and then disappeared. Then it appeared in front and it just rolled gently across and came to a rest on the left-hand side of the runway. I never thought about it exploding but if it had gone up, they wouldn't have seen us again!

Flower and his crew had had a lucky escape, but the crews of the Liberator and the Fortress that had collided were not so fortunate.

All the bodies dropped around our aeroplane. There was one bloke parachuting down who'd had his legs blown off and he died on the way down, but he was the only parachute that got out of those two aeroplanes. They just fell all round us. I always remember there was a WAAF who appeared in a little Bedford van, and she went round covering all their faces. She was fantastic, just getting on and doing that, only a young girl.

The presence of the WAAFs on the stations was certainly welcomed by the airmen off duty as well. For Alan Bryett, the nights when he wasn't on operations were an opportunity to get away from the station.

You'd fly maybe one night and then have two or three nights off, where you might get a forty-eight-hour pass and go into York or we'd go into Bridlington. There were lots of Women's Auxiliary Air Force on the station and you would go out and meet them. The squadron was very much like a huge family. It was a very big family, maybe twelve hundred people, with a large number supporting the two-hundred-odd who were flying on ops. There was a certain amount of sadness because the permanent staff got to know their aircrews very well and they'd fly five, six or seven ops and then they'd disappear. The young ladies would get friendly with the aircrew and the chaps would disappear or be killed and it was a sad time but they grew very hardened towards it. It was a pretty tough life for them as well.

As the crews made friends in the villages and towns surrounding their squadron bases, there was great kudos for local girls and WAAFs alike if they were asked on a date by an airman. The rumour went round that the RAF was lacing the airmen's tea with bromide to curb any excesses. They probably weren't. Those girls who did embark on wartime romances had to get used to the airmen not returning. Roy Finch would leave one date disappointed when he went on his third operation in November 1941.

I was in the mess, bored out of my mind, because yet again my name wasn't on the battle order. Twice previously it had been on only to be taken off again. The phone went, I got up and answered the phone, and it turned out to be a very attractive barmaid from the local pub in Cambridge who wanted to speak to one of the men. I told her, 'I'm sorry, he's not here, he's flying.' Anyway, we had a bit of a chat, and she agreed to let me come and meet her instead. I thought this was marvellous, I'd better go and get ready. Then somebody came along and said, 'You're on battle order tonight!' I replied, 'No, I'm not, I've checked.' 'You'd better go and check again, your name's on battle order.' So I went and had a look and sure enough somebody's name had been crossed off and mine put on. So I had to rush over to get myself ready to be trucked over to Bourn, and I'd no way of letting her know, I just hadn't time. I was very sad about that, because she was a very attractive young lady.

Soon Finch was in a Wellington as second pilot in a six-man crew on his way to Hamburg. At first, it seemed an unremarkable trip.

I was standing in the astrodome, bored out of my mind, when suddenly the skipper called out, 'Can you come up front, we've got a bit of a problem here.' The artificial horizon, which was one of the instruments for flying on, had packed up. Then the port engine started to play up a bit, and again he called me up front, and together we went through all the normal drill but eventually the engine just packed up completely. There was no alternative but to turn back for home. Now, with Wellingtons, we had a lot of training for flying on one engine, but for some reason this aircraft would not maintain height and we started getting lower and lower. Soon my job was to throw out everything that was loose, to lighten the weight. The first things that went were the bombs, but we were still losing height, so the final things to be thrown out were the parachutes. At last the realisation came that we weren't going to make it, we were going to ditch. When you land on water, it's almost like coming to a full stop immediately, and all this water came rushing in.

Finch crawled along the fuselage, making his way towards the rear gunner, who was already in the dinghy.

He called out, 'Hurry up, man, I can't hang on.' Eventually I managed to get there and literally went head first into the dinghy. Together we tried to hold on to the tailplane, but there was an enormous swell running, and we just couldn't hold on. I remember seeing three other poor fellows in the water, floating, I didn't see the fourth. On board there were no paddles, no rations, no Very pistol or flares. We tried to paddle with our hands, but could make no progress whatsoever, and bit by bit we drifted farther and farther away. It was terrible. I could see three of these poor devils, in the water, each wearing their Mae West life jacket with a little floating light, but we were just completely powerless to do anything about it. I'd no idea where the fourth was.

Finch and his rear gunner floated in the dinghy for the rest of the night, sitting up to their waists in water in the bitter cold of the North Sea at the end of November. When daybreak eventually arrived, the swell had subsided, and they were picked up by Danish fishermen, who put them in warm clothes and fed them.

I remember going up on deck a few hours later, and the feeling of exhilaration, to still be alive, was absolutely fantastic. They agreed they would try to smuggle us across Denmark and into Sweden. We arrived at Esbjerg port, and standing on the quay-side were all these Germans, grinning like apes. We discovered subsequently there were actually three little fishing boats. We were the last ones to dock, and somebody in one of the others had tipped the Germans off. That was it, we were in the bag.

It was Roy Finch's twenty-first birthday, and he would spend the rest of the war in a prisoner-of-war camp. The attractive barmaid never did discover what had happened to the mysterious airman who'd persuaded her to go on a date and never turned up. Despite such incidents, Bomber Command's presence on the home front helped win it the affection of the wider public. Until the run-up to D-Day, the army was largely based overseas, its victories in remote places such as North Africa and Burma.

Bomber Command was very much in the eyes of the public. We were stationed at Oakington in Cambridgeshire but we flew from Bourn, which was a satellite station. We used to be taken to Bourn in RAF trucks and in many cases the village would come out and applaud. So I think at that stage we were held in fairly high esteem. I think the civilian population realised that it was a fairly hazardous period and a hazardous job for us, but that we were really the only ones who could carry the war into Germany.

Aircrew were greeted warmly by the public. Long before that fateful night in the North Sea, Roy Finch had discovered that the significance of his new uniform was instantly recognised and curried favour even before he'd been on an operation. 'I remember going back to London with a girlfriend I had at the time, and we went into a pub. Everybody was wanting to buy us drinks. I said that I hadn't done anything yet, but they still wanted to buy us drinks.'

In public, the bomber boys benefited from the affection and admiration the 'Brylcream Boys' of Fighter Command had earned in 1940. Within the RAF, a friendly rivalry existed between the two groups of airmen. Those in the know could always distinquish between the two as the fighter boys invariably left the top button of their tunic undone. There were far more Bomber Boys, though, not least thanks to the seven-man crews of the heavy bombers.

By the late summer of 1941, Bomber Command had been transformed from the organisation it had been at the outbreak of the war. Technological improvements typified by the new aircraft being introduced, new crews better trained than ever before coming on to the squadrons and a more effective organisation were all having an effect. An ever higher bomb tonnage was being dropped on the enemy. Of course, not every crew was hitting the target, and some aircraft would always be forced to turn back because of poor weather conditions or mechanical failure. The Luftwaffe's night fighting force was becoming more effective, resulting in higher casualty figures. Yet Sir Richard Peirse must have felt he had good reason to be optimistic. With Stalin's Red Army now engaging a large part of the Wehrmacht, and for that matter the Luftwaffe, the way was open for Bomber Command to make a real breakthrough in the war.

Then, in August 1941, came a devastating blow to Bomber Command's confidence. Lord Cherwell, Churchill's scientific adviser, had commissioned a survey of recent photographs taken from the cameras attached to some of the bomber aircraft. The Butt Report was nothing less than a deep shock for those reading it. It analysed 4,065 photographs taken on a hundred night raids during the course of the previous two months. Only one in four of the crews who claimed to have bombed their target in Germany were found to have got even within 5 miles of their target. One in three of the crews didn't even claim to have reached the target. Bomber Command was aiming for specific strategically important targets, and yet five out of six of its crews weren't getting anywhere near them. It was much worse than that, though. Day after day, crews were being sent out on operations and not coming back, something that the crews were increasingly aware of, and it was beginning to affect their confidence badly. Their loss rates could hardly be justified in the face of the little damage being done to the enemy.

The Air Ministry and Bomber Command had known that accuracy was a problem, which was why there had already been an implicit sanction of area bombing objectives, but the study left little hope that any strategic bombing raids were leaving any real impression – come to that, even area bombing raids were unlikely to be making that much of an impact in the right places. The reports of the crews returning to their stations had been wildly optimistic, and the reports that had filtered through of the ineffectiveness of key raids could no longer be ignored. Typical of the problem had been a raid on Frankfurt on 21 July. Thirty-seven Wellingtons and thirty-four Hampdens set out to bomb the city, but Frankfurt recorded little damage. It was Darmstadt, a town 15 miles away, which suffered the blow: fifteen buildings were reported damaged, and sixteen people killed. Bomber Command's continual failure even to get to the target was not going to win the war. Darmstadt was unlucky; on most bombing raids the chances are that most bombs were falling in empty fields. The morale of Bomber Command's leadership reached a new low in the wake of the Butt Report; its very worst fears had been confirmed. As the shock waves reverberated around the Air Ministry, there seemed little sign of improvement. After a disastrous raid on Berlin on 7 November, when twenty-one aircraft were lost, 12.4 per cent of those dispatched, the Prime Minister summoned Sir Richard Peirse to Chequers. The evidence was overwhelming, and there was little Peirse could say to explain away his command's performance. Shortly afterwards, the War Cabinet ordered Bomber Command to scale down its operations dramatically until a new policy could be formulated. Bomber Command would have a quiet winter as it contemplated its future contribution to the war effort. It was a heavy draw on Britain's wartime resources, and that was going to need to be better justified by its results.

By the end of 1941, Britain overall could face the continuing war with a new optimism. Hitler's decision to attack the Soviet Union had backfired badly. Now he made another crucial error. Days after the Japanese attack on Pearl Harbor in December, he declared war on the United States, bringing the country that had so far remained neutral right into the war, and not just against Japan. Hitler had given Britain a powerful new ally which could be called upon for help overtly. Clandestine aid, such as the Arnold Scheme, could be exchanged for a proper commitment by the USA to help bring Nazi power to an end. The question for Bomber Command was whether it could do much to help end what had now truly become a world war.

5

Enter Arthur Harris

'The primary objective of your operations should now be focused on the morale of the enemy civil population.'

Directive to Bomber Command, 14 February 1942

The wreckage of Robert Kee's Hampden after it crashed on ice in the North Sea off the Dutch coast, February 1942.

The year 1942 marked a major moment of transition, not just for Bomber Command but for the whole war. For the British, though, it would mark a new nadir, despite the entry into the war the previous year of first the Russians and later the Americans, giving Churchill the superpower alliance he had been working so hard to achieve. British forces were on the back foot everywhere they were in action; disastrously so in the North Atlantic, as thousands of tons of vital supplies were sent to the bottom of the sea by prowling U-boats. In the Far East too, and in North Africa, British armies were struggling badly against the Axis powers that now included the Japanese. Not only did the prospect of mounting a successful continental invasion look impossible, risible even, the simple business of staying in the war at all looked hard enough. If, on top of that, the RAF had been forced to shut down its lacklustre bombing offensive, the whole war effort would have been declared terminal. The only alternative was to dig deep, and fight for a reversal of fortunes across all these vital fronts, bombing included. For Churchill it was clear; the road to victory lay across the waves of the North Atlantic, the deserts of North Africa, the jungles of the Far East and, above all, across the skies over Germany. Only then could the eastern front be pulled into the wider war.

So Bomber Command was given another chance to prove its rhetoric right, to show that aerial devastation could do to the vast German industrial war machine what her U-boats were doing to Allied shipping. It was clear that there would need to be changes, first to the leadership, and second to the technology; not just to the aircraft, but to the electronics that would help deliver these aircraft to the correct location. The result would be that Bomber Command would go on to have its best year ever, and see its place in the Allied war effort secured.

It had been a close-run thing. The War Cabinet and the Air Ministry had spent the previous autumn debating exactly what Bomber Command should do, and even whether a large bombing force was necessary. After all, daylight raids had already proved too dangerous for unescorted bombers, and night-time raids had proved too ineffective to justify the cost in crews and aircraft. With Britain's wartime resources now stretched to their limit, Bomber Command was beginning to look to some like a force that could be dispensed with. So Bomber Command's saving grace was not that it was able to refute this allegation, but that Britain had little alternative to continuing with a bombing campaign. If Britain and its allies were going to win the war, the war had to be taken to Germany. It was also of the utmost importance that, within the alliance, Britain could demonstrate that it was still playing a full part in the war. It would be vital to continually make evident to Stalin in particular that the millions of Russian troops dying on the eastern front were not a forgotten cause. Bombing the Reich remained the only way Britain could achieve this until an invasion became a possibility. Apart from the practical constraints that in any case meant an invasion was out of the question, many military chiefs feared the prospect of an invasion as much as the aircrews. They, too, were desperate to avoid the endless horror of trench warfare that had been the touchstone of the First World War, and Churchill was determined to resist an invasion for as long as possible. While Bomber Command may not have looked like the most effective fighting force in history, it did at least offer some hope, however optimistic, of a different way of winning a war. By now, the optimists also had technology on their side. New aircraft, and particularly four-engine heavy bombers, were coming on to the squadrons. They had significantly better performance standards than the aircraft available to date, and they could carry much larger bomb loads.

New navigational aids on the horizon offered the promise of actually getting the aircraft to the right targets. So there was a strong case for persisting with bombing Germany after all.

Following the disastrous collapse in confidence that had swept through Bomber Command in the wake of the Butt Report, the Air Ministry worked hard to redefine its game plan. Under the influence of Sir Charles Portal, a radical plan for relaunching Bomber Command's offensive was devised in late 1941. A list of forty-three leading industrial German cities was chosen, to be subjected to continuous air attack. In this plan, attempts to bomb individual military targets and factories are conspicuous by their absence. No one made any official declaration about this, of course, but area bombing was now going to be pursued unashamedly. Portal claimed that under this sustained area bombing Germany would collapse in just six months. All he needed was a force of 4,000 bombers. Churchill wasn't quite convinced: 4,000 bombers would be a big commitment, very big. Ten times Bomber Command's current front-line strength, in fact. Even if the crews were available, and the aircraft could be built quickly enough, it would consume too big a proportion of Britain's resources to be a palatable option. Yet while Portal would be denied his pipe-dream 4,000-bomber force, he did at least secure the backing of Churchill for Bomber Command's continuing offensive, albeit on a rather more modest scale.

Leadership and technology were only a part of the new strategy by which Bomber Command would push on with the war. There was one last terrible issue that would need to be resolved before the bomber war could recommence. That was the question of *what* the Allies thought was the nature of their targets. Factories? Or entire cities? Was 'precision' bombing worth trying to achieve, or was it to be swept under the 'carpet' bombing advocated by more militant voices in Bomber Command? It would mark the start of a long quarrel not only with the Americans, who would try to distance themselves from the doctrine of 'area' bombing for as long as possible, but with posterity too.

The year 1942, however, would mark another change in the war, one that was to lend a terrible context to this decision. Ever since the Germans had invaded Poland, and especially since their invasion of the Soviet Union, the east had witnessed barbarism on a momentous scale, exposing the true nature of the German war machine, and the aims behind it. Some of the older, more traditional German army generals had been aghast at the speed with which Hitler had opened up this eastern front, before they had had the chance to consolidate their hold on the west. They were to be even more horrified when they realised just what kind of war they would now be expected to fight – a war not just for territory, or for retribution for past perceived wrongs, but one of genocidal liquidation. Any notion that there existed some kind of gap between military and civilian collapsed. The atrocities that had started in Poland almost as soon as the Germans had arrived now multiplied tenfold, as first tens of thousands, and eventually millions, were murdered: Soviets, Slavs, communists, priests, gypsies – and especially, of course, Jews. While life in the occupied west remained apparently less savage (except for those groups earmarked for continent-wide destruction, 'combed from east to west' in Heydrich's phrase), with German officers holding doors open for Parisian women, there was no question that a conflict that had begun in a bid to reverse the outcome of the Great War had become something altogether darker, and different. This was a war no longer being fought between armies, or even between governments; it was being fought for the right to live at all, and it would swallow entire peoples, including, eventually, the Germans too, pulverised by Russian shells from the east, and by Allied bombs from the west. There were enough on the Allied side to have intuited this shift to give real and desperate impetus to the will to fight, to commit whatever it took to wrest Europe away from this terrible fate. All their earlier inhibitions went by the board. The bombers would be instrumental in this war plan, by virtue of levelling whole cities. It would mark a definite hardening of British attitudes towards the prosecution of the war, the recognition that the stakes were being driven higher by the month, that more than just national survival was genuinely and terrifyingly at stake. After two and a half years of endless setback, there was increasingly little interest in being precious about how the German war machine might actually be tackled and destroyed. If the only way to strike back was against German cities, then so be it.

Portal's plan was reformulated into a fresh directive issued to Bomber Command on 14 February 1942, which made clear for the first time officially that area bombing was now the primary objective of the bombing campaign. The crews would concentrate on the general bombing of the most densely built-up areas of a list of German cities, and the directive made explicit that civilian morale was the target, in the hope that Germany would be prevented from continuing the war if its population's homes were destroyed, particularly those among the industrial workforce. 'It has been decided that the primary objective of your operations should now be focused on the morale of the enemy civil population and in particular of the industrial workers.'

That the intention was to target the industrial workers' homes, and not just their factories, is made transparent in a note Portal wrote to Air Vice-Marshal Bottomley concerning the new directive. 'I suppose it is clear that the aiming points are to be the built-up areas, not, for instance, the dockyards or aircraft factories . . . This must be made quite clear.'

Once the RAF had begun the area bombing of Germany, they would stick with it until the end of the war. Nor would the strategy be subject to much debate once embarked upon. There was nothing like the levels of moral agonising over it that would ensue after the war was over, least of all in Downing Street or the Air Ministry. What opposition there was came from the mouths of individual critics, some of them highly outspoken, such as Richard Stokes, a Labour MP, and the Bishop of Chichester, but they were in a minority. For the most part, politicians glossed over the implications of the bombing campaign to the point of deceit, Deputy Prime Minister Clement Attlee telling the House of Commons, 'There is no indiscrimate bombing,' in May 1943, for example. Those with a hand in policy were dispassionate about it. Lord Cherwell, who remained an enthusiastic supporter of Bomber Command despite having commissioned the Butt Report, talked with relish of making the German people homeless, though he stopped short of taking public pleasure in the numbers that were being killed.

Bomber Command's new directive would not only be pursued, it would be intensified and expanded under a new commander-in-chief. Sir Richard Peirse had already departed, removed from his post on 8 January. He was not sacked as such, being moved on to other senior posts, but confidence in his judgement and leadership skills had been fatally undermined after the Berlin raid on 7 November 1941. It wasn't just that the raid had been a disaster with high losses; more pertinent from Peirse's point of view had been his decision to go ahead with the raid despite a late weather forecast that had been very unfavourable. One week after the area bombing directive was issued, on 22 February 1942, Air Chief Marshal Sir Arthur Harris was appointed as his successor. It is worth reiterating that Harris was not himself the author of the area bombing policy, despite his reputation being entirely equated with it. He was appointed to implement a policy that was already formed. The strategy's architect was Sir Charles Portal, working with his colleagues in the Air Ministry, and it came with the wholehearted support of the Prime Minister and Lord Trenchard among many others.

One of Britain's most single-minded leaders, Air Marshal Sir Arthur Travers Harris would transform Bomber Command's fortunes – and in so doing mire it, and himself, in controversy. Born in 1892, he spent time in Rhodesia, seeking his fortune in gold mining, driving horses and planting tobacco, and joined the 1st Rhodesian Regiment shortly after the start of the First World War. Determined to be part of the war effort, he persisted in his application after being told that the regiment was already fully subscribed, eventually filling a spare place as a bugler. Harris did not take to army life, though, the hours of marching combined with meagre rations making a long-lasting impression, and he became increasingly dissatisfied fighting 'the Boche' in Africa when he knew that the real war was taking place in Europe. So in 1915 he returned to Britain, but, 'determined to find some way of going to war in a sitting position', he enlisted in the Royal Flying Corps. By January 1916, just a few months later, he was a fully qualified pilot and was soon taking on the Zeppelin night fighters that were terrifying south-east England. He later went to France with No. 45 Squadron, where he saw the trenches for himself, an experience that forged his later conviction that bombing was the right strategy, and a better way to fight a war. Undoubtedly an able pilot, Harris cemented his reputation with five victories in less than four months, the criterion for qualifying as an 'ace'. He was also emerging as a strong leader, strict in terms of imposing discipline but forever thinking about ways of doing things better. With an inventive mind that was always prepared to challenge convention, Harris devised technical improvements throughout his RAF career and was never shy about suggesting them to his superiors.

Harris stayed with the RAF after the war, serving in India and Iraq in the 1920s, as well as commanding squadrons in the UK and spending time at staff college. He was undoubtedly a rising star in the force, noticed by Trenchard, and pointing the way to the future. His insistence on preparing for operations at night, combined with his advocacy of the importance of good navigation and accurate bombing, demonstrates his foresight about the kind of future war the RAF should be preparing itself to fight. He went overseas again in 1930, this time to Egypt, and commanded a flying-boat squadron before being called up to the Air Ministry. As Deputy Director of Plans between 1934 and 1937, he put practical experience to invaluable use. Officially, of course, the country was pursuing a policy of appeasement and putting its faith in diplomacy and the League of Nations. But privately, the military leadership could see the threat coming, and the Air Ministry knew that Germany was developing an air force soon after Hitler came to power. As plans for rearmament were quietly drawn up, Harris pushed for the development of heavy bombers, better navigation and specialisation in the crews, all factors that would be crucial in making Bomber Command effective. In 1937 Harris, now an air commodore, briefly took over the leadership of 4 Group, where once again he pursued the interests of his crews as a top priority, and became highly regarded by his pilots, who noted his operational experience and saw him as 'one of us'. In 1938, he was sent to the USA to negotiate orders for aircraft. He was unimpressed with the American air force, but the friendships he cultivated with senior US airmen would stand the RAF in good stead a few years later.

After the start of the war, Harris was appointed as AOC 5 Group, where once again he badgered for improved conditions for his crews, and particularly for modifications to the Handley Page Hampdens that his squadrons flew. During this appointment, he developed a strong working relationship with Charles Portal that would endure throughout the war, and gained a favourable reputation with Churchill. There was then another spell in the Air Ministry, this time as Deputy Chief of the Air Staff. During the Blitz, Harris's role embraced all the RAF's activities, but its bombing capability was clearly his preoccupation. He retained a clear-sighted belief in the potential of bombing which had held for a quarter of a century already. He didn't enjoy staff work, though, and must have been relieved in 1941 when he was asked to lead the RAF delegation to Washington, where once again he was successful in building up important alliances, and in fostering goodwill for the British war effort that could be exploited to the full after Pearl Harbor. It was from Washington that Harris would be recalled in February 1942 to take on Bomber Command.

The impression one gets of Harris is of enormous energy combined with a forthright approach. He had a reputation for being cold and abrasive, and the duodenal ulcer that dogged him throughout the war years doubtless did little to improve his short temper or intolerance of the shortcomings of others. He was certainly not always the easiest of subordinates, lobbying furiously on behalf of his crews, but his dedication helped earn him their loyalty and respect. Like most Bomber Command veterans, Fred Stearn retains that respect to this day. 'I think he had his duty to do, I mean he was a man of his honour and we followed him. It's easy to criticise afterwards but most of the bomber crews held him in high esteem.'

Bill Burke is also a great admirer of the commander-in-chief who would lead Bomber Command until the end of the war.

> There was great affection for the commander, Harris. He was called Burt Harris by his friends, Bomber Harris by the civilian population, and the bomber crews called him Butcher Harris. I wasn't clear whether 'Butcher' was because of the civilians killed or the number of aircrew that he sent to their deaths. I thought he was a remarkable man. He was one of the great commanders of the war. I thought he was very badly treated at the end of the war.

If history has blamed Harris for a bombing offensive with which people are undoubtedly uncomfortable, this is partly due to Harris's refusal to offer euphemisms, or distance himself from it. He was blunt about the real nature of his strategy, and was happy to be fully identified with it. Politicians were much more successful at skirting round the issue, leaving Harris to address it head on. A telling Harris legend concerns his being pulled over for speeding by a policeman, who reproached him with 'You might have killed somebody, sir.' Harris was quick to respond. 'Young man, I kill thousands of people every night!' It wasn't that he treated the job lightly in any way, simply that he never wavered from his belief that bombing could win the war, and more quickly and at less cost than an invasion. In fact, for Harris any effect on the morale of the German population was incidental; for him bombing was about destroying the Nazi's capacity for production by decimating the factories, and the cities where the factory workers lived. One successful consequence of his hard-headed single-mindedness was that it spared his crews any mealy-mouthed dissimulation about the true nature of their work. They could see at first hand what effect their bombs had, and respected the fact that their commander-in-chief refused to pander to those who would rather have been spared the knowledge. The fact that he never wavered in his belief that these bombs were paving the way to victory also helped the crews' morale. High losses are hard to take, high losses with little point impossible. For Harris the point of Bomber Command was clear cut, and of momentous significance, and his crews agreed.

Harris developed the policy he had inherited throughout 1942. Although the idea of 'area' bombing was not his, it would be he who would perfect how the strategy was executed. There was a paradox at its heart which he helped unravel; area bombing only worked if it was concentrated on as small an area as possible. It was about overwhelming single, easily attainable targets. Everything would be geared to that end. The aircraft would be massed into as tight a bomber stream as possible, and timed to arrive over the target in as dense a formation as could be achieved. Whereas previously a raid might have lasted for several hours, Harris pushed his crews to do the job in two hours or less. Eventually the raids would take just twenty minutes, even when they involved several hundred aircraft. While this did increase the risk of collisions, it greatly reduced the impact of Flak. This was a safety-in-numbers principle; there was also safety in speed. It also meant that flares could be used more effectively to ensure improved accuracy in the bombing.

Another important Harris tactic was the use of incendiary bombs. There is no doubt that the bombing raids were now being carefully choreographed to cause maximum carnage. The first wave of bombers would drop high-explosive bombs which would cause large-scale destruction of the city's infrastructure.

Craters would form and roads would be blocked, preventing the emergency services from getting across the city. Then came the second wave, dropping blast bombs that destroyed roofs and blew out windows, and incendiary bombs to start fires in the buildings that were left. By now, of course, the fire-fighting services had been immobilised. It was a clinical, and appallingly effective, use of bomb combinations.

Harris did not rush into his new tactics. He continued to be hampered by the poor weather that had so hindered his predecessors, and operating without moonlight was still a challenge. Important breakthroughs were made that spring, though. In March, 223 aircraft bombed the Billancourt Renault factory just outside Paris, which was being used to build lorries for the German armed forces. It was a record-breaking operation: the most aircraft to be dispatched to a single target so far, the greatest tonnage of bombs dropped, and 40 per cent of the target destroyed. Then came Bomber Command's first major success against a German target, one that showed another aspect of Harris's skill: his ability to play to the gallery of world opinion. Harris wanted to create a signature raid, one that embraced every aspect of his new doctrine and tactics, and one that both British and German populations would notice, and be awestruck by. He required the right target; put crudely, a city his bombers could find and, once they had found it, could incinerate; preferably one that wasn't too heavily defended. Ideal would be a medium-sized city, on the coast (making it far easier to pinpoint than an inland city) and comprising a closely packed town centre of wooden buildings. In the spring of 1942, he found it: the ancient Hanseatic city of Lübeck. As Max Hastings would put it, a city bombed not because it was important, but important because it could be bombed.

On Palm Sunday, more than 400 tons of bombs were dropped on the Batlic port, two-thirds of which were incendiary bombs. Thousands of buildings in this historic city were destroyed, many considered to be of important architectural value. The result was a horrifying vindication of Harris's calculations. The city went up in smoke, and the propaganda value was immense. The era of Harris's area bombing conflagrations had arrived. In April, similar raids were carried out on a similar city, Rostock, this time over four nights. Another historic city was set ablaze, causing thousands of people to flee. Both cities had been on the official list of area bombing targets, and both had contained war-industry factories, but their real significance was to prove to the world that Bomber Command could unleash untold destruction on an enemy that until this point had remained remarkably unscathed by the war it had started. Harris had sought these targets of lightly defended, compact medieval cities that would burn easily to prove to his crews that they wielded a truly terrible weapon; after their completion he considered Bomber Command to have been well 'blooded'.

The raids on Lübeck and Rostock had brought the success that Harris craved for his command, but now he needed a bigger gesture. Bomber Command hadn't yet sent as many as 300 aircraft out on operations on any one night, but Harris calculated that if every possible aircraft was mobilised, it would be possible to launch a thousand bombers. It was a totemic number. Again, Harris had his eye on the headlines, aware of the power that such a monumental gesture would have on the country as a whole. He would need not only the command's fleet of 400 bombers, but also Coastal Command's fleet, and aircraft and crews from conversion units and Flying Training Command using instructors, many of whom were themselves former aircrew. It was undoubtedly a bold plan, but Harris secured Churchill and Portal's backing. Then Coastal Command pulled out. Harris furiously recalculated the available crews and worked out he could still pull off a thousand-bomber raid, although he would need to rely much more heavily on the training units and use untrained crews and pupil pilots. The raid would last just ninety minutes, giving little opportunity for the city's defences to react. With so many aircraft over the target area in such a short space of time, many of them manned by novice crews, collision was once again a real danger. So Harris devised the bomber stream, a tactic that would be used for the rest of the war on major raids. All aircraft would fly a common route and at the same speed. They would be allocated a height band and a time slot. This may not sound particularly revolutionary, but in the early years of the war the crews had acted fairly independently of each other. Now they would be brought together to act as a unified whole.

The first Thousand Bomber Raid took place on 30 May 1942, on Cologne, having been delayed for several days by bad weather. It was followed by raids on Essen on 1 June and Bremen on 25 June, although Bomber Command didn't quite achieve the magic thousand figure on either of these occasions. While the Cologne raid was a great success, the other Thousand Bomber Raids were hindered by thick cloud cover. The details of the raids, however, are far less significant than the turning point that the three Thousand Bomber Raids represented for Bomber Command. It was a huge morale boost for the crews, the group commanders and squadron leaders, the RAF and the war effort as a whole, and a considerable amount of favourable publicity was garnered. It was a real statement at home and abroad, to allies and foes, and there could now be no doubt about what bombing could achieve, or about Britain's commitment to the war. Arthur Harris was dubbed 'Bomber Harris', an affectionate nickname for a national hero who had secured Britain's first decisive victory over Germany within the European theatre of war since the Battle of Britain.

The Thousand Bomber Raids were a stunt that wouldn't be repeated, although by the end of 1943 raids with 700 or 800 aircraft would be common, and a number of important raids towards the end of the war featured more than a thousand bombers. In the summer of 1942, however, Bomber Command's resources simply couldn't be committed on such a scale on a regular basis, most large raids including somewhere between 200 and 300 aircraft. Mounting the Thousand Bomber Raids had also been demanding for the ground crews, as John Holmes experienced.

> When the thousand night bomber raids were on, I never left the hangar for five days at all. Meals were brought up and I slept on the flight office floor. I was a corporal rigger; we were getting all the old aircraft they were roping in from OTUs and all over the place that hadn't been on operations for years coming into us and we had to get them operational ready. We were working round the clock, doing everything, changing wings, changing tanks.

The Thousand Bomber Raids also helped introduce to the Allied public, the latest stars in Bomber Command's firmament: the four-engine heavy bombers, and in particular the aircraft that would do for the bombing campaign what the Spitfire had done for the Battle of Britain, the Avro Lancaster. The tired old Hampdens and Whitleys could at last be phased out, and not a moment too soon, to be replaced by aircraft as big as Harris's ambitions. None more so than the Lancaster. Designed by Roy Chadwick, it was developed from the altogether less successful twin-engine Avro Manchester. The Manchester's main shortcoming was its Rolls-Royce Vulture engines, Rolls-Royce being too preoccupied building its more famous Merlin engines to develop the Vulture properly. Subsequently, on operations, Manchesters suffered engine failure at an alarming rate and the squadrons equipped with them frequently found themselves grounded. Continual modifications did eventually improve the Manchester's performance, but its reputation had become tarnished beyond redemption. In the end, only 200 Manchesters were ever produced, and the last operational flight by a Manchester was during the Thousand Bomber Raid to Bremen.

So when the aircraft that Avro had developed as the Manchester III began operational duties, it was given its own distinct name to ensure that the new aircraft would be taken seriously. The Avro Lancaster would go on to become more closely associated with Bomber Command than any other aircraft. This time, the troubled Vulture engines were abandoned by Rolls-Royce in favour of four Merlins. The prototype Lancaster, which made its maiden flight on 9 January 1941, had owed much to the Manchester, using many of the same components in a bid by Avro to reduce costs and trim the schedule for producing the new aircraft. The second prototype, though, produced in May 1941, featured a number of improvements, including larger tail fins and a new undercarriage. By Christmas 1941, No. 44 (Rhodesia) Squadron had become the first squadron to be equipped with the new Lancaster, its operational induction coming on 10 March 1942, on a raid to Essen. During 1942, other squadrons replaced their aircraft with Lancasters, greatly increasing Bomber Command's capacity, as it was the only aircraft that could carry bombs weighing more than 4,000 pounds. For airmen like Fred Stearn, the Lancaster was *the* aeroplane of Bomber Command. 'Everybody wanted to fly Lancasters. We were like kids at the Lancaster finishing school. We went up three times on the first day, three times on the second day. We loved it. It was a beautiful aeroplane to fly.'

That famous roar of the Merlin engines resonates in Stearn's mind to this day. 'When they land the engines splutter and you think they're packing up but they're not. Those four Merlins would start up and the power! Even now you can feel it. It was marvellous. We'd made it once we got on the Lancasters.'

The superiority of the Lancaster compared to the other aircraft Stearn had been in during training was immediately obvious.

It was terrible in the Stirlings, I mean they were always crashing. They were really second-hand kites that had been taken off ops and of course all the engines were rough and it took time to get Stirlings airborne, but once you got in a Lancaster, you'd feel safe. They could fly on one engine, no bother. They eventually did take the Stirlings off duty because the losses were too great as they hadn't got the speed and they hadn't got the height. The

Wellingtons were very good bombers in their time but of course they all got sent to OTUs for training, which finished their operational duties.

Pilot John Whiteley had seen the Lancaster flying for the first time as he completed his training in Lincolnshire. 'The Lancaster really was a marvellous sight. It seemed very manoeuvrable and the sound of the moving engines was something out of this world, they were most reliable engines. I thought the sooner I can get onto the Lancaster, the better. I was flying Stirlings at the time. They were a lovely aeroplane once you'd got them in the air, but very difficult to manoeuvre.'

Sure enough, Whiteley was soon at the controls of the Avro Lancaster. 'You had to learn to fly Lancasters very quickly. You had three circuits and three landings and then you're on your own with your crew, and you had the same at night.'

From his point of view as a pilot, the contrast with the Stirling couldn't have been greater.

The Stirling would swing to the right. The Lancaster swung the other way to the left, so that's the first thing you noticed. The cockpit of the Lancaster was much better arranged, and it was much easier to taxi. Having got the thing lined up for a take-off, you got on to the end of the runway and made sure the nose was pointing down the runway and opened up two thousand revs against the brakes. Then you released the brakes to see which way the aeroplane was going to swing and corrected for that swing. I never had any problem with it. I used to have a half-crown bet with my flight engineer that we'd go straight down the dotted line of the runway. I never lost half a crown! The hydraulic braking system on the Lancaster was also much better. On the Stirling it was pneumatic and you had to keep watching your brake pressure. If you'd been using a lot of brake pressure, you'd get down to the minimum and have to call up flying control to send out the ground crew with a bottle to top up your braking system again!

The most important advantage of the Lancaster, however, was the height it could reach, something Fred Stearn would quickly appreciate. 'The higher you go, the better. On our first trip we were supposed to bomb at twenty thousand feet but because of the cloud we had to come down to sixteen thousand feet so the ack-ack guns could pick us more easily, and it didn't take the shells so long to get up.'

Leonard Miller, another pilot, relished the handling of the aircraft. 'When I first saw the Lancaster, I drooled. It was *the* machine, four engines and it was terrific in handling with all the weight it could carry. It was beautiful to fly. As much as Spitfires are admired, so is the Lancaster. It was a perfect design. The power that surged through the machine was terrific. Such an easy aircraft to fly, it was wonderful.'

Former navigator Bill Burke is also an ardent enthusiast of the Avro Lancaster.

> The first time I went on board a Lancaster, I realised what a wonderful aeroplane it was. It's impossible to over-emphasise the importance of Lancaster bombers. It totally transformed the damage which could be done by bombing operations. I always felt that I was very fortunate to be flying Lancasters. I knew that its performance was so much better than a Halifax's or a Stirling's, and that really helped to decide whether you were going to live or die. A Lancaster could get much higher up than the others, and if you get that high, nobody is going to drop a bomb on top of you.

It's easy to forget how large the mighty Lancaster was. It dwarfs Bomber Command's early aircraft, and makes the Spitfire look like a scale model. The wheels were almost as tall as the airmen. It was an awesome, inspiring aircraft for the crews who flew in it. The Lancaster's reputation would be cemented in 1943 when Lancaster pilot Guy Gibson was chosen to form a new elite squadron in 5 Group, No. 617 Squadron, to raid three dams in the heart of the Ruhr in the hope of bringing the region's industrial production to a halt. The result was, of course, the most famous bombing raid of the entire war, the legendary Dambusters with their bouncing bombs breaching the dams in spectacular fashion (though German industry proved more resilient, recovering fairly quickly from its drenching). The Lancaster's fame was secured, though, as was that of the growing band of elite bomber pilots and their crews, now starting to rival the fighter boys for glamour and celebrity. Flying at up to 20,000 feet, and carrying up to 22,000 pounds of bombs, the Lancaster was leaps and bounds ahead of Bomber Command's earlier aircraft. No wonder it became integral to the rest of the bombing campaign, with a total of 7,000 aircraft built altogether. Astonishingly, just two airworthy Lancasters survive today.

The Lancaster's considerable charisma does an injustice to another important four-engine bomber, the Handley Page Halifax. It would play the same role that the Hurricane had in the Battle of Britain, indispensable, but somehow less glamorous. It may not have attained the limelight, but it was virtually as important in the raids, with more than six thousand aircraft delivered to the RAF. Developed from the same Air Ministry bomber specification that led to Avro building the Manchester, the Halifax was also originally due to fly on two Rolls-Royce Vulture engines. Handley Page were quicker than Avro to spot the Vulture's problems, and as early as 1937 had already switched to a design featuring four Merlin engines. The first Halifax prototype flew in October 1939, but it wasn't until the end of 1940 that No. 35 Squadron took the first delivery of finished aircraft. It was taken on operations from 1941, but continued to be subjected to a series of modifications, and by 1943 the Merlins, which had suffered from a lack of power, had been replaced by Bristol Hercules radial engines. This greatly improved the Halifax, which could fly at an altitude of up to 22,000 feet, and was faster than the Lancaster. Nevertheless, the Halifax couldn't quite reach the overall performance standards of the Lancaster, carrying a bomb load of only 12,000 pounds and suffering higher loss rates, although many of its veterans point out that in the event of a crash the survival rates were higher in a Halifax than in a Lancaster, the aircraft being somewhat easier to escape from. For Tom Wingham, who completed his first tour of operations on Halifaxes, the aircraft remains an impressive memory. Like the Lancaster, the Halifax dwarfed any aircraft he'd come into contact with up until that point.

> One was impressed by the size of these monsters all round the airfield. This was a marvellous aircraft, we felt privileged to be going on it, and it was great to be able to fly them. They were a lot more comfortable aircraft than the Lancaster for the crew. We had more space and you could move about freely. When we were on OTUs, we were flying Wellingtons and needed fur-lined trousers and coats to keep ourselves warm because there was no heating. It was a great delight to get into a Halifax and find that you didn't need all that clobber, a sweater was good enough. You still had a Mae West on top and then your parachute harness, which used to be a bit of an encumbrance for moving about.

Mindful of its relative obscurity, Halifax veterans are fiercely protective of its reputation, and are quick to point up the air-craft's virtues. Maurice Flower is typical of many.

> I personally would never have wanted to fly in a Lancaster. We loved the Halifax. Everyone I've known that flew Halifaxes loved them, apart from the Mark Is, which had the Merlin engines. They weren't so good, but once they got the Bristol Hercules engine, they were a real winner. They would take an awful amount of punishment, very strong aeroplanes. The Halifax didn't carry the load that the Lancaster did, mainly due to its construction, but it was a strong, robust aeroplane.

It was an obvious progression for Maurice Flower, having already served as ground crew, to become a flight engineer. The introduction of the four-engine bombers had made this role indispensable. 'Before the flight, you used to do pre-flight checks around the aircraft, checking everything. It's a routine that you get into very quickly and, having been ground crew, it's just second nature to look for the things you know have a tendency to go wrong on a regular basis.'

It was on the sortie itself, however, that the real work was done.

> We used to assist the pilot in take-off, opening up the throttles and correcting the swing on take-off that always happened with the Halifax. Then I'd work out, according to the distance and the hours that you expected to fly, what engine settings you would need for your trip, to make your fuel last out for the trip. I used to check the fuel, and keep a log of the instrument settings every half-hour. I'd change tanks as needed from one tank to another and carry out general maintenance.

As the bombers were often at the very limits of their fuel capacities for the longer operations, this was a crucial job, but one that was carried out in difficult working conditions.

> Changing tanks was quite a performance on the Halifax. First of all, you'd unplug your oxygen from the main supply and put on a bottle that you hoped had oxygen in it. You had to carry this little bottle and climb over the main spar, lie down on your stomach on the floor and reach underneath the main spar, and you had to do it all in the dark, just by touch. Over the target and during take-off and landing we used to fly on numbers one and three tanks, which were the main big tanks, and then we'd bring the smaller tanks in. It was quite a business.

As the role of second pilot had long since become redundant, it was the flight engineer who was effectively the relief pilot. 'If the pilot needed to go to the toilet, I had to sit in for him while he did that. Getting to the toilet was quite a job, as it was just outside the rear turret, so it was a long way back.'

The arrival of the four-engine heavy bombers would change

Bomber Command's war. For Wolfgang Falck, one of the leading Luftwaffe fighter pilots, their introduction across the squadrons would have a profound effect on the war in the air. 'It didn't only make the fighting more difficult, it was the beginning of the end of the air war as far as I was concerned. The Lancaster had a longer range, it could fly for a longer period of time, it could carry more bombs and it had good protection. That's why our losses became so high, and that's when we began to feel the superiority of the RAF.'

It wouldn't be in 1942, or even 1943, that the full effect would be felt by the Luftwaffe. The rolling out of the Lancaster was more gradual than that, but it was one of many changes in Bomber Command in 1942 that would have an impact for years to come. Falck, in the meantime, was highly influential in ensuring that the bombers would be continually challenged by the Luftwaffe. In 1940, he had been responsible for instigating the use of fighters against the bomber force at night, at a time when Luftwaffe pilots simply hadn't been trained to fly at night.

For many airmen, the Thousand Bomber Raids had provided the first experience of going on an operation. Hundreds of trainee crews had come out of the Operational Training Units and Heavy Conversion Units to make up the numbers, as even with the help of instructors, reserves and those who'd already completed their tours, there just weren't enough crews who had finished their training. Going on such big raids to such well-defended targets must have been a daunting prospect for a freshman crew. Normally crews were luckier. Raids on northern France, involving little time flying over enemy-occupied territory, mine-laying operations in the North Sea and dropping propaganda leaflets were all common briefs for crews on their first operation. Bill Burke was sent on a daylight raid to Brest for his first operation in August 1944.

> I can remember it very clearly. It was a very easy target; one of
> the aims on an operational squadron was to give a 'sprog crew'

an easy target to start off with. We put a couple of hundred bombers on Brest one afternoon, so you had no navigational problems, you could jog along with a gaggle of other Lancasters until you reached the target. It was an easy operation. I certainly learned very quickly that there were much more serious operations.

Going on that first operation was a chance for crews to assess just how effective their training had been. Even those who felt they were particularly well trained acknowledge the gulf between flying in training and going on operations. Maurice Flower went on his first operation in February 1944. 'You didn't really know what operational flying was. The first trip scared the hell out of you. You were flying along and people were shooting at you from all directions. I thought, I'm not going to survive this for very many trips! I think it was about the fourth trip before I looked out over the side. Before that, I just kept busy and pretended to do something to take my mind off all the bangs and crashes. It was a bit hairy really.'

When he went on his first operation in November 1941, Roy Finch was sent to bomb the invasion barges that still lay around Dunkirk. Finch was delighted when he saw his name on the battle order: he would be flying at last. He hoped to complete four or five trips as a second pilot before progressing to be first pilot on Wellingtons. 'When we arrived at Dunkirk, all this Flak was coming up at us and a lot of tracer bullets. It almost looked like a firework display, but we began to think, We've got to fly into that lot! That's when the realisation came that it was going to be a bit of a hairy experience.'

The sortie was going to plan, however. The crew arrived at the target, dropped their bomb load and avoided the Flak. Then, on the way back, they realised that they had got completely and utterly lost. They decided they would carry on flying until they recognised an aerodrome, where the goose-neck flares lined up on either side of the runway would guide them in to land. In the meantime it had become apparent why they had lost their way on a relatively easy trip.

We had to bring the navigator up front. This poor fellow was drunk, not through alcohol, but through lack of oxygen. He'd forgotten to take his oxygen mask with him, and was above ten thousand feet without oxygen. Eventually the navigator came to his senses, and three of us looked at the chart, trying to find out where we were. We couldn't find anything, but suddenly I spotted the shape of runways on an aerodrome down below. We landed at Boscombe Down, where we spent the night. The next day the six of us all went into town, wearing our flying gear because we had nothing else, and we went into the flicks. We'd no idea what was on, and we couldn't believe our eyes. Up flashed on the screen *Target for Tonight*, which was all about flying Wellingtons. At the end of the film, when they had 'God Save the King', we all stood up. It rather looked as though it had all been rigged!

Leaflet drops, known by the crews as 'nickel raids', had long been a mainstay of Bomber Command, but Harris remained sceptical of their value, and they would rapidly decrease in number. The crews weren't always convinced of their value either, if Maurice Flower's experience is anything to judge by.

One night we took leaflets and we had to crawl in through the front hatch because the whole fuselage was packed with two-pound bundles. The idea was you broke the paper wrapper around the bundles, and bunged them down the flare shoots, so they scattered as soon as they left the aeroplane. But we got a bit fed up with that and were just bunging them down as two-pound weights, hoping they did a bit of damage when they hit the bottom! They do say, that at North Creake there was a pile of second-hand bricks against one of the buildings, and as the war went on the pile of bricks disappeared. They'd all gone down the flare shoots!

Most crews went on a few mine-laying trips at some point, dubbing them 'gardening ops', and the bombs that were dropped 'vegetables'. They continued throughout the war. Robert Kee, initially a second pilot on Handley Page Hampdens, was sent on a mine-laying operation for his first trip in May 1941. He recorded the experience at the time in his diary.

Suddenly we were crossing our coast, a sharp evil line of pure black it seemed, and then for a long time it was eating chocolate, and waiting for estimated time of arrival, ETA. An occasional drift from a flamethroat, one of which I pushed out of the escape hatch. A rather terrifying experience, because I nearly pushed myself out too. Then waiting for ETA again, and a start on some more biscuits in the rations. There was a shattering moon, the sea looked pale and cool as we flew along just below light cumulus cloud at about 2,000 feet. I felt we were terribly naked in the strange, strong light. We must be clearly visible, I thought. Indeed, we were. We were within three minutes of ETA when a lot of things happened. The Frisian Islands had been visible in sight for a few minutes and twice a red Very light leaped up from the coast. Then quite suddenly I saw below about a dozen ships, a convoy immediately below us, and I was just going to remark on this to the pilot when I was saved the trouble. At first it was as if someone was striking matches round the aircraft, and then as the rest of the ships opened up on us, it was just a hell of a lot of sharp shooting, very accurately, with tracer bullets. We were obviously a clear target in their sights. The pilot dived with engines roaring and turned and twisted sharply away but still they were with us, hundreds of sharp little flashes in the darkness. I had time for once to feel really frightened, perhaps for two or three minutes, as we tried frantically to get away, but still they were with us. It was a miracle we weren't badly hit. As it was, I could hear a few bullets thudding into the aircraft. Then quite suddenly we were alone again and all was well. A few minutes later they started firing again but this time they were obviously only guessing our position, and the shooting was hopelessly inaccurate. It was only then that I remembered that of course we had a 1,500-pound mine, a magnetic mine, underneath us. We flew on and dropped it in the right position. We then turned for home, hitting our coast, a friendly black line this time, with the dark warmth of England behind it.

Even without such encounters, going on operations for the first time was always going to be an intimidating experience. For Arthur Smith, a relatively easy target gave the new crew a chance to acclimatise to operational flying. 'Our first operation was in broad daylight, sun shining, hardly a cloud in the sky, and we had quite a short trip over France to bomb what we called at that time a doodlebug base. We were flying in what we used to call a loose gaggle, it wasn't a proper formation, but there were perhaps a hundred Halifaxes, and we were quite excited.'

For Robin Murray, like Smith, after all the training, and the waiting, the chance to go on operations came as something of a relief, as it did for most aircrew. 'It was fear of what might happen, and relief as you're getting your first operation over, hopefully successfully. You didn't want to let the rest of the crew down by showing any fear or making any stupid mistake. You were rather on edge to do the right thing so that you didn't mess things up.'

Just about every airman felt fear, particularly on that first trip. When asked about it, most former airmen will tell you that anyone who claims not to have felt fear is lying; for some it was paralysing. Learning to control fear was just part of the job, and it wasn't an emotion that airmen such as Robin Murray ever wanted to express.

You were scared but you endeavoured not to show it because if you did it would spread amongst the other people. Everybody seemed to me to be very calm and collected. I suppose everybody felt the same, that they had to put on the front that everything was quite all right, you know, 'It doesn't bother me.' But it did deep down, you could feel your tummy turning over. The last place practically every aircrew went to before he came out for briefing was into the toilet. It was just one of those things you did. You never thought it was going to happen to you, though; that never entered your head. Stupid, but that was it.

That confidence was certainly tested on Murray's first trip, when he discovered that there would be no easy target for his crew to practise on.

My first operation was to Berlin, as a spare gunner, the front gunner in a crew. I was shit scared, to put it politely, as anybody was! Berlin was the one place you dreaded to go to because you had to fly right across Europe, right across Holland through the searchlights. So it wasn't the happiest of places to go to. But we went there and came back and we never saw another aircraft. It was just like a holiday flight and I thought, this is easy! But I was very lucky because I was with an experienced crew, so I was the odd one out while they all knew each other. They all knew what they were doing and it was a good bit of training really. But you were scared on your first trip, because you didn't know what was going to happen. After you've done your first trip then you realised what could happen and you were still scared, but you had some idea of what was going on.

Ironically, while Murray's trip to Berlin, a target that all air-crews particularly feared, had gone well, on Arthur Smith's trip to northern France, to a target that was supposed to be relatively easy, his crew had witnessed a terrible accident.

Suddenly in front of us a Halifax blew up, lots of black smoke, and we flew through this black smoke. At the time it was still pretty exciting, and we did our bombing run, everybody else did. We got back and found out eventually through various reports that a Halifax in front and above us had dropped a bomb which had gone through another Halifax, cut its wing off, and that wing had hit the third Halifax, so two of them were blown up.

For Smith and his crew, the adrenalin of the first operation was still rushing through their systems.

It was just like a huge firework, none of us had experienced anything like this at all, so we didn't appreciate the significance of it. We didn't know why the aircraft exploded, there hadn't been any Flak. It made us draw in our breath, but it happens in a few seconds, you go through the smoke and you're in clear sky again. I don't think that frightened any of us much at the time – we had to do quite a few trips before we realised that this was quite a frightening job.

It seems extraordinary, but Smith and his crew were not put off. 'The experience on our first operation with the Halifax blowing up in front of us was just something that happened. It didn't make me, and I don't think it made the others, think this isn't going to be easy. We knew that when we were going to bomb enemy territory we were going to meet with opposition and get shot at, and apart from the aircraft blowing up in front of us, it was an easy trip.'

Experience was no guarantee for a crew, but successful operations completed did seem to help to increase the chances of survival as crews perfected their ability to work together. Fred Stearn's crew, though, didn't get that opportunity. His was one of many crews that never made it back from their first operation. His pilot had already been taken out on a raid with an experienced crew.

The pilots would go out with a qualified pilot who had already done ops, to get some experience before he could take us out. So our pilot went on Wednesday to Bordeaux, on a daylight raid. 'Piece of cake,' he said. Then he went again on the Saturday. There weren't many of the old hands who liked taking anybody up because it was seen as a bad omen, but there were some Australian pilots on the squadron, and because our pilot was Australian, they said OK. So on that night he went to Rüsselsheim.'

Their pilot having now been out twice, Stearn and his crew were raring to go. 'On the Sunday morning we saw the battle orders; we were on ops. Of course, the pilot only got to bed about five o'clock, and he was still in bed when the battle orders came through, so we had to wake him up. "Come on, briefing in an hour, we're off this afternoon!" We were dead keen.'

Like so many first operations, it seemed like the 'piece of cake' that every crew hoped for.

First trip, it's more like a day out, like an ordinary cross-country flight, no bother at all. Over the sea, we'd got Spitfires that were taking us to the coast and we'd got Mosquitoes. We were picked especially because it was a very small target. We were chuffed to be going, I couldn't get airborne quick enough. It was a lovely, sunny day and I had no fear, I was just glad that we were getting it over quick enough. There were only about twenty aircraft sent out and I think eighteen turned up in the end because one or two turned back.

Stearn and his crew were in one of the aircraft to reach the target area.

Bombing a target, you have to go straight and level for at least three minutes. You can't deviate, you cannot take evasive action if you see a fighter. You've got to stick it out. We were on the bombing run and we noticed then they'd got predicted Flak. Predicted Flak is when they pick out one aeroplane and all these guns then coordinate on their radar, and they put a box formation up, in front of you. They know what height you are and you've got to keep going no matter what happens. We knew about it, and we saw it, but there's nothing you could do, you've just got to take your chance. Unfortunately they hit us the first time, just before we got to the target. The bomb aimer said, 'Bombs away,' but they didn't go, they were stuck up there.

At this point, the crew's inexperience became self-evident.

We tried to get rid of the bombs, but we couldn't. Our pilot, Joe, said, 'I'm going to sea to drop them over there rather than over the French.' I thought, That's very nice of you, Joe! We're all sitting here, there's two engines on fire and all the controls have gone. You think more of the French people than us! We were thinking to ourselves, Let's get out, but that's what the pilot said and whatever he said, we'd adhere to. So we went out to sea.

The pilot had made a crucial error, his Lancaster in no state to continue flying and drop the bombs.

The controls were all shot away and he hadn't got control so we turned back and he called us all up to get out. The bomb aimer went first. The navigator was sitting there, on the edge of the exit ready to go out with his arms folded, because his parachute had opened up in the aeroplane. But he'd got his flying helmet on. So I whipped his helmet off and pushed him out. I don't remember going out at all, or pulling the parachute. I must have just done it automatically, thanks to all the training, going out and pulling that rip cord and counting to ten. The only thing I remember was that suddenly I was floating down, and the Germans were shooting at us coming down, because we were in this fortified area right on the coastline. You could see these bullets whizzing by. I must have passed out then.

Unconscious, Fred Stearn drifted to the ground. He was now in enemy-occupied territory.

The next thing I remember was sitting under a tree, and I thought how four hours ago I was in England. The war hadn't touched me until then. There was no bombing over Cambridge and we'd had no real problem flying, so I couldn't get over it. I realised I still had some pound notes on me. I shouldn't have had them, of course, but on our first operation we were a bit green, so I tucked them up my thigh, in my pants. I thought, They're not going to find that. Of course, when we were captured, they stripped us and found pound notes in the tie under my collar. But they never found the ones in my pants!

Stearn had hoped at first that he could avoid being captured and, sitting under the tree, started to plan his escape route. 'I thought, It's not far down to Spain from Bordeaux, so if I keep to the coast, there won't be many Germans there. It'd be a piece of cake; I'd walk there in two days. Unfortunately it got a bit dark and I was going up this clearing when I bumped into this camouflaged tent. They came running out with their rifles and I put my hands up, I wasn't going to get shot.'

It had, of course, been a hopeless cause from the outset. Stearn and his crew had fallen in a heavily fortified area, surrounded by barbed-wire fences, German soldiers in abundance. The soldiers, knowing an aircraft had crashed, just waited for the crew to walk through to them. By the following morning, six of the seven crew had been captured. Only the pilot was missing, having fallen away from the fortified area, being the last to bale out from his aircraft. He alone would evade capture and return to Britain. It had been a swift conclusion to Stearn's operational career. 'What a come-down! The frustration was unbelievable. Once you join up at OTU, you are the best crew. We weren't going to get shot down at all, we were such a perfect crew. It was devastating to think after all the training that it would end like this. It seemed such an utter waste to get the chop on the first op.'

Fred Stearn spent the rest of his war in a POW camp. He was relatively lucky, shot down in 1944, when the war was already coming to an end. When he'd first crewed up at OTU, Adge Boal found himself in a crew in which the pilot, navigator and bomb aimer were all Canadian. On arriving at their squadron, the eager young crew had finished up waiting around for two weeks while the flight commander held out for what he considered a reasonable trip to send a freshman crew on. While they waited, Boal was unexpectedly called home.

I had a telegram and it read, 'Mum's had an accident. Can you get home for an hour?' So I showed this telegram to the flight commander and he said, 'OK, you've got a motorbike, haven't you? You can leave here at eight o'clock in the morning as long as you're back by eight o'clock tomorrow night.' So off I went, saw my mother, came back. I was back by seven o'clock. The place was pretty well deserted. I couldn't find the rest of my crew. I went into the mess and there was a crew there that had come back early. I asked about my crew. They said, 'Who are you?' I told them I was Adge Boal. 'You're the bloke everybody's been looking for.' It turned out my crew had gone out on ops. They'd desperately needed everyone to go to Magdeburg, deep into Germany. I thought I would get my leg pulled when they got back, being a sprog, when everybody else has been on the trip.

Boal's crew didn't return, though. The six men that Boal had been through training with had all been killed on that first trip, and it's a loss than Boal has felt ever since. He was sent on a week's leave before joining another crew, this time led by a pilot from New Zealand, with whom he would complete his tour of operations. Perhaps the experience explains Boal's particularly large collection of lucky mascots and flying rituals, and the dread he felt throughout his tour that he wasn't going to see his twenty-first birthday.

By the time Arthur Harris moved into Bomber Command's headquarters in High Wycombe, there were already nearly two thousand Bomber Command airmen in POW camps with a long wait ahead of them for liberation. Robin Murray had set out on his last operation on 12 February 1942.

We had been on stand-by since before Christmas 1941 because the German battleships *Scharnhorst* and *Gneisenau*, and her destroyer *Prinz Eugen*, had been holed up in Brest and the Allies were afraid that they would break out into the Atlantic to try and destroy the shipping which was bringing vital supplies from America. In actual fact, when they came out, they turned up in the Channel, which completely fooled the powers that be. Fighter Command missed them, everybody missed them in fact, until they got up into the North Sea and they sent Bomber Command out after them.

The *Scharnhorst* and the *Gneisenau* were of course by now well-known targets for the bombers, and the Germans had carefully chosen a day with low cloud cover to move the battleships. It was only late in the day that the British finally knew their new location, and the largest daylight bombing operation of the war so far was dispatched in three waves on a raid that would be dubbed 'The Channel Dash'. Murray's crew was in one of the ninety-two Wellingtons that were part of a 242-strong bomber force, and they went out full of optimism.

We were a night bomber squadron, we weren't a daylight squadron at all, but we were armed up with five-hundred-pound armour-piercing bombs to break through their armour-plated decks. In the event, it was ten-tenths snow-bearing cloud from nine hundred feet to nine thousand feet, and we just didn't see them at all, so we bombed on estimated time of arrival – ETA. We didn't know what had happended to the ships, but when we turned back to come home, we started to ice up, and when you ice up you can't do anything with the controls and we started to come down. Eventually we landed in the sea.

It was the problem that so many crews dreaded, and it was hardly the best time of year to crash into the North Sea.

It was February 1942, the coldest winter of the war. Snow was on the ground until the end of March that year in England. The pilot made a marvellous landing, because he brought it down tail first. When we finally came to rest, the dinghy automatically comes out from the wing, and they started to evacuate there. The two pilots got into it and the navigator and the wireless operator. I was caught, as when we hit the water I was pushed right back and I knocked myself out against the main spar. When I came to, I was under water but it was obviously the water that brought me to. I got out on to the wing and into the dinghy. There was Wing Commander McFadden, Squadron Leader Stevens, Pilot Officer Wood, Sergeant Andy Everett all in the dinghy and I got in. I was the fifth one, the last one into the dinghy.

In the freezing conditions, the crew now faced a fight for their survival.

We were all wet and it was very cold. It was an open dinghy, a big round boat, so we were still exposed to the wet and cold. You sat across the dinghy, so your feet would come up to the other side. You had rations in this tin, and the important thing was to try and stay awake. If you go to sleep and your temperature drops when you sleep, the cold will take over more than if you're awake. As a Boy Scout I remember being told that, so I tried to keep awake as much as possible. I used to doze off, but when I got to the stage when my head dropped down, I used to wake myself up again. Squadron Leader Stevens had a very bad bruise and a cut over his right temple and he'd obviously been badly concussed. He was the first one to die in the dinghy and Wing Commander McFadden also died soon afterwards. They had been delirious; McFadden was under the impression that he was in his car driving between the flights and the officers' mess. They went to sleep and they just faded away. I suppose you were lucky if you survived in that kind of situation, because if the cold takes hold of you, there's nothing you can do about it. Jimmy Wood died later and then the last one to die was Andy Everett, the other wireless operator. When you think of the ways people can die in a war, they were very lucky in a sense. To just go to sleep and not wake up again was such a calm, easy death. Sad as it is, they didn't suffer as so many people could do in war.

Robin Murray was now the sole survivor from his crew.

I felt a mixture of sorrow and thankfulness. Sorry that they're gone and thankful that I was still alive. I went to a very tough school, where you were encouraged very much to do your own thing and look after yourself, which stood me in good stead. Survival isn't physical, it's all in the head, it's about mental endurance. I suppose I had the right mental attitude from early training, I was lucky in that way, very lucky. It was about two or three hours before I drifted right inshore, near Flushing [Vlissingen]. That was my worst moment because I looked over the side of the dinghy and I could see all these big steel stanchions with barbed wire and little black boxes which obviously had mines on them. I thought if the tide doesn't go out, I'm going to get caught on one of those things and the bloody thing will blow up.

After seventy-two hours in the dinghy, Murray was himself at the very edge of survival, and he had no option but to get help as quickly as possible.

A German soldier came out of a hut and he started doing his exercises, so I got hold of the tin lid and got the sun on it and he saw me and waved. He went inside, came out with someone else and pointed down the coast. About an hour later a German Red Cross boat came out, all painted white with a red cross on it, and they picked me up. They towed the dinghy in and I was taken to the hospital in Flushing. I was in bed there and this very tall German officer came in and spoke with a perfect Scottish accent which completely floored me! Before the war he was a doctor and he'd done two years of his training in Edinburgh.

Murray would spend several weeks in hospital before being transferred to a POW camp. The three days he had spent in the dinghy left him with severe frostbite in his legs and feet, and his hands were also in a poor state. Even after extensive treatment, the effects of the frostbite would not go away. For the last sixty years, Robin Murray has been able to walk only with difficulty. The physical incapacity, however, is nothing compared to the terrible ordeal of having helplessly watched his crew mates die around him.

Robert Kee had already completed around twenty operations as a second pilot on Handley Page Hampdens when he converted to become a first pilot. For his first operation in his new role, he was sent to drop propaganda pamphlets over Paris.

It was a harmless trip. I think there were some searchlights round Paris, a certain amount of Flak, but I don't remember it as being difficult at all, as obviously the defence of Paris was not very great. For once it was possible to see the target quite clearly. The second pilot, who was acting as navigator, bomb aimer and second pilot, just pulled the bomb release and dropped a lot of pamphlets saying 'Join the Resistance' over the city.

With a successful sortie completed, Kee now hoped to complete his tour of operations as first pilot. The next job didn't appear to be too daunting either.

We were only trying to do exactly what one had done successfully on one's very first operation, namely to lay a magnetic mine off the Dutch coast. But this time it was different. This time I was the first pilot, and the navigation was very, very difficult. We had a very good second pilot/navigator and he got us roughly there on ETA. We were only flying at about a thousand feet, I suppose, because we had to come right down low to lay a magnetic mine. You had to drop them just above the water as they were magnetic mines and you couldn't let them come down like a bomb. The second pilot looked over the edge, and saw that the sea was all frozen. It was all icy below us, and that made it very difficult to know where to lay the mine.

Unfortunately, as Kee and his crew flew around the area, trying to work out where to lay the mine, they were picked up by the enemy. 'Some Flak opened up on us; they got us in the searchlights. We were obviously hit somewhere, because suddenly we were in a spin, and I did what I had been taught to do in my early flight training with a spin.'

Kee now called on some invaluable advice he'd received from his first flying instructor.

In initial training, on Tiger Moths, you have to learn all sorts of tricks that need to be common to all types of aircraft, and my instructor said, 'Well now, you must learn how to get out of a spin.' A spin is when you've lost flying speed and the aircraft is really flying by itself and usually twisting around, and you have to get out of that fast, and he said, 'Well, I'll show you how to do it.' You press the stick right forward, that increases your flying speed, and you press the opposite rudder to the way that the aircraft is spinning. He showed me that absolutely worked.

So now Kee did exactly as that instructor had taught him. 'I pushed the stick right forward to try and gain flying speed and pressed opposite rudder and we went flying down and then I saw the ground coming up. I thought maybe I've now got flying speed and I pulled it back. We had got flying speed so we crash-landed on the ice, which saved the lives of some of us because we slid on the ice. Somehow the magnetic mine did not go off as I thought it was bound to do.'

As the Hampden slid across the ice, it started to break up.

I had hurt my knee slightly, but otherwise I was perfectly all right. I got out, and found the navigator alive on the ice, and tried to pull him away because I was convinced that the mine was going to go off. Unfortunately, we could see that the two gunners at the back were dead. It was an extraordinary moment. I was just living in the present, seconds of the present. They were dead, but the main thing going through my head was that the magnetic mine was going to explode. Thanks to the ice, it didn't because it didn't get a really crushing blow, but I thought it might still go off.

As Kee surveyed the wreckage from the crash, he was found by German officers.

There were shots behind me, and I remember from seeing or reading books about being a prisoner of war in the First World War that if there was no alternative but to surrender, what you said to the Germans when they came up was '*Kamerad, kamerad!*' So I said '*Kamerad!*' to this fellow, and he put his rifle to one side and took me off to the German headquarters, where I must say I was met by an extremely intelligent and friendly German officer, who had been at Oxford, spoke perfect English, and was very sympathetic. The next day, they sent a little German plane with two officers in to take me to Germany. I'd heard one of the people in our squadron had the same thing happen to him, and in that aeroplane he had hit both the accompanying man and the pilot over the head, got hold of the aeroplane and flown it back to England. For a moment I thought perhaps I ought to do that, and then my thought must have been transmitted to the main officer, who pulled out his revolver and sat with it, perfectly politely.

By the middle of 1942, the bomber war had been firmly established. The early feints and thrusts, with inadequate aircraft and indeterminate strategies, had given way to what would become one of the war's major fronts. Coinciding with the moment when the war irretrievably changed its complexion, from an old-style territorial war of Blitzkrieg and contested borders to a world war that was going to be fought to the death, the bomber would play its role in keeping Britain in the frame, and in delivering to the Germans, to use Harris's phrase, the 'whirlwind' its armies had sown in 1939. By now it was also clear at just what price this aerial war would need to be fought. Behind the phrase 'a war of attrition' lay a casualty rate among officers that exceeded that of the Great War, which would scatter the aircraft and crews of the most highly trained, most expensively equipped British military force in history across the plains of Germany and the Low Countries. Increasingly, to be part of a bomber crew meant taking part in one of the largest mobilisations of men and equipment this country had ever seen, and with only a negligible chance of survival. Yet still they volunteered.

6

'Chocks Away!'

'They have sown the wind, and so they shall reap the whirlwind.'

Air Marshal Sir Arthur Harris

(top) Tom Wingham and his crew are waved off by squadron officials as they set out on the last operation of their first tour. *(bottom)* Jim Chapman during his training as a rear air gunner.

Harris's success at taking command of the RAF bomber effort, and stamping his authority on it, had not simply translated into a number of highly successful raids, it had also ensured the survival of Bomber Command, establishing it as one of the major British contributions to a war that now touched the entire globe. From now until the last day of the conflict, Harris would engage in a virtually daily ritual that would make him one of the war's most important personalities, able to inflict destruction on a scale unmatched by any other commander.

Every day had the same beginning. Harris would arrive early at his dour, cheerless bunker outside High Wycombe from which operations were coordinated. Then came the selection, made personally by him, of the target for that night. The range of targets varied according to the bombing directives of the moment, but of course it is the cities which are most associated with Harris's personal influence, and they remained his major priority for the rest of the war. He would weigh up the strategic issues, and the practical problems involved, such as the number of squadrons available and the weather forecast, before picking his chosen target from a folder of German cities. Nuremberg, Munich, Berlin, Bremen – there was scarcely a city in the Reich that did not at one time or another find itself plucked from Harris's files. After that, there would be relatively little for him to do. The machinery of Bomber Command would take over. There were thousands of men and women whose job it was to turn that city name into a real and terrible battle, and they would spend the rest of their day dispersing Harris's orders, translating them into specific mission plans, and mobilising the crews and

aircraft that would be needed to execute them. By the middle of
the afternoon, the target decision would have percolated down
to every bomber airfield in the country. At the sharp end, as
always, would be the bomber boys themselves. There would be
the dramatic, almost theatrical, moment at which the curtain
would be opened, revealing the name of their target, with accompanying maps; a moment at which to groan, or to sigh with
relief, depending on the difficulty to be encountered. By early
evening, the crews on operational flying that night would be
assembling, ready to board their aircraft.

It was usually with a sense of relief among the crew that
they finally found their places in the cockpits and turrets of the
bombers. After the tension of the briefings, and the nervous
anticipation that was endemic during the build-up to an operation, at last they were going to be on their way. The routine of
take-off soon became familiar to flight engineer Dennis Wiltshire.

> There is this constant smell. A lot of it is aviation fuel but with
> all the variety of instruments, there's a smell of engine oil, castor
> oil, lubricating oil and it all forms a smell that most aircrew
> know. When one takes off, one gets maximum revs on all four
> engines and, boy, everything moves in there, everything rattles.
> It's quite a frightening experience, especially when you reach a
> stage of what they call rotate. With everything at full power,
> you feel like the king of the air with it all under your feet.

As each aircraft was prepared for take-off, all focus was now
on the pilot, with the flight engineer to assist. The rest of the crew,
the navigator, bomb aimer, wireless operator and two gunners,
sat in quiet contemplation in their respective positions, ready for
their contribution to the operation that would come later on.
Lancaster pilot John Whiteley still has a strong recollection of the
checklist running through his mind at the start of the operation.

> First, I had to get the engines started. I had all the flying instru-
> ments in front of me, and the flight engineer would be sitting

on my right. Along that side, there would be another panel which had the dials for the cylinder head temperature, the oil temperature and the oil pressure. The flight engineer was in charge of the fuel gauges. Having got the engines started, we always took off on the number-two petrol tanks, having made sure that we've got all the right pressures and temperatures, and that the brake pressure was OK. It was also very important to make sure the oxygen was working because at night we took off with oxygen right from the word go. We had to make sure that the intercom was working, so I would call all the members of the crew to make sure that they answered; 'Skipper to rear gunner, are you hearing me?' and so on through the crew.

Having ensured that everything was in order, Whiteley could now start moving the mighty machinery of his Lancaster.

We'd taxi out to the end of the runway and we'd maintain wireless silence, with no communication between the aircraft and flying control at this point. You got to the end of the runway and there was an Aldis lamp. Once the aeroplane ahead of you was clear airborne, you got the green light and then you opened up and took off. Usually if it was dusk, a lot of the ground crew would have assembled there along with the WAAFs to give you a good wave off.

The crew would usually be in one of around twenty bombers going out from each squadron, all waved off by a crowd gathered at the end of the runway. The commanding officer, the padre, ground crew, WAAFs and girlfriends would all be there, waving the crews off as they disappeared into the darkness, hoping desperately that in a few hours' time they'd be welcoming them back. Now the rest of the crew relied on the pilot to avoid the potential dangers of take-off. Bill Burke waited patiently in his navigator's seat. 'The aeroplane taxied along the perimeter track, got to the runway and the pilot turned on to the runway and that was when anticipated danger turned to actual danger. If you had got a big bomb load on board, say twelve thousand pounds, you knew that as you tore down that runway if the Lancaster swerved on take-off, and it could do, or you got an engine failure, you were going to say your last goodbyes.'

The hazards of take-off became all too apparent to Ricky Dyson when he joined a crew as a spare gunner for a raid on Munich in November 1944. It was a late take-off, about eleven o'clock at night.

We hadn't been airborne for ten minutes when we crashed into high ground, on the Lincolnshire Leicestershire border. We were carrying a cookie, other high-explosive bombs, incendiaries, and a full load of petrol for the return journey, and it all blew up except the cookie. I was sitting in the turret one moment, listening to the air speed being called out, and then all of a sudden I could see a glimpse of trees and hedges when this huge bang occurred. I was knocked out and when I came to, I was encircled by noise and flames.

Dyson was still in his turret, but behind him a piece of the fuselage was alight, and it was getting nearer to him. He knew he needed to get out, but the turret doors were jammed. Dyson started to panic.

I managed to extricate the flying suit, and with the aid of an axe, which was in the turret, chipped away at the perspex. I made a hole big enough for me to slide through, and got out. All around me was an inferno. There was ammunition going off in all directions, bottles exploding, bombs exploding. It was a terrible sight. I ran for my life towards a hedge, but found I couldn't vault it. I looked back and then I heard the screams, screams of people being burnt alive.

The events of that night have given Ricky Dyson nightmares ever since. He rushed to help his crew mates, and managed to pull the pilot, who was trapped in his seat, out of the fire to safety. But one of the crew had already died and he couldn't free the mid-upper gunner trapped in his turret. He went to help somebody else whose clothing was alight. Incendiaries had landed on his stomach. Dyson put his hands down to extinguish the flames, but felt his hands disappearing into the airman's stomach. When he pulled them out, they were wet with boiling blood. Four of the crew died that night. Thanks to Dyson, the pilot survived, although he was severely burnt and later had to have his leg amputated. In the ambulance, suffering from shock, the pilot's main concern had been whether his moustache was all right. Years later, he would become godfather to Dyson's daughter.

So getting a four-engine bomber into the air required the full skill and concentration of pilots. For John Whiteley, it was important to get the flying speed right.

With a full bomb load and a full fuel load and the crew, the Lancaster weighed about thirty and a half tons. If you were taking off for operations at night, you'd got to make sure you kept the thing straight down the runway and you took off at about 110 mph. The important thing was to make sure that you built up the speed to a minimum of 135 mph because if you had an engine failure below 135 mph the chances are that you would crash because you hadn't got sufficient flying speed. But once you'd got up to 135 mph, you had sufficient speed to climb away on three engines, go out into the North Sea, drop your bombs and come back and land. Assuming that everything went to order, you would let the speed build up to 135 mph, and then bring the power back and bring the revs back. Obviously, you'd select your wheels up. Before you select your wheels up, they are revolving, so you press the brakes to stop that, otherwise you get oscillation in the engine. Then you climb up to about 160 mph.

As he thinks back, Dennis Wiltshire remains in awe of his pilot's skills. 'It was a mammoth task to take this thing into the air under the conditions of the time. Even to taxi round the perimeter track to get on line with your runway to take off is quite a skill in a Lancaster with the engine power involved.'

Having reached the desired speed, the pilot could now concentrate on heading out on the prescribed flight path. 'Normally going out on operations, I could go out three ways. One was southerly, going out over Reading and Beachy Head, which was the route if we were going to southern Germany. If it was mid-Germany, we would go out of Suffolk, and if it was going up towards Scandinavia, you just headed out over the North Sea towards Norway or Sweden.'

Being a good bomber pilot required far more than just being able to fly the aeroplane. The teamwork that had been built up so carefully at Operational Training Units, and then consolidated at Heavy Conversion Units, now came into play. Although the heavy bomber crews were carefully briefed on which route to follow, the navigator's input was still required. John Whiteley worked with his navigator to maximise their chances of avoiding enemy fighters.

> I had a marvellous navigator. We were given tracks to the target, but it wasn't the most direct route. For example, if we were going to Berlin, we never flew directly to there, instead we'd head off towards some other city, then branch off about fifty miles away. Even then, the navigator always used to arrange that instead of flying dead on the track, we used to be about three or four miles from one side or the other. I don't know whether that helped or not, but he reckoned it did and I trusted him, so I flew whatever course he told me to fly. You certainly missed the Flak as you went over small towns which had Flak areas in them if you were to one side or the other.

Trust was the quality that made a bomber crew. By the time they were going on operations, it wasn't just a question of each individual knowing his own job, they also needed absolute confidence in the ability of each and every one of the rest of the crew, and to be able to work with them, as a team, instinctively.

Once the bomber had crossed into enemy territory, there would be continued scanning of the night skies, looking out for the night fighters of the Luftwaffe. Here the pilot was totally reliant on his crew, and had to be ready to act quickly. This teamwork could, and would, mean the difference between surviving the operation and being shot down. Such was its importance that Ron Pitt recalls that a high-ranking pilot who took no notice of one of his gunners on one operation was reported at briefing and was taken off combat duties immediately. John Whiteley was well aware of the importance of teamwork. 'You have got to have implicit trust in all members of your crew. If they said there was a night fighter coming in right, you've got to be prepared to corkscrew.'

While flying bombers may not have the same suggestion of glamour as flying fighters, the role of the bomber pilots was far from being that of some kind of mechanical automaton. It took great skill to get these machines safely into the air, across to mainland Europe and back, never mind confronting the enemy. A bombing raid could mean hours of flying either side of the target, and it was not straightforward flying. Pilots who kept their aircraft straight and level wouldn't complete their tours of operations. Instead, like John Whiteley, they did everything they could to help their crew in that unending search for any sign of a fighter.

We did what they call a banking search. The blind spot of a Lancaster is right underneath it. The German night fighters used to formate underneath you, lining up their upward-firing cannons so they could fire their cannons directly into the bomb bays. We just didn't see them, and I witnessed so many Lancaster's shot down on operations in that way. So rather than flying straight and level continually, about every five or six minutes you would tip the aeroplane about sixty degrees to the port, and half the crew looked up and the other half looked down, and then you tipped it sixty degrees to the right and did the same thing, and the report came back, 'All clear down below, Skipper,' and so we resumed normal flight.

Leonard Miller, another Lancaster pilot, describes his usual flying technique as 'side slipping'. 'You're not actually flying in a straight line, but you're sliding sideways, like a greased slide. You're not going forward but you're going forward and down, with no lift on. If someone is trying to take an aim on you, they can't get a direct aim where you might be, because you're sliding out of their sights. Nobody was silly enough to fly straight and level.'

Banking searches and side slipping were key tactics employed by the most able pilots. For Maurice Flower's pilot, positioning the aircraft carefully was also important. 'You made sure you stayed within the stream, because if you go above or below it, you're going to be picked up. You also stayed in the cloud if you could.'

These tactics came easily to the more experienced crews. John Whiteley is sure that it was the failure to develop them quickly enough which led so many novice crews to disaster.

One classic mistake of a raw crew would be not to stay alert as to what was happening. It was very important to stay alert, and to keep performing banking searches regularly throughout the flight to make sure as far as possible that there's no German night fighter near by. I can only conclude that the new crews initially forgot to do these things. You want a lot of good luck on operations, and if you haven't got that, then the chances are you won't survive a tour of operations. I suppose bad luck must have been the biggest obstacle on first operations, and it meant that a lot of guys were killed. That was very sad.

Pilots did at least get the chance to go on operations before the rest of the crew. Flying as 'second dickie', every new pilot would be sent out with an experienced crew. This was when the novice pilot would realise the difference between the flying they had already learned and operational flying. It was an invaluable opportunity to observe the pilot at work and learn directly about the tactics that would be so important if their own crew was to survive the tour. The rest of the crew would wait nervously on their squadrons, anxious until the moment their pilot returned. John Whiteley went on his 'second dickie' trip in September 1944.

My first operation was as second pilot to Bergen in Norway. I felt quite a bit of apprehension when I went into briefing to be told where we were going, and I think there was a measure of tension. I was going with a crew who had done about twenty operations, so they were very experienced. The pilot did the take-off and I just stood at the back of the cockpit, behind him, standing with the bomb aimer. Once I had got inside the aeroplane and we'd got airborne, I seemed to relax a bit. I wasn't completely relaxed, but I certainly felt more comfortable than I had done before take-off, and I remained reasonably relaxed until we got close to Bergen.

Whiteley was surprised, however, to discover that he wasn't expected merely to observe the operation. 'As we got airborne and got up to our operational height, which I think was two thousand feet while we were flying across the North Sea, the pilot asked if I'd like to take over, which I thought was a bit unusual! I flew the Lancaster for about an hour and a half towards Bergen, and then he said he'd have to take over again.'

It would turn out to be a relatively easy sortie. 'I had no idea what was going to happen over the target area, so it was a journey into the unknown. When we got to Bergen, there was low cloud and a little bit of Flak, the first time I'd seen Flak. But it wasn't too bad, and as far as I remember we didn't see any night fighters.'

Whiteley experienced at first hand, however, the problems of poor weather on operations.

The master bomber said we'd have to abandon the operation because with the low cloud they couldn't see the ground properly, and they were fearful of bombing the Norwegians. So we abandoned the flight, still carrying the bombs, and brought most of the bombs back. We couldn't land at Strubby because I think it was either low cloud or fog so we landed at East Kirkby and spent the night there before flying back to our base the next day.

By February 1945, Whiteley was an experienced operational pilot, and he was asked to take a novice pilot with him as 'second dickie' on the infamous raid on Dresden.

The operation to Dresden was about my twenty-fifth or twenty-sixth operation, near the end of my tour. I was listed to fly to Dresden and the flight commander said, 'There's a new crew just joined the squadron, I want you to take the pilot on his first operation as second pilot.' That morning, my wireless operator reported sick and had been grounded, so I said to this pilot, 'I'm taking your wireless operator too.' I think that scared him!

Taking inexperienced crew members was always a risk; few established crews were keen to work with substitute members at the best of times. John Whiteley's novice wireless operator was soon in difficulty.

It wasn't exactly dark when we took off for Dresden, and the wireless operator had to listen out every half-hour in case there was a recall. A coded message came through on the wireless, but he told me on the intercom, 'I'm sorry, Skipper, I can't get the radio to work.' I replied, 'Keep trying, it'll work.' After an hour the same report came through, by which time it was dark. I could see we were in the bomber stream and everybody seemed to be going on, so I said we would try for another half-hour. So we pressed on and we went right over Dresden with no radio. I got on to the VHF which was a separate set, listening to the master bomber talking to the markers. But strictly speaking, I shouldn't have continued, I should have turned back.

There was a fine line between heroism and foolhardiness in such circumstances. Turning back, though, carried its own stigma. When Hal Croxson's rear gun turret stopped working and his crew was forced to turn back on their sixth operation, to Frankfurt, he feared his crew mates would question his courage.

As soon as we got over the Channel, my turret suddenly ceased to operate. I couldn't do anything about it so I told the skipper, and there was no point trying to proceed without a rear turret operating. So we did what is known in RAF terms as a 'boomerang'. We flew back up country to the squadron, put down, and I was then looked at rather sideways, I felt, by members of the crew. It was unsaid, but some of the looks indicated that they were wondering, Has Crocky just gone yellow? Is he trying to back out? But it proved otherwise, which I was very relieved about. The debriefing when we'd landed was very scrutinising; they wanted to know a lot of detail about it. In the morning, the ground crew reported that there was a hydraulic fault and that let me off the hook. Now I could smile! But it was a nasty little experience whilst it lasted because you didn't want to be the one that let the crew down.

In difficult circumstances, it was the pilot who held the crew together. Even if other crew members were more senior in rank, it was always the pilot who was the captain of the aircraft, and so he needed to be a strong leader as well as being able to master actually flying the aeroplane. From the moment the crew first came together at OTU, it had been the pilot who would be most influential in encouraging the teamwork that was so vital, and in keeping morale up. The airmen knew they were doing a dangerous job, and they looked to their pilot and captain for leadership in the long, dark hours on the bombers. The pilots were of course themselves young, and afraid. Yet many had completed tours of operations on four-engine bombers before they could even drive a car. Hal Croxson flew with a pilot who was just nineteen years old.

Jimmy was a pupil at Harrow School when he decided to pull out and join the service at sixteen. They believed he was nineteen. He was the only commissioned person in the crew, and gave us the lead. We were all older than him but followed him and that's why we were as successful in getting as many ops completed as we did. At nineteen years of age he was in charge of an aircraft with six other members, responsible for their lives. He wasn't the stereotypical officer, he didn't swagger in any way. I felt he wasn't really a military man, he always seemed just a shade untidy! But I had strong admiration for him and the way he conducted himself.

Admittedly Jimmy was exceptionally young, but many weren't all that much older, and crews in which the pilot was the youngest member were common enough. Most crew members had a firm sense of what made a good pilot. Arthur Smith has no doubt about the qualities he thinks were important.

Leadership, courage, patience, and a certain amount of what one might call 'gung-ho', but controlled gung-ho. That means if you've got a job to do, you never turn back, you do that job to your best ability, and he had to be able to control his crew, which he would be able to if he'd been all through training with them. If you didn't think your pilot was good, it wouldn't be a good crew, and you'd have to say something about it. The pilot was the linchpin.

So personal skills as much as flying skills were involved, and there's a sense that the best pilots had innate qualities they were born with. The ability to cope under pressure was vital too, as second pilot Roy Finch suggests. 'I think the main thing is having the ability to remain calm and just take stock of your situation at the time, and come to the best decision you possibly can, coolly and calmly. It's important not to panic, because if you panic, your mind just goes haywire.'

Of all the figures in the bomber crew, it was the pilots who usually cut a certain swagger. Inevitably, some of the glamour of the fighter boys rubbed off on their Bomber Command counterparts, most of the public unsure, and probably at the time unbothered, how to distinguish between the two divisions. In the public arena, where seeing men in RAF uniform was commonplace during the war years, a successful raid was down to the ability of the pilots, and it was they who won the more prestigious decorations. This seems a little unfair in retrospect. No bomber crew succeeded without the dedication of all its crew, but the captain who leads his men into battle will always in the end get the highest accolade. The pilots were also usually set apart from the rest of their crews on their squadrons, being commissioned officers. The special camaraderie of the bomber crew could, however, overcome the strict hierarchy at the heart of RAF life. Lancaster pilot Leonard Miller says he never pulled rank as far as his own crew were concerned, and was frequently told off for mixing too freely with his non-officer colleagues.

It was also the pilot who set the tone and mood during the operations. For Robert Kee, there had been an informality on the smaller bombers used in the early part of the war.

It was very intimate in the Hampden. You chatted a lot with the two gunners, and the pilot about what the drift looked like, whether the wind was as strong as we were doing the sum for, and that sort of thing. You always had something to do if you were a pilot. As a second pilot you were thinking about what the pilot was doing, and getting off the ground was always noisy. Flying through the air was noisy, but you were used to that.

That informal atmosphere is not typical, however, for the vast majority of aircrew who flew on the heavy bombers. Most of their pilots enforced a strong discipline aboard, all too aware that an enemy night fighter could attack at any time, not just over the target area. Captains who insisted on no chattering and no smoking were not always popular at the time, but they quickly gained the respect of their crews, and that respect is still held today. Talking was strictly limited to necessary communications over the intercom, and even the language used was indicative of the attitude that was expected of the crew. John Whiteley was typical in insisting on the correct form of address over the intercom. 'We never used Christian names. I was the skipper, and it was "Skipper to rear gunner", or "Rear gunner to skipper" if he wanted to talk to me. The important thing is, if they were not speaking, you had your microphone turned off because you could hear people breathing. Once the click went, particularly if you're over Germany, you'd think the worst is going to happen. So it was dead silence.'

Admittedly, some crews didn't stick to such rigid formality. British airmen serving with predominantly Canadian and Australian crews were often surprised to find the atmosphere somewhat more relaxed, with some captains from other parts of the Empire even allowing what most would have termed 'idle chatter' during the flight. Most, though, accepted, and indeed supported, the need for discipline, knowing only too well that all their lives depended on every member of the crew being fully alert. Off duty the crews could throw off the rigid behaviour required on operations, and a blind eye could be turned to those who relaxed more than might be otherwise expected in 1940s Britain.

During the flight, only the intercom kept most of the crew in touch with each other. For the gunners, including Robin Murray, and bomb aimers, take-off was the last time they'd see each other until they landed back at base. 'You weren't allowed to take off in any of the turrets, so you'd be standing up behind the two pilots, in the little cabin where the wireless operator and the navigator were. Then once you were airborne, the pilot would tell you that you could get into your turret, and the first thing you do is to make quite certain it all works.'

Now the crew were separated, each in their own corner of the bomber. This is where the scale of those heavy bombers is most resonant, most of the crew now working in their individual spaces, with no sight of their colleagues. It would be a lonely night. Far removed from most of his crew, John Whiteley had only the intercom as a means of contact, but he knew that each member was keeping his own lookout.

The bomb aimer would be lying prone on his belly in the nose of the aeroplane and through the front window he would be looking forwards and downwards. The pilot was on the left-hand side of the cockpit, the port side, and he could see forwards, sideways and slightly downwards. The flight engineer was sitting on the right-hand side of the pilot and he could see forwards, sideways and slightly downwards. Immediately behind the pilot and the flight engineer was the navigator, and on night operations he was curtained off, because he had to have a light to carry out his navigation. I remember on one occasion it was a fairly hefty target and I said to the navigator to come and have a look. He poked his head round the curtain, but he didn't want to know and he went back to his work. Immediately behind the navigator was the wireless operator. When we did a banking search, he got up into this astrodome and had a look out. The mid-upper gunner was in the top turret, and then the rear gunner, or 'Tail-end Charlie', at the back.

In the air, this lonely existence must have seemed eternal – just occasional communications over the intercom, but otherwise a long silence, the gunners and bomb aimer staring into the endless darkness. For Robert Kee, this was the moment of fear, as he recorded in his diary at the time. 'Fear is something cold and hard inside you, something smooth and calm. Sitting in the nose of a Hampden while tracer bullets flick round the perspex, and against the bomb doors, with absolutely nothing to do but sit and wonder whether they are going to hit you.'

It was like that for hours and hours on end. A longer raid, such as one on Berlin, might be a ten-hour round trip. Although confident of his crew's ability, John Whiteley never took their alertness for granted. 'I used to call up the gunners to make sure they were awake, because they were the eyes of the aircraft. They were very good and always answered back immediately so I knew they hadn't dozed off.'

As a Halifax bomb aimer, Alan Bryett had little to do for most of the flight, but along with the two gunners on his Halifax, he was kept busy looking out for enemy fighters.

On the whole when you were flying on operations, it was pretty deadly boring flying. You were flying at night, you could look out of the window and see one or two other Halifaxes or Stirlings two or three miles away. We were never attacked by fighters at all on our first six operations so we had no combat and it was rather boring. You were putting into experience all the training you'd had. For example, you don't fly straight and level for more than one or two minutes. You will change direction, you will change height and you're constantly moving about. You're not presenting a target to anyone who might be following you. I was invariably in the nose of the plane as the bomb aimer, just looking out and keeping my eyes skinned and trying to do map reading. The two rear gunners were going round in their turrets keeping their vision going the whole time. You were fully occupied and you never relaxed for a moment. That was very tension-making really, until you got near to the target.

Back in the rear gun turret, it was a miserable existence for Hal Croxson: cramped in a tiny space, cold, alone, with only the occasional glimpse of another Lancaster, always looking back, seeing what the aircraft has just passed.

You did have an intercom but you were absolutely on your own. It was likely to be thirty or forty below zero, so it was extremely cold. You had an electric suit which you couldn't have managed without and you were strongly advised never to take your gloves off. We wore three pairs of gloves. A silk pair close to the skin, a woollen pair over the top of that, then a leather gauntlet. If you touch anything up there that's metal, you freeze to it. Sometimes the clips on the oxygen mask would touch my cheek and that would give me frost burns on the cheeks and they would be there for two or three days.

The rear gunner quickly learned to keep moving the corrugated tube that fed the oxygen into the mask so that his breath wouldn't freeze on the inside. Ricky Dyson recalls continually having to remove icicles and having to take care that his face didn't get frostbite. Jack Eveleigh, another gunner, completed operations in both the mid-upper and rear turrets. Somehow, despite the conditions, he preferred acting as rear gunner.

Once you were in and shut that door, that was your territory, and I felt content in there. If I had to come out for some reason and crawl up through the fuselage, it was like being in foreign territory, particularly crawling over the main spar, which was a bit of an obstacle. Everybody had their own way of keeping warm. I wore everything that I could pile on, including a pair of pyjamas. First of all you had long johns and a long-sleeved vest, all made of a silk and wool mixture. You had the electrically heated suit which plugged into the electrics of the aircraft. Towards the end, they had ducts running along the inside of the fuselage which from the engines gave you some warm air. You had electrically heated gloves and silk gloves. I also had mittens over the top and then leather gauntlets on top of that. On your feet you wore electrically heated slippers which plugged into the electrically heated suit and you also had sea-boot stockings that came up to your knees, and fur-lined boots. Besides that you had your overall flying suit.

So Eveleigh was cut off more than most from the rest of the crew, sitting it out, watching for fighters, rotating in his turret. 'There was very little conversation when you were flying. You would hear the navigator giving a change of course, or the flight engineer and pilot talking about the fuel state, changing from this tank to that tank, and of course when you got close to the target, the bomb aimer would be giving instructions.'

The plight of the rear air gunner was not improved by an innovation that was introduced while Jim Chapman, another 'tail-end Charlie', was on operations. 'In the early days, I was encased in perspex with a clear vision panel in front which slid up and down. You could either close it or open it but people were opening fire on what they thought was an enemy aircraft and it turned out to be marks on the perspex. So the perspex gradually disappeared until you were literally sitting outside. That was cold, I can tell you! I just felt cold and uncomfortable, and I was afraid.'

As the captain of his crew, Leonard Miller was obsessive about making sure the perspex on their aircraft was clean. It was part of a rigid discipline to keep them prepared for any eventuality.

I used to be very strict with my crew, taking them out to the airfield in daylight and practising jumping out of the hatches with blindfolds on, finding your way around, finding your parachute, putting it on and jumping out the hatch. I used to make them polish the perspex windows to keep the grease and all the specks off. We had to have it absolutely clear, no scratches, no blemishes. We had paste to polish it and everybody else used to laugh at us, but it's the difference between living and dying.

For the rest of the crew, the cold wasn't as much of a problem, especially on the heavy bombers, which had much-improved heaters compared to the earlier aircraft. Rather, it was the darkness which Harold Nash hated, feeding his imagination, and his apprehension.

Darkness is all there is; the conversation of the crew had to be to the point and brief. Outside it was just darkness, and the noise of the engines. It's the unknown, 'Is there a German fighter out there?' You're not aware of anything, but when there's nothing there, your imagination fills the void and all your fears are experienced. If something was there, the fear might be reduced because you've got something to face, something you can combat. I imagined fighters below us, above us, and it was just silence.

Good night vision would be essential for those on lookout, indeed for the whole crew. The blackout was as important in the air as on the ground. Alan Bryett remembers the piercing darkness of those night raids. 'You had no lights at all, complete blackout, and in the aeroplane the pilot had a little light over his instruments but there were no other lights in the aircraft. As you were flying you could look to the left and the right and everyone would be looking out and someone would say, "There's a couple of Halifaxes about two miles to the left." We didn't fly in convoy but you would see one or two other aeroplanes.'

The Luftwaffe knew they had to compete with the bomber boys on their night vision skills, and paid particular attention to the challenge. Night fighter pilot Peter Spoden was trained accordingly. 'We sat in dark rooms as it was very important to be able to adapt to the dark. Some of them prepared before they flew by wearing dark glasses. Then there were some of us who ate carrots because of the vitamin A content and because the doctor recommended it. Nobody ever tested our night vision, but it was an indisputable fact that those with better night vision were better able to shoot, so this preparation was important.'

Like the bombers, the insides of the enemy fighters were completely dark. 'The instrument panel was painted with phosphorus but otherwise there was nothing. From the radio tower there was no light.'

Wolfgang Falck also recalls preparing for night-time flying in this way. 'We knew that the English night pilots were called rabbits because they ate so many carrots, and that in the preparation rooms they wore dark glasses most of the time so that

Bomber Crew

they would become very quickly accustomed to the darkness. We too wore dark glasses to become accustomed to the dark.'

Carrots were a staple of Jim Chapman's diet. 'I didn't do anything special to improve my night vision, I just ate my carrots! There were medical people involved in what you were fed and you could guarantee in any mess, where there's aircrew, there'd be carrots. That's why I don't like carrots!'

Crews were issued with flying rations for the sortie, usually consisting of ham or cheese sandwiches and a flask of coffee. Frequently, these wouldn't be touched, though, and many crews would open the flask only when they had crossed the North Sea for the second time and were back flying over their own territory. Maurice Flower remembers that there was another aspect of the flying ration.

We also used to get a chocolate ration. Civilians didn't get a chocolate ration, but we did. I never used to eat mine as it always used to make me thirsty. When we were flying out over Holland, I always used to bung my chocolate ration down the flare shoot, and I'd send the rest of the crew's chocolate down as well if I could cadge it off them. A couple of years ago we were in Holland on a reunion and I got talking to a man. I asked if there'd been any high spots during the war. The Dutch had had a terrible time, almost starved to death by the Germans. I met one old lady who had actually boiled her husband's boots to try and make some gravy. Anyway, this chap said he was coming home from school one day and he found two bars of Cadbury's chocolate. So at least I've met somebody who might have got my chocolate! He said that was the most beautiful thing he remembered from the whole war, those two bars of chocolate.

There's one other aspect of being on board a heavy bomber for hours on end that people like to ask about: was there a loo? Well, yes, every heavy bomber had its Elsan toilet, although they were rarely used. The bomber boys feared leaving their positions

222

even for a few moments and usually carried a bottle instead. In any case, in the thick layers of protective clothing and flying suits, using an Elsan was not entirely practical, and in the extreme cold probably not advisable. Leonard Miller always used a bottle. 'The Elsan was right in the rear of the aircraft, which means climbing over the main plane of the aircraft, inside the main beam. I never liked to leave my controls, even for one moment, because that's when you're most vulnerable. I was the pilot and if anybody attacked us and I wasn't at the controls, I'd never have forgiven myself.'

Ricky Dyson was similarly unprepared to leave his post in the rear gun turret.

> I was very proud of the fact that I never left the turret, not even to go to the Elsan. The Elsan was outside the turret in the main body of the aircraft, so it meant that if you wanted to go, you had to put your turret astern, open the doors behind you and lean out backwards into the main body of the aircraft. On one occasion I was taken short and I let go and drowned my trousers, having a good old wee. Little did I realise that it shorted everything out because I had an electrically heated suit on and there was soon a singeing smell! Of course, the uric acid on my legs was becoming very uncomfortable, and I was quite raw when we got back. So I never peed myself again.

Before any crew could hope to complete their bombing operation, they had to get to the target safely. As the war progressed, the German night defences improved considerably, but another old enemy didn't go away. The filthy weather that is so endemic to north European skies was a continual problem, making accurate bombing extremely difficult, if it hadn't already prevented the aircraft from reaching the target at all. Robert Kee had been on one daylight operation over northern France in August 1941 when the poor conditions made the raid more dangerous than it would otherwise have been. He recorded the raid at the time in his diary.

We were supposed to be bombing the aerodrome at St Omer as a diversion for a big Blenheim attack on Cologne. A beautiful day, until the French coast, where white cumulus cloud was stacked high behind the beaches at Dunkirk like bales of cotton in a warehouse. There were large gaps in the cloud and as the first black smudges of Flak began to unfold around the formation I thought that there would be at least a chance of seeing the target, for once. The Flak, though not intense, was very accurate, and I tried as usual to conceal from myself the fact that I was afraid. At St Omer we could see nothing but the large wood to the north east of the town so the leading bomb aimer gave the orders to bomb over the RT, radiotelephone, on an estimated position of the aerodrome. His pilot had left his RT in the transmitting position and when the Flak started again, as we got to the coast, getting away, we could hear the bomb aimer yell, 'I'm hit, sir', but when afterwards we discovered that he'd only been bruised in the bottom by a piece of shrapnel bursting through the floor, it was relegated to the level of a music-hall joke. This time the Flak was more vicious on the coast, and I could see it winking in spite of strong light as I had done that day at Brest. Suddenly the Wing Commander's voice came through gallantly, through the Flak, on the RT. He was like a leader of forwards in a rugger match. 'OK, chaps, everything under control, steady, steady, the bastards, OK, close in, close in, closer, closer, nearly through it now, come on chaps.' In a few minutes we were out again, flying past Dover, to Manston, at ten thousand feet. It later turned out that some of our fighter escort flying below us had seen our bombs burst. They missed the aerodrome altogether, but by an extravagant fluke hit a railway junction, so that in the newspapers the next day, it was 'Hampdens of Bomber Command were sent to attack rail communications near St Omer'. *The Times*, speaking of it as if it was giving away prizes on Speech Day, said, 'Hampdens also did well'. Our aircraft was hit eight times, once in the windscreen, a few inches from the pilot's head.

So much was improved in terms of Bomber Command's technical and operational ability during the five and a half years of the Second World War, but the weather never stopped being a menace. Even in the last few months, at the climax of the bombing campaign, operations had to be called off, or the bombing was a disaster, thanks to the weather. A late unfavourable forecast sometimes led to the cancellation of a raid even after the crews had got into their positions on the aircraft, ready for take-off. Close attention was paid to the weather forecast, but even though detailed meteorological reports were avidly studied in Bomber Command headquarters, and were part of the briefings given to crews, they were not always accurate. It was simply not, as Alan Bryett explains, possible for wartime meteorology even to get near to being an exact science.

> The weather was a terrible enemy because the meteorological forecast had very limited information to go on. Once the war started, the weather ships, which were in the Atlantic between New York and southern Ireland, were no longer able to be there because the submarines would have sunk them, and therefore the meteorologists had the problem of not knowing a great deal about the weather until it hit the west coast of Ireland. So the forecasts were not nearly as accurate as they are now. It didn't actually happen to us when we were flying but there were occasions when Bomber Command went out and then had to come back because the weather forecast changed over a period of two or three hours.

It wasn't just the unpredictable cloud cover over mainland Europe. At home, fog was the greatest meteorological problem faced by the crews. If it was heavy in the early evening, the raid could be called off, but once the squadrons were in the air, unexpected fog was a serious obstacle. Coming back from operations, at four or five o'clock in the morning, crews frequently found themselves unable to land at their own airfields and so had to be diverted elsewhere. The treacherous conditions that were especially prevalent in the long, cold winter months would be the cause of hundreds of aircraft being lost during the war. Some progress was made, with the introduction of FIDO, which by the end of the war had been installed in fifteen airfields around the country, mainly at those close to the coast. FIDO, or Fog Investigation Dispersal Organisation, was a sophisticated engineering solution to the problem, pumping high-octane petrol along a system of pipes that ran up the sides of the airfield's runway. The petrol was heated in the pipes, and as the vapours escaped, they were lit. The petrol flames extending along the runway became two walls of flame, which burnt away the fog, allowing aircraft to identify the runway in even the worst conditions. Thanks to FIDO, thousands of aircraft were able to be diverted to FIDO-equipped aerodromes and land safely, but it was an extremely costly device. Operating FIDO for one hour required 250,000 gallons of petrol, which even at the prices of the day meant a bill of £42,500. It was a price worth paying, however, for the number of aircrew it saved on the foggiest nights. Huge tanks on the airfields were built to store a million gallons of fuel ready for nights when FIDO was essential for the safe landing of the crews.

Even when the forecast was for clear weather, crews were still affected by the elements. Ice was a particular problem, and had plagued the early aircraft, as Robin Murray found flying on Wellingtons. 'It was very cold to start with, and you were flying in cloud a lot of the time. The trouble was that in very cold weather, the front of the turret would ice up and you couldn't see, so you had to turn it on the side as much as possible so you could see out of it.'

Ice was still a problem for the heavy bombers. It was the combination of bad weather and ice which made one of the operations Arthur Smith's Halifax crew went on particularly hazardous.

One of the more hairy trips, and there were plenty of them, was a night-time trip to Hagen. The weather wasn't good, there were cumulus clouds, and because it was night-time you didn't know really when you were getting into one. We didn't climb high enough, we got into a cumulus cloud, the aircraft started jumping about, iced up, and the ice was coming off the propellers and the leading edge and smacking against the fuselage, and that was a really frightening thing. We tried to climb to eighteen thousand feet but couldn't get above fifteen thousand feet, so we knew that all the other bombers were above us, dropping their bombs possibly on us. We got back, but that was more frightening in a way than actually getting hit by anti-aircraft fire, which we did once or twice.

If the weather was one enemy, engine problems were another. Even the impressive machinery of the Lancaster belies the nature of wartime flying. Design improvements were being introduced all the time, but aircraft were still relatively primitive. There was a lot that could, and did, go wrong. Maurice Flower witnessed one aircraft that got into difficulties on take-off.

On another occasion, we went for take-off at night, and there was a Wellington going to do something in the North Sea ahead of us. He went to the end of the runway, took off and, as his tail came up, his port engine caught fire. It was too late to stop, so he carried on and took off and of course the Wellington is a fabric aeroplane. The fire started to spread and he banked round to the left and went right round as the flame got bigger and bigger. It started to spread and he came round behind us and landed, and it was just a huge flaming cross. One of the crew had ejected and jettisoned through the astrodome, and he was sitting out on top of the aeroplane, holding on to the rim with his legs like riding a horse! The Wellington came in to land and crashed down on to the runway, on its wheels, throwing bits of burning stuff either side as it went down. It ran off the runway on to the grass and they all got out. No one was touched, not one burn, nothing.

The crew had been remarkably lucky on this occasion, and the incident had a humorous ending. 'My rear gunner leaped out and ran down the runway to see if he could help, but he tripped over something and fell on the runway. The ambulance arrived and he was lying on his stomach and they were trying to put him on a stretcher. He was trying to explain that the real recipients of help were farther down the runway!'

The cancellation of an operation at the last minute was welcomed by crews but, as Bill Burke points out, it wasn't without its own problems. 'There were occasions even when you're in the aircraft the raid was aborted and of course that was a cause for great relief if you're not going to fly. But on the other hand it wasn't so good if you were buzzed up to the eyebrows with Benzedrine to keep you awake.'

The Benzedrine tablets given to the crews were dubbed 'Wakey-wakey pills'. As a navigator, Burke had less need for them than the gunners.

> You could have Benzedrine tablets which kept you awake but when you're calculating winds constantly and making sure that you are on track heading in the right direction with a prospect of getting home, and nobody was keener on getting home than you were, it did command your attention. It kept you awake having something to do. I've flown for over ten hours, going down to attack Munich. At that time I was absolutely dog tired but you really had to concentrate as a navigator. It wasn't easy because you're only human beings and ten hours' flying in stressful conditions is very tiring.

The focus of attention on the bombing crews of the Second World War has always been on their work in Europe, not least the bombing of German cities. This, however, is something of a distortion of the diverse work of British bomber crews. Of all the tonnage of bombs dropped by Bomber Command during the war, less than half was dropped on the Reich's cities. British airmen were also part of bomber crews operating outside Britain.

Squadrons based in the Mediterranean played a crucial role in supporting the army's campaigns across North Africa, and in the defeat of Italy. Squadrons based in the Far East were an integral part of the war against Japan. These squadrons came under different commands, and their work is beyond the scope of this book, but their losses were also high, and their contribution essential to those theatres of war where they operated. Harris wasn't enthusiastic about his bomber squadrons being sent overseas, often including some of his most experienced men, but the army desperately needed their support.

Back in western Europe, one thing remained clear. No matter how high the casualty rate, it would be questions about 'precision' versus 'area' bombing which would threaten to drown out national appreciation of the sacrifices endured by bomber crews, and the contribution they made to the final victory. It would be an issue that would flare into life during the war too, especially marked in the increasingly bitter and vocal quarrel between Harris and his USAAF counterparts, who by 1943 were conducting their own punishing schedule of heavy bomber raids over Europe, though in daylight. It would also be a divisive quarrel within the Air Ministry during the second half of 1942.

7

'Green Markers Ahead, Skipper'

'When I arrived at the Squadron it was a matter of considerable pride if a crew brought home a photo showing the target area at all, but it soon became a matter of considerable disgrace if one failed to obtain a photo of the aiming point itself.'

Donald Bennett, Pathfinder *(1958)*

Bill Burke, a navigator on Lancasters and later Mosquitoes,
photographed in 1945.

The Thousand Bomber Raids in May and June 1942 had been a major success for Bomber Command and a significant boost to confidence for crews and the country alike. At the time, though, they were a stunt that the command had no hope of being able to pull off on a regular basis. Once the hype from Harris's spectacular early hits on Germany had subsided, and the bomber crews had returned to their regular routines, familiar problems returned to plague their efforts. Just as one obstacle was negotiated another, larger one would leap up in its place. So far Bomber Command had dealt with the issue of aircraft, leadership and public support. But there remained other problems that seemed absolutely intractable, no matter how fierce Bomber Command's resolve to throw itself into the bomber war. The news coming back to Harris's High Wycombe headquarters was far from encouraging. For one thing, just as Britain had done before the Blitz, the Germans were investing heavily, and increasingly effectively, in the defence of their homeland. Thousands of 88mm anti-aircraft guns were being deployed across the vulnerable heart of the Reich, forcing the bombers to fly only on moonless nights, and leading to the loss rate reaching an unprecedented 4.3 per cent between May and August 1942. This was not just appalling, it was simply unsustainable. If the command continued to lose crews at this rate, there soon wouldn't be enough left to continue the campaign. Worse still, accuracy was *still* eluding the bombers, even though the area bombing policy had now been fully adopted. It has been estimated that in those summer months between a half and three-quarters of the bombs dropped during night operations were not even hitting the cities being targeted. Until they got navigation right, every-thing else was a waste of aircraft and, worse, of crew lives. It was time to graduate from pencil and paper, and recruit the latest in electronics technology. The result would see the birth of modern avionics.

Yet while the current operational dispatches must have made depressing reading for Harris and his group commanders, there was cause for hope on the horizon: 1942 would be a watershed year in navigation, as it had already been in so many respects. It would take a year of development to get right, but once this was done it would provide huge dividends in the remaining three years of the war. Techniques would now progress rapidly, firmly leaving behind the era when the navigator, then also fulfilling the function of observer, had had no mechanical aids. It had, quite frankly, been a miracle that so many aircraft had reached their targets at all. There had, of course, been some gifted observers who, with the help of their crews keeping lookout, could work with dazzling accuracy. Robin Murray had been lucky enough to have had one in his crew.

> Our navigator would say, 'If you look at ten to ten you should see a church spire coming up,' and I would look out at ten to ten and there was this church spire in the distance coming up, in this little village. Those are the sort of things he'd say, 'Look out for so and so and let me know when you see so and so', so that he knew exactly where he was, and he was a very good navigator. He always seemed to know where we were, which wasn't always the case for navigators! They had a very difficult job, let's face it, but the front gunner kept a lookout because he had the first view of everything, so he tried to keep the crew informed of what he could see.

Most observers were not as successful, however, and even if they could navigate reasonably well in daylight over Britain, converting their skills to operate over enemy territory at night was another matter. The principles of navigation were basic enough, as Bill Burke, who was a navigator towards the end of the war, discovered.

Air navigation is fundamentally very simple. You know where you're starting off from and you measure the direction, the speed and course which you're travelling on. You can then measure where after a given period of time your position would be if there was no wind. That's known as your air position. You've then got to determine what your ground position is, in other words where you've actually reached after that period of time. Having identified the ground position, you put these two points on a chart, draw a line between them and you can tell the direction the wind is blowing you, and if you relate the distance you've been blown to the time taken, you can work out the wind speed. So therefore you know the speed of the wind, you know the direction of the wind and you can build that into your plan of what course you should steer so that you actually reach your target.

Knowing the wind is in fact the key to aerial navigation, to allow the pilot to steer the correct course. The job of an observer, such as Peter Baker, was to give his captain the heading, in other words the direction the aircraft should point in. 'It's not always easy to keep to a flight plan. The track is what was called the direct line between A and B. The course was slightly different in that it allowed for wind. So that if it was fairly high wind coming in from one side, you'd have to correct for that and that was the course rather than the track.'

As wind speeds changed over time, ideally a navigator needed to be able to continually recalculate his course, as Bill Burke explains.

Knowing the track which you wish to follow and the wind, you can then determine how you're going to offset the courses you're steering to allow for that wind. So fundamentally both in training and operationally the problem is in identifying your ground position, and identifying what your air position would be if there was no wind. Now that sounds very easy but in actual fact it's very far from easy, particularly if the aircraft is being thrown about following different directions very speedily. It's very difficult to identify what your air position is, and flying over Germany at night in the winter it's very difficult to identify where you are.

Without any mechanical aids, there were three ways the navigator could try to work out his position.

The means of navigation on which you're trained are first of all map reading, secondly radio fixes and thirdly astro-navigation. Now that sounds fine, but you can't do much map reading over the sea, and if you're going to a target like Bremen, you're going over a lot of the North Sea. Once you're flying over land, you can't see very much of the ground in normal winter conditions over Europe because of cloud. Astro-navigation is a very cumbersome process to perform in an operational situation and is totally impossible if you've got high cloud: you can't do astro-navigation if you can't see the stars! That only leaves radio fixes. The first problem with radio fixes is that their range was very limited, and secondly it was really a shade crude. You need to have two radio bearings in order to identify the particular spot, and you couldn't do that on operations.

So whenever there was heavy cloud cover, the navigator's options were pretty limited, and there was little hope of being able to follow the correct course.

The only means at your disposal of directing the aircraft was to take the winds which you actually found getting to the enemy coast, comparing that with the forecast winds and identifying a correction factor. In other words, if you found the winds were blowing twenty degrees farther round than the met forecast, twenty miles an hour faster, you could then use that for what's called dead reckoning. What you did, you just allowed for your corrected winds and steered on the basis of that correction. But without possibly any means of identifying precisely where you were on the ground, there could be considerable errors.

Faced with these difficulties, Peter Baker, who had worked as an observer, usually finished up relying on dead reckoning in an attempt to locate the target. Experience certainly helped him to become a better navigator.

In the early days whilst you're training and lacked experience, it was not terribly easy, but in the latter stages it became almost routine. You knew the dangers and the possibilities of mistakes. You had to determine the winds very accurately. If the forecast was good you would arrive at your finishing point on time. If the wind forecasts were inaccurate, which they often were, you wouldn't. The radio sets in those days were large, heavy and fairly elementary, and they used to break down quite often as well. So bearings were not always as accurate as they might have been. We depended really on dead reckoning, using astro, radio and visual pinpoints to an extent when we could. If you were lucky enough to get pinpoints, in other words recognition of ground features or crossing the coast, that was always useful, especially crossing the enemy coast. If you got a fix on that you could determine the effect the wind had had on you and you could compare it with the theoretical forecast winds which you were using. You could then adjust accordingly on the run-up to the target.

If the observer's job wasn't difficult enough, the problems were only compounded by his dual role. Once the crew reached the target, the observer would have to abandon his navigation to act as bomb aimer over the target. Having joined the RAF in 1940, Peter Baker completed his first tour of operations in 1941 and 1942 as an observer on Wellingtons.

The navigator's desk in the Wellington was in the body of the aircraft, and as we approached the target I used to come up and stand next to the pilot to get my eyes acclimatised. That was generally speaking five or ten minutes before we reached the target. It was always a bit frightening to watch the Flak coming up left, right and centre. Then, as we approached the target, I'd go down into the well and lie on the escape hatch and set up the bombing pattern.

As Bill Burke points out, moving from one part of the aeroplane to another was hardly ideal if the observer was going to be an effective navigator during the most crucial part of the operation. 'Over Germany, it was very dangerous for the navigator to wander away from his desk, say fifty miles from the target, drop the bombs and then spend time getting back to his desk when they were desperately anxious for accurate navigation in and out of the target. So that's why it was important that they introduced the trade of bomb aimer.'

With so few crews able even to reach the target in the first few years of the war, mounting properly coordinated mass attacks was impossible, and bomber crews were tacitly given considerable freedom during their operations, as Baker found.

We were almost freelance. There wasn't the accuracy and the restriction on individualistic feelings. We were certainly given a route to a target but it was left largely to us to divert to some extent from it. On one occasion, we were flying to the Ruhr and we saw an aerodrome beneath us. It was obviously a fighter aerodrome so we diverted a bit from our course and dropped a bomb on it. I don't know whether it did any significant damage, but it put all the lights out.

Baker cherished such opportunities. 'It was freer; it was an exciting period, in spite of the fact that the losses were very high at that stage.'

The flexibility allowed to the crews at the time was small compensation for the inaccuracy of the bombing, and meant that some damage to the enemy could be inflicted on nights with the worst cloud cover. In fact, this sense that it was better to do some damage to the enemy, whatever that damage was, rather than no damage at all, lasted throughout the war. Such operational freedom was, however, out of the question by the time Baker returned for his second tour of operations in 1943 and 1944, this time as a navigator on Halifaxes. 'Later on, following the introduction of the Pathfinder Force, we were to within ten seconds at any turning point on the bombing run. So we were much more controlled on the second tour than we had been on the first. We were under instructions and given the exact route, we were told the heights, we were given times, we were given the bombing height. You didn't deviate from it except to take evasive action.'

By now, mechanical aids had been introduced which certainly made the navigator's job considerably easier. He still needed to pay close attention to the winds, however, and unsurprisingly, Peter Baker and his fellow navigators would be listening particularly carefully to the weather briefing on the afternoon of the operation.

> We had the meteorological forecast and they would forecast the winds at different heights, depending on what height you were flying. Sometimes they were accurate; sometimes they were totally inaccurate, which could result in disaster for Bomber Command on some occasions. The meteorologists were working under very difficult conditions because not only could they not get advance information from the Atlantic, but they couldn't get information from the continent either, as it was occupied by the enemy, so it was not always easy to forecast the winds accurately. Modern-day aeroplanes fly so high and so fast that they're hardly affected by wind, but in those days, when the speed of the aircraft was relatively slow, around 200 mph in a bomber, you would be affected fairly substantially.

Bill Burke became a navigator in 1944, and soon found with experience that he could achieve a degree of navigational accuracy that had been undreamt of just a few years previously. Now the ability to operate the mechanical aids was of prime importance.

Like so many other things, the more familiar you become with a problem the faster you become. Experience affected how well you can operate a *Gee* set, for example, or the more skilled you are in operating an H2S set. That experience builds up until you become more and more competent. When I first started operating, if I found a wind every ten minutes, I thought I was doing pretty well. But by the end of the tour of operations, I was finding winds every six minutes.

Burke claims that most 'ordinary, average guys could become quite competent navigators' by this stage of the war, but nevertheless, the personal skills of the navigator were still important if the precision that was now possible was going to be achieved.

A knowledge of elementary arithmetic is very helpful. What you're aiming to do all the time is to determine what are the wind speeds and the wind directions in the locality in which you're flying and on the route which lies ahead of you. If you don't measure those reasonably accurately and adjust the pilot's course accordingly, you're going to wander way off track, and that applies from the moment your aircraft takes off from your aerodrome to the point when it returns. It's as simple as that. So it's a continuous operation, you've got to be doing it all the time.

The introduction of *Gee* in 1942 had been the first major navigational breakthrough for Bomber Command. This electronic device received three pulse signals sent out from different transmitting stations based around Britain. The navigator could see the blips on a screen in front of him, which allowed him to identify the position of the aircraft over the ground. It was nothing short of a revolution for the crews using it. Peter Baker had had an early insight into the workings of *Gee*. 'It was almost at the end of my first tour. I was in one of six crews that were trained on *Gee*, which was the radar navigational system. It was highly secret at the time. We were only carrying flares. We'd navigate to the target using *Gee*, and then drop the flares to light up the target with the main force coming in behind us. I like to think that we might have been a forerunner of the Pathfinder Force.'

The device did have its restrictions. Even from the outset it had limited range so it was only ever of use for the less distant targets. Admittedly these did include the cities of the Ruhr, which were so imperative. Worse, though, the Germans quickly learned about *Gee*, and so by the time Bill Burke was using it in 1944, its range had been reduced even farther. 'Unfortunately *Gee* only operated satisfactorily as far as the enemy coast because the Germans found a way of jamming it. But outside enemy territory *Gee* was a very accurate means of identifying where you were.'

Despite this drawback, *Gee* was still a significant boost to the crews as it at least allowed them to get a decent navigational start, and to guide them back to their bases. The next break-through quickly followed. *Oboe* was conceived as a blind-bombing device which was fitted directly in the aircraft, but controlled from ground stations in Britain. Again, it worked on the basis of pulses being transmitted from ground stations in Britain, being picked up by the aircraft and then being trans-mitted back to the ground stations. By measuring the time taken for the pulses to return to two or three stations, it was possible to calculate the exact position of the aircraft. Initially *Oboe* was intended to be used to send a signal to the aircraft at the moment the bombs should be released over the target, and with an average error of less than 300 yards, its potential was obvious. Again, though, the range was limited, as the pulses couldn't be carried over the curvature of the earth, and as only eighteen aircraft could be controlled by the device at any one time, it helped one particular revolution in bomber tactics spearheaded by the RAF. If finding the target was so important, and if it remained so difficult even for veteran crews, never mind the inexperienced, why not create an elite whose role would be to specialise in this one job of target location and illumination, on behalf of the main bombing force? Why not equip them with all the latest electronics, the best pilots and navigators, and free up the rest of the force to simply get close to the target, which even average navigators could do, leaving the last stage to the experts? The result would be the Pathfinder Force, the cream of Bomber Command crews, flying both Lancasters and the smaller, quicker Mosquitoes. This debate would be important in 1942, as we shall see, and it was made possible only as the practical challenges of navigation were overcome. There was another advantage of fitting *Oboe* to Mosquitoes: they had a far higher flying ceiling than the four-engine heavies, or even the Wellingtons that had first used the system. Increased altitude allowed the electronic range to be hugely extended, and so from December 1942 this became standard practice. The Mosquito's superior speed also made it less vulnerable over the target area, where the device required the aircraft to fly straight and level for several minutes. After D-Day, *Oboe*'s range was further extended as transmitting stations could finally be established in France, allowing the pulses to get to targets much deeper into Germany. Remarkably, the Germans never learned how to jam the device. By the end of the war, Tom Wingham was a navigator on Mosquitoes specialising in *Oboe* marking.

> Without *Oboe* we would never accurately have been able to put the Ruhr out of action. It was very accurate and with it accuracy really did improve. Without *Oboe* and the experience which we'd gained with it, I think it would be true to say that Normandy could never have happened. Bomber Command was given thirty-seven railway targets to knock out. Now even Harris himself didn't think at that time that it could be done but we knocked out all thirty-seven. With the coastal batteries, we were given ten large coastal batteries and knocked out nine, and the other one was very badly damaged. That's how good our accuracy was by the end of the war.

Another navigational device being tested out in 1942, and available for operational use from the end of January 1943, was

H2S. That year, every Pathfinder Force aircraft was fitted with the equipment, and by early 1944 it had been rolled out to the whole of the main force as well. Bill Burke was one of the navigators able to benefit from the aid.

> H2S was an airborne electronic device which enabled you to see on the screen an outline image of the ground below. Built-up areas would be bright, lakes and the sea would be dark. You could see coastlines, wide rivers and city outlines. H2S sets were used extensively by the Lancasters on Pathfinder Force, and they carried an additional navigator, whose job was solely to operate the H2S set because it was absolutely vital that somebody should find the target, and in fact not only did the Pathfinders use the H2S sets for navigational purposes, they used them for actually dropping bombs. They could bomb blind using H2S.

Although it was a primitive tool compared to the more advanced ground-scanning radar gadgets that have been developed since the war, it had the advantage of an unlimited range as it didn't rely on contact with any ground stations in Britain. With aircraft using *Gee* and *Oboe* to get them on the right course to start with, and over to the enemy coast, H2S proved an invaluable addition to the navigator's range of equipment for maintaining that course as the aircraft penetrated deeper into the Reich.

In the air, on course for the target, crossing the North Sea coast was a significant moment for the crews. How many airmen must have looked back at the British coastline and wondered whether they'd ever see it again? Crossing the North Sea itself brought its own particular dread; the airmen knew that engine problems here and a subsequent ditching, especially in the winter months, meant they'd be lucky to survive. Of course, it wasn't nearly as dangerous on the heavy bombers as it had been for the light and medium bomber crews, but it could, and did, still happen. The dangers kept increasing. As the crews crossed the coast into Europe, they were now flying over occupied territory. For Robin Murray, the immediate intensity of enemy activity had been unexpected. 'There was an area of searchlights and Flak over Holland, which was about fifty miles deep and two or three hundred miles long. So you had to fly through that and with all the Flak guns which were coordinated with the searchlights. It could be a little unpleasant at times going across there.'

This band of searchlights was known as the Kammhuber Line, after the commander of the German night fighters, General Josef Kammhuber. Since his appointment in October 1940, he had been charged with protecting the Reich from the Allied aircraft. As the bombing offensive over Germany increased its momentum, the few night fighters in his command were having little effect. In any case, these interceptors would be just as vulnerable to searchlights and Flak over the target cities as the bombers they were supposed to be hunting; much better, then, to get the bombers before they even got to the cities. The belt of searchlights was, however, a stopgap measure, not a long-term solution, as there was little time over the line of searchlights for the night fighters to do their job. So the next innovation had been to establish a chain of radar-guided 'boxes' to help direct the fighters onto the bombers and keep with them through the searchlights. It was this innovation, known as the 'Himmelbett' system, which had been disastrous for Bomber Command, leading to the loss of hundreds of crews over Holland. It was only when the bomber offensive increased in scale in 1943 and 1944 that the bombers were able to overpower the system. For Bomber Command, bigger raids would mean not just bigger hits on the target cities but safety in numbers for the crews as well. The introduction of these defences made reaching enemy-occupied territory an intimidating prospect for Bill Burke.

Assuming you got the aircraft into the air, you made your way over the English Channel, or whatever the route was towards the enemy coast. You knew by then that the German radar had picked you up. They knew where the bombers were likely to be coming over and they were alerting their coastal batteries and their fighter squadrons to prepare for action. You knew they were trying to kill you. That makes your adrenalin run a bit. So you then hit the coast and when you hit the coast the coastal batteries opened up on you, and they could be very accurate in their fire. I remember speaking to a chap who on his first operational trip was shot down as he crossed over the coast. After two years of training, his total operational flying time over enemy territory before he was taken prisoner was less than ten minutes. So there was a degree of danger there, and you knew that really was a taste of what was coming.

As Alan Bryett discovered, it wasn't just night fighters and searchlights which posed a danger as crews crossed the coastline.

When you had your briefing the commanding officer had a huge map of Europe and the anti-aircraft batteries were marked and of course they were fixed anti-aircraft batteries. One of the notorious ones was the islands of Sylt off Denmark, a long string of islands which were ringed all the way down and had anti-aircraft guns. Going anywhere near Sylt was asking for trouble. The Germans also had anti-aircraft batteries on trains, and these would move about. You flew over the North Sea, which on the whole was fairly quiet. I would normally be at the front and I'd see enemy coast ahead, or the navigator would say, 'Right, we should be getting within sight of enemy coast', and you would begin to see the anti-aircraft guns. You were routed away from town conurbations where it was known the anti-aircraft would be, and you'd see aircraft searchlights sticking across the sky.

With the reinforcement of the German defences under the influence of General Kammhuber, it wasn't just as the crews crossed the coastline and flew over the target area itself that Bill Burke found that his aircraft was vulnerable to attack.

Going to a target like Burnswick, you'd have a flying time of about five hours over enemy territory. Two and a half hours to the target, two and a half hours back. The danger beyond the coastal area was not anti-aircraft fire, because they would route you to avoid anti-aircraft concentrations. The problem was night fighters. Now anti-aircraft fire is very impersonal, it's not shot at anybody directly. Fighters, though, are a different matter. It's very, very personal. There's a guy coming in to attack you, and it's hand-to-hand combat really between the fighter pilot who wants to kill you and your pilot who wants to escape. On your way to the target you would see aircraft which had been unsuccessful in fobbing off night fighters that were on fire or exploding and going to the ground. That didn't make you particularly happy, and it made the adrenalin run. When you got to the target area, you knew there were going to be no fighters because if a target was worth attacking it was worth defending and therefore you'd get massed anti-aircraft guns. You'd get a hail of fire and the night fighters didn't want to share that experience with you.

For John Whiteley, the evidence of enemy action was also too common a sight as he flew across enemy territory. 'You'd see aeroplanes shot down, particularly near Kassel. On the northern route we seemed to go very close to Kassel and there always seemed to be quite a few aeroplanes being shot down. I used to estimate the distance to where the aircraft had gone down and tell the navigator to plot the position, and his plot would go back to headquarters so they would be able to pinpoint the position of the aeroplane that was shot down.'

It was a horrifying sight, but it wasn't something that anyone could dwell on if they were going to be able to continue flying on operations themselves.

Initially you'd just see a small flame, and it got bigger and bigger. Then there'd be an enormous explosion, because it had obviously got at the bombs. I felt very sorry for the crews but I just tried to forget it because my job was to look after my own crew. As long as I could get back and they could get back, then that was going to be a success. I suppose later on, when one thought about it in the small hours after you'd got back, you'd think, thank goodness it wasn't me, it could have been me. It's true to say that at the time I had no idea of the bomber losses. That didn't hit home until after the war was over. And there was no shortage of aircrew for Bomber Command; they seemed to be queuing up.

For many of the crew, seeing other aircraft exploding was a trauma they could do little to avoid, but navigators enjoyed the small mercy of being one step removed from the action. Stuck in their cubicles, head down over their calculations, they weren't able to see what was happening outside, which for Bill Burke was a welcome relief.

For me one of the great benefits of being a navigator was that I could sit in my office, not really bothered about what was going on outside. You had a nice desk with all your equipment. There was your air position indicator, your *Gee* set, your H2S set, and you could sit there ignoring what was going on outside. That was the problem for the rest of the crew. My problem was to navigate the aircraft and therefore I was constantly working, calculating wind speeds, directions and new courses for the pilot to steer. I was kept fully occupied.

Burke admits to deliberately burying himself in this work. 'I thought it better not to know what was going on outside. I didn't really want to see all these shells exploding or all these aircraft being shot down on the way to the target. I wasn't happy about that. I thought I was much better off concentrating on getting the hell out of there.'

This wasn't the case for Peter Baker, though, who'd been used to seeing the target area for himself during his time as an observer. 'I personally would rather have been a bomb aimer. I would rather have been able to see what was going on outside. Normally once we'd got over the target area, I used to go up and stand next to the pilot and simply watch the pyrotechnic display going on around us.'

At this point, Baker could take advantage of the fact that he didn't *have* to be absorbed in his calculations. 'You had done a pre-flight plan, so you knew what the course was out of the target. Once you were on the target and I had identified it, I would give the pilot the next course out of the target, so there wasn't really very much to do for the navigator at that stage.'

The wireless operator had something of a similar advantage, being able to avoid the worst of the spectacle of battle outside the aircraft if he so chose, but that didn't stop Jim Rogers taking a look. 'I was cocooned up to a point. In the Halifax I could only see out of this little window, and in the Lancaster where my seat was, there was the astrodome above me. I used to constantly stand up and look out of the astrodome and helped to pick up fighters, so I could see the raid going on. But my navigator only ever saw one target. He looked out from his curtains, got up and looked out and went straight back in again!'

It wasn't just the introduction of *Gee*, *Oboe* and H2S to the main force which would revolutionise the navigator's role. During the autumn of 1941, an ambitious former squadron leader posted to the Air Ministry started to advance an even more radical plan for improving navigation. It was nothing short of a completely new approach to the organisation of operations. Group Captain Sidney Bufton had recently been appointed as Director of Bomber Operations, but he had extensive operational experience, having previously commanded Nos. 10 and 76 Squadrons. During this time he had experimented with using some of his most experienced crews to drop flares and coloured Very lights over the target area to guide the rest of his force. Now he proposed to extend this principle across Bomber Command by creating a Target Finding Force who would fly out ahead of the main force, dropping flares for the rest of the crews to follow.

From the outset, Arthur Harris was vehemently opposed to the idea. Supported by all his group commanders, he argued that the creation of an elite corps separated from the main force would leave the regular squadrons short of the experienced and able crews that were vital for helping the novice crews as they arrived out of the training units. This could have a devastating knock-on effect on morale, undermining Bomber Command's whole foundation. Bufton persisted, though, persuading his new colleagues in the Air Ministry to support the innovation. He found himself pushing an open door; nobody in the Air Ministry was under any illusions about the gravity of the problem of target location, and they seized on Bufton's innovations with missionary zeal. It would lead to a bitter stand-off. During the early summer of 1942, a vociferous debate resonated around the Air Ministry. It was coloured by a sense of 'them and us', the ministry's staff officers in one corner, Harris's operational team in the other. Harris's intransigence was only increased by his habitual resentment of the Air Ministry's staff, whom he characterised as meddling bureaucrats, never mind the fact that this Pathfinders suggestion struck at the core of his own dearly held policy. Those who signed up for Bufton's proposal were generally of the view that area bombing was a short-term expedient that would be superseded as soon as accurate bombing became realistically possible once again. Harris, meanwhile, was perfectly convinced that area bombing was a war-winning strategy in and of itself.

In the end, Air Chief Marshal Sir Charles Portal, who as Chief of Air Staff was effectively head of the RAF, was forced to adjudicate. Faced with Bomber Command's continuing struggle to find targets, he became convinced that the formation of an elite force offered the best chance of reducing the terrible loss rates of the crews, and Harris was ordered to set up the force. Though he always gave the appearance of a stubborn lack of grace in arguments, Harris would show a remarkable willingness to support this decision once he realised he had been overruled. Admittedly in this case he insisted that the new force be given his preferred name, the Pathfinder Force, rather than the Air

Ministry's suggestion, Target Finding Force. He justified the change by arguing that their job wasn't just lighting up a target but helping muster and organise the entire bomber stream that had been Harris's own most innovative strategic development. Beyond semantics, it was also, of course, a way for Harris to save face, having already been made to back down, and his name was allowed to stick.

Nevertheless, Harris showed his support for the new force in other ways, negotiating with the Treasury to secure better pay for the crews to compensate for their longer tours. And if this force was going to have any chance of success, then Harris would also choose the right commander for it. In this, too, he would prove inspired, selecting a man who would become a Bomber Command legend, Donald Bennett. He had to fight for his chosen appointee as Bennett, while an experienced pilot, was still a relatively junior officer. But once Harris had made his choice, he was unshakeable, telling Bennett 'he would support me personally in every way'. Harris's confidence in Bennett dated from before the war, when the latter had served under Harris in the flying-boat squadron he commanded briefly in the 1930s. By 1942 Bennett was widely recognised as a first-class pilot and navigator with considerable operational experience, far more useful skills in Harris's mind for making the new Pathfinder Force work than the administrative experience that many in the Air Ministry argued would be necessary.

The Pathfinder Force was inaugurated in August 1942. At first, despite the contentiousness that had surrounded its creation, it seemed little more than a gesture rather than a war-winning elite force. The PFF was not yet a group in its own right, its four squadrons (each drawn from one of the night-bombing groups) reporting directly to Bomber Command headquarters' planning staff. It was equipped with the mighty Lancaster and the rapidly improving Halifax, but its fleet also included the rather less state-of-the-art Stirlings and Wellingtons. The bombs it was dropping, the so-called 'Pink Pansies', designed to illuminate the target area for the main force, were crude adaptations of 250-pound and 4,000-pound bombs. All that would soon change, and the PFF rapidly progressed to become the elite force promised. It was soon allocated its own group, becoming 8 Group from January 1943. Now it positioned itself to take full advantage of the navigational innovations of 1942, and the majority of the main forces' crews could take advantage of the skills and equipment of the most experienced crews which hitherto had been denied them. Despite Harris's insistence on the name Pathfinder Force, target-finding and marking would become the PFF's most useful role. There was another contribution that accurate marking would make, and that was to help counter what by this point in the war was being seen as an increasing problem: creep-back. So nerve-racking was the final approach that it became irresistibly tempting to drop bombs prematurely, sometimes just by a couple of miles. But of course aircraft behind the first wave would also tend to drop short, culminating in a huge proportion of a raid missing the target. The Pathfinders would help counter that, even if it meant dropping the markers just beyond the target. In any event, their role would soon become indispensable, as Peter Baker explains. 'The PFF dropped red and green markers. The red markers were calculated as being accurate, whereas the green were not quite as accurate. If you couldn't see the target, which we often couldn't, you ran up to the target and bombed on the red or green marker. With PFF, bombing became very much more accurate.'

Those picked to join the Pathfinder Force were usually already experienced crews embarking on a second tour. After his first tour of operations, Bill Burke volunteered for a second tour, and was chosen for the Pathfinder Force. It was a considerable honour, indicative of his status as one of the command's best navigators. 'Without doubt, I was proud to be with the PFF to the point of arrogance. One was proud to be in Bomber Command and in aircrew anyway. To go onto Pathfinders and get to the absolute sharp point of Pathfinders, which is actually dropping the target indicators, made you immensely proud.'

Those who had made it into the PFF were instantly recognisable to anyone in the RAF, and their PFF status instantly commanded reverence.

> You wore a little badge on your left-hand lapel and you were really proud to do that because you knew that even within Bomber Command, Pathfinders were highly respected, and regarded as an elite within Bomber Command. Wherever you went amongst aircrew, they could identify the significance of the badge that you're wearing. You were a Pathfinder and you were one of the guys who was facing not a thirty-trip tour, but many more. Sometimes as many as sixty trips were expected of people in Pathfinders. In other words it was recognised that you were prepared to volunteer for an especially dangerous role within Bomber Command.

Burke wasn't in fact part of 8 Group. The 8 Group Pathfinder Force believed in high-level target-marking, dropping target indicators from over 20,000 feet in what was known normally as 'blind' bombing. If there was heavy cloud cover, preventing them from actually seeing the target, it was possible to use the H2S sets to bomb blind. With a lot of experience, 8 Group found that it could mark very accurately. Meanwhile, over in 5 Group, low-level target-marking techniques would be developed under the influence of Leonard Cheshire. First used in April 1944, low-level marking would be a vital development for Bomber Command's support of Operation Overlord, the invasion of Europe launched by the Allies on D-Day. It was a 5 Group PFF squadron which Burke joined.

Cheshire was one of Bomber Command's most outstanding pilots, and he was obsessed with the technology and techniques available to the men in his squadron. He had joined the RAF at the outbreak of the war, and by August 1942 he had been promoted to squadron commander of No. 76 Squadron. In March 1943 he became the youngest group captain in the RAF, aged just twenty-five. Despite his elevated status, he never shied away from operational duties himself, insisting on going on some of the most dangerous raids, and by the end of the war he had completed more than a hundred bombing sorties. As Peter Baker says, 'Cheshire was a colossal bomber pilot, a very brave man.' It was after being given command of No. 617 Squadron in November 1943 that Cheshire would develop the low-level marking techniques. Bill Burke is full of praise for his role here.

Leonard Cheshire was the second commander of No. 617 Squadron and he was a very remarkable man. He was recognised even amongst aircrew as somebody who was a totally exceptional, brave and competent man beyond belief. He was regarded as a hero, somebody who led an elite squadron. He had such a magnificent past record and collected so many medals that he was really unbelievable to average aircrew. How anybody completes a hundred operations without dying is beyond me. He collected a VC, a DSO and two bars; he was of that calibre and quality, as well as being a superb commander. It was whilst he was in command of No. 617 Squadron that they dropped the tallboy bombs, the twelve-thousand-pounders, on targets like the submarine pens at Le Havre and other targets which called for that force of bomb.

No. 617 Squadron had been established to carry out the famous Dam Raids in 1943, and after that was assigned a series of special operations. Yet Cheshire's influence extended well beyond that squadron.

He was a master bomber and insisted that we could mark more accurately than had previously been achieved. This was particularly relevant later on in the war, when we were bombing French targets which required absolute precision because the politicians were very disturbed that we might kill a lot of French civilians. All that had gone before was really either marking from twenty-four thousand feet or blind on H2S or Oboe. But Cheshire said you can mark more accurately if you go in at low level, identify the target visually and put down the target indicators. And he proved it. He took three more crews from No. 617 Squadron and they went down to Munich and actually did it. The results were tremendously good, it was very accurately marked and from there he built up the practice of low-level visual marking.

Under Cheshire's influence, low-level marking would be perfected, further tightening the vice-like grip the bombing campaign now had over the German mainland, and No. 627 Squadron, which Burke would eventually join, was among the squadrons specially charged with using the technique.

Cheshire said, 'If low-level marking is as good as that, we shouldn't be relying on one man and two or three others who are really Lancaster pilots. We need some people who specialise in this form of marking.' That was when it was decided to create No. 627 Squadron for the specific task of low-level visual marking. I knew that the squadron that I was on was an elite squadron, and I knew that the station that I was on was possibly Bomber Command's most elite station because on the other side of the aerodrome we had No. 617 Squadron, the Dambusters.

Integral to low-level marking would be the De Havilland Mosquito. In many ways it was an extraordinary aeroplane. An all-wooden, unarmed bomber can hardly have sounded like the high-tech solution that Bomber Command needed, and it was only with some reluctance that the Air Ministry finally ordered fifty aircraft from De Havilland in March 1940. Its great virtue was that it was unlike any other bomber being produced. Its two Merlin engines gave it almost fighter-like handling, while its top speed of 415 mph allowed it to outpace the best of the German night fighters. It made its debut on a sortie to Cologne on 31 May 1942, the day after the first Thousand Bomber Raid, and it made its first low-level attack on the Gestapo's headquarters in Oslo on 25 September. It would become highly valued in the remaining years of the war as part of the Pathfinders' cavalry, and in the Light Night Striking Force in 100 (Bomber Support) Group, which was inaugurated towards the end of 1943. Here the Mosquito took part in spoof raids, aiming to convince German radar (and succeeding) that a major raid was about to hit (usually, Berlin). The night fighters were put on guard, the Mosquitoes evaded them, partly through speed and partly through utilising the Mosquito's 37,000-foot flying ceiling, and the real raid of the night continued elsewhere.

Bill Burke was delighted when he was told that he would be flying in Mosquitoes for his second tour of operations. After the mighty Lancaster, though, he was in for a shock.

> I was immensely excited. When I went down and actually saw a Mosquito, some of the excitement wore off a bit. The entry to our Mosquitoes was in the nose and you climbed up a little ladder through the nose and I was horrified to find out how close the propellers were, death-dealing propellers, and then when I got into the aircraft I was horrified about how small it was. I had to force myself through a little hatch door to get into the aircraft, whereas I'd been used to roaming about in a Lancaster.

His impression of the Mosquito didn't improve when he came to look for the navigator's desk.

> What appalled me most of all was that I was used to the office on a Lancaster, a sort of Rolls-Royce-standard office, where all your navigational kit was around you. There was your nice desk and you could lay out your pencils and your rulers. I couldn't see anything like that on the Mosquito and I asked, 'What am I to navigate on?' and I was given a board to put on my knee. I couldn't credit that anybody could be expected to navigate in those conditions.

While the navigating conditions seemed rather inferior, Burke did enjoy flying in the 'Wooden Wonder', as the Mosquito was dubbed by its crews.

When we became airborne, I realised what a wonderful experience flying in a Mosquito really is. It's absolutely superb, it's
exciting and exhilarating, but just not so good from the point
of view of a navigator, particularly navigating at night, because
my pilot would really have preferred me to navigate in the dark.
If you put on the slightest bit of light, he'd shout out, 'Are you
trying to attract the whole of the Luftwaffe night fighter force?'
So navigating Mosquitoes wasn't my favourite sport, but flying
in Mosquitoes was a wonderful experience. It was one of the
finest aircraft of its day.

By the end of the war, Burke found that he had become very
fond of the Mosquito. 'I thought it was a wonderful experience
to have been privileged enough to have been able to fly in Mosquitoes, and an enormous, exciting experience beyond words to
be a low-level visual marker. It was quite far and away the most
exciting experience of my life. I realised aged twenty I'd already
experienced the most exciting things that life had to offer!'

Having spent most of his operational career as a Lancaster
pilot, Leonard Miller retrained on Mosquitoes at the end of the
war. He quickly fell in love with the aircraft. 'It was the most
wonderful aircraft in the world at that time. It could soar and
outfly anything the Germans had. The control you had was
marvellous. Being all wood, it was a superb, light, quick aircraft;
you had the power, the height and the speed to get out of trouble
and it was very agile. I was also very pleased that I didn't have
a seven-man crew that I was responsible for as you only had the
navigator and yourself.'

The speed of the Mosquito must have been awe-inspiring at
the time. Pilot Stephen Nolan flew thirty-nine operational sorties
with No. 142 Squadron, which from October 1944 was a specialist Light Night Striking Force based at Gransden Lodge. On
5 March 1945, such was the speed of the Mosquito, he was able
to bomb Berlin twice in twenty-four hours. With his navigator,
Nolan took off at 1 a.m., bombing at 3.30 a.m.; he set out again

at 6 p.m., bombing at 8.30 p.m. Later in the month, they recorded a total sortie time of four hours and fifteen minutes for another raid on Berlin, approximately half the time the heavy bombers would take. Nolan went straight from training on to Mosquitoes, but many of its crews were already experienced heavy bomber pilots. Ivor Chambers, for example, completed a first tour of operations on Wellingtons and Halifaxes between September 1941 and September 1942. He took part in all three Thousand Bomber Raids, and numerous other trips to German cities, particularly in the Ruhr Valley, many of which were successful. Although he was offered promotion and a second tour on heavy bombers, it had been a tough tour for Chambers and he turned down the opportunity. Instead, he became a Mosquito pilot, also with No. 142 Squadron. He completed a second tour of thirty-four operations, many of which were to Berlin, where the Light Night Striking Force kept up the pressure on the German capital even when the main force couldn't get there. He was also involved in a number of other diversionary nuisance raids.

It wasn't just the airmen of Bomber Command who admired the Mosquito. Luftwaffe fighter pilot Peter Spoden was impressed with the way it overwhelmed the German fighters.

> They were far superior to what the Germans fighter pilots had. They were faster, more manoeuvrable, and the radar was much better. We were terrified of the Mosquitoes. Towards the end of the war we had a warning system, an acoustic detector. The sound increased when we were near a Mosquito. Then we turned off and went away. We were afraid of the Mosquitoes, particularly when we landed. The Mosquitoes waited over the German air bases and we had huge losses.

Wolfgang Falck agrees with Spoden on the importance of the Mosquito. 'That aeroplane was much too fast, flew much too high and was far too difficult to catch with radar. It was a superb aircraft. When the Mosquitoes arrived, all we could do was shake our heads. The Mosquito was unique.'

With the introduction of the Mosquito, and the development of Pathfinder techniques, the organisation of the bombing runs was to become extremely well orchestrated. In 5 Group, Bill Burke was part of a Pathfinder Force that included both Mosquitoes and Lancasters.

We sent nine aircraft into the skies, and three aircraft were to go fairly near the target. They would arrive there about twenty minutes before 'H hour', 'H hour' being the moment when the bombs were due to start dropping. That's when the first wave of main-force bombers would arrive. These three aircraft would circle over a flare, and they would try to identify, accurately, the wind in the locality at that height for the bombers. That information could be fed at 'H minus 20' to the leading aircraft of the three, who averaged out the three wind finds and then broadcast at 'H minus 10' to the master bomber the wind that the main force should use on their bomber sights, because obviously the wind direction and speed affect the fall of the bomb.

While the wind was being calculated, the target-marking would begin.

At 'H minus 13', the two Lancaster squadrons that supported us arrived and, again blind-bombing using H2S, would drop green flares in the locality of the target, so that our six target-marking crews could start to approach the target area. At 'H minus 11' the first of the heavy Lancasters dropped flares. These were illuminating candles on little parachutes which fell down towards the ground and really turned the area, if not as light as day, certainly as light as the brightest moonlight, so you could see all the details on the ground. By this time the Mosquitoes had already come down from around twenty-five thousand feet to about five thousand feet, and after the flares were down we were in there at 'H minus 10' to visually identify where the target indicators were to be dropped.

An easily identifiable location in each city would already have been chosen for the target markers.

When 'H hour minus 10' arrived, we were in there like little rabbits, looking for the particular point where we were to drop the target indicator. It would be something that we could readily recognise when we were travelling at two or three hundred knots at five hundred feet. Typically, it would be something pretty conspicuous like a sports ground or football stadium. When we attacked Würzburg, we put the target indicators into a football ground. You had half a dozen aircraft milling around at about five or six hundred feet, hunting for the point to be marked, and there was great competition to be the first person to identify the aiming point and mark it. Everybody wanted to be the first person to spot it so they could shout out 'Tally ho!'. That was really an instruction to the other crews, 'Stand back, give me air space, I'm going to mark.' He would then dive down from around a thousand feet to nearer four or five hundred feet and dive-bomb his target indicator.

Then the other target-marking aircraft would get their chance. 'The marker leader would come along and inspect where the target indicator had fallen and how near it was to the required aiming point. If he thought it was fine, the rest of us would be instructed to come in and back up that single target indicator with further indicators of the same colour. If it was not sufficiently accurate, somebody would be called in to mark again alongside it with a correction factor.'

Different-coloured flares were used to indicate different degrees of accuracy in the marking.

If it wasn't accurate, then he might say, 'Mark again, this time with yellow flares,' and by then they'd be satisfied that they'd got the target indicators in the right position. The marker leader would then tell the master of ceremonies, flying in a Lancaster, who would then call the main force and tell them to bomb on the reds, the greens or the yellows, or whatever they were to mark on, and he'd ask permission from the master of ceremonies for you to buzz off, in which case you turned on the taps and rushed home as fast as you could. Those ten minutes were exhilarating beyond belief because there were hails of tracer fire coming up, streams of it. You think it's only moving very slowly but when it got near you it zapped past at speed. To fly through that and also to be competing with your mates for the privilege of being the first marker was like a ten-minute white-knuckle ride.

Flying at such a low level gave the Pathfinder crews a much more detailed view of the city waiting below than was possible for most of the bomber crews.

As we came down at that level we could see everything. At five hundred feet, with all that amount of illumination and light, you could see particular individuals walking about or shooting at you. All the time, you're getting anti-aircraft fire around but you could see every detail. Sometimes you could see remarkable things. We marked a marshalling yard somewhere in Czechoslovakia, and you could see these little ants of people buzzing around. You identified, pretty quickly, that they were trying to get an engine out before the bombers arrived. That added a new dimension because you became intent that they were not going to get that train out. We were going to get the main force going in quickly enough to blow them up, which at the time was all tremendously exciting.

The kind of low-level marking practised by Burke had become extremely accurate.

We'd aim to have the target indicators within one hundred yards of the aiming point, and in some cases it was absolutely spot on. For example, one of the problems when we marked the Dortmund-Ems Canal was that one crew, at least, put their target indicator down into the canal. Again on one of the French targets, I think it was when Leonard Cheshire was doing the marking, they put their target indicators right down on to the factory roof. They went through the roof and burnt inside the factory, so they couldn't be seen by the oncoming bombers! But I'd say that normally we'd get within a hundred yards or so of the target.

In fact, it was sometimes considered better not to drop the target indicators exactly where the bombing was intended.

The main purpose of the squadron was to drop target indicators at a particular point which would guide the bombers to the target. When it became more sophisticated, the target indicators would be put down at a point short of the target area because if it was in the target area when the bombs started dropping, they would blow the target indicators away. So by dropping the target indicator just outside the bombing area and telling the crews to come in, on different courses of action, you spread the bombing widely over the target area and you didn't blow your target indicators out of existence.

In charge of the marking was the master of ceremonies. Bill Burke still has a great deal of admiration for the men who performed this role.

The master of ceremonies would be circling over the target, not merely whilst the marking operation was taking place. He would be there to control the bombing itself, shouting out to the crews, 'You're dropping short.' This was one of the great problems with bombing. There's always creep-back, because the crews wanted to drop the bombs and get the hell out of there as quickly as possible. The master of ceremonies stayed there possibly for thirty or forty minutes until the raid was over. The chop rate amongst them was terrible, and they were required to be very brave men to do that.

With the marking completed, it was time for the Pathfinder crews to get out of the target area.

Once the master of ceremonies was satisfied that the target had been marked appropriately, with a particular colour, he called out over VHF, because we were all VHF connected, to the main force, 'Bomb on the reds,' or 'Bomb on the yellows.' By that time we were scudding off home because it was highly dangerous to be in that area when they were going to start bombing! The marking force never hung around because there might be six hundred aircraft thundering towards you, and they weren't going to dawdle, they were going to be dropping their bombs at 'H hour'.

So as the crews of the main force approached on 'H hour', they would see the flares lighting up the target. Lancaster pilot John Whiteley felt the tension he'd experienced at the start of the operation return, but it certainly wasn't an emotion he was able to show at this point.

The fear dispersed a little bit after take-off until we got nearer the target, then it used to build up. There was apprehension, and I think everybody experienced the fear. The guy that went on to operations who said he was never afraid never existed. The important thing from my own point of view as captain was not to expose the fact that you were afraid because I am sure the other members of the crew were going through the same experience. I kept everything to myself and I think that was terribly important because you can't have fears going right through the crew because then they would be useless. So there were never any complaints, and the crew would come with me through thick and thin.

During the latter part of the war, when raids with several hundred aircraft became commonplace, the main bomber force wouldn't all descend on the target at the same time, as Whiteley explains. 'You went in three waves. There were three hundred aircraft in the first wave and that would take place over about three minutes, so that's a hundred aircraft a minute.'

While the marking was being carried out, Bill Burke would see the main force in the distance. 'The main force of bombers were chugging along at 180 miles an hour towards the target and they'd know that they had to be on the target at a particular time. They would see the marking operation in the distance. They could be twenty minutes or more away from the target, but the light being created by the illuminators dropping the flares could be seen from many, many miles away.'

The target area would soon be crowded with Bomber Command's aircraft. Pilots would need to concentrate hard to avoid disaster.

Over the target area, there were special dangers. First of all, in order to bomb accurately you had to fly straight and level for four or five minutes, which made it much easier for predicted gunfire to hit you. The second thing was you had a mass of aircraft going over the target area in very concentrated fashion. Towards the end of the war they would put two hundred aircraft over a target in twenty minutes. So there was a mass of aircraft milling around, and there was always the danger of collision. The third thing was that there was a danger of bombs being dropped from above you. I had a friend who had a wing clipped over the Ruhr at twenty-four thousand feet. The aircraft, with a full bomb load, went into a spin and the pilot just couldn't get it out. It was falling and you can imagine what the centrifugal forces would be aboard that aircraft. The flight engineer got alongside the pilot, and between them they succeeded in pulling it out at six thousand. So they'd plummeted the best part of eighteen thousand feet.

By the time the second wave of bombers came in, the target would usually be well alight.

In the main, the attacks on towns and cities were intended to be concentrated incendiary attacks. So when the first incendiaries and a few high explosives had been dropped in the burning areas, the towns started to burn, so there was not merely the bright illumination over the target, but the burning fires on the ground, and the bombs exploding as well. The cities wouldn't become a sea of fire to start off with, even at Dresden. The fire would build up, but when a four-thousand-pound cookie lands, or an eight-thousand-pound double cookie goes off, you can see it from a fair distance.

The development of the Pathfinders and target-marking was nothing short of a total revolution that would transform Bomber Command's fortunes, and more potently those of the German cities below. For Horst Hirche, who served as a Flak gun operator towards the end of the war, the image of the Pathfinders has endured.

During night raids the Pathfinders flew ahead, dropping their incendiary devices, which we called Christmas trees. For us it was a terrifyingly beautiful sight on the one hand. When we saw them it was like watching a fiery umbrella slowly falling to earth. That memory has stayed with me. I couldn't or didn't want to see fireworks any more. If fireworks were ever let off, no matter what the occasion, for years I avoided them. All I could see was the incendiary devices and how awful and dreadful they were.

With the navigator having directed the aircraft to the target, and the skipper having managed to throw off any night fighters and searchlights, all eyes were now on the bomb aimer. It would be his job to provide the raid with its explosive climax, through the lens of his bomb sight, delivering as much of the payload as possible down the throat of the areas below lit up by the Pathfinders. This too would require a skill it took months to acquire.

8

'Bombs Gone!'

'There are a lot of people who say that bombing cannot win the war. My reply to that is that it has never been tried yet. We shall see.'

Air Marshal Sir Arthur Harris

Jim Rogers, a wireless operator, in his full flying kit,
photographed just before going on an operation.

Now was the bomb aimer's moment. The training, the briefings, the tedious hours of flying and staring into the darkness had all been leading up to this: the bomb run. Success or failure now rested not with seven crew members, but with just one. If the bombs brought all the way from their home base were now to miss their target, all of Harris's fighting words, and all the nightly sacrifices endured by Bomber Command, would come to nothing. No wonder the bomb aimer's training programme lasted nearly as long as the navigator's. After several hours waiting, helping the gunners look out for night fighters, spotting landmarks for the navigator and relying on his fellow crew members to get him to the target at the right time, that training would reach its crunch point when at long last the bomb aimer took his position, and guided the aircraft into position for its final four or five minutes of the outward journey. By the time he saw the target, the Pathfinder Force should have been and gone, their flares left lighting up the target below. For those coming in on the second raid, the target would already be a blazing inferno. As a bomb aimer on Halifaxes in No. 158 Squadron, Alan Bryett waited nervously and patiently for this most critical time to arrive.

Before the bomb run, you're in the front, in the nose. In the Halifax you had a perspex nose and you are looking out. Flying over the North Sea, you can't see very much until you get to enemy coast, and you're trying to do map reading. Some nights you could do a certain amount of map reading, mainly from rivers or from contours of islands and things of that sort. The navigator is droning in every now and again, 'We are now over so and so town,' or 'We are fifty miles south of the town, we're on course,' and he'd also be telling you how you were going with timing. It was important you got the timing within a minute or two of your scheduled time.

The target area must have been on the bomb aimer's mind more than most of the crew's throughout the operation, but Arthur Smith found that the other roles he was expected to perform were not just a way of keeping him occupied in the meantime.

An air bomber, or bomb aimer as you may call it, was essential. He assisted the navigator in the aircraft, he had done a gunnery course, because he had to be able to fire guns in the bomber, and he had done a bomb-aiming course, because he had to know all about the bombs and dropping the bombs. In Halifaxes he could also act as a second pilot, in an emergency. You had been trained as a pilot, and you went on what was called a linked trainer, which was ground training in a darkened room, but with all the controls. So I could have flown the Halifax, although I couldn't have landed it at all.

As the aircraft came within about fifty miles of the target, Smith would see where the Pathfinder Force had placed their target markers. On night-time raids, it was an end to the hours of darkness the crew had experienced since take-off. 'Half our operations over enemy territory were in daylight and about half at night-time. At night you didn't see much until you got to the target. You could usually see the target coming up in the distance, a glow. You'd gradually get over there, see the markers going down.'

Now the bomb aimer moved into position for the bomb run itself, lying prone in the front turret. Alan Bryett vividly recalls doing this on each of the seven operations he took part in during the summer of 1943.

It was a bit hairy lying on the perspex looking down. Fortunately the anti-aircraft fire always seemed to be bursting below us, because in Halifaxes we could fly sufficiently high to be above most of it. Generally speaking you never had a head-on attack from a German fighter. You were moving so quickly they couldn't do it, but you were looking ahead. There was apprehension which I don't think one would have admitted to the rest of the crew because it might have made them feel a bit nervous as well.

Peter Baker flew as an observer during his first tour of operations in 1941 and 1942. Once he'd moved down from his navigating position, he also felt the apprehension, and indeed terribly exposed, as he lay prone in the front of a Wellington ready for the bomb run. 'As the Flak came up, you'd turn on to your side to reduce the target area. It didn't do any good at all, of course, but you would protect what you considered to be the more important parts of your body. You could at times be fascinated by the sight below, particularly if the target was burning.'

If the bomb aimer was going to bomb at exactly the right point, the contribution of the pilot was essential. It would be the pilot's job to fly straight and level for the several minutes of the bomb run. It was an unnerving time for any experienced pilot, forced to abandon his instinct to weave at the very time when the Flak and searchlights were most intense. Lancaster pilot Leonard Miller knew, though, that the bomb aimer would be preparing for the bomb drop.

The bomb aimer gets his bombs fused up by pressing all these electric panels which make the fuses on the bombs ready and live. As you start your run, you've got to get straight and level and you had the master bomber above you calling out which markers to go for, where the heaviest bombing had to be. You opened your bomb doors, made sure they opened and you started your run and from that moment on the bomb aimer was then in control. As you were running towards the target, the key man was the bomb aimer, and everyone was feeding every bit of information in to make sure he didn't muck it up at the last minute.

This is where the trust that was so integral to the camaraderie of the crew once again really mattered. The pilot was still operating the aircraft, but he was handing over control to the bomb aimer. In the most effective crews, the teamwork that had been so carefully nurtured in the training units and on the squadrons could, over the target more than ever, become the factor which ensured that the crew survived. As a bomb aimer, Arthur Smith knew that he had the trust of his pilot.

> When I was doing the bombing run the pilot had to do exactly as I told him. He would see the target in front lit up by markers, or if it was daylight he might see the actual target itself. I would start saying, 'Right, steady, there's the target ahead,' and I would guide him on to the target by saying, 'Right, left, left, right,' and he would guide the aircraft according to my instructions. According to the tone in my voice, he would know how much to turn it, because he had got so used to me in training. If he was getting way off and had to turn it a lot, I'd say so quite loudly and urgently. When you said, 'Bombs gone!' that's when the yellow cross on your bomb sight intersected with the target or the markers.

In the noisy environment of a four-engine bomber, it was vital that bomb aimer Alan Bryett made his directions to the pilot clear.

> You would have a code for speaking to the pilot. If you wanted the pilot to fly left, you'd say, 'Left-left', for right you'd say, 'Right' [drawn out]. It sounds simple but on operations when there's lots of noise about, if you heard 'Baa-baa', then you knew that was left whether you could actually hear the word 'left' or not, and 'Baaaa' would be right. So it was simple but quite effective for operations. When you were in the correct position, you'd say, 'Steady-steady.' Sometimes all the pilot would hear was 'Er-er, er-err'.

The bomb run lasted just a few minutes, but for Tom Wingham, who was a Halifax bomb aimer on his first tour, and the start of his second, it always seemed far longer, as it must have done for bomb aimers universally. 'The bomb run seemed interminable. From when you were getting the thing in your bomb sight, to actually releasing the bombs, time just seemed to absolutely stand still. You could always smell cordite when shells were near you as it used to permeate the aircraft at times.'

The smell of the cordite, the sight of the Flak barrage, the roar of the engines – it took nerves of steel for even the most calm and experienced pilot to maintain his flying position over the target area. For John Whiteley it wasn't just that he knew that it was dangerous, he could see that all around him, but he had to overcome his instincts and ignore it.

> Once the bomb aimer said, 'Bomb doors open,' I was flying on instruments. I could be flying on instruments for the next couple of minutes because to get the best bombing results one had to have that aeroplane straight and level. So I took no notice of what was happening outside. If there was Flak coming up, I just had to ignore it and get on with the job until the bombs had gone, and you'd probably have to fly on for another fifteen or twenty seconds to get a photograph and close the bomb doors. Then you could dive out of the target and get away from it. So on the bombing run I saw very little of what was going on outside, I was just concentrating solely on my flying instruments.

All concentration was now on the bomb aimer, aligning the aircraft over the target. By the last few years of the war, he could rely on the sophisticated Mark XIV bomb sight, a vast improvement on what had been available in 1939. Then, the early Mark VII bomb sight had been, like so much else about Bomber Command at that time, dismally elementary. The Mark IX, introduced soon afterwards, was a considerable improvement, but it was with the Mark XIV that bomb aiming would reach its apogee. First introduced in August 1942 with the Pathfinder Force, by 1943 it had been installed in all the RAF's heavy bombers. As one of the first uses of a mechanical computer, the Mark XIV could be programmed to take account of wind speed and direction, removing so much of the inevitable human error that had dogged early bombing accuracy. His bomb doors already open, Arthur Smith now looked through his bomb sight in the final moments of the bomb run.

> You see either the markers or the target coming up, gradually getting in line with a line on your graticule, and you just know that you've got to drop the bombs when the target or the markers hit the intersection on your bomb sight, that's when you press the bomb tit. There's no two ways about it, that's what you've got to do. We were told always to bomb the markers. Through your bomb sight you see a lot of closely lit lights, all in a little group, and you would go for the centre of that little group of lights, if they're of one colour or another.

Back in the cockpit, Leonard Miller and the rest of the crew would immediately feel the impact of the bombs having been released.

> When he pressed his tit to say 'Bombs gone', you feel the jolt of the bombs leaving the aircraft, because there was a release of weight. The aircraft would jump a bit; the sensation was like going over a speed bump these days. The next job the wireless operator did was put his head down in the hatch where the bombs were to make sure there's no hang-up and they'd all gone. A hang-up inside could be deadly. Then you could shut your bomb doors and get the hell out of it.

Like any other crew member, wireless operator Jim Rogers hoped desperately there wouldn't be any problems with the bombs being released. A hang-up meant more time over the target, more time for the aircraft to be at its most vulnerable. 'You're flying straight and level with the bomb aimer in command; you feel vulnerable because once those bombs doors are open, you can't do much about anything coming on. So we're thinking, Get rid of those bloody bombs quickly!'

Bomb aimers and crews alike dreaded the bombs not dropping. If they weren't over the target, or if the release mechanism failed, the aircraft would have to circle round and try again. If one bomb run was frightening enough, having to do it a second time was terrifying. Even if the release was working correctly, there were occasions when Alan Bryett wouldn't drop his bombs on the first run. 'Sometimes the wind would blow the aeroplane about, and by the time you got near the target you'd be blown off course. You wouldn't drop the bombs because you'd miss the target, so you'd have to go round again. It was a tedious business and rather frustrating to start with because you were making mistakes, but after two, three or four times you really got the hang of it and it wasn't terribly difficult.'

There was tremendous pressure on Bryett, and no doubt on every other bomb aimer, from the rest of the crew to get the hang of it pretty quickly.

> You would get a hell of a bollocking from the rest of your crew if you had to go round again because it was terribly dangerous. It would be treated in a very good-humoured way but when you got home you'd have to buy drinks for the rest of the week. It was fortunate on the whole because, with the exception of Peenemünde where we were flying very low and it was easy to bomb the exact target, you were bombing cities and towns where it was such a big area that even if you were half a mile off, you were still over the immediate dock area.

Anxious as they were to drop the bomb load as quickly as possible, it was all too easy for crews to fall for a favourite deception of the Germans: bombing false flares that they had laid down. The give-away clue was the difference in the colour of the flares, but sometimes the difference wasn't that pronounced, and if the crew were having a rough ride over the target it was a trick that could catch an anxiety-ridden bomb aimer out. Tom Wingham made this mistake in a raid over Nuremberg. It was his fourth operation. 'I saw a red flare going down and hurriedly turned my pilot on to it. It was only as I pressed to release the bombs that I realised I'd fallen into the stupid mistake of bombing a phoney German flare, which they sometimes used to put down.'

This was one of those occasions when such a mistake seems entirely understandable.

At that time, instructions were that you couldn't bomb on anything other than Pathfinder flares, and the PFF were late. For twenty minutes we were just circling. I was stuck up in the nose of a heavy bomber, circling around with at least another hundred aircraft all doing the same thing. A near-miss was if the aircraft didn't actually hit you! All the time for twenty minutes I was seeing black shadows passing. I was more scared of dying that night than any other time in my life.

To have to circle the target for such a long period was admittedly unusual. Nevertheless, Leonard Miller felt more fear on the bomb run than at any other point of the operation. 'Flying straight and level, you seem to be naked and you can't do much about it. You've got to hold it in that position and that's when you're most vulnerable to the night fighters and all the defences. The crew is a very close-knit family; you're like a set of brothers really. You're there together and you're facing the same fears and you know exactly what each other is thinking. We were very close as friends.'

Miller's fear was borne out on one terrible night for his crew.

We were on a bomb run to Berlin that particular night. A shell came through into the cockpit and hit the flight engineer in the head. We only assumed he might have been wounded, so we wrapped him in the all warm clothing that we had, our Irvin jackets and blankets, rolled him up and put the portable oxygen cylinder on him to help him breathe. It was a very stressful time; we didn't know if he was mortally wounded or just badly wounded. So the best thing was to get back home with him as quickly as possible. He died beside me on the floor. He had been a very close friend and we had plans to do things together after the war.

The Flak barrage wasn't the only concern. With the growing ambition of Bomber Command came growing risk. The increasing scale of the raids in the last three years of the war meant that the bombing made a greater impact than had ever been seriously imagined in 1939. Measures had of course been introduced to accommodate the magnitude of the operations: flying in a stream was now common practice; each aircraft bombed at a specified height issued in the briefing; the master of ceremonies flew above the bombers in a Mosquito to direct the mass of aircraft below. But as the stream converged over the target, the presence of hundreds of aircraft in a relatively small flying area still made the possibility of collision serious. Trouble with searchlights, the Flak barrage and night fighters all interfered with the blueprint for the perfect raid as the bombers were forced to take evasive action for their own safety. Rear air gunner Ricky Dyson's operational career ended in tragedy in 1945 when his Lancaster collided with another. The operation had started much like any other.

Take-off time was about eight o'clock in the evening. It was a cold February night. It wasn't a bad night as far as visibility was concerned. I made sure that my guns were in the upright position, which they had to be after two accidents earlier on where in the excitement the gunners had inadvertently fired their guns and caused havoc on the ground! We had a good take-off. I remember seeing the party on the flare path. As you went down the runway, one bit of fear came and I was very grateful when I heard the air speed being called out, which was just above stalling speed. Over Reading there was a rendezvous, where all these bombers came into one stream. As part of the stream, there was safety in numbers and you felt quite comfortable. When I was flying, France was occupied by friendly forces so it wasn't until you reached Germany that you were over enemy territory. You were then conscious of the Flak and the possibility of fighters, and so you were very much alert and you'd already tested your guns over the Channel to make sure all were firing OK, and that your gun sight was in good working order. Then it was just a matter of keeping a cool head and searching and keeping in touch with your mid-upper gunner.

After passing over the English Channel, Dyson's crew flew into bad weather.

We were into cloud, flying at about twelve thousand feet, when we found we'd got icing in the cloud. The icing got a bit worse and I could see we were going through an electrical storm. There were little pinpoints of light around the propellers which I could see and also off the tail, and the aircraft started to buck about in the cloud. The pilot was striving to keep the aircraft straight and level, and to climb out of the cloud if possible. We were relying on the navigator to keep on the course, which under those conditions wasn't easy. The storm got less and less, and we got safely through that cloud, which lasted about half an hour.

The weather then improved, and the stream of bombers progressed towards the target in fairly clear sky. They were heading into southern Germany, to Karlsruhe, an industrial city that had been targeted numerous times by Bomber Command. As it happened, the 250 Lancasters heading there on this particular night in February 1945 were taking part in the last major raid on Karlsruhe of the war.

We went into another bank of cloud before we reached the target. When we got over the target, we found that we were silhouetted against thin cloud below. Then the reverse happened; we had thin cloud above and a full moon shining through and we felt quite naked, silhouetted. The searchlights were on, and as far as I can tell we dropped our bombs on the target, and then as we turned to go home, it happened.

Dyson has never been able to establish beyond doubt what happened, but after studying the records for that night he's fairly sure that his Lancaster collided mid-air with another, which itself had probably been caught in searchlights and forced to take evasive action.

All I know is that we were leaving the target and then there was this terrific blackness. I thought it was cloud, but then there was a huge explosion. I felt myself going upwards and at the same time being forced downwards. My last conscious vision was seeing my four guns in the turret, leading me in slow motion, just floating away into the sky just before I lost consciousness. I thought to myself, This is it. This is what it's like to die. I came to in mid-air, conscious that I was still alive, but I didn't know what was happening. I looked up and saw the ground, looked down and saw the sky. The next second it was the sky and the thing was converse, and I realised I was somersaulting. There was a parachute behind me and I felt for it with my hand. It was still there, and there was a chromium-plated D-ring on the front on the harness. I pulled it and when I looked down at it, a piece of wire was on the end of it. I thought I'd broken it. Then all of a sudden I looked up and saw a little parachute waving in the wind above me. That was the pilot chute pulling out the big canopy, and once the wind got underneath it, it opened up and there was a huge tug under the crotch. I became upright and there were guy lines either side of me. I pulled on one and went to the left, pulled on the other and went to the right. I was gradually descending and I could see the target area all alight around me. I saw searchlights and Flak but thought this was no place for me, so pulled on the right line to get away from it. So I steered myself away for a few seconds. It was a nice sensation but I realised my feet were cold, and I looked down to see that I was barefooted; no shoes, boots or socks. Then all of a sudden to my right I saw a burning box. It was like a Catherine wheel with bits flying off it. It was going through cloud, and I looked transfixed at this, and then as it disappeared I realised this was probably the Lancaster with my crew aboard it. I was sure they'd be killed, and I was pondering this while still falling through the sky.

Dyson didn't have long to contemplate the fate of his crew mates before landing.

The ground started getting near. I was going through lighter cloud and saw trees and buildings. The next thing I knew, the ground came up to meet me. I landed in a ploughed field in February, on a cold night, and the ruts were frozen. How I didn't break anything, I don't know. I felt around my face and tasted blood and mud. I heard screams, barking and whistles so I thought the best thing was to lie low. I used my jackknife to cut some silk off the parachute to bind round my feet and then I hid the parachute. I thought of the fact that I was going to get frostbite so went looking for some shoes. I must have waded about for a few hours, falling in ditches, and I can still hear the dogs barking, people calling to one another, and I knew they were looking for anybody that had survived. I eventually came across a shed and looked for some clogs, and while I was there a German soldier came up and told me I was his prisoner.

Dyson's reaction to being caught was one of annoyance.

I thought I could have been more careful. I should have stayed in the spinney. I thought I'd done the wrong thing and was blaming myself. I was frightened and I was alone, not knowing whether I was going to be shot. I was taken to a farmhouse, where there were two ladies in the kitchen. Old ladies to me, but probably only about fifty. In my dishevelled state, I must have been a picture, covered in mud, and although I hadn't injured myself, I had cut myself so there was blood down my face. The shock made me want to vomit. They got me a receptacle, and I was slightly sick. They also gave me some sugar soaked in cinnamon which had the great effect of settling my stomach. After some time, two German soldiers tried to interrogate me. One could speak a little English, but not a lot, and I just answered my number, rank and name. Then they took me to an army barracks and put me in solitary confinement.

Ricky Dyson spent the next few months as a prisoner of war. He was fortunate as the war was nearly over. Even more fortunately, he was the sole survivor of his crew. The bodies of his other six crew mates were found in various villages in the hinterland of Karlsruhe. All had been badly burnt as the Lancaster fell, the pilot identifiable only by his clothing. Dyson's Lancaster had been one of four aircraft lost that night by his squadron, No. 189, from the nineteen they'd sent on the raid. The heavy cloud over the city meant that the operation had in any case been a failure.

Such failures due to poor weather conditions over the target had become increasingly rare by 1945. The contribution of the Pathfinder Force, combined with the improved bomb sights, allowed bomb aimers such as Arthur Smith to bomb with what was beginning to become a degree of precision. 'When we bombed, if you could see the target, or the markers, and you were confident that your graticule and your bomb sight crossed them at the right time, you were confident that your bombs were within distance to do a lot of damage to the target. You didn't really think that you'd made a pinpoint; you'd know from all your training that there is always a few yards' error, perhaps a few hundred yards' error.'

Bombing cities, even with a hundred yards' error, however, the bombs could do a lot of damage. The heavy bomber's arsenal included 4,000-pound high-explosive bombs, the 'cookies' or 'blockbusters'; 8,000-pound bombs had also been introduced in 1942; much larger bombs were used for specific operations. The heavy bombs were dropped along with incendiaries, which had been developed in the early years of the war to ensure that fires would spread as quickly as possible. As the high-explosive bombs and incendiaries had different terminal velocities, they had to be dropped separately. The high-explosive bombs would fly through the air horizontally for some distance, whereas the incendiary bombs would more or less drop vertically. So to achieve co-ordination of the two sets of bombs, the bomb aimer would release the high explosives first, and then count for so many seconds before pulling the pin to release the incendiaries.

One problem Bomber Command had to contend with was a psychological rather than a technological problem: the almost irresistible tendency that badly shaken bomber crews had to jettison their bomb load too quickly, what came to be called 'creep-back'. On a bad night, entire raids could find themselves having missed their objective by 4 or 5 miles, enough to make even area bombing ineffectual. Arthur Smith was only too conscious of what caused this impulse.

> You wanted to get rid of your bombs as soon as possible, but you had to conquer the instinct to drop them a little bit too soon. Some people wouldn't do that, they'd drop them a little bit short, so that they could get away quickly, and if several people did it when there were hundreds of aircraft, you would get fires that looked like markers short of the target, and the rest of the bombers coming over would start bombing on that glow, and so you wouldn't get a good hit on your target.

As Alan Bryett recalls, bomb aimers were continually warned about the dangers of creep-back in briefings. It was particularly important to avoid creep-back on the raid to the rocket research establishment at Peenemünde in August 1943. Away from the urban sprawls that Bomber Command was becoming used to, the creep-back effect might mean missing the target altogether.

> On the Peenemünde raid, we came from the north and we bombed down as far south of the Peenemünde area as we could. I remember being told, 'You're all going to begin by bombing as far south as you can, because we know your bombing will

creep back and you will creep back nearer and nearer towards the actual hangars where they are making the V2s. So even if you do creep back, don't panic, you're still going to bomb what we're looking for.' Whereas if we had started bombing on the experimental stations, we might have crept back off the aerodrome altogether.

Of course, no one admitted to being susceptible to creep-back, and it's unclear how much of a problem it really was. As Peter Baker observes, in the intensity of the target area it's unsurprising to find that some bombs weren't dropped at precisely the right moment, however advanced the bomb-aiming mechanism, however diligent the crew.

There was an inevitable tendency to avoid danger, and the sooner you could get in and out, the better. So there was a tendency to bomb the outskirts of the conflagration rather than go through it to the other side. As far as our crew was concerned, and I think it's fair to say the majority of the crews, we tried to do a conscientious job. We were given a pinpoint to bomb and we would try and bomb it. But it wasn't always easy, and the fact that you're being shot at is not particularly pleasant. It was as easy to release bombs twenty seconds later rather than creep back. We bombed simply as accurately as we could.

Occasionally, the confusion of the bomb run could result in another disaster for the bombers. Rear air gunner Hal Croxson had a lucky escape when the Lancaster flying above him dropped its bomb load. 'Over Milan on one occasion, the mid-upper gunner screamed into the intercom to say that there was a bomber directly over the top. He'd got his bomb doors open and then the next thing he's saying, "The cookie has just gone right between the front and the tail wing," and it had missed them by a few feet. One aircraft unloading a bomb load on to the top of another sometimes did happen.'

As the bombs descended, the crews would look down on the

burning city below. It was a sight that stunned rear air gunner Jim Chapman.

Over the target area I was terrified, but I wouldn't let it be seen, it could affect my crew. And I'd volunteered for that job so I had to stick with it, we were all volunteers. One could volunteer out of the job but there was no way I was going to do that. When I first saw what was below, it was really awesome. Everywhere is on fire and you think it's reaching you as well. It's too much to take in until you've been a time or two and got away with it.

Even from 20,000 feet above the city, flight engineer Dennis Wiltshire could begin to visualise the impact of the bombing, although as with most of the airmen, it was only later that he really considered the human element of the terrible drama unfolding below him.

At the height we were, it looked like one huge gigantic red blob, but because of the intense heat and flame you could see a lot of damage had been caused. What the damage was, obviously one couldn't tell from that height. You couldn't see people, just this red glow and an occasional outburst of flame. Then, whilst you're making a left turn away from the target, you're suddenly confronted by people behind you dropping even more bombs down. That's how I imagine Dante's Inferno. Just fire and flame in one concentrated spot. I was glad I was not down there, but I didn't consider human people down there until a long time after I came back.

'Dante's Inferno' is frequently cited as a metaphor for the cities under attack, and it's the image that comes to Jim Rogers' mind when he recalls looking down over the target area.

It was an awesome sight and almost indescribable at times because you had the fires on the ground, the searchlights, the Flak coming up, the fighter flares over the top, and in between that you're there and the fighters are there. The flares and streaks of light from the anti-aircraft guns were all vivid colours. You see fire on the ground, explosions on the ground, explosions in the air, aircraft going down on fire. You see an aircraft blow up, tracer bullets flying all over the sky, and the chandelier of fighter flares which lit the sky up as well. It was absolutely a picture of flame. You didn't have a lot of time to think about that, and you knew you had to go through that, because that was your course.

The scene below on Harold Nash's first raid on Germany is still fresh in his mind.

It was black and then suddenly in the distance you saw lights on the floor, the fires burning. As you drew near, they looked like sparkling diamonds on a black satin background. I had no thoughts for the people below at all. My thought was, Let's drop the bombs and get out. I didn't realise there were people below, it never entered my head. All I thought about was my skin. The instructions were coming from the bomb aimer, 'Left-left, right', and the pilot saying, 'Get a move on.' I remember on one occasion the bomb aimer saying, 'We've overshot, we'll have to go round again.' I can't repeat the captain's reply, but it was to the effect of 'Drop them, we're going!' and I thanked him.

For Ricky Dyson, there was an awareness of the people below, but he knew he was doing the job he'd volunteered for, a job that was an essential part of bringing the war to an end.

The thump of the bombs going down all over the target area; showers of sparks; it was the greatest pyrotechnic show I've ever seen in my life. Rivers of gold, rivers of red, black acrid smoke. It was like hell's inferno and then you pitied the people below, but you knew it was your job and you were upstairs and it was impersonal. It crossed your mind that people were losing their lives down there, but they were the enemy. It meant that those people wouldn't be able to go to their factory the next morning because either their home was bombed or the factory was bombed, or you'd disrupted German communications and they couldn't get the train or bus. That was part of your job.

Maurice Flower had some idea of what it was like to live through an air raid. He'd been in London during the Blitz. He was there only one night, but the experience had left a deep impression, having 'scared the hell out of me'. At 18,000 feet, he too was far enough removed from the victims of the bombing to think much of the scene being created below. Once again, it was a case of the insulating effects of altitude and distance which all bomber crews become familiar with. 'It's one good thing about being in an aeroplane at war, you never touch the enemy. You never see the whites of their eyes. When we shot a Messerschmitt Me-109 down, it was shooting an article down, it wasn't shooting a person down. You were hitting another aeroplane. You drop a four-thousand-pound cookie and kill a thousand people but you never see one of them.'

By 1943, the bombing of German cities was reaching a new concentration that was set to increase for the rest of the war. For the German population, there would be less and less respite from bombs missing their target and dropping harmlessly on deserted surrounding countryside. The great majority of British bombs now fell on populated areas, and the cities simply had to brace themselves for a long and terrible war. Horst Hirche lived through many of the air raids over Germany as a teenager, before becoming a Flak gunner in 1944.

> The attacks terrorised the civilian population. We had to witness how so many private houses, not barracks or military targets, were deliberately targeted. We saw how entire residential areas were bombed to the ground or were destroyed by fire or bombs. When we were called up, we felt it was our duty to do our utmost to protect the civilian population – women, children and older people. We were told it was our duty to shoot down as many enemy planes as possible. We had to fight against this bombing terror.

Based in Berlin, Hirche was one of more than a million Germans who were employed by 1945 to man the Flak defences and searchlights.

During the heavy raids, the Flak units shot continuously. The impression we got was that the attacking bomber squadrons just casually flew over the area of Berlin despite being fired on by the Flak. The attacking squadrons hardly took any notice of us. They continued flying, keeping to the course assigned to them by their superior commanders or by the Pathfinders. Then they simply dropped their bombs and tried to get home safe and sound. We were always ready for action and we had alarm bells in our quarters. So if attacks were reported on the north German coast, the advance warning went off. We took our helmets out of the closets. In winter we also had thick overcoats and then we went up to the anti-aircraft guns. Here every single person had to carry out a certain function and this was checked and reported to the anti-aircraft commander that we were ready to fire. He then had to report this farther up the line to the battery chief. At first, the defences were covered with tarpaulin but it was very heavy to remove, especially if it was wet, so later it was dispensed with as it wasted too much time. Then we received the information that the Allies were flying in the direction of Berlin. Then we received the first electronic and optical values from the main tower. We could calculate the coordinates, the altitude, their time frame. The guns were adjusted accordingly. When these groups had reached a certain distance from Berlin, or had entered the range of our grenades, we shot group fire. If it was a large-scale, heavy attack then we employed continuous fire.

The raid was as short and intense for the Flak gunners as it was for the bomber crews. Hirche waited in trepidation for the advancing armada.

As the bombers came closer, there was an almighty humming noise in the heavens, the sound of a thousand aircraft. It was a sound that for us was quite normal. When the alarm went off we knew it would always be followed by the same humming noise. When they entered our firing range, we shot at them. We were covered in gunpowder smoke and steam; sometimes it was very difficult to breathe. When we had to fire continuously the empty grenade cartridges lay all over the place. But everything lasted only a few minutes and it was very hectic. None of the comrades I fought with were afraid. We had been trained to do our duty – it had been drummed into us in the Hitler Youth – and that's what we were doing. At the age of sixteen, we were all far too young and completely unaware of the danger we were in.

Hirche and his fellow Flak gunners would watch the searchlights carefully to ensure that the Flak was not directed at the Luftwaffe's night fighter force.

The first catch was the most important one for the searchlight unit. It was very dark and it was the duty of the people who manned the searchlights to try and catch as many bombers as possible. They were awarded points, and referred to in terms of points, 'He was a 150 or a 200 points searchlight.' When a bomber was caught in the beam, others in the vicinity got involved. We sometimes understood that the pilot in the bomber was trying to use different manoeuvres to try and get out of the beam of the searchlight. It was important for the Flak gunners but also for the fighter bombers to know this. It was very important for the defending aeroplanes not to be caught.

As he worked, Hirche couldn't avoid being aware of the impact the bombs were making on Berlin. 'The whole place stank of sulphur and it was full of smoke and fire. These smells were very nasty and sometimes the smoke was so thick we could only see the other teams through a kind of a fog.'

Wolfgang Falck, known as the 'father of the night fighters', spent little of the war in German cities, but on one occasion he saw the devastation in Berlin for himself. 'I'll never forget the people sitting on a chair or a sofa they'd rescued in front of their burning houses. It made a huge impression on me.'

The raids had a high personal cost for Falck. Yet just as the Blitz had led to so many British airmen volunteering, the bombing raids over Germany only encouraged him to continue his own war work.

> My mother was dead and so was my brother. My father was bombed at home and he was buried in the basement, but they dug him out and saved him. You could get angry. Not hatred, but rage, and not against the crews. They are soldiers and they are carrying out orders. It is the leadership that is to blame. They have the responsibility, no matter what the state. The people in charge are responsible for the way war is conducted. In the Luftwaffe we fought for our country, we did not fight for Hitler. We tried to protect the German people, and the towns and the civilian population of Germany. The pilots saw the cities burning and knew that down there their parents or relatives lived. When they attacked their home towns they were very bitter.

While 1942 had been a year of enormous progress for Bomber Command, the full area bombing offensive really started only in 1943. The experimentation with new techniques and the introduction of new aircraft and technology were brought together in what Arthur Harris called his 'main offensive'. From March, for four months, the bomber crews continually pounded the cities of the Ruhr. It's likely that Harris saw the Ruhr offensive as a dress rehearsal for the bigger battle he was already planning: Berlin. Attacking Berlin would need the longer nights of winter, and for the crews to be experienced in all the advances the command was benefiting from. In the meantime, there was the Ruhr. The area had of course long been targeted by Bomber Command. Its twin attributes of being relatively close to Britain and being a sprawling conurbation of important industrial cities made it an obvious point of attack. Now there was the additional advantage of the Ruhr being within the range of *Oboe*, and so an extensive series of attacks could be mounted – the Battle of the Ruhr. Of the forty-three major raids between March and July 1943, two-thirds were concentrated on the Ruhr: Essen, Duisberg, Dusseldorf, Cologne, Dortmund, Wuppertal, Bochum, Krefeld and Mulheim were repeatedly hit. If the Ruhr was a dress rehearsal for Berlin, it was a pretty thorough performance.

Bomber crews dreaded operations to the Ruhr. The heavy defences of this dense urban sprawl had prompted the area to be given its own ironic nickname, 'Happy Valley', long before 1943. As befitted an area of exceptional industrial significance, the Germans provided these factory cities with the best defences they could muster. The experience of the next four months would do nothing to alter its reputation. At briefings, Alan Bryett remembers the particular reaction as the curtain went back over the map of Europe to reveal a Ruhr target. 'If it was the Ruhr you'd hear a moan going up. There was always a great deal of apprehension if you were going to the Ruhr. The Ruhr was very heavily defended and the losses would always be great.'

For Peter Baker, the prospect of a trip to the Ruhr was equally forbidding.

> The Ruhr was one of the worst targets. You were flying over enemy territory from the coast and there were searchlights and fighters and so you had a fairly hectic couple of hours' run in over this part of the country to the target. Once you got over the target it was even worse. The Flak was intense, the searchlights and fighter activity were intense. In fact, as you ran up to the target at times you wondered whether you'd ever get there, far less get back.

Many didn't. Going over the Ruhr, Baker found that it was virtually impossible to avoid the Flak. 'You would see the Flak bursting and you would know that you had to go into it. You would wonder whether you'd ever manage to come out. It was in fact surprising how many times you flew into the barrage and came out unscathed. Certainly there were times when we were hit but very often you'd fly straight through it.'

Few airmen who visited the Ruhr more than once got away completely unscathed, and during that spring especially crews returned time and again. On one raid that Jim Chapman and his crew went on, they brought their Lancaster back with plenty of evidence of how the Ruhr's defences had lived up to their reputation. 'There is a single target which I always remember, Leverkusen. We got badly shot up that night. Having got back the next morning, when we eventually reported to where our aircraft was situated, they wanted to know what we'd been doing to their aeroplane because ground crews always considered the aeroplanes were theirs. They only let you fly them, and we'd got twenty-two holes!'

So notorious was the Ruhr that it was awarded the dubious honour of its own bomber boy song. Hal Croxson was among the airmen who sang it on the nights they weren't on operations.

Every blooming evening at half past blooming eight,
You could hear us on the runway with the throttles through the
    gate.
Get up, you big black basket, we're twenty minutes late
And we've got to bomb the Ruhr in the moonlight.

Flying o'er the Ruhr shovelling manure.
You could hear us do our little bit,
You could hear the cuckoos clang as they go bang-bang
It's the James crew shovelling out tissue paper, marmalade and
    jam.

It wasn't just the Flak which was intense in the Ruhr. The searchlights were particularly strong as well. Like any other air-man, Tom Wingham knew that some crews would get caught; all he could hope was that it wouldn't be his.

As you got within sight of the Ruhr, you saw massive amounts of searchlights just waving idly in the sky. Often we used to see a blue light, which we were sure was a master searchlight radar. It used to fix on the aircraft, and then all the others congregated on the aircraft. Once you'd gone into one of those, there was only one thing to do on the Ruhr and that was turn round and get the hell out, and start again. We developed a practice in the Ruhr of watching all these searchlights and waiting until they'd got somebody else, and then we would nip past in between the gaps.

One night over Dortmund, Wingham wasn't so lucky. His crew was coned in the deadly beams.

We had just finished our bomb run when there was a hell of a bang and we were falling out of the sky. We were at seventeen thousand feet, we'd turned west to come home and we dropped ten thousand feet. At seven thousand we were coned by everything that was available and everything was getting chucked up at us. Fortunately our engines started to pick up, but being coned at seven thousand feet over the Ruhr, we weren't just getting heavy Flak, we were getting light Flak as well. I think light Flak, although it's not so dangerous, is the most frightening thing because they have incendiaries and coloured lights in amongst the bullets. So you see this flight of light coming towards you and then at the last moment it sort of falls away, but it's frightening looking at it. Anyway, we managed to get back home, and found that we'd had a near-miss. The aircraft looked like a pepper pot and one great chunk of Flak had come and cut three of the fire extinguishers. Engines don't particularly like foam instead of petrol, so they'd packed up and we'd flown home on one engine. We met the engineering officer the next morning, who'd learned everything had to be done by the book. We found him wandering around the aircraft, poking his finger into holes, and then we had the most extraordinary conversation I can ever remember. He turned to my pilot and asked what had happened. He said, 'Could an aircraft fly on one engine? No, I don't think so! You've had three fire extinguishers go off in your engines, now what's the rule for when you've had fire extinguishers set off? The book says you can't use it again. Now tell me, could you have flown home from the Ruhr on one engine? I don't think that would be possible. You've had three fire extinguishers set off, you only had one good engine, it couldn't have happened!' With that, he turned on his heel and walked away.

The difference in scale between what Bomber Command was able to achieve in the Battle of the Ruhr compared to its attainments just a year previously was staggering. Then, a thousand-bomber raid had called on every reserve the command could lay its hands on, including over forty crews who were still in training. On 2 May 1943, more than 800 aircraft could be sent to Dortmund, drawn just from front-line units. Raids of 500, 600 and 700 aircraft were now becoming regular features of the bombing campaign. The number of aircraft wasn't the only difference. Photographs of the damage inflicted on cities such as Dortmund show how much more penetrating the raids had become. Nearly two thousand buildings had been destroyed there in one night, demolishing large areas of the city centre. Industry was severely affected, the Hoesch steelworks forced to cease production. This was a decisive blow for the Nazi war effort, a raid achieving exactly what Bomber Command existed for. Throughout 1943, the command's resources had continued to grow at an impressive rate. Nearly six hundred aircraft had been available in March; by the end of May it was eight hundred. And increasingly, the aircraft were four-engine bombers dropping much heavier bomb loads. A record 1,000 tons of bombs were dropped in a raid in February; by the climax of the Battle of the Ruhr, that record had been doubled.

From this point on, the area bombing of cities dominates the perception of what Bomber Command was setting out to do, and it was certainly the cities which received the overwhelming share of the tonnage dropped. This perception, however, was not entirely representative of the command's activities, as a range of other targets continued to be prominent and important. Not least among these was the famous Dams Raid of May 1943. Back in March, Wing Commander Guy Gibson had established a new squadron, No. 617, to train for this most daring of operations. Gibson had been in the RAF since 1936, and a bomber pilot from the start of the war, winning a DFC in July 1940. He then joined Fighter Command before returning to Bomber Command, to lead No. 106 Squadron. He was already a celebrated bomber pilot before the establishment of No. 617 Squadron. The purpose of the new squadron was to train selected crews from 5 Group intensively over six weeks to bomb four dams in the Ruhr Valley. The crews would have to perfect flying at low level, not only to escape the Luftwaffe's night fighters but also to ensure that the bombs were released just above the water in the dams. This was not part of Harris's Battle of the Ruhr as such, but if the raids were successful, it was hoped that industrial production in the region could be brought to a standstill. On the night of 16 May, No. 617's nineteen Lancasters set off, loaded with Barnes Wallis's famous bouncing bombs.

It has been fashionable in recent years to point up the failings of the Dams Raid, no doubt partly as a backlash against the distorted idealism of the famous 1954 film. It is well known that the stirring patriotic tone and rousing music of *The Dam Busters* camouflage more than a few factual inaccuracies, but the raid was nonetheless far from being a failure. It's true that the Sorpe and Schwelme dams survived the raid. It's also true that it was a very costly raid. Eight of the Lancasters were lost that night, with fifty-three of the fifty-six crew members killed. Yet the Möhne and Eder dams were breached, and large parts of the surrounding area were flooded, with a significant impact on the Ruhr's production capacity. Bomber Command achieved the dubious record of more civilian deaths that night than for any other night of the war so far. Gibson was further fêted, receiving his VC, and the raid was a momentous success in the newspapers, a propaganda triumph and a boost for morale throughout the command and across the home front. Once again, the contrast with what had been possible a year before is striking. No. 617 Squadron emerged as a *corps d'élite* within Bomber Command and completed many more special operations during the war. Gibson became a Mosquito pilot, acting as master bomber, but was killed in 1944.

While No. 617 basked in the glory of the Dams Raid, the main force turned to Hamburg as their next major target. Like the cities of the Ruhr, Europe's largest port (and Germany's second-largest city) had been in the sights of Bomber Command many times already. But it had so far eluded the big hit that Harris was determined to mete out to it. It wasn't for want of trying; only bad weather had prevented Hamburg being the first target for the Thousand Bomber Raids; now, in Operation Gomorrah, there would be four raids in ten nights. The result was a devastating firestorm, final proof of just how destructive the Second World War bomber raid could be when every single contributing factor worked the way Harris had planned that it should. Hamburg wasn't an aberration; it was what happened when everything went to plan, and the resulting devastation remains among the most horrific of the entire war. Jim Chapman went to Hamburg on three of the raids of July and August 1943. 'The worst raid was Hamburg. We carried lots of incendiaries and the idea was to put down heavy blast bombs, like four-thousand or eight-thousand-pound bombs. We set fire to the place and that was uncanny, watching Hamburg burn. It wasn't nice watching anywhere burn, but this place was particularly bad.'

Many of the airmen on operations at that time, including Maurice Flower, saw the accumulative effect of so many raids in such a short space of time. 'We went to Hamburg three nights out of the four and the Americans went during the day. The last night that we went we could see the fire from 150 miles away, we could see Hamburg burning. It was just awful, a terrible sight. It was like flying into a holocaust. Hamburg was just awful, just one huge fire, and it took several minutes to fly over this fire.'

The firestorm hadn't been specifically planned; it was simply a consequence of a terrifying combination of factors that helped magnify the destructive potential of the kinds of payload Bomber Command could now unleash. The weather conditions were favourable, the German defences were weak, and the bombs were dropped on the target area accurately. The result was catastrophe. In the midst of a midsummer heatwave and high humidity levels, the temperature soared as the fire rapidly took hold. The continued bombing created many smaller fires which rapidly joined together. As the force of the flames increased, the oxygen from the air below was drawn upwards, creating a vacuum. Many of the estimated 40,000 who died were poisoned by carbon monoxide as they sheltered in deoxygenated cellars below street level. For those who struggled out on to the streets in search of air to breathe, death came in the form of violent 100 mph winds sucked in by the rising vacuum, creating hurricanes of scorching air, stripping flesh off bodies, and hurling victims back into the raging fires. A huge proportion of the firestorm's victims were simply vaporised, or reduced to small blackened heaps, in a ghastly premonition of the kinds of scene that would be visited upon Dresden, and even Hiroshima, later in the war. Hamburg ensured that the word 'firestorm' would be added to the list of horrors that set this war apart from anything the world had previously experienced.

The raid on Hamburg had also seen the introduction of another military innovation, one that briefly eradicated the power of the Luftwaffe fighters, another major reason for the Hamburg raids having the effect they did. *Window* was designed to fool enemy radar. Maurice Flower was among the first to use it.

> We used to drop *Window*, which was like strips of aluminium foil. We used to drop that by the ton and it appeared on the German radar screens like a huge bomber force, even though it

was just one aircraft. So they'd send their fighters up to intercept this bomber force which didn't exist because the *Window* just drifted to the ground and then suddenly disappeared, but they'd used up all their petrol and had to go back and refuel. While they were doing that, the real force was carrying out a raid elsewhere.

Although this device had been developed and ready for use as early as April 1942, the RAF had resisted using it for fear that the Germans would quickly develop their own version and use it in a fresh round of Blitz raids on Britain. Now that the Luftwaffe was mainly occupied in Russia, its use could be contemplated without running the same risk. It completed baffled the German radar, the operators literally seeing thousands of 'aircraft', and the operational chain of the night fighter force was paralysed. Luftwaffe pilot Peter Spoden was among those left unable to operate against the bombers effectively thanks to *Window*. 'It was a huge shock. Suddenly we were blind, all our radar equipment just twinkled. The ground control could no longer tell us anything. I remember when I landed that everybody was furious. It was something we hadn't expected.'

It's thought that *Window* saved hundreds of Bomber Command's aircraft and crews over Hamburg. The Luftwaffe quickly learned how to get around the tactic, but its short-term impact was marked. The war in the air had become a conflict of electronics, fought between the boffins of either side, as well as a war of bombs and cannon fire.

During the summer of 1943, Bomber Command also played a significant part in bringing about the Italian surrender. The raids on Milan and Turin felt very different to the crews from those on the German targets they were used to. Alan Bryett went to Italy soon after taking part in the Hamburg raids.

We raided Milan in northern Italy. It was a hell of a long way to fly from Bridlington, across Europe to northern Italy. The navigator had really got to do a first-class job to find Milan and there was great excitement that we were actually going to Italy, and we'd been told at the briefings that if we could bomb Milan really well, it would probably knock Italy out of the war, which really is exactly what happened. Within two or three weeks Italy had dropped out of the war and that was very exciting.

For Jim Rogers, the Italian raids were considerably less taxing than the other operations he'd been part of.

Turin was an easy trip, a lovely trip. We went across southern France on a lovely moonlit night. We never operated in moonlight normally, but there were no fighters around to worry about. We crossed the Alps and I could see lights in Switzerland. The only sign of any life was a small machine-gun post on the Italian side which opened up on the stream, but it was obliterated by all the bombers with their gunners opening up on this hut. If they'd stayed in the hut and done nothing they'd have been OK! When we got to Turin, we got hit by Flak, but only a small amount.

For once, the problem Rogers' crew had was nothing to do with the target itself. It was getting back to base which caused difficulties.

We'd had diversions coming back because ground mist had appeared in most of the counties and our base was fogged in. They gave us some coordinates in code, which I decoded, but after a while I thought we should be able to identify where we were, and we couldn't. The navigator had also lost track of where we were. We called up and they gave us a bearing to land at RAF Church Stanton, an air base in Devon. It wasn't a proper air base, and they had no lighting, so we had to go down as low as we could and find this aerodrome. We made the landing, but were out of petrol as we rolled to the end of the runway. They came out and refuelled us so we had enough fuel to get back in. I think we were airborne for eleven hours on that trip.

The Italian raids were an undoubted success for Bomber Command and were widely credited with helping to bring about the Italian surrender on 8 September. Alan Bryett's next target was to be another of Bomber Command's great triumphs. At Peenemünde on the Baltic coast, a German rocket research establishment was developing the deadly V2 rocket. For aircrews used to bombing the cities, the order to attack this secret research centre was somewhat baffling.

> There was great consternation at the briefing when they took the curtains off the map of Europe, as they always used to, and said, 'You're going to Peenemünde.' Everyone's reaction was, 'Peenemünde? Where's that? Never heard of it!' There was complete excitement; it was obviously something very special. We were told that the Germans were cooking up secret weapons, we had no idea what they were – a lot of us thought that they were gas shells or something of that sort but it was obviously a very important secret weapon.

The importance of the raid was reinforced to Bryett by his station commander.

> I remember being told by him, 'You must bomb Peenemünde tonight, you must absolutely wipe it off the face of the earth because if you don't you will have to go back tomorrow. And they'll be waiting for you tomorrow and more and more of you will get shot down.' And I remember thinking what a dreadful thing to say. He's virtually saying if we don't do it tonight we're going to be killed when we go tomorrow night, but that actually was very true.

Precision would be vitally important at Peenemünde, a strategic target that covered a relatively small area, and it would demand different bombing tactics to the ones crews were used to. 'The other thing which caused great consternation was that the pilots were told they could go in as low as eight thousand feet. As we normally bombed at twenty thousand feet, eight thousand was perilously low. We had no thought of what the danger was, it was a case of "Goodness me, we're going to do something which is really going to help the war and this may even shorten the war."'

In order to ensure accuracy, at Peenemünde the Pathfinder Force used a master bomber for the first time, flying separately from the main raid, and charged with coordinating the whole attack. The meticulously detailed planning of the raid paid off, as did a diversionary raid over Berlin. Peter Spoden was among the Luftwaffe pilots caught out.

The British tricked us. There were two hundred fighter planes over Berlin being held by six Mosquitoes. I was there. Then we saw that it was on fire in the north, but it wasn't Berlin. They had ordered us to stay in Berlin, and it had started to burn in Peenemünde. We flew there very fast. I shot one down. At that particular moment you don't think about the other crew. You have to shoot between the two engines and we had been trained to do that. He used to say, 'Shoot between the two engines, it will go on fire, and they will have a chance to bale out.' So I shot between the two engines to give them a chance to bale out.

For Spoden, the chance to claim his first bomber at Peenemünde couldn't have come soon enough.

I trained for twenty-seven months to be a fighter pilot and joined the night fighter squadrons. The first attack was on Hamburg, but I couldn't find anyone because of *Window.* Then Peenemünde came, which was a kind of relief. When I shot somebody down I was so excited, I landed and went to the crash site and spoke to one of the survivors. I felt free, as if I had achieved what I had been trained to do. How can I explain how I felt? Like an avenger for Essen.

The Luftwaffe used less gentlemanly techniques at Peenemünde than Spoden employed. This was the night when the deadly tactic of *schräge musik* (See Chapter 9) was used for the first time. It meant there would be a relatively high loss rate for Bomber Command, but nevertheless it had been a great conquest for the bombers. The crews had taken the grim warnings about the price for failure to heart, and had succeeded in inflicting large and accurate damage to the rocket-building facilities. They are credited with delaying the deployment of the V2 rockets by several months, maybe as much as a year. The rockets were finally used for the first time only in September 1944, and the 1,100 which reached Britain in the six months in which they were used killed 2,724 and seriously injured a further 6,000. Without the raid on Peenemünde, they would have killed and injured many thousands more.

There was another twist to the procedure of the bomb run which would put even greater pressure on the nerves of the bomber crews. By 1943, it was normal practice for the aircraft to be made to carry on flying straight and level even after the bombs were gone, instead of being able to swing out of the way and head home. This was to ensure that the aircraft were in the best position to photograph the detonation of the bombs as they hit the ground below, and provide the necessary confirmation that the attacks had worked. Over Peenemünde the photographs were more than an aid to the intelligence reports that were compiled after every raid. If they had shown that the crews had missed the target, they would be returning the next day. By then, the advantage of the surprise attack would be lost, and bombing at such low levels would mean the aircraft wouldn't be able to perform their standard evasion manoeuvres to avoid the Luftwaffe fighters. The crews knew this, and celebrated their success all the more. It was Adge Boal's job as wireless operator to make sure that the photo was taken on the raids he took part in. 'We used to carry a thing called a "photo flash" which exploded with the power of a five-hundred-pound bomb. It was at the back of the aeroplane in a chute. When the bomb aimer released the bombs, the photo flash went down and the wireless operator was supposed to make sure that the photo flash had actually left the aeroplane.'

The photo flash was supposed to show the exact area where the crews' bombs had struck. 'That was fine, of course, if it was clear. The intelligence people would analyse the photo to see if the bombs had dropped where they were intended. If you're bombing through cloud, the exercise was completely wasted.'

Boal was shocked when he saw the results of the photo flash after one raid.

We were sent to Rouen when the Germans were strengthening their Normandy defences. Rouen was a very important railway junction, and it had about five bridges going across the Seine. The object of the exercise was to remove those bridges and destroy the marshalling yards. We came back at the end of the raid, were debriefed by the intelligence people and they analysed the photographs. While we were being debriefed, the bomb aimer was called away from us. He came back looking pretty sick and he said, 'We've bombed the cathedral.' We'd come back with a perfect photograph of Rouen Cathedral, right in the middle of the photograph, which was the point where our bombs dropped. In the paper that night, it said, 'Rouen Cathedral badly damaged in an RAF raid'.

It was a terrible discovery, an inadvertent act of war that Boal still regrets.

The photo flash complete, the crew could now turn for home. For crews, the moment couldn't come too soon. The business of leaving the target area was particularly dangerous, though, as Bill Burke testifies. 'When you came out of the target area, of course, the fighters knew where you were and roughly where you were going so that was when the night fighter attacks tended to mount. People were tired on board the aeroplane and they were strained. But it was absolutely imperative to keep alert, to pick out these fighters.'

By 1943, *Window* was not the only device being employed by Bomber Command to disrupt the German defences. In a bid to make the target area safer for the crews, Bomber Command had started to develop a range of jamming devices. The first of these was *Corona*, which used German-speaking operatives based on the ground to imitate the German night fighters' controllers, broadcasting false instructions to the pilots. This concept was taken further by No. 101 Squadron with *Airborne Cigar (ABC)*. Now the crews took the German-speaking operative with them. Sometimes these were British servicemen who spoke particularly good German, but among the special operatives were German and Austrian defectors as well. Peter Spoden was among those who fell victim to the decoy manoeuvre. 'The British were very clever, and had German immigrants on board with them. They gave their orders in our German code words. We'd land only to find out that the order had not come from Germany, it had come from some other broadcasting station. It was only after the fact that you could judge. By then you saw the cities on fire and realised that all hell had broken out.'

Inevitably, the Germans learned to see through the deception. Their answer was to start using female operators instead. Surely there would be no way the RAF would put women on their aircraft and place them at such risk over the target area? At least, that's what Spoden and his colleagues believed.

The day before one of the raids, we received an order to only obey the codes given in women's voices. We were told these were real German operators and this is a binding order, 'Do not obey the codes in male voices.' We complied with that order, but on that particular night the British even succeeded in using female operators. We were absolutely baffled. We only received the order that women's voices would be used one hour before we took off. I think that the British must already have had women on board.

Now the Luftwaffe had to resort to other codes in order to avoid the British counter-measures.

We used different types of music to pinpoint the area where the British had massed. If they were positioned over Vienna, we played Strauss. For Berlin we played Brandenburg marches. For Cologne we used carnival marches. The radio operator had to listen in and obviously had to have some knowledge of music to know exactly where the British were. We used this tactic in order to combat the decoy manoeuvres of the British.

In No. 192 Squadron in 100 Group, Maurice Flower was also involved in special operations.

We were called 'Bomber Support'. We were in support of the main stream, jamming the German radar, interfering with the German fighter command broadcasts. One or two aircraft from my squadron used to fly into the target, with maybe five hundred Lancasters. We'd fly independently of the bomber stream into the target and then circle the target. That was quite hair-raising because you'd got five hundred aeroplanes channelling in over a target, and you are going in with them and then turning left, across the front of them, and then going up the opposite way and then turning left again across them, and flying round and round whilst the raid is in progress.

His crew also carried an eighth member, although Flower and the rest of the crew were largely oblivious to exactly what work they were engaged in.

As a squadron, we didn't normally carry bombs. In between the front spar and the rear spar, you had a rest bed at either side normally, but on our aircraft this was devoted to all the equipment the special operator carried, and you had to squeeze past them if you were going to the loo or whatever. He had all these little green cathode tubes and screens lined up in the rest position. He used to sit there hunched over them with a rubber face piece on, staring into these little green cathode tubes and twiddling knobs. I really didn't know what we were doing on any one trip, but apparently it was important. I'm sure that none of the rest of the crew knew what we were there for either, only the special operator actually knew.

The special operators didn't only take part in the raids over German cities. 'We did trips down the Bay of Biscay. We used to fly down from Cornwall and we'd do about an eight- or nine-hour trip, so tedious trips. The Germans were bringing ball bearings from Sweden down to Spain and Portugal and they used to fly up the Bay of Biscay and home on a beam. We used to pick up this beam and bend it out into the Atlantic so that these Condors, big four-engine things, used to fly out and run out of petrol halfway to America.'

Not all the decoys used by Maurice Flower were quite as technical. 'We used to pee in cider bottles and bung them out through the flare shoots. If you left the bung off, they used to whistle on the way down.'

A number of bomber crews apparently did something similar. The whistling sound of the falling projectile sounded like a falling bomb, and it was hoped that some of the less experienced search-light operators would be fooled accordingly and switch off their searchlights.

By the autumn of 1943, Arthur Harris was ready to launch his next major offensive, and his most ambitious, the Battle of Berlin. Some preparatory raids had not proved entirely successful and the squadrons involved had endured heavy losses. Berlin was a beast of a target for British-based bombers. The distance meant they were flying at the outer limits of their range. The city was deep inland, on the north German plains, depriving the navi-gators of any readily detectable natural features – even H2S would be beaten. Its layout too made bombing difficult. It was a large modern city, spread out over many square miles, with long wide streets separating many of its major centres, and as such hard to overwhelm or set on fire. The weather too would be no friend of the RAF; Berlin winters habitually covered it for months at a time in impenetrable cloud. And it would be defended to the death, by experienced anti-aircraft forces now recovering from being wrong-footed by the earlier use of *Window*. Nor could approaching bombers hope to fool these defences into thinking this was a feint, with another target being the real victim. By the time they got within 100 miles or so, their intended destination would be crystal clear. Yet still Harris maintained that Berlin should be the next big target, especially as he now had the promise of American help.

The USAAF Eighth Air Force had first begun operations in August 1942, and had joined Bomber Command for the first time over Hamburg. From the outset, they had operated with the same determination as the RAF, sharing the same commitment to the idea that bombing would play a major, if not decisive, role in defeating the Germans. But they prosecuted their bombing offensive in very different ways. Like the RAF they had four-engine heavy bombers, particularly the Boeing B-17 Flying Fortress, and later the B-24 Liberator. But unlike the RAF, they would fly only during the day, in open defiance of both RAF and Luftwaffe experience of doing this earlier in the war. They would also persevere until the end of the war with the idea that precision bombing remained the best (and most civilised) strategy for a modern air force, although the difference between the American and British bombing is more apparent from the rhetoric than the results. Not surprisingly, their early attempts at making these daylight strikes work proved highly costly. Even bristling with .50-calibre machine guns, and able to fly at over 30,000 feet, they were easy meat for Luftwaffe fighters, earning them the sympathetic bemusement of Bomber Command's airmen, including Ron Pitt. 'They were very heavily armoured, but they didn't carry very a big bomb load. We used to laugh and there was a song, "Flying ******* Fortresses, at forty thousand feet, and they'd only got one little bomb, pop!"'

The turning point for the USAAF came later in 1943 and was consolidated in 1944, with the introduction of escort fighters capable (with the introduction of long-range, disposable fuel tanks) of accompanying the bombers all the way to Berlin and back, and of overpowering the Focke-Wulf Fw-190s and Messerschmitt Me-109s that were sent up to intercept them. Most notable of these would be the legendary North American P-51 Mustang, taking over from the earlier Republic P-47 Thunderbolt and Lockheed P-38 Lightning. Flying together all the way to the target, the USAAF's aircraft could now make a real contribution to the Allied bombing campaign. For many airmen, including Harold Nash, the knowledge that Bomber Command had a committed and active ally was a boost to morale. 'We knew that they were coming in. On the night we were shot down, we were told there'd be four Flying Fortresses coming with us. We never saw them, of course, but you did feel that things were coming on our side, and you were encouraged by the fact that you'd got an ally in the air.'

Once early reservations about the potential of the Flying Fortress had been allayed, Ron Pitt also welcomed the help of the Americans. 'It was marvellous to have their support, to see their bomber fleets flying over, hundreds of them, in the daylight raids, and we just wished them good luck.'

Bomber Command's crews were all too aware of the additional dangers the USAAF faced on daylight raids. Hal Croxson certainly wasn't envious. 'I think they had a tougher time doing it by day than we had by night. I wouldn't want to have been doing that. Their aircraft were bristling with guns in the fuselage but wouldn't you want them! They used to have to fly in strict formation and that to my mind was ridiculous because it didn't give anybody a chance to get away from the fighters.'

The brash confidence instilled by flying in formation wasn't lost on the Luftwaffe's airmen either. As a fighter pilot, Peter Spoden regularly had to confront the American bomber raids.

The American flying tactic was completely different to that of the British. The British flew in a stream, by night. But the Americans flew in a kind of a box so that there were about twenty-five B-17s grouped together like a swarm of bees. In January 1944, we fighter bombers had to fight the American B-17s during the day. They shot from behind and it was like a shower. They had many more machine guns on board. Somebody was always firing non-stop. During a day raid that was particularly spooky as you could see the white plume, which I never saw by night.

With the attack now coming not only by night but by day as well, and in such large numbers, Spoden found himself barely able to make a dent in the Allied bombing operation. 'Our feeling was to fight to the very end. I was a trained bomber fighter; it was my duty. Our only aim was to shoot down as many four-engine planes as possible. But there were far too many, we were outnumbered. From the south, the Americans came from Italy in their thousands during the day, and they had escorts. We couldn't do anything.'

By day, Horst Hirche would watch the approaching armada of bombers with trepidation.

We had a fantastic view of the advancing aircraft. We could see the trail of condensation and their silver tails shimmering in the sunlight. We could recognise them and it was like watching a flying parade because they did not deviate for a second from their course. We might as well have given up on the war there and then. The American bomber streams were becoming more protected. There were so many Mustangs around the fighter bombers, they were like a swarm of bees. The German fighters had major difficulties penetrating these units. We knew from the aircraft recognition servers that these were very efficient aircraft. They were very successful and were increasingly used.

By the end of 1943, the signs that the beginning of the end of the war had arrived were slowly becoming evident. Wolfgang Falck was aware that the omens were not in Germany's favour, and that the Luftwaffe was effectively beaten. 'It was on a beautifully clear day; it must have been in late 1943 or early 1944. The US Air Force attacked in broad daylight with B-17s. I saw the bombs being dropped on the centre of Berlin, and there wasn't a single German fighter. Hundreds of Flying Fortresses. On that day I thought, Poor old Germany.'

The end was still some way off, however. During the coming months, the scale of the bombing raids would increase even further, and by substantial margins. More aircraft would be sent to each target, dropping more bombs. In 1943, Bomber Command had dropped 157,457 tons of bombs; the USAAF 44,192 tons. That was considerably more than in any previous year. In 1944 Bomber Command dropped 525,518 tons; the USAAF 387,501. Yet while Germany's chances of winning the war had evaporated, the Nazis fought on. As the bombing campaign reached its zenith, so too would losses among airmen.

9

Schräge Musik

'It is my firm belief that we are on the verge of a final showdown in the bombing war, and that the next few months will be vital.'

Sir Arthur Harris, in a letter to Sir Charles Portal, 12 August 1943

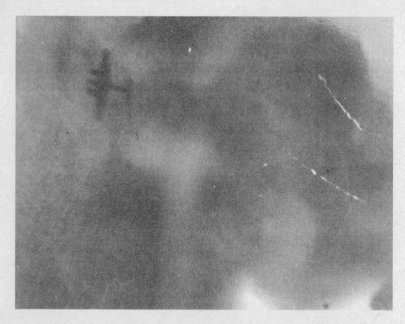

(top) A close encounter with a Junkers Ju-88 fighter captured by the photo flash of John Whiteley's Lancaster.
(bottom) Hal Croxson inspects a damaged mid-upper gun turret.

If Bomber Command's losses had been devastating in the first half of the war, they would be truly catastrophic in the second part. The aircraft were indeed more reliable, and the average crew's ability to deal with bad weather was by now much improved, but against that had to be set the fact that German defences had increased spectacularly, in quantity and in quality. By this point in the war, the Luftwaffe really knew what they were doing, and the RAF was paying a heavy price. By now too the average nightly raid was significantly larger than earlier in the war, which may have masked the level of casualties understood as a percentage of a raid, but the crews themselves were under no illusions. In absolute terms, many more of their number were being killed, or being forced to abandon their aircraft over occupied Europe. In the first three years of the war, Bomber Command's losses had already more or less doubled year on year. Between September 1941 and September 1942, the period in which Sir Arthur Harris had taken over the command, a total of 8,018 airmen, trainees, ground staff and WAAFs had been killed. Two years later, the equivalent figure was 18,948.

During the winter of 1943 and 1944, these losses would reach their peak. It now became an absolute rarity for a crew to get through a whole operation without having to encounter ferocious enemy action of some kind. It was taking a terrible toll of aircraft and lives, and the pressure it inflicted was remorseless and without respite. Just as traumatic was the nightly spectacle for the surviving crews of other RAF aircraft being torn to shreds all around them. What used to be a one-off shock was now a nightly routine, as aircraft after aircraft in the densely packed bomber stream fell victim to Flak or night fighters. When Peter Baker had been completing his first tour in 1941 and 1942, seeing other aircraft shot down over the target had been rare; by his second tour in 1943 and 1944, it was a sight that had become all too common. 'A lot of my friends were killed. Over a target you could see aeroplanes being shot down. Sometimes you'd see the crews baling out; at other times they didn't get out. They would either be shot down by Flak being fired from the ground or, more likely, they'd be shot down by fighters.'

Like many wide-eyed airmen straight out of training, rear air gunner Jack Eveleigh had eagerly counted the aircraft falling around him when he started flying on operations in the autumn of 1944.

> Our crew was pretty well disciplined, we didn't chatter too much on the intercom. We only spoke when there was something to say. The mid-upper gunner and I had to report any time we saw an aircraft hit or on fire or anything like that. All you'd see was the tracer coming suddenly from nowhere up into the sky, and the next thing either a ball of fire or an explosion. After we'd seen about seven aircraft go down, the skipper said, 'Right, stop, that's enough. We don't want to know any more.' We didn't report any more after that.

It was usually the job of wireless operators to keep a count of aircraft going down so that the crew could report back at debriefings to the intelligence officers compiling the records of each raid. Shut off in his little cabin, the wireless operator could see the carnage outside through one small window. Crews could no longer remain oblivious to the extent of the losses, and on Adge Boal's squadron, working out survival rates had become an obsession. 'A lot of the guys used to work out percentages. The operational tour was thirty raids, and according to the Bomber Command hierarchy, five per cent casualties were acceptable. If you're going to do thirty raids, and five per cent casualties were going to be inflicted each night, in reality, once you'd reached your twentieth operation, you were living on borrowed time.'

It soon became a Bomber Command truism that alongside teamwork simple blind luck remained the most important factor marking out those crews that survived from those that did not. There were better and worse aircraft, easier and harder targets, benign or unpredictable weather conditions, but none of these was in itself enough to dictate who lived and who died. Even to this day, there are veterans who still cannot believe the manner in which they evaded near-certain death, close escapes that defy the imagination. Rear air gunner Hal Croxson is one such.

> We got shot up once. Bullets went through the centre of the mid-upper gunner's turret and behind him, shattering his turret completely, but he wasn't hit. He had bullets going right across the back of his neck and they missed him! When we inspected the aeroplane the next morning, the ground crew showed us three bullets directly within a foot of my rear turret, several holes in the fuselage and across the port wing which went through the petrol tank. We couldn't believe we were so lucky that we got away with it.

The luxury afforded earlier bomber crews of the easy first trip, mine-laying or leaflet dropping to help them acclimatise to operational flying, had long vanished. When Adge Boal and Ron Pitt flew on their first operation together, it was on a major raid to Berlin. Forty-three aircraft were lost that night. Then they visited Schweinfurt, where thirty-three aircraft were lost, and Augsburg, where another twenty-one went down. In the time it took them to complete their first dozen operations, Bomber Command lost nearly five hundred aircraft. That meant the loss of five hundred crews; 3,500 airmen either dead, in a POW camp or, in just a few cases, on the run evading capture. Simply to have survived a dozen raids now marked this crew out as exceptionally lucky, and they knew it.

Boal and Pitt's first operation to Berlin had come towards

the end of what had been Bomber Command's most ambitious offensive yet. Having paved the way for a sustained offensive on the German capital with the Battle of the Ruhr and some preparatory raids to Berlin in the summer, the Battle of Berlin, as Harris dubbed it, began in deadly earnest on 18 November 1943. Nothing had shaken Harris's iron conviction that bombing not only worked but would prove decisive in winning the war on its own, and he was determined to show Churchill and Portal over the next few months that he wasn't bluffing. He had no illusions that these raids would cost up to five hundred aircraft, but compared to the many tens of thousands of soldiers who would certainly be killed in a land invasion, these were numbers he was prepared to tolerate. So, for the time being he was given free rein to pursue the plan, launching sixteen major raids on Berlin in the following four and a half months. Berlin wasn't the sole target that winter. Sixteen major raids were dispatched to other major cities, as well as a plethora of smaller raids, but Berlin was the primary target and crews were sent there whenever weather conditions allowed.

Berlin's special status as a target hardly needs explaining. It had been the subject of numerous raids since 1940, but now Harris wanted to take it out of the war completely. Robin Murray had been on some of the earliest operations to the Reich's capital, and for him it was the sheer length of the trip which made it such a formidable target.

On the long trip to Berlin, there was an awful lot of time when you could almost go to sleep, but you had to keep your eyes open all the time. You were bored stiff because there was nothing going on until you got near Berlin and then you could see everything going up. I had a friend who was shot down in the September 1941 Berlin raid. He landed in a cemetery in Berlin itself, and he hid there for about a week until on the Sunday they all came round to visit the graves and he was picked up!

Besides their obvious propaganda value, the raids on Berlin still hadn't achieved anything particularly significant by 1943, certainly nothing as dramatic as Harris now promised. The Nazi state was still operating unimpeded. In the summer of 1943, it was clear to bomb aimer Alan Bryett, as he was briefed on his first raid to Berlin, just how important a target the city had become from the point of view of the Allies' military strategy. 'At the time of the Berlin raid, I can remember being told at the briefing, if this Berlin raid is a success then the German people will collapse. They've had their capital city destroyed; it will be the end of the war.'

This gave Bryett and the rest of the crews a real sense of what they could contribute to the war. 'There was no alternative; we had no ways of winning the war at that stage other than by the RAF. In the bombing campaign I had the feeling that I was doing a particularly useful thing in ending the war. What amazed me is that the war went on so long after the devastating raids of 1943. I never thought that any nation would put up with bombing for so long and not surrender.'

So it was not going to be quite as easy as Harris had hoped. Long before the real Battle of Berlin began, Bryett had been shot down and was stowed away in a POW camp, and he was far from alone. Many crews came to dread Berlin even more than the Ruhr Valley. Not only could it match the Ruhr in terms of heavy defences, but it was so much farther away from the security of their squadron bases in Britain. The aircraft may have improved dramatically since Robin Murray had gone to Berlin in his Wellington, but the length of the sortie was still daunting. This meant even longer flying over enemy territory, twice as long as going to the Ruhr in fact – twice as long to fall victim to the German defences. It was the longest trip that most Bomber Command airmen would go on, and in the winter of 1943 many crews found themselves heading for the German capital on a regular basis. Wireless operator Jim Rogers is among those air-crew who counted Berlin as the worst target. 'Invariably we lost thirty or forty aircraft on Berlin, more at times. I went there twelve times, and actually reached the target on ten of those occasions. It was always a daunting trip.'

One of those trips to Berlin was more daunting than any of the others for Rogers.

We were flying Lancasters, and always kept our own aircraft, but on this trip ours was in for service. We were given 'C for Charlie', but as we were warming up the engines they started overheating. So we had to call the ground flight sergeant and he told us to shut down the engines. It looked like we would be scrubbed from the trip, but then the flight commander came along. His navigator had gone sick and he said to take his aircraft. We got out of our aircraft with all our equipment, transferred on to the coach to take us to this other dispersal and got into his aircraft. By the time we'd finished the changeover, we were somewhere in the region of twenty to twenty-five minutes late on take-off. The squadron leader said, 'It's a good aircraft, you'll catch up!' but we never did.

By the time they crossed the Dutch coast at Texel, Rogers reckons that his crew were between 60 and 80 miles behind the main force.

Over the North Sea, we could see the Flak coming up from Texel. It all stopped, and then when we got there, we had the benefit of the lot coming up again. We saw the flares go down on Berlin and the bombers dropping their bombs but we were still way behind. We arrived on the target just as the actual raid was finished. The Flak guns had stopped, and all of a sudden, as we made our run in, they all opened up. Our pilot announced, 'We're not messing about. We're going straight across the target. Nose down as fast as we can, get the bomb doors open and get the target in sight and away.'

The dangers of being a lone bomber over such a major target were soon apparent to the crew.

I had a little radar tube fitted called 'visual Monica' and could pick up aircraft up to a thousand yards away. If they were slow, they were bombers; if they were fast they were fighters. There was an aircraft coming up fast on the port side above us, so I alerted the rear gunner. As he locked on to him, I got another one coming up the tube on the starboard side below. So I had to alert the gunners to watch for the two aircraft. Our bomb doors were open, and we were willing the bomb aimer to hurry up and press the tit to get rid of the bombs. He did and we felt the jerk as we went up and then the pilot started corkscrewing. That's when I suddenly heard these thuds coming through the bomb bays, obviously cannon shells going through the aircraft. The rear turret was firing and then stopped.

As Rogers looked up into the astrodome above his wireless operator's seat, he could see a Junkers Ju-88, a twin-engine German fighter. It was one of the most versatile and long-serving aircraft of the Luftwaffe's fleet.

He'd overshot us and the mid-upper gunner depressed his guns and fired straight into him. We saw him on fire, going down. We identified the other one as a Focke-Wulf Fw-190. He came in on the other side and opened fire. Our starboard inner engine caught fire but we had to keep on, staying in the dive, hoping that the flames would go out, which they did with the force of the wind. There were huge holes in the wings. We managed to shake this other one off but we couldn't get any response from the rear turret so I got an oxygen bottle but I couldn't get into the turret. It was jammed. So we assumed Pedro, the rear gunner, had been hit. We were gradually losing height, because we'd feathered the engine so we were on three engines. As we got lower we suddenly heard Pedro on the intercom. He'd passed out through lack of oxygen but come round as we got lower.

Remarkably, the crew got back to their base. When it was examined, the aircraft was found to have 156 holes in it; the rear had disintegrated, the armour plating having been shredded. The guns had gone too, and the rear air gunner had made the return journey sitting in what was left of his turret with just a seat belt around him. Rogers recalls that the squadron leader who had lent the crew the aircraft was not best pleased.

Berlin certainly had some damage inflicted on it that winter. Thousands of houses were destroyed in some of the raids, reducing whole districts to rubble; casualties were regularly in the hundreds; there were incidents of firestorms; government and civic buildings, military headquarters and factories housing important war industries were all destroyed. Even though cloud cover rendered some raids redundant, there were plenty of other occasions when the bombing force was able to deliver its full potential. And yet by the spring it was clear that it had failed to deliver Harris's decisive blow. Berlin was still standing in parts, able to function. There was absolutely no sign of the German surrender that would have vindicated Harris's strategy. Bombing alone was not, after all, going to win the war. Lancaster pilot Leonard Miller has one explanation to offer as to why the German capital was to prove such a difficult target. 'Berlin was known as the "big city". The trouble with Berlin was that it was so spread out. There were a lot of parks and lakes in between various areas, so you could never concentrate on one area. Several sections of Berlin were difficult to hit because it was spread out over such a large area with wide open spaces.'

The Battle of Berlin also coincided with the epiphany of the German defence system. The Flak anti-aircraft guns were at their most effective. There was of course nothing new about Flak. It had been a menace back in 1941 when Robert Kee had been a second pilot on Hampdens.

The enemy was *Fliegerabwehrkanonen*, anti-aircraft fire, or Flak as it was known, and that was unpleasant. It was extremely good on the whole from the German point of view, very often quite accurate, nasty stuff. It seemed to us at the time that their technical facilities were slightly superior to ours. In the beginning one would hear distant bangs, and then you immediately saw a great explosion like a star exploding, some way away. They were occasionally closer, of course. I remember at least one occasion when the pilot had the front part of his sight taken away by a lump of Flak.

Those early crews, however, were not peppered with Flak in the way that the crews over Berlin would be. Roy Finch experienced some on his first operation, to Dunkirk, but none on his longer second trip to Mannheim. Robin Murray saw some over Hamburg, where the pieces of shrapnel hit the canvas of his Wellington with a ping, but crews could go for several operations in a row without being hit at all. Robert Kee is aware that his encounters with the German defences were rare compared to what later crews would face.

Casualties certainly occurred, but they were nothing like what they were to become later on as the bombing intensified. We only saw one German night fighter, and that was because we nearly collided with it. They got much, much better at night fighting, and their Flak was always accurate. I got several bits of Flak through the navigator's position, but it never hit me. Every now and again, a bit would come through, and of course you never knew when one of those lumps of metal was going to hit an absolutely disastrous part of the aeroplane.

During the Battle of Berlin, rear air gunner Jim Chapman went to the city eleven times. He saw a much greater intensity of Flak, his aircraft hit by it many times. 'It feels like your aircraft is being buffeted about, and you can even get the smell of cordite off Flak at that height.'

By now, there were two types of Flak, as pilot John Whiteley explains. 'One was predicted Flak and the other was barrage Flak. If you were flying towards a target area where they were predicting Flak, you dived away from predicted Flak and hoped for the best. With barrage Flak there's nothing very much you could do about it, you just had to keep going straight and level and hope for the best.'

Flying through the Flak barrage had become an intimidating experience for the crews on a regular basis. There was little they could do but to fly right through it, as Hal Croxson testifies.

> You just fly on, doing exactly what you'd been doing before you got to the barrage, and ignore it. You can't do anything about it except carry on weaving and rolling and just hoping you weren't hit. We had occasions when we didn't think we were going to get home and only just managed it. The Flak barrage was about a couple of thousand feet deep. It's a big box in the air that might be a couple of miles long. We flew through it because that's what we're there to do. When we did come out the other side, we'd say very casually, as Englishmen do, 'Flak was a bit hard tonight, wasn't it!' You may have been hit once or twice or a dozen times, but as long as it hadn't done anything which will interfere with the airworthiness of the aircraft, you were on your way.

Sometimes, however, the Flak could wreak very serious damage to the aircraft. Bomb aimer Arthur Smith's crew came under particularly heavy Flak on a couple of occasions.

> We got what they call predicted Flak. You could hear it banging outside. That is quite frightening, when you hear the Flak, you know it's much too close, and one or two bits came through. One bit went through the lapel of my battledress. Another time we were going to bomb Münster in daylight and were on the bombing run. There was a little bit of Flak but not a lot, when suddenly there was a great crash, and the aircraft lost about three thousand feet. Flak had hit our radar dome on the bottom of the fuselage, blown that off, made a lot of other holes, put the hydraulics out, and stopped one of the engines, amongst other things. We had to go back practically on our own in broad

daylight, too low, and of course scared that the German fighters might come up. The gun turrets wouldn't work without hydraulics, and I think two other Halifaxes escorted us back. We had to land at an emergency aerodrome on the coast, and the aircraft turned out to be a write-off, with about three hundred holes in it.

Smith had had a lucky escape with the piece of Flak that had gone through his battledress.

I've still got the piece of Flak. I should have been dead, because I usually knelt up in the nose when I was going to bomb, but I went to get a better view, and was looking down when the window shattered and the Flak came in. At the time, I knew a window had shattered, I didn't know what else had happened. Later, on our way back, I was getting up out of the nose, and as I passed the pilot he pointed down at my lapel. I looked down and it was completely torn up. He said I went white. The next day, we went out to the aircraft to see where this piece of Flak went. We got a line of flight, followed it and found a hole in the bomb aimer's curtain behind me, and a strut practically holed right through, and another strut damaged, and that was where it apparently ended. If I'd been in my normal position, it would have gone straight through my heart.

For Smith, that piece of Flak became a treasured possession.

When I found the piece of Flak, I said, 'That's my lucky piece of Flak, I'm keeping that for ever.' We were very fed up with our pilot because from another trip he had kept one large piece which he found inside the aircraft. One night in the pub someone said to him, 'I'll give you a pint of beer for that piece of Flak,' and he said, 'OK,' and handed it over. We didn't half tell him off for doing that. Most people had one or two superstitions. I had to carry that piece of Flak in my tunic and I had to wear that tunic on trips.

Flak was fired continually up at the crews over the target area, and it could hit any part of the aircraft, making its consequences unpredictable. One veteran recalls an operation to Hildesheim in March 1945. As the Lancasters circled the target, dropping their bomb loads, the Flak guns were firing. One shell went into the open bomb-bay doors of the Lancaster ahead. The Lancaster exploded shortly afterwards. As the Flak had got heavier, so the searchlights had become brighter; the threat of being 'coned' by them was an ever greater dread for the bomber crews. Even in the early years, Robert Kee had been impressed with the searchlights. 'They were very good, we all commented on that. We thought they were superior to ours, they seemed very accurate.'

By 1943, when Alan Bryett was flying as a bomb aimer, they were even better, especially over Berlin.

> The searchlights were really quite devastating, terrifying really, and once you were caught by one, the only way was to fly fast and get out of the range of the searchlights, but over Berlin there were so many searchlights that you were within range for several minutes. Had it been over one searchlight battery in the back woods somewhere, you could have got out of it and you'd be in the safety of the darkness again, but we weren't.

As a pilot, Leonard Miller found himself evading the searchlights on several occasions.

> Being coned was like being in a car with all the headlights shining through the windows at you. You couldn't see the instruments, and you felt you were right at the centre of everything. The night fighters were trying to home in on you, and all the Flak used to seem to come round to you. You had to recognise the limitations of what the searchlight could do. It seemed to follow you like a magnet, so you knew it was radar controlled, and we were dropping *Window* to blur up the radar control. If you could throw up enough of that and turn back into it quickly, you could probably lose the main searchlight.

John Whiteley found that the best method for getting out of a searchlight was to dive. 'They were lethal weapons. If you were coned in a searchlight, you felt the whole of Germany was looking at you. If you saw a searchlight coming towards you, you dived through it to put him off. Once they'd got one or two on you, you'd probably find you'd soon got about fifty on you and it was damned hard work to get rid of them. Once you were coned in searchlights, the Flak opened up.'

However skilful the pilots, it became impossible to evade being caught by the searchlights altogether. Earlier crews had had some success looking ahead and trying to weave their way round the searchlights, but by this point in the war they were simply too numerous for that. For Adge Boal, the worst encounter with searchlights was as his crew made their way to Berlin for one of the major raids of 1944.

> Going over, we drifted way to the south, flying between Osnabrück, which was well known for its radar control searchlights, and the Ruhr. The whole of that area was just one cauldron, completely lit with searchlights everywhere. Just above us was another Lancaster. He was coned not just by one searchlight, but probably a dozen, and the whole area around that particular aircraft was lit. Even if he weaved or dived, he was in the lit area. We saw a fighter cruise up behind him and open fire. That was the end of it; gone. The crew couldn't do anything about it; the gunners were completely blinded when they were illuminated. That was a sad sight to watch that one go down.

Like many airmen, Jim Rogers realised that the accuracy of the searchlights was a result of their radar control. 'The radar-controlled searchlights had a blue searchlight which would come up almost directly on to an aircraft and then the rest, maybe twenty or thirty searchlights, would concentrate on that one aircraft caught in the blue beam. It was a terrible sight.'

The operation of the German defences absorbed very considerable amounts of German manpower and resources. By 1945, more than a million people would be employed manning the Flak guns, searchlights and balloon barrages to defend the Reich. In the Luftwaffe itself, 35 per cent of its personnel were manning the Flak guns alone. So a significant proportion of the German armed forces were kept on home defence as a result of the Allied bombing campaign. More than that, a significant proportion of industrial production was directed at building, maintaining and loading the 20,625 anti-aircraft guns and the 6,800 searchlights. On average as many as 3,343 shells were fired for every Allied bomber shot down. As he operated the Flak guns, Luftwaffe veteran Horst Hirche admired his colleagues manning the searchlights. 'The people who manned the searchlight units were so well trained that they could do all the manoeuvres in their sleep. When the searchlight teams worked well together, it was very difficult for a pilot to extricate himself. When a bomber was caught in the searchlights, it was confirmation that the searchlight teams were doing their job. They also received praise from their superiors and points towards medals of excellence.'

The searchlights didn't discriminate between friend and foe. They lit up the night fighters as effectively as the bombers, allowing an eager air gunner to take aim. Whereas once the night fighters had largely avoided the targets themselves for their own protection, by the latter part of the war the Luftwaffe aces had become much more daring. But it took all the experience of the best fighter pilots to keep out of the searchlights, and the full force of the aircraft's strength to get out of the cone. In August 1943, Luftwaffe pilot Peter Spoden was yet to reach that level of experience.

It was one of those heavy raids where seven or eight hundred aeroplanes flew over. The Pathfinders dropped the incendiary devices – the Christmas trees – and in a very short time everything on the ground was in flames. The Flak guns started shooting. Then the fighters came in and were shooting. The aircraft were all shooting at one another. Green and red lights, it was terrifying. We were absolutely shattered, and then I was shot down. It all happened very quickly. All of a sudden there was this very bright light. A searchlight officer had caught me in his beam.

It was a terrifying experience for Spoden. Somehow he managed to get away, and he was soon back with the rest of the night fighters, waiting for the searchlights to illuminate their next victim. The night fighters had been reorganised in 1943, and they emerged as a much more powerful force, by now attracting not just the best pilots, but equipped with cutting-edge electronics. They had even learned how to get around *Window*, which had blinded them so successfully just a few months earlier. Now the fighters came out of their box system and emulated their 'Wild Boar' colleagues, the single-engine fighter pilots who roamed the skies as freelance fighters. In fact, the twin-engine 'Tame Boar' fighters turned out to be superior, using the very latest radar equipment, along with a new generation of radio and navigational devices to locate the bombers.

The role of the gunners, on lookout for the fighter attacks, was becoming ever more important. Jack Eveleigh was always scanning the skies, alert to any sign of a fighter. 'We were taught not to look at the fires, and not to look at the searchlights because it would destroy your night vision. But we still did. The Flak was just flash, flash, flash. There was no sound. If you could hear it, it was pretty damned close. The sound of the engines, and the fact that you were wearing your helmet and your earphones, drowned out the sound.'

The Luftwaffe, of course, knew the importance of the gunners. Night fighters would deliberately aim first for the rear turret, then the top turret. Once the gunners were taken out, the already limited defensive powers of a heavy bomber were virtually extinguished. Who would warn the pilots to corkscrew now? Who would fire back as the fighters came in for the final blow? This had long been established as their best line of attack. Once the turrets were out of action, there was precious little chance for the rest of the crew. As the rear turret was the easiest to hit, the resulting loss rate among rear gunners in particular was appalling. It became a particularly grim feature of operational life to see aircraft returning with rear turrets utterly shot to pieces. In particularly ferocious attacks it was frequently the case that the only way to remove the remains of the poor gunner was with a hose. Flight engineer Dennis Wiltshire was among the many airmen who felt for the rear air gunner's predicament. 'They always went for the rear gunner first because they had to approach from the rear and they knew he was our main way of getting them out of the way. We really respected the rear gunners, sat on that little canvas seat for six to eight hours. I don't know how they did it, I really don't.'

Ron Pitt and his crew were left without their rear gunner when they were discovered by a German fighter one night in 1944.

I remember very clearly the time our rear gunner got wounded, on a trip to some marshalling yards in Paris. A couple of the crew were down the back, taking him out of the turret because he was wounded. While that was happening, the fighter attacked from our port side and all I saw was the tracer flying above my turret. We couldn't corkscrew because three of them were down the back, so I told the skipper, 'You'd better dive into that cloud below, because someone just had a shot at us.' He dived into the cloud and we got away.

Thanks to the efforts of the crew, the rear gunner survived the operation, but he would never fly on operations again. So the rear turret was the most vulnerable place to be, and it was also the most uncomfortable. In those cold winter months over Berlin, the temperature regularly fell as low as minus 40 degrees flying at 20,000 feet. The electrically heated flying suits, gloves and boots helped, of course, but it was still a bitterly cold experience, and if the electrics failed, the gunners were left with frostbitten fingers and toes. As if conditions weren't bad enough, the gunners had had a 'clear vision panel' created inside the turret. This was designed to alleviate the problem of weary gunners shooting at flies, specks of dirt on the perspex or just about anything else in the mistaken belief that they had spied a fighter. In fact, all the already frozen gunner did was remove the perspex altogether, exposing himself to the sub-zero wind without any protection. But at least he could see. He was also the member of the crew farthest away from his parachute. In the event of having to abandon the aircraft, he would have to crawl ten feet back into the fuselage just to locate it, then put it on, before finally trying to extricate himself from the aircraft. Difficult enough in broad daylight, but at night, in a bomber by this point almost certainly spinning or diving, it would be almost impossible. No wonder he was called 'tail-end Charlie'. Many didn't make it. Ricky Dyson survived his aircraft's collision with another Lancaster only because by the time of his last operation, in February 1945, this problem had been addressed.

> The commanders had realised they were losing too many gunners for no good reason. They couldn't bail out because they were trapped in the turret. A new type of harness was manufactured on the same system as the pilot's harness, which was a seat parachute. The parachute itself was attached to the harness and was used as a seat cushion. So I went out with the parachute attached to the harness and that's what saved my life and the life of many other gunners.

Despite the conditions, some gunners were able to achieve considerable success. Leonard Miller remains in awe of his rear gunner. 'One of our gunners shot down five German aircraft, which was unusual because he was very accurate. Every time we came back from a trip, he used to take the guns out of his turret, put them in canvas bags, take them back to the billet and take them to pieces, oil them all up and service them before he'd take them out again.'

The teamwork between pilot and gunner was essential for a

gunner to get so many direct hits. 'My gunner and I were very close in the aircraft. We sensed if there were any enemies around. It was like inbuilt radar to us and we'd sit there in the dark, in the quiet, and I'd say, "I think there's somebody around," and he'd confirm it. Out the back would come the machine-gun fire from the fighter and he'd give me instructions to corkscrew.'

It wasn't just the gunners who were on the lookout for fighters. It was the responsibility of every man in the crew with access to a window to be vigilant whenever he had the opportunity. Flight engineer Maurice Flower had occasion to see the enemy in their midst one night.

We were flying along quite quietly, nothing wrong at all, and in the flight engineer's position there was an astrodome where you used to hang the sextant to do your star shots. I used to stand up in there and have a look around every now and again, just to check there was nothing loose or flapping around. On this occasion, just out of the corner of my eye I saw this movement at the trailing edge of the port wing. My first thought was that the flap was loose, and then I saw this wing appear and I realised it was a Junkers Ju-88 lining up to give us a squirt. I just shouted to the pilot, 'Corkscrew port!' and he corkscrewed immediately. As he went down, the rear gunner saw a Messerschmitt Me-109 coming in from the starboard side.

These two aircraft were clearly working together.

The Me-109 came in from behind on the starboard quarter and started to fire but we'd gone down to the left. He started to follow us down, but he had to turn on his back and Jim, the mid-upper gunner, just raked him from front to rear. The cockpit cover came off and the pilot came out. His parachute streamed and he hit our port wing and we actually brought his flying boot back, it was stuck in the wing. I don't suppose he survived it. He hit the wing and disappeared into the dark; his aircraft went down in flames.

It was in split-second moments such as this that the training and the teamwork of the crew were tested most. Every gunner knew to shout the 'Corkscrew!' command immediately; any pilot who wanted to survive obeyed immediately without questioning his gunner's order. The corkscrew itself was the one tactic the pilot could employ in a desperate attempt to lose a fighter, and pilots quickly learned too that for it to work they needed to hurl the aircraft round as hard as possible, even if it meant, as it often did, that rivets went flying. The rest of the crew hung on like mad as they were rolled about, G forces having a dramatic effect. The pilot who hesitated, though, or who operated the controls at all gingerly, did not survive long. Without any power assistance to the control column, it was also something that required brute strength. It was eloquent testimony to the quality of the construction of these aircraft that, even fully laden, they could survive the violence of these manoeuvres. It was a tactic Leonard Miller found himself performing in his Lancaster on several occasions. 'If there was somebody firing at you, you'd go into a corkscrew, which was a combination of climbing and sideslipping, going through the air like a corkscrew. It was very difficult for a fighter pilot to sight up on you during that manoeuvre, because where you were at any moment on that flight path was unpredictable.'

Everything depended on the reaction time; the pilot's, and before that the gunner's. Hal Croxson knew that he could rely on his pilot to respond to him instantaneously.

If you spotted a fighter, you immediately screamed at the skip-per, 'Corkscrew starboard!' or 'Corkscrew port!' We were actu-ally flying as a fish swims, which gives everybody a view, and the skipper is also rolling the aircraft slightly, both left and right, so that we get a chance to look underneath the aircraft. If I screamed 'Corkscrew starboard!' he would do an immediate dive to starboard and enter into what is called a 'corkscrew'. He would then pull over to port and then dive to port with a view to shaking off the fighter, during which time if you can get a shot at the fighter then, of course, you do.

When pilot John Whiteley encountered a night fighter on a sortie to Leipzig, he had only the corkscrew manoeuvre to fall back on, as the gun turrets had already become inoperable.

It was a very long operation, about five hours from take-off to Leipzig, and about three and a half hours over Germany. We'd got at least an hour and a half to go to the target when the two gunners reported that their turrets were not operating. The hydraulic operator to swing them round wasn't working, and there had obviously been a hydraulic failure. Now I had a decision to make. Do I go on another hour and a half, virtually with no guns, or turn back? I was always very conscious of 'lack of moral fibre', people who were scared and turned back, so I pressed on, and after about another half an hour the gunners reported this German night fighter was about to attack us. I went into the corkscrew and eventually lost him. We went on and bombed this target near Leipzig and came back to base. When we got back, the crew reported to the squadron commander that we'd flown a lot of the way with the gun turrets out of action, and the station commander heard about this and said, 'Good show for carrying on.' But the gunner leader took a rather different view. He got hold of me and said, 'You don't believe in gunners, then!'

Whiteley had been walking the fine line between pressing on heroically and the kind of foolhardiness that could endanger the lives of the men whose lives he, as captain, was responsible for. 'I always took the view that once I was airborne, I was determined to get through to the target, be that what it may. As long as the aeroplane would fly I was quite happy to fly it.'

Towards the end of 1944, Whiteley received his DFC, the citation including a reference to that raid to Leipzig. 'His keenness and gallantry in the face of the enemy', it recorded, 'have set a stirring example to all members of his squadron.'

Although the corkscrew was the manoeuvre most frequently performed by the bomber pilots, it wasn't the only one. During a raid on Berlin in August 1943, Luftwaffe pilot Peter Spoden witnessed an extraordinary sight as a Lancaster flew a loop.

There were seven hundred bombers and around a hundred fighters. It was complete pandemonium. Then I saw one Lancaster caught in the beam of the searchlights. The fighter pilots would be on top of him, he was easy prey. But he escaped the beam by flying up. It was an unusual manoeuvre, but the British were excellent pilots. They were able to do acrobatic manoeuvres that you could only do with model aeroplanes and escape that way.

During 1943, a particularly deadly form of fighter attack had been introduced which would render even the most effective lookouts and the corkscrew manoeuvre virtually obsolete. For some reason known as *schräge musik*, meaning jazz music, it was a technique that would cause the loss of hundreds of crews and was first used during the raid on Peenemünde. Fighters were fitted with upward-firing cannon. Positioning themselves underneath the bomber, they could fire upward, either at the petrol tanks or straight into the bomb bays. The bomber crew didn't stand a chance, and more often than not would not even have seen their attacker. It was a technique that Peter Spoden was able to use to great effect when he infiltrated the bomber stream during a bombing raid in December 1944.

When you got into the bomber stream, which wasn't very easy, you saw more aeroplanes. But you have to be very careful. You go in and look around and get out again right away so they won't see you. Then you attack and shoot the first one immediately. On that raid, in the two or three minutes after getting inside the bomber stream, I had shot down three fighters using *schräge musik* within ten minutes. I didn't miss any of them, but after those three hits I was absolutely exhausted. I was trembling, so I landed very quickly. There were fighters who got five or more, but I didn't have the nerve.

It was the development of *schräge musik* which more than anything else would account for the escalating bomber losses during the period of the Battle of Berlin. Many crews were unaware of the tactic until it was too late. It's unclear how quickly the Air Ministry knew about it. Some airmen remain convinced they withheld information for some time; if they did, presumably it was to protect the crews' morale. In any case, there was little the crews could do about it other than the customary banking rolls that they had been advised to carry out for years. By 1945, when Jack Eveleigh was on operations, crews were certainly being warned about *schräge musik*.

> The German fighters would be directed on to the stream. They were flying against the ground underneath, which was absolutely dark, and you would be silhouetted against the stars or moonlight. So you didn't see him. Most of the boys got caught that way, their aircraft just exploded in mid-air, and they knew nothing at all about it. We were told about it, and we saw it in action. One night coming back from Kleve, we saw about fourteen cases of aircraft exploding in mid-air. We were told that the best way to avoid it was to do a 'rolling search'.

The ruthless efficacy of the *schräge musik* attack did not discriminate between novice and veteran crews; both were equally vulnerable. This was even more shattering to the bomber crews, who had started to believe that skill and experience would enhance their chances of survival. Not even a seasoned pilot and crew could know if there was a night fighter beneath them, in their blind spot, particularly a fighter flown by a German pilot who was by now an expert in evading detection, masking his presence by blending his speed and movement with those of the bombers. Even the best-executed banking roll wouldn't be enough. Hal Croxson and his crew became victims of *schräge musik* in January 1944. It was their twenty-third operation, and their seventh consecutive visit to Berlin. Having completed the bomb run, they left the city and about fifteen minutes later they were attacked.

> There was just one thump. The entire aircraft shuddered and then carried on. The bomb aimer bellowed into the intercom, 'We've got fire in the bomb bay!' He had fire there and some hang-ups, bombs that hadn't been released because of the very low temperature. The gear that releases the bombs would freeze solid, so there would often be odd hang-ups. At the same time, the navigator said he'd been hit in the leg with a piece of Flak and the flight engineer said one engine had gone down. All this had happened in the few moments after the thump.

After the initial shock of the attack and the panic that ensued, the situation hadn't seemed quite so serious. 'The bomb aimer came back and said it was OK, he could deal with the fire through the inspection door, which he did, and at the same time he'd managed to release some of the hang-ups. The wireless operator said he was dealing with the navigator's wound and that he would be OK. The pilot reckoned even with three engines we'd be perfectly all right to fly on home.'

The crew's optimism would, however, be short lived. About twenty minutes later, another engine packed up. The aircraft was going to struggle to maintain enough height to be able to make it home. 'The skipper asked me to leave my turret for a while and just empty anything I could out of the fuselage and jettison it. So I did that, I got the flare shoot away and I got the Elsan out. I thought, I wonder whose head this will land on! I also got the arrest bed out and twelve thousand rounds of ammunition which would feed the rear turret, but leaving the channel with several hundred rounds should I need them.'

By now the aircraft's condition was really desperate. Flying on two engines, it had fallen to just 4,000 feet. Worse, Croxson knew they would soon be flying over the high ground of Bavaria. 'As I got back into the turret I took the parachute, which was carried in a little rack outside the turret with elastic ropes over it, and clipped it on to my harness. I got in the turret and at that point the skipper called out, "I've got to go. Good luck, chaps, and everybody out."'

The crew proceeded to bale out. The bomb aimer got out through the front; the mid-upper gunner came down from his turret and managed to get out of the side door.

I brought my turret round to full port, opened the slide doors at the back, took care to get hold of my oxygen feed, my electric suit, my intercom cord and get it all out of the way. Then I got my feet on the gun butts and kicked myself out into space. And that was it. I remember doing that, but I don't remember what happened next until I suddenly found myself hanging in the air in total silence. Away in the distance to my right, I saw the sky light up and I knew that was the aircraft. They hadn't made it. I was just swinging there with the breeze swishing through the cords of the parachute, an enormous black cloud above me. The next thing, I thumped to the ground – when you bale out at night, you don't know when you're going to hit the ground.

A month later, in February 1944, Jim Chapman and his crew also fell victim to *schräge musik*. On a raid to a ball-bearing factory at Schweinfurt, they suddenly found themselves under attack. Chapman would also bale out, but not without a fight.

There was nothing happening in our vicinity to suggest we were likely to be under attack, then suddenly I'm gazing out the back, operating my turret, and I hear a noise in the back end of the Lancaster. I can only describe it as like somebody rattling a dustbin lid. That was followed by a glow from underneath the rear end of the aircraft. It wasn't until then that I realised we were under attack. I realised this noise was his cannon fire. The mid-upper gunner had picked him up as well, and within seconds the captain was ordering, 'Bale out!' Those were the words I never wanted to hear.

Chapman managed to open the doors of his rear turret, ready to evacuate the burning aircraft.

I disentangled myself from belts of ammunition, got onto the bulkhead. I thought, The engines are still running. Are we so badly off? That was in spite of looking down the left-hand side of the aircraft and seeing there was nothing there. The enemy aircraft had targeted our fuel tanks, setting fire to the petrol tanks and the incendiaries in the bomb load. I got back in my turret, plugged the intercom in and called the captain. He thought there was a ghost in the aircraft! 'What are you doing there? I've told you to bale out!' I asked him, 'What's our position relative to the Swiss border?' He knew the way my mind was working; I'd heard these stories about living a life of luxury interned. However, he left me in no doubt I'd got to get out. Coming along the aircraft to the exit, towards me, was the navigator, in flames. The wireless operator was badly wounded in the neck. I watched them bale out.

Before he exited the aircraft himself, Chapman had one last job to perform as a rear air gunner.

I heard the mid-upper gunner's guns and he was speaking on the intercom to me, not that I could really decipher what he was saying. I just gathered what he was saying, and squeezed the triggers. The next thing, my .303 guns were belting, and the attacking aircraft was belching great black filthy clouds of smoke. As I squeezed the triggers, I felt the severe vibration of the machine guns. For a moment I felt real power, not that I wanted to dwell on it because I was thinking about getting out myself. I thought the parachute might not open, so to make sure it did, I put my hand through the D-ring and wrapped it round my finger. I anticipated losing consciousness and thought the slipstream would throw my hand away, and that would operate my parachute, and that's what happened. I slid on to the step looking down. We were hit at twenty thousand, by now we were down to about twelve thousand. I have no recollection of those first seconds of my actual parachute fall, I was unconscious. My parachute had hit my face.

Chapman hadn't realised it at the time, but that operation had been his thirtieth, the end of his tour of duty. Instead of earning a rest period, he was now yet another prisoner of war. The rest of the crew survived, apart from the flight engineer. In the panic of the attack, the eighteen-year-old mechanic had leaped from the aircraft – without his parachute.

To maximise their chances of taking the bombers out of the war, the Luftwaffe's fighters would act in pairs. The first aircraft would aim to be deliberately spotted by the bombers, knowing that the two gunners would open up with a burst of fire. The fighter could rely on its greater firing power to resist the attack. The gunners' readiness to defend their crew would prove to be their biggest mistake. In opening fire, the bomber had revealed its position, and the second fighter could position itself underneath and fire upward.

With experience, crews learned about the night fighter tactics. Training had taught each airman only his own job; the real education came during operations. It was on the tour of duty that the airmen discovered how effective the Luftwaffe were, and what their pilots were capable of. Most aircrew reckoned that the first raid was the most risky of all, but that if you could survive your first five operations you were beginning to learn enough to give yourself a much greater chance of survival.

Wireless operator Adge Boal was lucky enough to have a good pilot, who taught the rest of the crew about tactics. 'On one particular night, the rear gunner called up the pilot, "I've got a fighter in my sights, about six hundred yards away, what shall I do?" "Leave it alone and I'll edge the other way." Had we opened fire on him, his pal would have seen our tracer and attacked us. So that was one thing you learned, never open up on a fighter unless you're actually being attacked.'

Although the gunners could fire back, the fighters always had the greater firing power. The fighter also had the advantage of speed, particularly when the bomber was weighed down with a full bomb load. This was another thing the crews learned with experience: only open fire if you could get really close to the attacking aircraft.

In a bomber, you're a sitting duck. There's very little defence. We were attacked on the way back from Aachen by a Focke-Wulf Fw-190, at the time probably the most feared German fighter. He opened up on us but he didn't run really close because we'd got six .303 guns firing towards him. The maximum range of a .303 turret was six hundred yards. A German fighter not only had machine guns but it was fitted with 50mm cannon shells with a range of a thousand yards. So if the German pilots were switched on, all they had to do was to cruise up within a thousand yards and open fire, and there was absolutely no chance that the bombers could reach them.

As his crew gained experience, Boal became aware of another Luftwaffe tactic. 'Coming out of the target, they would lay down a line of flares and it looked like driving down Piccadilly. The whole sky was lit up, and the bombers used to fly between the flares. The fighter pilots were sitting up above and as soon as they saw you, away they'd go.'

It wasn't just over the German targets that the crews had to be careful. Flying over Paris on D-Day, Boal's crew came under a burst of Flak, swiftly followed by an attack by a fighter.

These bursts of Flak appeared all the way round us and the intercom went dead for a minute or two. We tried to call everyone in the crew and Ron [Pitt], the mid-upper gunner, said that the rear turret wasn't moving. The skipper said, 'Adge, boy, get down and have a look at him.' I went down and he was slumped over his guns. I had to try and get him out, but the snag was that all the hydraulics had been shot away and the turret was actually swaying. I had to tell the pilot not to corkscrew or weave, because once I'd undone his parachute harness and the straps holding him in, he could have fallen out of the aeroplane. It was while that was going on, and the pilot was flying straight, that we were attacked by a fighter. The only thing we could do then was to dive into the cloud and we got away with it. The rear gunner was very badly injured; apparently one shell had exploded just between his knees. I managed to get him out and he survived, but he never flew again.

In avoiding *schräge musik* and the dangers posed by the fighters acting in pairs, the real skill for the gunners often lay in not firing at all. Indeed, they were encouraged not to fire if at all possible. Instead, they served their crews more usefully with a prompt call to corkscrew. To this day, many Bomber Command gunners are proud to be able to claim that they never once fired their guns in anger, Hal Croxson among them. 'The whole of the twenty-three operations that we flew, I never once had to shoot my guns in anger. Occasionally we agreed it's a good idea to test your guns whilst you're out over sea, but never to fire them in anger. When we were shot down, we were hit by something that nobody ever knew existed.'

It's a claim that Ricky Dyson is also proud to be able to name.

I never fired my guns really in anger. I took evasive action twice and the only time I really fired my guns was over the sea, testing them. I'm very proud of the fact because I was obviously doing my job and avoiding other people. My job, and the whole job of the bomber crew, was to drop the bombs and get the aircraft back safely to bomb on another occasion. These bombers weren't cheap and aircrew lives weren't cheap.

When all else failed, the call to bale out always came from the pilot as captain. It must have been one of the greatest tests of their leadership skills, knowing that they were sending their crews parachuting down into enemy territory. In just a few seconds, the captain had to battle his compulsion to help the rest of the crew whilst also ensuring his own survival. The decision to order a bale-out fell to Leonard Miller on his thirty-second operation.

We were attacking Friedrichshafen, on the night of 27/28 April 1944. We were suddenly hit by a whole hailstorm of cannon fire and bullets from beneath and it set our petrol tanks on fire. I gave the order to bale out. The flight engineer clipped my chest chute on and the bomb aimer put his chute on but he couldn't get the hatch open at first. He said it was stuck, but I realised that because we were going down in a heavy dive, the suction was holding it. So I pulled the nose up and he got it free and out he went. The flight engineer sat on the edge of the hatch and was waiting to go. I could see him sitting there so I came up behind him, put my boot on his back and pushed him. Then I thought the other crew hadn't moved, so I went back to the cockpit to see what was happening, but they were slumped over in their positions. I assumed very quickly that they'd been hit by the cannon fire, because all the intercom and electrics had gone out, and they couldn't hear me on the intercom. At that point my earphone controls got whipped up round the control stick and I couldn't get away from it. So I ripped it off, breaking the cord, and made my way down to the hatch and pushed myself out.

Miller had had a very close escape. As he left the aircraft, the tanks exploded. As he descended from the burning wreckage, the moon shining above him, he felt for his parachute. 'It was about three or four feet above my head, having come off the clips on my chest harness, just hanging on the strap harness above my head. So I pulled the thing down to my chest by the straps and pulled the rip cord and it didn't open. So I had to rip open the chute by hand, and luckily enough it opened up.'

Miller landed on the ground just moments later. He estimates that his Lancaster had already fallen most of the way down from 20,000 feet, and that he probably fell just the last 1,500 feet.

Aircrew who baled out earned the right to join the exclusive Caterpillar Club. Established in the 1920s, its founder was Leslie Irvin, who had made the world's first free-fall parachute descent in 1919 before establishing a factory for the mass production of parachutes in 1926. Parachutes from the factories of Irvin, and GQ, another British parachute manufacturer, saved the lives of thousands of Bomber Command aircrew who baled out over northern Europe. The Caterpillar Club continues to this day for all those whose lives have been saved by parachute, members receiving a certificate and a distinctive golden caterpillar badge. By the time of VE Day, 20,538 badges had been awarded. Jim Chapman still wears his Caterpillar Club badge with pride. 'That little badge means more to me than any medal because in that confined space behind there is my rank, name and number. Campaign stars don't have your rank, name and number on.'

Baling out from a burning aircraft thousands of feet above ground made parachutes essential for survival, but there is one extraordinary tale of an escape without a parachute. Nicholas Alkemade was a rear air gunner with No. 115 Squadron. He joined the RAF in 1940, and served in Air Sea Rescue launches before transferring to Bomber Command. On the night of 24 March 1944 Alkemade and his crew were shot down in the Lancaster 'S for Sugar', shortly after dropping their bomb load over Berlin. It had been a difficult operation, twenty-one-year-old Alkemade's thirteenth. The aircraft had been hit by Flak over Frankfurt before they got to their target, but they reached Berlin to complete their bomb drop close to midnight. Then came the attack from a Junkers Ju-88. 'S for Sugar' sustained damage from cannon and heavy machine-gun fire, with the starboard wing and fuselage catching fire. Alkemade's rear gun turret received a direct hit from a cannon shell, blowing out all the perspex and setting part of the hydraulic gear system on fire. Alkemade returned fire at the Ju-88 and saw its port engine burst into fire, and the aircraft dive away.

The attack was over, but 'S for Sugar' had sustained terminal damage. With the aircraft on fire, and losing height rapidly, the crew had no choice but to bale out. For Nicholas Alkemade, however, there was a serious problem. Like all rear air gunners at that time, he wasn't wearing his parachute. It was still stashed away in the fuselage, apparently ready for an emergency. Alkemade went to fetch it, but the wall of flame between the turret and the rest of the aircraft made it impossible. As the smoke filled the gun turret and the flames reached his gas mask, he faced an unthinkable choice: burn to death, or throw himself clear and hope mercifully to pass out before being killed on hitting the ground. By now his clothes were already alight, and his face and hands seriously burnt; he decided that the prospect of dying by fire was simply too horrible. So, without a parachute, and with no possible chance of making it, he threw himself out into the night-time sky, some 18,000 feet above the ground. Blissfully, he did indeed pass out. And then, in one of the most extraordinary miracles of wartime survival, he came to, three hours later, on the ground. He was still alive! His fall had been broken by fir trees and deep snow cover, and his 120 mph terminal velocity had been safely cushioned by foliage and branches. Indeed, what injuries he had sustained mostly came from the on-board fires, and not the fall. He had first-, second- and third-degree burns on his face and hands, and burns on his legs. His 18,000-feet free fall, however, had resulted in a twisted right knee, a deep splinter wound in his thigh, a strained back, and slight concussion!

Unable to move far from his landing spot, Alkemade blew his whistle to get attention; all airmen wore whistles attached to their collars so that they could keep in contact with their fellow crew members in the event of ditching at sea. When he was found by local members of the equivalent of the Home Guard, he was smoking a cigarette; when they picked him up, he fainted. When he was subjected to the usual interrogation by Nazi intelligence officers, it was quickly assumed that he must be either mad, or a spy, as spies dropping into enemy territory often buried their parachutes. In Stalag Luft III, he was placed in solitary confinement. Yet he stuck by his claims. Eventually the harness of his parachute was examined, and the Germans realised that his story must be true.

Alkemade was one of just three members of a seven-man crew to survive from 'S for Sugar'. It had been a terrible night for Bomber Command, one of the worst of the war. Powerful winds from the north scattered bomber crews far away from their target, and the raid was quickly remembered as the 'Night of the Strong Winds', the last major RAF raid on Berlin of the war. Alkemade and his crew were in one of seventy-two aircraft lost on the raid, from a total force of 811 aircraft. The lost rate of 8.9 per cent was exceptionally high. Adge Boal was also flying on operations that night. His crew too was blown well off course, having received readings from the station commanders which woefully underestimated the true strength of the winds.

> The winds which were given to me, which I passed to the navigator, were completely wrong. I panicked. I thought I'd given him the wrong information but when we got back the navigator was crying, a grown bloke of twenty weeping. I asked him what the matter was. He replied, 'I should have had you guys killed tonight. We came out way south of the area we should have come out. I don't know what I've done wrong, but I let you all down.' Later, in the parachute room, we were taking our parachutes and Mae West life jackets off, and there were a couple of Canadian navigators chatting and saying they didn't know what had gone wrong, they couldn't understand it. My navigator heard this, so he went and chatted to them and of course they realised they'd all had problems and cheered up.

Boal and his crew had been lucky. Somehow they had survived an operation that had left the aircraft and crews even more vulnerable than normal. 'The winds given were completely wrong, so instead of being a column, the whole bomber force was a gaggle of aeroplanes cruising along, about twenty miles wide and seventy miles long, spread out right from the north of Osnabrück to the south of the Ruhr. A lot of them came through the Ruhr. It just shows if the weather was wrong, the whole thing was badly affected.'

The Battle of Berlin was now over. It had achieved few of its desired results. To make matters worse, just days after the 'Night of the Strong Winds', on 30 March 1944, Bomber Command faced another disastrous night. A raid on Nuremberg went seriously wrong, resulting in the loss of 95 bombers, 11.9 per cent of the force sent to the city. Bomber Command lost more aircrew on that night alone than Fighter Command had lost during the entire Battle of Britain. A combination of heavy cloud cover over the target and strong winds, again badly forecast, meant that many of the bombers never even got to the target. Meanwhile bright moonlight and cloud below had combined to silhouette the bombers perfectly for the night fighters prowling to intercept them. Ron Pitt and Adge Boal flew together at Nuremberg. Pitt remembers that the Luftwaffe were waiting.

They knew we were going to a distant target and the German fighters were just cruising around waiting near the river. They knew we were going there despite a couple of dummy raids by Mosquitoes. It seemed a long trip to me, I think about seven hours. Our bomb wasn't very well directed either, so a bit of a waste of time on our part. But we were so fortunate, because the weather closed in just before we got back and out of the fifteen or so aircraft that left Waterbeach on that trip, only three of us got down before the weather closed in. We were the third crew in, the others landed at various aerodromes around the country.

For Boal, that raid on Nuremberg is one he'll never forget. 'The odd thing about it was that it was a brilliant, moonlit night. Normally, Bomber Command hadn't operated during the moon period and I can remember walking to the briefing room, looking at the sky and thinking there's something wrong here. The bomb load indicated that it was going to be a major target and there was a full load of fuel so before we got into the briefing room we knew it was a deep-penetration raid.'

He also recalls the waiting night fighter force.

As we got to the south of the Ruhr, the whole sky lit up, the whole airway covered in tracer and aircraft started going down. They were going down so fast you couldn't believe what you were seeing. When we got to the target that was complete chaos, the whole of the area illuminated with searchlights and Flak all over the place. I watched several of the bombers go down. Having bombed the target, or what we thought was the target, which in our case was about forty miles beyond Nuremberg, we turned round and came home. On the way back we began to get a bit worried because it had been a long trip, we'd been weaving all the way after the Ruhr, and used a lot of petrol up. Had we got enough fuel to get back? We got back all right. Over the Wash we called up control and they said to land wherever possible as there was a snowstorm. Bomber Command couldn't operate effectively for about three weeks after that.

Various theories have been put forward as to why things went so drastically wrong that night. Even Arthur Harris began to doubt the bombing campaign after two such appalling nights in the space of a week. The heavy losses suffered over the winter had also prevented the bomber force from growing as quickly as he'd anticipated. Hundreds of new aircraft were rolling out of the factories, but they were doing no more than simply replacing those lost over the Reich. Harris's crisis-ridden bombing campaign would now be saved only as it changed direction in the run-up to D-Day.

In the aftermath of operations such as the 'Night of the Strong Winds' and the Nuremberg raid, it's no wonder that the nervous trepidation of the first operation evolved into a paralytic fear for many of those in the more experienced crews. All airmen knew that luck played a large part in their survival, but the more operations they survived, the more they began to realise it was simply a question of when, not if, their luck would run out. Navigator Bill Burke thought that moment had arrived on a raid to Bremen.

I wasn't scared, I was terrified. We were on the first wave to Bremen and we got a fighter on the tail. He opened up with his cannon machine guns and did quite a lot of damage, cutting the oil pipelines to the rear turret, so the turret was inoperable. The rear gunner was shrieking this out and I really thought that I was about to die. It seemed to me to be inevitable that the fighter would just pull closer, press the tit and a hail of cannon fire would sweep down the fuselage, eliminating us all and setting fire to the aircraft. Then at that very moment we went into cloud. The sense of relief and release from paralytic fear was incredible. You were going to live another day.

It was a lucky escape, but such lucky escapes could play even more on the nerves. Burke had a friend in another crew who had an even more terrifying ordeal that night in Bremen.

They were attacked by a night fighter which did terrible damage to them. The captain of the aircraft said, 'Abandon aircraft.' The mid-upper gunner unplugged his intercom, and let himself down into the bottom of the aircraft to find that the bottom of the aircraft was largely missing. As he went through, his parachute harness got caught on projecting pipes and he was left swinging at twenty thousand feet. He managed to get back and by this time he was in a total state of shock. He climbed back into his turret, plugged in his intercom to find that the captain had cancelled the order to 'abandon aircraft'. He never flew again after that shock to his system.

The more operations he completed, the more Harold Nash noticed the increasing fear. 'I used to tremble. I hadn't realised we were losing so many airmen. When I got to No. 10 Squadron, it was a good squadron. They had had no losses for two months and I thought, This is the place. On our first few operations we all got back, then we were changed to the third wave, and we began to lose crews.'

It was only the airmen's youthful naivety which allowed them to go on at all. Nash was himself shot down on his thirteenth operation, on 27 September 1943.

It was a Focke-Wulf Fw-190 who came up through his own Flak and got us from beneath. Behind us was a Junkers Ju-88 acting as a decoy. The aircraft began to burn, and the calm voice of the pilot announced, 'Prepare to abandon.' The intercom cut out; obviously the small fire was eating through the electric wires. I gave him his parachute. The chap next to me was badly wounded. We couldn't open the trapdoor and I can remember thinking, I'm going to die. With that thought, I experienced an inner peace which is indescribable. It was probably one of my calmest moments in the air. Someone managed to open the trapdoor and I helped the wounded man out. I went second. The bomb aimer's parachute was all over the bomb bay, I don't know whether he panicked. As I fell, I had no sensation, but I must have been turning head over heels because at regular intervals I saw the fire of the aircraft. I counted to ten and pulled the rip cord. I thought it had broken, but suddenly the parachute opened. It was such a shock. I floated and I thought I was looking at the clouds below, but it was trees. I had pulled the cord almost too late and landed in a corner of a field. I hid my parachute under a bush and was there in Hitler's Germany with one boot on and my summer flying suit. No one around, deadly stillness, a barking dog in the distance.

Nash was one of just two members of his crew who survived that night. Two other aircraft from the same squadron had also been shot down, but only one airman from the other two crews survived.

The increasing fear was never articulated, but it did show itself in other ways. Airmen could see it in colleagues' faces, hear it in their speech, or watch it in their movements. Jim Rogers remembers his mid-upper gunner obsessively feeling down for his parachute throughout their operations together. On one occasion, he picked it up by the rip cord and it fell open in the middle of the aircraft. He also remembers the airmen lighting up cigarettes in the debriefing room after they'd landed, still shaking, their hands barely able to hold the cigarette steady. Yet fear remained a taboo subject. For many, the greatest fear of all was anyone finding out that you were afraid. Adge Boal recalls the sense of relief when his bomb aimer inadvertently revealed his fear.

> We were waiting to get in the aircraft one night, when this New Zealander suddenly said, 'Oh, come on, let's get in. If they don't get us tonight, they'll get us some other night.' I listened and thought, Brilliant, he's scared stiff too! On another raid, things weren't going particularly well. As I handed my navigator the wind forecast, he was praying. Excellent, Eric's scared stiff as well! That cheered me up no end. As you discover other people are afraid, you still don't talk about it but you feel a lot better because you know there's nothing wrong with you after all, you're not unique.

The cold, awful reality of being in a bomber crew had hit Hal Croxson one morning as he arrived to prepare for that night's raid.

> At first, we were excited to get into it, but after we'd done a few operations we began to feel this is a bit serious, we're not going up there to have a giggle. Something that hit me was when I went out on a morning inspection. The ground crew were swilling out the rear turret with a hand pump and a hose. The water that was running away was pink. I looked at the guy

doing the job and he looked at me, but neither of us spoke. I just carried on with what I was doing, but it gets to you a little bit.

The way the fear could manifest itself in aircrew wasn't always predictable, and it certainly wasn't controllable. On one particularly difficult trip, Maurice Flower saw how fear could show itself.

We were coned one night over Dusseldorf by about fifty search-lights. Another navigator timed us and said we were in this cone for twelve and a half minutes. The normal survival rate for being trapped in a cone before you were shot out was three minutes. We got out of the cone eventually, but the aircraft was just a mess. Everything that was loose was stuck to the roof or under the spars. We had done every manoeuvre you can think of to get out of it. The pilot climbed and dived and rolled for twelve and a half minutes, which when you've got thirty ton of aeroplane is hard going. He was just exhausted, and suddenly said, 'I've had enough of this.' He jettisoned the top hatch and decided he was going to parachute out. I grabbed his legs and the bomb aimer came out and helped, and we threw him down the stairs.

As flight engineer, it fell to Flower to take over the controls of the aircraft. He flew it halfway back over the North Sea, by which time the pilot had recovered from the ordeal enough to be able to take control back and land. The pilot was lucky to have recovered. He was even luckier that his crew stood by him, keeping the incident to themselves. 'We didn't mention it when we got back. If we had done, he'd have been grounded. We were fairly well through the tour by then and well knit, and he just cracked, he'd had enough. You couldn't blame him. When we got back, we just debriefed and went to bed and that was it. The next time he was fine, he just carried on for the rest of the tour, no trouble at all.'

It was far from an isolated incident. Having spent most of the war as ground staff, and for two years based with the training units in Canada, Dennis Wiltshire had returned to Britain in 1944 and applied to be a Flight Engineer Aircrew on Lancasters. He was accepted, and soon found himself on operations. After years working on the ground, it was a relief for Wiltshire finally to be airborne, the whole aircraft shuddering and rattling, the engines roaring as they prepared for take-off. The first two operations went well, but on the third, a raid on Cologne, Wiltshire felt an overwhelming sickness as the Lancaster neared the target. Longing to be back at home, he found it difficult even to repeat the Lord's Prayer to himself. As the bomb aimer hailed, 'Bombs gone!' a piece of Flak flew into the aircraft, hitting the bomb aimer. His flying suit soon caught fire. Wiltshire's pilot asked him to go and see how the bomb aimer was.

> I reported back, 'I'm sorry, Skip, it's not good, he's finished.'
> With that, it was the pilot's turn to negotiate the return home.
> There was a terrific gale blowing through the front of the kite
> which made it difficult to stand up and the pilot was in the
> throes of making a left-hand turn with seventy or eighty other
> aircraft. I got back into my seat and then I felt absolutely
> terrible. The skipper asked me, 'Are you all right?' I didn't say
> anything, I just put both thumbs up. Then quite suddenly, this
> is where the story comes to an end. I don't know what happened.
> I've been told that I took my harness off, got out of my seat,
> and walked aft. Apparently, I fell over the main spar span and
> the navigator came to help me. He spoke to me, but I didn't
> answer him. I couldn't talk to him. I have no further recollection
> of that flight.

Exactly what had caused Wiltshire's total blackout remains a mystery to him. Perhaps it was the cumulative stress, perhaps the fate of the bomb aimer. Yet he had felt perfectly fit on take-off, and had been there to help the bomb aimer. Something had triggered his mental collapse, however. Wiltshire understands that the navigator then propped him up on the deck by the main spar so that he could get back to his duties. By the time they arrived back at their unit, the crew had radioed ahead for an ambulance, which took Wiltshire and the bomb aimer off to the station's sick quarters. 'I was there only a few days before they sent me into an RAF mental hospital at Matlock in Derbyshire. It was not very nice what happened there. I saw some quite unpleasant things. The hospital was specifically for people who had suffered any mental stress. I was at Matlock for some time.'

One day, a nurse dropped a dish on the floor in Wiltshire's ward, and he started screaming, 'There's another poor sod going down, look at the flares! Look at the flares!' His trance was finally broken.

I do remember coming to after that. There was a nurse sat by my bed. I can remember this beautiful white bedding and this nurse in her uniform shouting, 'Doctor, he's come around!' I passed out again but it was not for long. I had all kinds of treatment after that, very unpleasant treatment. I was wheeled down to the basement where they decided to give me shock treatment. I had been completely stripped with just a white gown on and I went into this small annexe. There was a bed with just a rubber-covered mattress and a pillow. An orderly came in with the doctor and they put some form of gel on both my temples. Then the doctor gave me an injection in my left arm. I went out like a light but I had seen other people have this treatment and it's pretty horrific. I was quite poorly for a couple of days, I did a lot of vomiting, and it didn't do what I think they were trying to do. They were trying to make me remember what I had forgotten. In the end they realised they could do nothing at that time and I was sent home.

Wiltshire was only sent home, however, once the RAF had established that he was suffering from a genuine medical problem.

I had no uniform other than what I had worn there. They gave me a new suit of hospital blue, a new pair of shoes and a new forage cap. I had to go before a tribunal. There were wing commanders, air commodores, all asking questions, and in the end I was told by a flight lieutenant to go back to my room. He came along later and informed me that I had been relieved of my duties in the RAF Volunteer Reserve and that I was to be returned home. I had been invalided from the service.

This was, of course, long before the concept of 'post-traumatic stress' was widely accepted, but Wiltshire found himself surrounded by people who were clearly suffering its symptoms while he was at Matlock.

We went for a meal and they used to stack up all the plates on the hotplate to keep them warm. Somebody knocked one of these stacks of plates on the floor with a tremendous crash. One fellow just went deathly white, almost to a shade of green, and he stood up and screamed and dived under the table. He was crying out, 'Shoot the bastard down, shoot the bastard down! Why just sit there?' The medical orderlies helped him up, took him away, but no one else at that table said a word about it. In fact it went eerily quiet. Another fellow very regrettably jumped out of the fourth-floor window. There were so many sad cases there.

After the war, Wiltshire was certainly not the only veteran of Bomber Command to find himself in a mental hospital under heavy medication. Eventually he was able to resume a successful engineering career. That night still haunts him, and the memory of coming under attack and the Flak flying into the Lancaster remains as harrowing and lacerating as ever.

Dennis Wiltshire was classed as mentally disturbed, and there's no doubt that he was genuinely suffering from an extreme psychological anxiety. The greatest stigma was reserved for those who were not believed to have a medical condition as such, labelled instead as suffering from LMF, a 'Lack of Moral Fibre'.

Those three letters meant an undignified end to an RAF career, with those who succumbed being stripped of rank and quickly marched off their stations. Such cases were generally kept very quiet, although there are also examples of LMF-branded airmen being humiliated very publicly in front of their squadron colleagues. The RAF's commanders stamped down on any signs of cowardice harshly, dreading that it would spread, bringing Bomber Command grinding to a halt. So cases of LMF were rarely obvious, but there was always suspicion over any airman reporting sick, and there were rumours of crews getting only as far as the North Sea, dropping their bombs and returning. Engine failure would be claimed – after all, a plausible enough problem. Consequently, reported cases of engine failure were checked very meticulously, the ground crew left to distinguish between those that were genuine and those reported by crews who might be LMF. Robert Kee's squadron had one such incident.

> It never occurred to me that anyone wasn't doing their duty. It did come out later that one crew in the squadron had been taking easy trips, knowing perfectly well they weren't going near a target and coming back and saying they'd been there. There was one squadron leader who had a slight reputation of finding it too easy to leave the target rather early, but I don't know whether that was justified. I think it was very, very rare.

There was a standard drill when cases of LMF were discovered, as Bill Burke recalls. 'They were court-martialled, stripped of their stripes, reduced to the lowest of the low in terms of rank, and then they were assigned to the most unpleasant tasks or ejected from the RAF altogether. One chap I heard about was sent down the mines, which I think was a terrible thing to happen to people who had got it in that fashion, serving their country and accepting very great risk in the process.'

Peter Baker saw for himself how cases of LMF were treated when it affected members of his squadron. 'It was a very unkind thing because some men were simply not cut out to face the dangers of flying. It didn't mean to say they couldn't play an active part in the war. I knew men who were accused of LMF and were posted from the squadron in disgrace. Some of them lost their rank. They disappeared, posted to other duties. You didn't really have time to question where they went.'

The authorities' eagerness to stamp down on suspected cases of LMF was also apparent to Adge Boal when his bomb aimer completed his tour.

Now he was a great guy, loved life, hadn't got a care in the world. Yet as soon as the raids were over, he disappeared from the station the next day. He thought he'd done his thirty trips, that was him finished. Apparently the police caught him on the railway station about to get on to a train. I don't think he really knew where he was going, but unfortunately for him, he was sent to a place in Sheffield which was a disciplinary camp. Lots of people had nervous breakdowns, but it was when they gave up that it usually had the most effect.

It started to affect Arthur Smith long before he was due to give up. He found that the more operations he went on, the more fearful he was becoming.

I became rather frightened of what was going on, and I thought I wasn't going to survive, especially in daylight, when you saw it all. If you were in a mass formation, a gaggle as we called it, over a target that was particularly well defended with Flak, you could see the spent shells. The smoke from the spent shells would form a grey cloud in the daylight sky. This was a fantastic sight, and a frightening sight, but you'd got through it. I gradually got more frightened. I realised it wasn't just fun and exciting. They talked about what the opposition was expected to be like at briefings, how the weather's not going to be too good, and you'd think, Oh, I don't want to go out on that again.

Despite having these misgivings, Smith was bound by silence; fear was not an emotion to be openly discussed.

I never spoke to anybody about it. But when we got through to our twentieth op, I decided I couldn't stick it any longer. I didn't dare say this to anybody. We were going to a very tough target, we got into the aircraft, at night-time, and as we got up, before we had crossed the coast, I just became a dummy. I was absolutely frightened and couldn't do anything, shaking. I was just trying to pluck up courage to say, 'Turn back', but I couldn't say it. Eventually my physical condition took over, and I just froze solid with fright. I didn't know what to do, and I couldn't operate the *Gee*. The navigator said to the pilot, 'Something wrong with Smithy. I think we'd better do something about it, he can't do anything.' They thought I was seriously ill and turned back. I can't remember the precise procedure. All I know is that I was whisked away on my own. I wasn't allowed to see anybody at all, even my crew. I was taken to our billet, told to pack all my stuff in my kitbag. I went to see the commanding officer, who tore me off a terrific strip. I felt an absolute fool, but knew I couldn't do anything else. He said, in the First World War, if you turned your back on the face of the enemy, they shot people for that, and so on.

Smith was then bundled into a waiting truck with a flight sergeant, who apologised for arresting him, and drove him to see a psychiatrist. By now, it was late in the evening.

It wasn't a very long drive. We went into an office with a psychiatrist in RAF uniform who interviewed me for about an hour. His attitude was very sympathetic. He went through my life, my background, my parents, and so forth, to see what sort of person I was. In the end, I told him that the real reason I packed up was that I was scared and didn't know what to do. He told me that I'd be stripped of my rank, everybody would know about it, I'd be on some menial job in the RAF somewhere, and I wasn't going to see my crew any more. Did I realise this? Of course I didn't realise this, I thought they'd just give me another job. He asked, 'Would you like to see if they'll take you back?'

I said, 'Yes,' so he rang up the CO. The CO, surprisingly, said, 'Yes, I'll take him back if his crew will, and he makes a promise not to duck out any more,' so they rang up the pilot and the pilot asked all the rest of the crew. They all said, 'Yes, of course we want Smithy back, if he's going to be all right,' and I went back. I knew that I could face my fear rather than be labelled a coward, because this is what I thought I would be, a coward for the rest of my life. My family would know what I'd done, all my friends would know, it was a terrible prospect. I thought, I've only got ten more trips to do. It didn't cure me but I knew what I had to do, like knowing you've got to go towards a certain goal. So I just used to shut my eyes if I knew anything was happening outside and conquered my fear.

Smith had come very close to being labelled LMF. He didn't really understand what LMF was, but like all aircrew he knew that it was whispered about as something terrible. Many other squadron commanders wouldn't have been so sympathetic, but Smith was quick to take the opportunity of returning to operational duty. He was accepted back by his crew; the camaraderie within the crew ensured that. With typical wartime resolve, no one talked about the incident.

It seems brave of me to have gone back; it wasn't. My fear got worse, trip by trip. Some were easier, daylight, short trips. The way I used to fight it was to concentrate on what I was doing, forget what was happening outside my aircraft, and my crew never said anything. We didn't have any trouble at all, and if things got too bad and I didn't have to concentrate on something, I would just shut my eyes. Having made up my mind that I was going to stick it to the end of our tour, I knew I would be able to do it. When we finished our operational tour, I was extremely relieved not to go up again. I've never flown unless I've had to since then. It's just the feeling of being in an aircraft. I wasn't meant to be a bird, I was meant to keep my feet on the ground.

History has judged men like Arthur Smith more sensitively than the mood of the 1940s allowed. As we have come to understand what being a member of a bomber crew entailed, so we have come to revere those men who were in those crews, and show consideration to those whose courage wavered. Cowards wouldn't have completed twenty operations before their feelings overcame them; cowards wouldn't have been able to continue their tours.

It had been Bomber Command's most demanding winter. By now the sheer weight of the British war effort that lay behind Harris's strategy meant that the RAF would have to remain committed to it, even if there had been second thoughts. Though few crews were in much of a position to appreciate the fact, actually their attacks were beginning to take their toll on the German war effort. For two years they had taken the war to the Nazi mainland, striking back in a way impossible for any other Allied force, and in the process they were helping to pave the way for the plan that would see the opening of the Second Front, the land invasion of continental Europe.

10

'For You, The War is Over!'

'We applaud your continuous and sustained bombing of German war industries and the effect this has on the German war effort.'

Letter from Field Marshal Sir Bernard Montgomery to Air Chief Marshal Sir Arthur Harris following D-Day

(top) Roy Finch *(front row, far left)* with fellow prisoners of war in Stalag 383.
(bottom) Tom Wingham's false Belgian identity card, used while he was
evading capture after being shot down.

Bomber Command may not finally have delivered the decisive blow against Germany that Harris had long boasted it would, but the pulverised cities that greeted the advancing Allied soldiers in late 1944 and early 1945 provided sobering proof of just how devastating the bombing campaign had been. The RAF had clearly long since left behind their early days of inaccurate and frequently ineffectual raids. Harris's whirlwind had indeed been terrible; large sections of the Reich's industrial capacity lay in ruins; whole cities were virtually decimated, their populations' homes and factories destroyed. Even though German production had managed to rise, there was little question as to how much more fiercely they could have opposed an Allied invasion had they not had to divert so many resources to make that rise in production possible in the face of such a sustained bombing campaign.

So back in the spring of 1944, when preparations had begun in earnest for Operation Overlord, Bomber Command was given an important and central part to play. Even Harris now conceded that his bombers would not be able to win the war on their own, as he had told Churchill in 1943; a land invasion was inevitable. This didn't spare Churchill the nightmare he and Harris both shared, namely that such an invasion could still all too easily degenerate into the horror of a First World War-style stalemate across northern France, a repeat of the Somme. His diplomacy was subsequently directed throughout the year at preventing this happening, at all costs. In any case, he knew he no longer had the luxury of postponing the invasion indefinitely. The pressure from Stalin was intense, the Red Army and the civilian population of the USSR suffering most at the hands of the Wehrmacht. The Second World War would cost the Soviet Union over a tenth of its population, more than 20 million people in all. Stalin was understandably anxious for a Second Front to be opened up as soon as possible; the longer the delay, the more suspicious he became of his western allies. At the Casablanca Conference of January 1943, Churchill and Roosevelt had agreed to postpone the invasion until 1944, but when they met Stalin in Tehran in November 1943, it was clear that they wouldn't be able to postpone it again. By now, Stalin had become increasingly frustrated at the seemingly endless delay, and it was agreed that Operation Overlord would go ahead in 1944.

The run-up to the invasion would cost Harris his operational independence, however. Despite his vociferous objections, he would now be under the command of General Eisenhower, who had been appointed Supreme Allied Commander in Europe. Bomber Command would be joined there by the USAAF. Their commander, General Carl Spaatz, had in fact shared Harris's doubts about the merits of diverting the bomber forces from the continued assault on Germany, but in the end both agreed to follow the directive that would prepare the way for the invasion. The principal bombing target would now be the German air force, followed by the railway and communications systems. Bomber Command's ability to bomb specific, strategically important targets was to be exploited as the major raids on German cities were suspended. This was, of course, something of a relief to a command that had been struggling in the first few months of the year as a run of unpredictable weather and the Luftwaffe's defence system at its most successful conspired, resulting in Bomber Command's most serious losses of the war. So now, instead of the cities, there was to be a range of smaller, more focused targets requiring precision bombing: major railway lines, to prevent the mass movement of German troops, and to ensure that those based in Normandy on D-Day itself would be isolated; military camps; ammunition depots; radio and radar stations;

coastal gun batteries; explosives and armaments factories – all targets that required the sort of accuracy that had eluded the bombers for so long, particularly as many of the targets would be in the occupied countries of Europe, where civilian deaths needed to be kept to an absolute minimum. The targets weren't just around the Normandy beaches; communications around Calais were bombed just as fervently as part of the successful attempt to deceive the Nazis' military leaders into believing that the invasion would take place there.

Bomber Command's contribution in the weeks leading up to D-Day was pivotal in allowing the invasion to take place successfully, more effective in fact than anyone had really expected. The combination of low-level marking techniques and the use of master bombers led to unprecedented accuracy rates, while the much shorter distances across enemy-occupied territory helped to ensure that Bomber Command suffered considerably fewer losses than it had become accustomed to. The availability of fighter escorts for the bombers also allowed daylight raids to be introduced again, greatly increasing the number of raids that could be mounted. In fact, over these weeks the crews went on more raids than in any equivalent period before, sometimes going out twice in twenty-four-hour periods. It is noticeable, talking to veterans who were active during these weeks, just how quickly they completed their tours of operations.

It had been years since the RAF had last mounted daylight raids. Most airmen active at the start of 1944 had never experienced one, having long believed they were too dangerous. For Arthur Smith, the most striking thing about flying during the day was the realisation of just how large the bomber force was.

When we went over on a raid at night-time you felt very much alone because you never saw or practically never saw another aircraft. If you did, he was much too close and you should get out of the way. In daylight, it was a fantastic sight, you'd be in a gaggle of maybe five hundred aircraft, and I always wished I'd had the courage to smuggle my camera up and take a photo or two out of the window of this amazing sight, but we weren't supposed to have cameras.

Daylight raids could, however, be more frightening for the bomber crews. Suddenly, rear gunner Jack Eveleigh could see exactly what conditions he was flying in.

As you go into the target and the bomb aimer takes control, you fly straight and level no matter what's being thrown at you, and you don't say anything. You just sit there and bear it until you are out the other side. On the first daylight raid we did, we got some predicted Flak coming up. I'm afraid I broke the rule and said, 'Predicted Flak!' We got a bit of a pounding but still went on, and when we landed we could see we'd taken a battering.

In broad daylight, on the same sortie, Eveleigh also witnessed another Lancaster being hit by a bomb dropped from an aircraft flying above them in the bomber stream.

I saw a Lancaster above us open its bomb doors flying in on the bombing run. The bombs dropped. They cleared us OK as he was slightly behind, but one of the bombs dropped through the wing of a Lancaster that was on our starboard side. The bomb didn't explode; it just dropped straight through the wing. The Lancaster just banked over and disappeared. I reported it at interrogation so it would have been logged, but I don't know what happened to it.

Despite these incidents, Eveleigh also found it comforting to see the whole bomber stream.

It was like a flock of starlings. Several hundred aircraft flying down, the whole stream around you, behind you, above you, below you. It was a very comforting sight. We didn't fly in a formation. We flew in what we called a 'loose gaggle'. In other words, we got as close to each other as was comfortable. We weren't trained for formation flying like the Americans. The

Americans were good at formation flying, but we were trained
mainly for night flying.

On 6 June, D-Day itself, Bomber Command was again at the
forefront of the offensive. A total of 1,211 sorties were launched
the night before the landings, ensuring that many of the German
army's resources were destroyed. Troop strongholds and gun
positions, ammunition dumps, oil supplies and road and rail
communications were all targeted. This was followed up by more
bombing on D-Day itself, and support for the land forces as
they advanced across occupied Europe. Flight engineer Maurice
Flower and his crew were among those on operational duty on
6 June 1944. 'One of the longest trips was D-Day. We did six
hours, thirty minutes flying up and down parallel to the beaches,
jamming the German radar. The Germans didn't know the operation was on until they appeared right in front of them. In fact
we didn't know they were coming until the sea was just black
with ships.'

As the Allies had prepared for the invasion, the Nazis had
fought on, but it was already clear to many Germans that the
war was drawing to a conclusion, and that they weren't going to
be on the winning side. By the spring of 1944, Luftwaffe pilot
Peter Spoden was no longer flying in the belief that Germany
could win the war.

In the last two years, we had battle fatigue and Germany was
so devastated, the cities in flames. We didn't regard this as a
victory any more but as a necessity. To the very end, we wanted
to show the RAF that we were there and we were protecting
our wives and children. We didn't feel any great joy in 1944,
and 1945. What I had felt at the time of Peenemünde was gone.
We just wanted to show them we weren't going to let them
shoot everything to bits.

As Bomber Command bombed by night and the USAAF by
day, Spoden could see that Germany had been defeated. 'The

German fighter bombers couldn't do anything. As one city after another was burnt to the ground, we knew the fate of the air war was sealed. However, a huge amount of propaganda continued at that time. The rockets that they fired on England were a faint glimmer of hope, "Maybe we can still pull it off!" These were the so-called revenge weapons, but it was much too late.'

The V1 flying bombs, popularly known as 'Doodlebugs', that were launched against London from June 1944 may have been too late, but they did inflict on the capital a grim reminder of the Blitz, a taste too of the destruction being meted out to German cities. Launched from fixed ramps, these unpiloted monoplanes carried a 1-ton warhead and were a terrifying menace at 8 metres long with a 5.5-metre wingspan. The 1,435 bombs that hit south-east England that summer sent the population into total panic, causing thousands of Londoners to evacuate. Yet thanks to Bomber Command, the Doodlebugs were never as destructive as intended, already delayed following the Peenemünde raid in particular. Two Mosquito squadrons were employed to shoot the bombs down, while the main force was sent out to destroy the launch pads, mainly in the Calais area, that were firing these dreaded bombs. The bombers also destroyed many of the launch sites for the V2 rockets that would arrive from September. Navigator Peter Baker was sent on several daylight raids to the V-weapon launch sites. 'Around D-Day, I did six or seven trips in Halifaxes bombing the sites which were hidden in woods in northern France. It was tremendous being able to see. At one time I was a navigator for the wing commander and we led the wing, and it was an extraordinary sight to look back on these three or four hundred aeroplanes in the sky behind you.'

The bombers continued to support the invasion in the weeks after D-Day. With their help, the Allied armies were gradually able to set about the liberation of Europe, more than four years after its rapid fall. For the troops, seeing enemy-occupied territory for the first time must have been an eye-opening experience.

It was a landscape that many of the Bomber Boys had seen for themselves in the preceding years as they parachuted down from the wreckages of the aircraft. Most airmen would be picked up quickly by the search parties sent out as soon as an enemy aircraft was seen falling from the sky. After baling out, Jim Chapman had landed in a six-foot snow drift that turned out to be in the middle of the Black Forest. There was no sign of the rest of his crew. He soon heard German voices, and two elderly gentlemen appeared. It was clear that he had no choice but to surrender. 'I was escorted by these men to the nearest police station. It was a bit of a palaver, a lot of "officialdom" with each other. I got the idea half of them didn't understand what the other half was saying, but by the time we came to leave that station, they'd got the captain, navigator, mid-upper gunner, wireless operator and myself.'

After losing consciousness during his parachute descent, Hal Croxson, another rear air gunner, had come round and landed safely.

I thought, The whole of Germany will know I am here, so I'm waiting for them to come and get me. I took my revolver out and loaded it, laid it beside me, ready if anybody wants to come aggressively, otherwise I can hand it over. I then took stock. I think I had seventeen cigarettes in my packet and a few other things which were going to be useful to me, including the RAF escape kit. With a scout knife that I used to carry, I cut the bottom of the flying suit off and made it a jacket length. I took the electric suit off and got rid of all the kapok that's in the suit, round the neck and the chest, and rolled it all up. Then I discovered I was bleeding from my right hand, so I ripped a strip out of the parachute and bound it up. I cut off all the cords of the parachute, pulled my shirt up, and wound them round my body, thinking they'd probably be useful to me at some point. I'd lost a boot. It was common to lose one during the violent pull-up that you get when you jump out in a parachute.

At this point, Croxson had no idea what had happened to the rest of his crew. It was only when he met his crew's mid-upper gunner and bomb aimer in a prison camp that he discovered that they were the only three survivors. 'One of their parachutes hadn't opened properly. He'd fallen into trees and fortunately the trees had held him, otherwise he would have hit the ground without the 'chute opening. They were the only two alive. The rest had gone with the aircraft, which was very sad. They were smashing blokes and I enjoyed their comradeship and friendship very much.'

As the airmen were captured, they came face to face with the enemy for the first time. Until now, this had been an impersonal war for the men of Bomber Command. However aware they may have been of the people living where their bombs fell, they never saw them, let alone spoke to them. Few people at that time knew much about Germany other than what they remembered from reading about the First World War. It wasn't just that the Germans spoke another language, the 'Hun' belonged to another world, his culture a mystery to most of the young men who had volunteered to take on Hitler. The initial response many airmen felt on encountering Germans in person for the first time was one of shock at the hatred felt by the Reich's civilian population towards them. As he was finally taken out of the village police station, Jim Chapman experienced that hatred for himself.

We were called 'murderers', and I was called that to my face. The inhabitants of that village were waiting for us to emerge, because we were being taken to the Central Interrogation Centre for Allied air prisoners, and I heard the German word for 'murderer' accompanied by spitting. That's what they thought of us. I can only think that's what our people thought of them when they bombed London, Coventry, Liverpool and Birmingham. Our people were crying out, 'Where's our Royal Air Force?' You had to live with it and hope they didn't catch up with you. While we were being transported from one place to another, we had to go through Frankfurt, which was absolutely wrecked by the bombing, and we saw an RAF flight lieutenant in his uniform strung up, dangling on the end of a pole outside an upper window. It was safer to remain in the hands of the Luftwaffe officers and the ordinary servicemen.

The anger directed at the crews came far more strongly from the civilians than the enemy's own airmen. The civilians, after all, knew as little about the British as the British knew about them. What they did know and think was heavily influenced by the propaganda machine of Joseph Goebbels. But among the airmen of both sides there was a certain understanding, an appreciation that whichever side you were on an airman was a fellow trained professional who deserved to be treated with a degree of respect. No doubt they were only too aware of how soon they too could be meeting the same fate as those airmen they encountered as prisoners of war. Luftwaffe veterans such as Wolfgang Falck had had friends in the RAF before the war, and had visited Britain in 1939. 'Both the British and Germans were soldiers, and in the time of war we fight for our country. We don't fight personally against one another. We don't hate one another, even later we didn't hate one another. We didn't fight the people, we tried to shoot down the aeroplanes, hoping the crew or the pilot could bale out.'

In 1940, Falck had felt the difference between civilian and air force attitudes for himself.

One of the pilots was late reporting to me. He explained that he had shot down a Blenheim in broad daylight right outside Dusseldorf. He told me the aeroplane was still there with its crew. We both went there. The Blenheim was still held together, although severely damaged. The place was full of people and police. It was a Sunday and one of the passers-by started to kick the body. So we shouted at them to leave the bodies alone, that these were dead pilots. The passers-by shouted at us, screaming that we supported Churchill. We had to retreat to our cars very quickly. The people were out of control.

As a young Flak gunner operator, Horst Hirche felt that empathy for his fellow soldier, when he witnessed two American airmen parachuting down over the Flak tower where he was stationed during a raid on Berlin in January 1945.

On that occasion we shot group fire. Those were our orders. I looked up at the aeroplanes and saw two parachutes dropping right on top of us in the Flak tower. I thought, 'Hopefully they won't be shot.' Thank goodness this didn't happen. The two parachutists were safe and landed between our tower and the church. My colleagues freed them from their parachutes and then they were captured. At that time, the people really hated the Allied bombers. They were very angry, they had lost everything. We heard that a lot of ugly things happened which shouldn't have happened. But we were told afterwards the two airmen had removed their parachutes, held up their hands and surrendered. They came into the Flak tower and about ten soldiers had to protect these men from the people. They accompanied them up to the fifth floor, which was a military zone and off limits for civilians, and locked them in. We had to stand guard in front of this room so they couldn't escape. I stood there for a whole hour. I only saw them very briefly in their leather jackets and fur collars. Their clothes were new, and they couldn't have been more than twenty years of age. They were just young people, four years older than I was. It really upset me. The following day, they were transferred for interrogation.

As the airmen came across Germans, they noticed the similarities between the people of two nations at war. This was certainly the case for Robin Murray, the sole survivor of a Wellington crew that had crashed into the North Sea in February 1942. 'The Germans I met, quite truthfully, were no different from you and I. They were at war but they no more wanted it than we did. They were just ordinary, normal people who in any other time you could have got to know and liked or disliked. In fact I met some very nice people over there.'

Murray had sustained serious injuries before being captured which had to be dealt with before he could be taken to Lamsdorf on the Polish–Czech border. He recalls the wonderful treatment he received at Luftwaffe hospitals in Amsterdam and Frankfurt. Roy Finch, who also ditched over the North Sea, similarly remembers a certain camaraderie between airmen, even enemy airmen, after he was captured in November 1941.

We were taken along to the local Messerschmitt fighter squadron, and we stayed the night there. They treated us very well and we had bacon and eggs, which of course was difficult to get in England. The next day, they took us to Dulag Luft, the interrogation camp. We went third-class carriage, sharing the coach with two Messerschmitt fighter pilots, who we got on extremely well with. Every time they smoked, we smoked. We had a lot of banter with my little bit of German and their bit of English about the pros and cons of the Spitfire and the Messerschmitt. I even exchanged names and addresses with one of them, the idea being that after the war we'd get in touch with each other. When we got to Hamburg, we had to change trains. They went their separate ways, but they helped carry our kit. I remember thinking at the time, Why are we fighting these people?

It was sobering for the airmen to realise that those fighting for the enemy were also young men. Robin Murray found himself guarded by a corporal who was only around twenty years old.

He'd been wounded seven times, blown up in a jeep, all up his left side. His left leg was useless, his left arm in a sling and he'd got a glass eye. He was still in the forces, in spite of all those wounds, having got the highest decoration he could get. He couldn't understand this chaining-up business, said you just didn't do it to people, but it didn't affect us very much. The long chains had handcuffs each side, and you could open them with a bully-beef tin key. You could take your handcuffs off, put your hands in your pockets and walk about looking as if you'd got handcuffs on.

By 1944, Robin Murray, Roy Finch, Jim Chapman and Hal Croxson were among thousands of Bomber Command airmen being held in prisoner-of-war camps. Murray would spend three long years as a prisoner.

I was a POW from 15 February 1942 until 17 April 1945. The main thing about being a prisoner of war was that you had to muck in with everybody. If you felt you wanted to say something to somebody, you had to hold back because that would create bad feeling and maybe a quarrel, a fight even. We did have some terrible fights amongst people. So you had to watch what you said. I suppose it was like being at boarding school, where you couldn't do as you really wanted all the time but then you had a certain amount of freedom. You could wander about as you wanted to in a very restricted space, you got friendly with people in other billets and you went for a brew and a chat. There were some people there who had talents which they never even dreamed of. The Bank of England clerk we had with us turned out to be an expert forger given a quill pen and the ink. Where the Germans were silly was they had these working parties out in various factories, including one where the pens were produced, and another where all the ink was produced. So of course we had the correct paper with the watermark on it, the correct ink and these forgers made it look as if the stuff had been printed.

How airmen were treated as POWs varied from camp to camp, much defending on the individual guards in charge of them. Roy Finch has no fond memories of the camp where he spent his first nine months as a POW.

They shouldn't have made us work, with the rank of sergeant and above, but they did. We had to put up a new compound for some Russian prisoners they were expecting. Being clever, I thought as I'd learned a bit of German I'd be an interpreter. The more I asked one German guard to speak slowly, the angrier he got, and suddenly to my horror he pulled this pistol out and stuck it into my stomach. I thought, This is it, I've had it! Fortunately, another fellow came along who spoke fluent German, and took over. I promptly disappeared behind everybody else, which was the end of any ambition to become an interpreter. I began to realise that nationalities are not important. If people are nice, they're nice, if they're not, they're not.

It wasn't just the Germans who caused problems. Finch found the behaviour of some of his fellow POWs caused tensions.

The latrines were a cesspit arrangement with a boarded cover over them. In the first winter, the fellows were very short of fuel for the stove in each hut, and they took the wooden planking off the cesspits. Then they complained bitterly because the so-and-so Germans wouldn't replace them. At another camp, the working parties stripped all the lead piping down because they could melt down the lead and use it for all sorts of things. The people remaining had to put up with having no piping. So there wasn't much camaraderie about this, each man for himself.

It wasn't always like that, however. Some veterans go as far as describing POW camps as almost like holiday camps, and more comfortable than the squadron bases they'd been used to at home. Robin Murray had a rather more pleasant experience than Roy Finch in his first camp. 'It got to the stage after about six weeks where it was a farce. We had a little room at the end of one hut. There were six of us who slept in there. This German used to come in, put his gun in the corner, take his jacket and hat off, and we'd brew up and sit there having a cup of coffee and a cigarette. It was as easy as that.'

There was a whole hierarchy to the system of POW camps. Separate camps were established for army personnel and air force, for officers and sergeants. Nicholas Alkemade, the rear air gunner who'd baled out without a parachute, finished up in Stalag Luft III, a camp normally reserved for officers, despite being only a sergeant – such was the power of his special status in the eyes of the Luftwaffe, his extraordinary escape earning him special privileges. He became a celebrated figure among his fellow POWs.

There was a routine at POW camp, just as there had been on the squadrons, even when the regime was relatively relaxed, as Robin Murray experienced.

At seven o'clock in the morning, you had *Appell*, a roll-call, where you were counted. You stood in fives and there was a bloke in charge of the RAF compound, known as 'Ukrainian Joe'. He was a big, dim Ukrainian and he hadn't got a brain in his head. We used to take the mickey out of him something rotten. For instance, we heard there was going to be an inspection of arms for the compound guards, so we took out his gun and put a wooden one in its place. He did three weeks in the cooler, you know! They were there for baiting, you see. We'd got nothing else to do, but you'd brew up and there were one or two people there who had various skills. Two or three schoolmasters there, for instance, and they would take lessons in various things which people felt they needed or wanted. We used to mix amongst ourselves and if it was fine, we'd walk around the compound.

While the guards may have counted the prisoners in theory, Murray recalls that they didn't have as much control over them as they thought.

They never knew how many people were in the camp. In the summer of 1944 they decided to have a count, so everybody in the compound had to line up, give their name and prisoner-of-war number. We all went outside and came back in again, but more people came in than went out. So they had no idea really how many people were in the camp, it was too big. At any one time, there could be nine thousand people in the camp. There were thousands of what were known as 'Dunkirk Harriers', the people who were captured at Dunkirk. Anybody from corporal or below was entitled to go out on working parties and they just didn't know how many people were there. The German girl who ran the card system was madly in love with a little RAF pilot. He was a good-looking young lad of about twenty and she used to stand out there and gaze at him with her mouth open! So of course we played on that. Cards used to be swapped and all sort of things, because the only way the RAF could get out on working parties and make an escape was to change over with an army bloke.

In captivity for years on end, the airmen were living out their youth. Robin Murray had been relatively old when he joined at twenty-three, but most of his fellow POWs were younger.

I was a poor old soul compared with most of them who were eighteen-, nineteen-year-olds, but that's where I was lucky as I'd had a bit of experience of life. Some of these poor sods that were killed hadn't lived really. Some of them hadn't even had a girlfriend. I remember friends who had their twenty-first birthdays in prisoner-of-war camps. They were so young when you think of those that were killed or even some that were wounded so badly, their lives were destroyed virtually.

Many POW airmen had been badly wounded in their last minutes as members of bomber crews. Although the German authorities saw that injuries were treated as well as medical science at the time would allow, during the course of the war, many POWs would die as a result of their injuries, and many others spent their years in captivity in considerable discomfort. Robin Murray was left with permanent mobility problems from when his Wellington had crashed. 'In the dinghy because it was so cold, I got severe frostbite from my legs downwards. In fact I had very little feeling in my legs and I still can't move my toes, they're locked. The Germans excused me all parades. There were several of us who were like that and they counted us in the barracks and then a guard was put on the door to make quite certain we didn't get out.'

There were many far worse injuries, not least the severe burns that affected so many airmen in aircraft that crashed, whether shot down or not. Hundreds of the worst burns cases were treated in POW camps by Major David Charters, a surgeon who himself became a POW in 1941. With equipment provided by the Red Cross, he led a medical team, becoming a pioneer in reconstructive surgery, including many eyelid and facial operations. There were other teams in the POW system making the hundreds of artificial limbs required by airmen. Charters' work mirrors that of Archibald McIndoe, who ran a treatment unit for burns victims in East Grinstead. McIndoe was able to develop even more advanced surgical techniques; he continued the treatment of POWs after the end of the war, as well as of those who were repatriated while the conflict continued.

For those who hadn't suffered such severe injuries, the worst part of being a POW was often the endlessness of it, months turning into years with little to do. Roy Finch tried to occupy himself usefully.

I made use of my time by studying French, German and Spanish. I worked in a bank before the war, and took a bookkeeping exam there, arranged by the Red Cross. I used to teach a bit of French, and we spent a lot of time playing bridge, which I considered afterwards a complete waste of time. I should have been learning! The big problem was not knowing when it was going to end, 'Am I going to be here for ever?' It's not like serving a sentence as an ordinary prisoner where you have a definite sentence and you know by good behaviour it will be shortened.

By 1944, it was clear even to the POWs that the war was not going to continue for ever, but the hope offered by D-Day quickly turned into disappointment. 'After the invasion, we'd all made up our minds that the war would be over by Christmas, and of course in the event we were still stuck in Germany, with no sign of it ending.'

In the routine and drudgery of camp life, it's the meagre diet provided by the German rations that stands out in Robin Murray's memory.

You had a mint tea – ersatz mint tea – which used to come up after the parade. Then at twelve o'clock the German rations used to come up, which might be a two-pound loaf of bread shared between seven or eight of us. You'd get a little bit of cheese, about two inches by an inch, a bit of ersatz butter, and a biscuit. Maybe, if you were lucky, it'd be one of these Canadian white-flour biscuits, big oval biscuits, which were marvellous because if you pounded them down you could make wonderful cakes with them, as we did for birthdays. One of our muckers was a baker in civilian life, and he used to make these beautiful cakes.

With such meagre rations coming from the airmen's captors, the supply of Red Cross parcels became essential to a POW's survival. 'We lived on those parcels. The Red Cross in theory supplied POWs with one parcel a week. It had a tin of bully beef, milk powder and various things like that. They were all vitaminised, so I understand. It was a great help.'

Having been known as Tubby throughout his service career, Robin Murray found that even with the succour of the Red Cross parcels the sustenance was hardly sufficient. 'There was enough food to keep you alive. You didn't need to take an awful lot of exercise or do an awful lot. You spent a lot of time on your bed, lying in your pit for quite a few hours a day reading. You didn't take a lot of exercise because you knew your food intake wasn't that much. Nine times out of ten you got a parcel a week but you didn't always.'

So enough food to keep you alive, but little more than that. Other prisoners recall that the rations consisted mainly of a thin

---

Bomber Crew

soup, leading to a grim existence. Then there was the frustration for the POWs that they could do little to help the war effort. Hal Croxson consoled himself with the knowledge that running ever larger POW camps was itself diverting the Nazis' resources away from the front line. 'We were told by people who'd been there longer to keep as many guards round you as you can. Every guard you've got keeping you in place is a guy who's not doing something else for the war effort. So we used to devise all sorts of thing to keep as many guards around us as possible, to disrupt their organisation as much as we could. That was the only way we could contribute.'

Even escape attempts were all part of this strategy. 'Immediately there was an escape, hundreds of German personnel were put into action searching and that took in the local police, railway personnel at ticket offices and guards and the military, of course. So we always felt that was a worthwhile effort. If you've got two or three hundred chaps looking out there for you, they're not doing something else.'

With so much time on their hands, it's no wonder that many prisoners' thoughts turned to attempting to escape. Some, indeed, felt it was their duty. Robert Kee, who'd been a POW since his Hampden had crashed on ice in February 1942, was among them. 'Everybody wanted to escape. It was just part of being there. You didn't actually have orders to, but that's how we were meant to behave.'

There were many audacious escape attempts, although few were successful. Whole legions of airmen put their minds to thinking up the most elaborate plans, and inventing the most cunning deceptions. While some prisoners worked on lone escapes, Kee was part of a much more ambitious scheme.

I was part of a big escape, organised by someone very brilliantly when I was in a POW camp in Poland. It was a tunnel from the lavatory, which had taken about five or six months to build, and we'd all taken part in that. It was very tight in the tunnel, and

376

one did wonder whether one was ever going to be able to get out, but I think that over sixty of us did. People who remained in the camp said it was wonderful the next morning, because the Germans hadn't realised it had happened at all until only half the camp turned up at roll-call.

It was a great feeling to be released from the confines of the prison camp, but as with so many other attempts, Kee's liberation was not to last.

We were free for around five or six days and thoroughly enjoyed ourselves until they finally caught us. We'd travelled by train all the way right from Poland across to Wuppertal, in the Rhineland, and for once we faced a more intelligent policeman than we'd had until then. They'd always looked at our false papers before and been taken in by them, but this fellow looked at them and said, 'Right, thank you, you'll be coming along with me to the police station.' When we got there, he took out some magnifying glasses and looked at them. 'Yes, forged papers.' I don't think anyone got back to England.

It wasn't the end of Kee's escaping career. He tried on another occasion, but this time was caught almost as soon as he had boarded the very first train. There was no surprise in being caught. After all, the local authorities were usually quickly alterted to prisoners on the loose, and, as Robin Murray recalls, it was hard for a captive airman not to look conspicuous.

We were way out in Poland. There was nothing for miles around except villages and in a village everybody knows one another, so a stranger must have been a Kriegy on the loose. As the German Camp Defence Officer said, 'You English have a natural arrogance. It's no good pretending to be a French peasant. You could dress like a French peasant, but your attitude won't be like a French peasant. You know you are good, and it sticks out like a sore thumb to anybody who is trained.'

It didn't stop the attempts, however, and some endeavours defied most prisoners' imaginations.

We had a Royal Australian Air Force sergeant who in civilian life worked in the circus. One day he literally went over this barbed wire which went all round the compound. Over a fence, then over coils and coils of barbed wire and then another fence equally as high. He went over the lot and disappeared into the woods, down to the railway station, caught a train, got up to Stettin. The thing to do if you got to Stettin was to get to the brothel area, find a suitable girl – most of them were Swedish – who would get you on to a Swedish boat, take you to Sweden and they flew you home from Sweden. In six weeks he was home in England, just like that.

Yet in a sense, escaping was not so much about getting back to Britain – plenty of airmen were party to escape attempts without really believing they would make it all the way. It was a distraction from the endless ordeal of being a POW, and the terrible conditions of their captivity. For Robert Kee, escaping was almost a sport, a way of occupying the minds of the young prisoners. 'RAF morale was very good in camp. The Germans were meant to come in looking for our tunnels. We all said, "We know what you're here for, you're looking for the tunnels, aren't you? We haven't got any!" We'd say this to tease them, and we became rather fond of them.'

Then one escape changed every prisoner of war's mind. This was no longer a game. In Stalag Luft III, the most daring of escape attempts, known ever since as the Great Escape, had started like so many others. Alan Bryett, captured after baling out of his Halifax in August 1943, was one of the prisoners involved.

Once you became a prisoner of war and went into the compound, there was a feeling of terrific frustration that you were not going to be able to do anything useful in the war. It was because of the frustration that senior British officers decided that there would be a tunnel on which a large number of people worked. You could vent your frustration on doing useful work in trying to escape. These were bright, young men in the prime of life, not able to do anything useful.

The plan was for 220 prisoners to escape during one night in March 1944. Over the course of eleven months, three tunnels were dug out, named 'Tom', 'Dick' and 'Harry', the earth that was removed carefully concealed to avoid arousing suspicion. The escapees were issued with forged papers, passports and German money that had all been painstakingly manufactured within the camp. On the allotted night, everything seemed to be in order, but then the camp was thrown into darkness as a result of a major air raid on Berlin. The escapees were thrown into confusion, and after just seventy-six of the prisoners had got through the tunnels, the German guards caught the rest as they waited their turn.

It wasn't the fact that the tunnels were discovered which sent shock waves around the POW community, or that of the seventy-six who had got out of Stalag Luft III just three managed to get home. What nobody had expected was Hitler's personal order to shoot fifty of those who had been recaptured. It was only because he was one of the prisoners still in the queue to get into the tunnel when it was discovered that Alan Bryett survived that night. Robert Kee was also in Stalag Luft III at the time of the Great Escape, and although he wasn't involved in the attempt, three of his best friends were among those shot. Escape would no longer be worth contemplating. 'Nobody tried again after that. Most people would say that until the awful shooting everybody wanted to escape, it was rather fun. I remember the commandant of the camp, who announced that shooting to us on *Appell*. It was a great shock, one couldn't believe it. He read out the names, but he obviously didn't approve of it.'

In the bleak aftermath of the Great Escape, the prisoners could at least sense that their release might finally be on its way. It was a boost to Robert Kee's morale that he could sometimes hear the work of his successors in the bomber crews.

> We heard a lot of bombing. We were always pleased to hear it, and one night after we'd had to move from Stalag Luft III to another camp because the Russians were advancing, I remember we heard the most fantastic bombing we'd ever heard. Everyone roared and cheered, and actually it was the bombing of Dresden, which wasn't all that far off. We didn't know it was Dresden, but I remember we were very pleased to hear the bombing.

It was a relief for Roy Finch as well. For two years he had been in a camp in Bavaria, too far away from the bombing targets to hear anything, but now he too had been moved to another camp as the Third Reich retreated. 'When we heard the Allied bombers coming over, we'd all come out of our huts and cheer.'

Perhaps, finally, they were nearing their liberation. A small but significant minority of airmen who baled out over enemy-occupied territory had already found theirs, evading capture and avoiding POW camps altogether. The airmen had been taught about evasion during their training, and issued with escape kits in the hope that they might be able to make hasty returns to Britain. When Harold Nash had been shot down in his Halifax on a raid on Hanover in September 1943, he had been determined to put this part of his training into practice. 'I tried to get to Holland. We were taught to hide ourselves away and sleep in the daytime, and move at night if you were in Germany. You could go in the daytime in occupied territory, it was thought, if you could hide your uniform. I was walking along in the night when I met a gun pointing straight into the sky. I was afraid to go on and so I reconnoitred. But it wasn't a gun at all, it was a road barrier sticking up!'

After the tension of the bombing missions, and everything that had happened on the last one, evading airmen were suddenly faced with a profound sense of loneliness as they found their way around the darkness of enemy territory on their own. They were also exhausted, physically and mentally. Most had little idea of the fate of the rest of their crews. It was only after the war that Harold Nash learned about his. The pilot had nearly managed to land the aeroplane in a field. In the darkness, how-ever, he hadn't been able to see the tree in the middle of the field, which they hit, and the four remaining members of the crew were all killed. As he walked across Germany Nash didn't know this, and could only imagine what might have happened.

> I thought about them, especially the pilot, and the bomb aimer, who I knew had managed to bale out. I wondered where he was and got no sight of him. He told me after the war he'd been slightly wounded, and I think he'd gone to a farmhouse and been taken to hospital. It was a feeling of loneliness, of being lost, of having been abandoned, being all alone in Germany. I was also thinking about the girl I was due to meet that evening in York. We'd been given a week's leave but one crew had reported sick so we were only called in at the last minute. I don't think I got very far that first night. With dawn I got into a wood, and lay down behind a bush.

In the bright sunshine of late summer, Nash found he couldn't sleep during the day as he planned.

> I remember lying there, looking at my watch, and then four boys came by, playing at soldiers. One had got a wooden rifle. The last one saw me and he stood looking at me, yards away. He must have thought I was a forced labourer, and then he went on to join his mates who had gone on. I decided to change my position, and as night fell I went on again. I was tired. I remem-ber falling asleep going under wire and waking up. I'm sure a cow that was standing near to me had been licking my foot, which was then nearly bare.

Nash's socks had worn through with all the walking, even though he'd worn several pairs around his neck on operations in case of such an eventuality. He did still have his escape kit with him, however.

It was a little box which fitted into the pocket. In it was an amount of money, French francs, Belgian francs and Dutch guilders. There was a rubber bottle and tablets. You could put sewage water into that bottle, put a tablet in, let it stand for half an hour and in spite of the taste and the awful odours, you could drink that water without doing any damage to your health. We also had concentrated chocolate; they told us a couple of squares would keep us going for twenty-four hours. They said to try and pick up food on the way if we could. I remember crossing a field with beet in it and trying to eat some raw beet, but I couldn't. There were three silk handkerchiefs, two of which were maps of Germany and France, and I had three photographs so the underground movement could make false identity papers. Like most of the airmen, I had two press studs which in reality were compasses. You could remove them quite easily. The upper part was marked with a white point and that was attracted to magnetic north. It was a good approximation if you had no sun or stars.

Making use of his escape kit, Nash made his way across Germany. By now he had been on the run for three days. As he made his way across some fields, he spotted houses in the distance.

Suddenly a door opened and light streamed out. I heard voices and realised a man was coming on a bike. I just threw myself on the ground and tried to look like a heap in my brown flying suit; the wife came past me quite close. When the door had shut and I started to walk, the door opened again and the light streamed out. No voices this time and the door shut again. Then I heard a locomotive shunting backwards and forwards and realised there was a railway there so I skirted round this settlement. On the other side of the road below the lines was a river, and beyond that a copse. I was very demoralised by now so I got into the copse and stayed there for the day. Then I did sleep. Frankly, I was exhausted. I was awakened about two o'clock in the afternoon. There were three ladies sitting talking about ten yards from me with a dog. Fortunately the breeze was coming from them to me because the dog didn't sniff me and after two hours they went. I came out of my hiding place and a bike came along, so I darted back.

Nash continued up the road, but despite having finally got some sleep he was totally exhausted by the experience of the last few days. He had been kept going by the fear of what the Germans might do to him if they caught him. He saw a bike in front of a house and, remembering how they had been counselled to steal a bike if possible to enable them to move more quickly, he sized it up. Then the door of the house opened.

I remember thinking, This is it, I'm finished, the war is over for me. This chap came out and I was stood by his gate. He opened the gate and was about to walk straight past me, not taking any notice. There were so many forced labourers out there. So I said slowly, 'English airman.' He didn't speak English! So I showed him the wing on my uniform and he understood. He took me into his house, which was so poorly furnished. That made me think, If this is Hitler's Germany, I don't think much of it. There was his wife, a wooden table and one or two wooden chairs and in the corner a wooden box. In it was a baby. He left me with his wife.

Eventually the man returned, bringing a policeman with him. The policeman tried to interrogate Nash, but he had only school-boy German at the time, so the policeman's daughter, who was about the same age as him, acted as interpreter.

I kept saying name, rank and number and he got angry with me and handcuffed me. Then, I shall never forget, the daughter came to my side and stuffed an apple in my pocket. Her father couldn't see it. That apple tasted gorgeous in the cell. I spent the night in a night fighter aerodrome. A fighter pilot came down to talk to me in English, very good English. We weren't supposed to betray any knowledge of German and only talked generalities, nothing about the war. He wanted to practise his English, I think.

The next day, Nash was taken by rail through the Ruhr, the area that had been so devastated just a few months before. As he stared out at the bleak landscapes created by the bombing he'd participated in, Nash was the recipient of an act of kindness that would have a profound impact on him after the war.

In the carriage was my guard sitting at the side of me, a middle-aged man from the Luftwaffe. We were at Essen changing trains and there was no place on the train. Yet I got the carriage to myself. The guard said we'd let some people on. In came three women dressed in black, obviously in mourning. I can remember this man standing at the window shaking his fist at me with rage. I remember this man looking at me and spitting on the floor. We went through an area where our chaps had obviously raided the night before, and I felt very embarrassed. I think the Germans cleared up the debris as quickly as we did, but there was an arm or a leg sticking out. Were these women going to start cursing me amidst these ruins? I was looking very dishevelled, hair all over the place; I'd got a beard and was dirty. I think it helped those women take pity on me. Suddenly, one of them plunged her hand into a big black bag and took out a piece of bread. With the agreement of the other two women, she offered me the bread. The guard said '*Nein*!' and I didn't get my bread. The gesture of these three women changed my attitude to war and to the German people, although not until years later.

Harold Nash's bid to evade capture had ended in failure, but the maps printed on silk scarves that were part of an airman's escape kit did help hundreds of men to avoid spending the rest of the war as POWs. Sixty years on, Maurice Flower still has his map, and it's in perfect condition, with a plan of Germany on one side, and the Nazi-occupied countries of mainland Europe on the other. If airmen were captured, they could soak the scarf in water and wash out the ink, leaving them with a plain white scarf. Flower never had reason to use his silk map, but a gunner from his squadron did after being shot down over Berlin, and made a bold escape from Germany.

He said he couldn't sleep in daylight, so he used to sleep at night and walk during the day. He turned his battle blouse inside out and that's how he walked back, taking about four months. When he came to the Rhine one Sunday afternoon, he needed two pfennigs to get across the bridge. We used to be given money, but it was all in notes and he didn't have any change. There was a German officer striding along the towpath with two soldiers, and he noticed as he passed all the sentries were saluting him so he fell in behind him and he marched across the bridge behind this officer and didn't have to pay his money! But due to that experience, they started to give us small change as well as the big notes. He was walking along the road. There was a farmer in a field who'd left his bike at the roadside, so he pinched his bike and he rode through the Siegfried Line. The sentry was talking to two girls at this border post so he rode on to the footpath; through the gate, past this sentry!

Having escaped the Reich, the gunner came through Spain, and presented himself at the British Embassy in Madrid. The Germans had men hovering around the embassy, waiting for escapees, and those last 50 yards into the embassy had the reputation of being the most dangerous part of the whole trip, but the airman got through.

When Leonard Miller landed in a forest after baling out of his Lancaster, his first emotion was one of anger at having been caught out by a fighter. It was absolutely pitch black, but Miller quickly realised that he was hanging in his parachute harness from a tree, upside down.

I had to swing myself towards where I thought the trunk was. I grabbed the trunk, which I could feel in the dark, and followed all the instructions about letting go your 'chute harness and falling out of a tree. So I gripped the trunk like mad and slid down ever so slowly. But I was only about two feet off the ground which I couldn't see at all in the dark! I sat there for a minute and had a laugh. You had to at that stage. I could hear water running and found a stream near by where I had a drink. Then I walked down the stream, away from the area in case they had dogs. I kept on going until I found a holly bush, which is a very good place to hide, being hollow inside.

Miller had come well prepared for an escape. As well as his standard RAF escape kit, he had large pockets sewn inside a set of overalls which he wore over his flying suit, where he had stashed extra chocolate and malt tablets. In the seams were small bar magnets so he could make a compass. In fact, he could see the Pole Star clearly, and was able to make his way by following the night sky. Miller had seen two of his crew mates come down on their parachutes, so he hoped they would be safe. As his aircraft had crashed some way off in another wood and was burning, he knew he had to get away from the general area as soon as possible to avoid the Germans, who would be searching for its crew.

Once I'd got away from the area, I was on the road. The first instinct is to go across the fields to keep off the roads but that's wrong because you don't move very quickly through a field. So I kept to the road and came to a small village. Ahead of me was a German on a bicycle, with his helmet on his back and gas mask. He called in at a cottage and left the bike outside by the kerb. So I nipped on the bike quickly and cycled off quick as I could, riding south, because I could see the Alps in the distance. At the same time, I was looking out for an airfield in case there were any aircraft I could pinch to get home. I wasn't going to walk if I could help it! And if you got home in a German aircraft with all their latest equipment and radar, it would have been a plus for us. As I was going along, I was throwing rocks at the telephone wires and all the electrical installations hanging down, scoring quite a good lot of hits. I thought, I'll do as much damage as I can!

Miller kept on cycling south. As he was still wearing the rather grubby overalls he had first had as an engineer over his RAF uniform, nobody took any notice of him. He even cycled through major towns without being questioned. Then having crossed into occupied France, he was stopped. 'The town was Mulhouse, on the Rhine farther south, nearly on the Swiss border. I was stopped by a German officer wanting to know where Grossman's Platz was. I don't know German but I understood his interrogation and "Platz" and said, "Yah, yah," and pointed across the road at another road. Off he went and left me to it!'

From that point, Miller cycled like mad to get out of the town. By now he was eager to get to the Swiss border, where he could cross to safety. He knew from the barbed wire that he'd reached it.

The barbed wire separated this village in two halves. I thought there might be a guard's point so I had to be very careful. I ditched my bike and walked back out of the town, following the wire into the countryside. When I got out there, the fence was about three metres high and four wide with sloping phalanxes of wire up each side. It was bright moonlight, so I was sitting in the shade of a tree. A guard came along the fence and stopped on the other side of the tree, and I thought, Ready for a fight now. But he was just peeing on the other side of the tree and off he went. I thought, Get over this fence quick! Where I was positioned with this tree, the sapling growing through the wire, I was able to walk up the wire and stand on the top of the first post. I could see the tops of the other posts, ran across them and dived off the end of the last post into Switzerland.

Leonard Miller had made it into neutral territory. He was found by a Swiss guard, who interrogated him and sent him to a holding camp in Switzerland. From there he crossed into France, worked with the French resistance and finally returned to London in September 1944, five months after he'd been shot down. Remarkably, Miller's wartime flying career was not yet over. Back in Britain, he retrained as a Mosquito pilot, and completed a couple of operations on Mosquitoes just before the end of the war.

After being shot down over Dusseldorf in April 1944, Tom Wingham was reported missing. Once again, his crew had been victims of *schräge musik*, two of the crew killed as the aircraft crashed. Like so many other next of kin, his mother received the usual, rather officious, telegram to report the fact. It must have been a terrible ordeal for any parent to read such a bleak, impersonal and rather cold communication. Nor was there much comfort to be had from the fact that final knowledge of an airman's fate remained speculative; 'missing in action' all too rarely meant 'still alive'. 'Regret to inform you that your son Sydney Thomas Wingham failed to return from an operational flight against the enemy on the night of 22nd/23rd April 1944 STOP Letter follows STOP Any further information received will be communicated to you immediately STOP Pending receipt of written notification from the Air Ministry no information should be given to the press STOP Officer Commanding, No. 76 Squadron.'

It is a rather extraordinary experience to read the telegram, and the collection of letters of sympathy sent to Wingham's mother, sixty years later, as he describes how he survived the attack and spent five months on the run before returning home.

I got myself down into Belgium and I then went back to Holland with the Dutch police. The Dutch police were a bit dubious about coming to my rescue because the woman I'd contacted was the most notorious gossip for miles around and he was a bit worried about that! When I got there, it was the beginning of May and there was a ban put on movement by London of all aircrew. The bombing had made life very difficult for the Germans in France, smashing all the railways, so it took too long and was too dangerous going through France. So I was stuck in this house for seven weeks initially. It was a peculiar situation because I was sleeping in the second bedroom of the house, and the husband didn't know I was there. I often asked people what would happen if he found me. They said he'd probably tell me to go. Wouldn't he tell the Germans? No. Then why wouldn't he let me stay? Ah, he's neither for the Germans nor against the Germans, neither for the English nor against the English.

The husband may have kept quiet, but someone had raised the Gestapo's suspicions that there was someone hidden in the house. One day, while Wingham was on his own and about to listen to a BBC programme on the wireless, there was a squeal of brakes followed by the hurried footsteps of a Gestapo officer. Wingham sat by the front door as the officer approached.

There was bashing at both the back and front doors. The idea was that in the event of a raid, I was to get out of the bedroom window at the side of the house and go up into the woods. I went upstairs and opened the shutters only to find there was a Gestapo guy on the outside, trying to get in. I thought, That's it, I've had it. However, I rushed downstairs, where I thought there was a cellar, although I'd never been down there before. I found the cellar, all dark, solid concrete steps going down, nowhere to hide, a few beer crates around. I could hear them by this time in the upstairs room. Suddenly I was conscious that at the back of these solid concrete steps there was an alcove, about four feet high, about the width of my shoulders. So I piled up two piles of beer crates, hurriedly got in here and pulled the crates up to the concrete. As I did that a couple of Gestapo came down. You always had to have luck with you, and it was summer so they hadn't brought any torches. They walked round the cellar and came right up to these beer crates. I could see them through it, striking matches, but they decided the bird had flown and left me!

It was only later that Wingham discovered how his cover had been blown.

After a couple of weeks in the house, somebody had wanted to have a chat with me about joining the White Brigade. I agreed to see him. It was just after D-Day and he told me they were forming the White Brigade in the Ardennes in the event of prolonged fighting. Would I join them? I felt it was far better to have a .303 in my hand and in the open than be tied up in a house so I agreed. What I didn't know was that this guy had two mistresses, one of whom was of German extraction. About that time he dumped her. He'd talked a lot to her about his activities, and kept a book with names, so she went to the Gestapo and lodged information about him. They picked him up, extracted all the information, and came round chasing up all the places that he'd got listed. I was in one of them. So it was a case of the old story of a woman scorned.

Tom Wingham would finally make it back to Britain, where he too would resume his operational flying career.

For those crews who had completed their bombing runs, and survived everything the target area had to throw at them, there was still the journey back to base to complete. It was always a relief for Alan Bryett to be on the way home.

Once you'd left the target at twenty thousand feet, in general terms you stayed at height over Germany, but once you started coming over Denmark or France you were losing height. As you were losing height, you were going faster and by the time you were coming over the North Sea, you were preparing to land. You had your oxygen masks on the whole time and there were oxygen plugs all the way through so as you walked down the aircraft, for example to go to the toilet, you plugged in the thing. You had to have oxygen if you were more than ten thousand feet and if you didn't have oxygen you began to lose your efficiency. So if an aircraft was badly damaged and lost its oxygen, you would have a worry there.

With the adrenalin of the bomb run subsiding, this was when the tiredness, boredom and cold could set in for a crew. Yet they were still vulnerable, and it was vital for gunners such as Ricky Dyson not to slacken off in their searches of the dark skies surrounding them. 'On the way back, you had to be more alert than ever because there was always a chance that you're going to be jumped by fighters. So no crew really relaxed on the home leg.'

The flying might be made all the harder if the aircraft had been hit by Flak or forced to corkscrew to avoid a fighter during the operation. Navigator Bill Burke was sympathetic towards those crews that ran into difficulties on their way back from the target, perhaps getting lost. 'I never got lost myself. But if an aircraft had been attacked by a fighter and thrown about the skies, they'd head off in any direction to escape and then there were cases when an aircraft had been attacked and the gyro compass might have been blown out of operation.'

It was when the aircraft had crossed the enemy coastline once again that many crews finally opened the flask of coffee that was part of their flying ration. For Tom Wingham, the journey back was also the time to take the 'Wakey-wakey' Benzedrine pills that bomber crews were issued with. 'I never used mine until after we'd bombed because I always felt that was when you needed them most. On your way back, you were relaxed and it would be easy to nod off, so that's when I used to have my coffee and Wakey-wakey pills; most of my crew used to do the same.'

Yet even once the crew were past the enemy's coastline, a safe landing was still far from guaranteed. It was a lesson Burke learned on his own station.

Your final hurdle was the enemy coast where they shot at you again and then you're thinking, I am going to make it. All is well, you're over the Channel and you knew you were safe, but in actual fact you were not safe, because when you got back to the aerodrome you'd have something like thirty-five aircraft milling around and that was dangerous because all of them wanted to get down on the ground as soon as possible. I remember when I was operating out of Spilsby, two of our aircraft collided. Both aircraft were destroyed, fourteen aircrew killed.

Maurice Flower witnessed another accident as his crew came in to land after one raid. 'A Halifax landed on top of a Mosquito. The Mosquito had just landed and the Halifax didn't see him and he touched right on top and the cockpit of the Mosquito came up between the inboard engine and the fuselage of the Halifax and so both pilots were sort of looking at each other!'

It wasn't just accidents among the bombers which aircrew had to be wary of once they were back over their own territory. The danger from the Luftwaffe's fighters was not yet over. 'The Germans sent over intruders who'd get into the bomber stream, position themselves against an aerodrome, wait for a Lancaster to be about to land with its flaps and undercarriage down, so it was really defenceless, and then just move in and blow it out of the air. So it was only when you got two feet on the ground that you were really safe.'

It must have been so easy to be complacent. After ten hours in the air, how many young aircrew would be sufficiently conscientious to be fully alert in those last minutes in the air? The need to remain vigilant to the very end of the trip became apparent to Alan Bryett only when he witnessed one particularly terrifying fighter attack over a bomber station.

The Germans were very brave and would send in a Dornier. No one would look carefully on the way home and the Dornier would actually circle while the other aeroplanes were trying to get in, and they would shoot a bomber down. On one occasion we got back to our aerodrome near Bridlington and one of our own aeroplanes was circling to land, and suddenly the pilot shouted out to the control tower, 'We're being shot at! There's an enemy in the circuit somewhere, for goodness sake do something!' It was the most terrifying thing I've ever heard in my life.

As he prepared to land after one trip, Maurice Flower and his crew had to unexpectedly divert to another aerodrome at the very last minute.

When you came back and you were maybe one of five or six aeroplanes all coming back to the same station, you used to try to get the first call in. First call was first man in the queue. We came into the circuit one night; there were seven aircraft in the circuit. They put the runway lights on. They didn't put them on until you came into the circuit and then you were told to put on your navigation lights. Up to that time you'd been in total darkness. Suddenly this Junkers Ju-88 came from somewhere and he shot four down in the circuit. We tore away and landed at North Creake, a few miles away, shivering. We stayed there until daylight and then came back to our own airfield. All the crews were lost in those four aeroplanes. That was thirty-two men, quite a tragedy.

Such attacks were terrifying, and there was no chance for the pilot to perform an evasive manoeuvre as he could at 20,000 feet. Terrifying not just because seeing a fellow bomber crew being shot down was always terrifying; it was compounded by the irony of it happening right over your own base, your place of safety. It was bad enough encountering the danger when you'd flown hundreds of miles into enemy territory, but unbearable when the threat followed you back home. For Leonard Miller it was one final possible distraction just as he came in to land, one of the moments of an operation which was in any case most demanding for the pilot.

You picked up the code of your airfield from the top of the control tower, which used to flash the code letters for the airfield and you know you were home. So you used to join the circuit or call up to the watchtower and get your circuit order. Once you were in the circuit you knew you were home and dry, almost. But I never let up even then, because that's when you're most vulnerable. You're coming in at a very low speed over the edge of the airfield and that's when the night fighters pounced. You're unmanoeuvrable; you can't get away from it. It's a big sigh of relief when you touch down and hear the squeal of the tyres on the tarmac.

Such last-minute fighter attacks were thankfully rare enough. For Ricky Dyson, as the bomber ground to a halt on the runway at the end of another operation, there was the comfort of finally having landed. 'You were grateful to be back. Some people kissed the ground when they got out of the aircraft. It was a great relief to get back home safely. It never occurred to you that you were going to be killed the next night.'

Finally, the crew could get out of their turrets and seats. After all those hours, there's no surprise about what Leonard Miller remembers happening next. 'I think everybody wanted to have a pee! Then you cleared out all your parachute and gear that you had with you and your flight bag and made your way to the waiting transport. If there was a WAAF driver that you liked, you used to cheer and whistle!'

Before they could relax, all aircrew had a debriefing, a meticulous recording of every detail of every operation. It must have seemed a tedious affair. Leonard Miller went through the routine time after time.

Debriefing was in a big room where the intelligence people were. They had separate tables all round the room and you were designated to each table as a crew and you reported what you saw and did to the intelligence officer. He made a record of that and of course he in turn was collecting all this information from other crews as well, so they could formulate how successful the raid was, how concentrated it was and how effective the enemy's defences had been.

Debriefing was one of the few unchanging elements throughout the bombing campaign. It had been as important when Robert Kee was flying operations as it was at the end of the war. 'They took details of what you thought had happened. You told them whether you thought you'd hit the target, or if you'd bombed on ETA, that sort of thing. Then you went to bed, and the next few days you'd be leading the same sort of life as before, going to the pub, going to the cinema, being with friends, getting a bit plastered sometimes, and then a few days later you might be on operations again.'

Often the intelligence officers were members of the WAAF, and on Tom Wingham's squadron there was a treat for the crews as they reported back on the raid.

Sometimes you'd have to wait for an intelligence officer but there was always coffee laced with rum, usually administered by the padre. He'd be running around with a bottle, topping your coffee up with it. The intelligence officer would have a set number of questions, in particular the trip out, any new guns or new sightings of defences, any observation of aircraft shot down on the way, any observation of anything else that had any effect, such as the positioning of Pathfinder markers, and then of course the time, heading and speed of when you were bombing. Your review of what had taken place at the target, whether it was accurate or not, whether the disposition of the markers was concentrated or spread out and anything to do with the success or otherwise of the raid were all asked about.

The records that Adge Boal remembers his crew keeping during the operation itself would prove invaluable during debriefing. 'The navigator had to log almost everything that happened. If we were attacked by a fighter, he'd have to log it with the time. He would have to log any Flak that was seen, along with a note of the intensity, and that would all be discussed. They would compare what our navigators said with every other log, so they got a pretty good idea of what the German defences were and what tactics they were using.'

With debriefing out of the way, the next item on the agenda was one part of the operational routine that every airman had been looking forward to, probably for several hours. They may have taken flying rations with them, but it was the breakfast waiting for them when they got back which Robin Murray enjoyed. 'The one good thing about being aircrew was breakfast because you always had bacon and eggs and fried bread and anything else that was going, whereas that was a luxury in those days. The breakfasts were always something to look forward to, you know, when you got back.'

After the reserved, nervous atmosphere of the briefings and pre-operation meals, Leonard Miller remembers an entirely different mood at breakfast. 'It was all swapping of stories. I think it was a lot of bluff about "What I did" and "What I didn't do"! There was always a competition between the crews, how many crews did this many ops, and who was going to be the next to have done thirty. There were long trestle tables in the mess, and everybody was chattering at the same time. The WAAFs used to bring round your tea.'

As the crews celebrated their own successes, there was also the dawning realisation that other crews hadn't made it. Miller remembers checking what had happened to the rest of the squadron during the intelligence debriefing. 'You used to ask, "Is so and so back?" and they would say, "Yes," or "No, but he's still missing, not reported in yet." You had it at the back of your mind that they probably wouldn't get back.'

By the time breakfast was being served, these absences were all the more potent. There was always that parting optimism, 'See you at breakfast', between the crews, but now some of the crews weren't there. Of course, there was still the chance that the other crews would turn up late, or that they had been diverted to other stations because of the weather, or had made emergency landings after Flak damage. Ron Pitt would look at the board to see who hadn't returned. 'You'd know the ones that were missing as we had a battle order and they'd put up the time of landing for the crews that came back. Then you'd get messages if they'd landed at another aerodrome. You'd soon know about crews not coming back, because you knew the amount of petrol they had, so if they couldn't get any farther, you knew they wouldn't be coming back.'

As the minutes ticked by, no news was bad news. By now, the missing crews' whereabouts would be known if they were going to return. The crews would go off to sleep desperately hoping that these last stragglers would have come back by the time they woke up, but knowing that the chances were increasingly slim. The only hope would be that the individuals had survived their aircraft crashing and were POWs. It was that hope which kept the airmen going. They must have known it was largely a delusion, but it was another shield against the harsh reality of Bomber Command's losses. Such concerns in other circumstances might have kept airmen awake, but after an exhausting trip Tom Wingham had little problem sleeping. 'After breakfast, we'd be very happy to turn in, get to bed and forget things until we woke up the next day. One always slept well; normally you were quite tired because you'd had to concentrate. Sometimes you did wake up the next day to find that you had to get over to the briefing room because you were expected to be flying again, but that didn't happen too often.'

The Nissen huts could tell their own stories, though. Usually two crews shared a hut, and there was no disguising the sight of empty beds, which could mean only one thing: their occupants had not returned. The losses became achingly personal. The service police would come and discreetly gather together all their belongings. Little was said, but everyone knew. Still, the hope that they'd survived and been captured lingered. It would be weeks before confirmation either way would leak back to Britain. By then the survivors would themselves have long moved on to other bases, or become casualties themselves. No wonder that many would have to wait years after the war before they finally discovered what had happened to their squadron colleagues. Bill Burke had a belated pleasant surprise.

The worst experience of all is when your crew share a hut with another crew and that other crew don't come back. We were great mates with a crew who didn't come back in that fashion and we just assumed that they'd died. After the war we discovered they had a remarkable experience. They had been badly damaged over a target somewhere in the Baltic, and were limping home. They got across Denmark, flying on two engines in daylight, when a Focke-Wulf Fw-190 came up behind them. They thought, This is it, he wants another one for his victories. In actual fact there was a lot of mutual respect, you see, with the Luftwaffe and vice versa. The pilot drew alongside them, pointed down and they ditched, and as they were ditching he gave them the thumbs-up sign. But you didn't know that when they went missing.

In the meantime, losses had to be dealt with in a matter-of-fact, unemotional fashion. 'You really mentally equip yourself not to become involved in deep sorrow when a crew didn't come back. It's not possible to do that if you're going to do thirty operations, when the likelihood is you're going to lose a crew on virtually every operation. You've just got to accept that that's going to happen to you.'

That's another reason why the camaraderie in the crews was so important. It wasn't just that they had to work together as a team. They stuck together for emotional security. If they were shot down, at least they'd all be shot down together. The atmosphere in the squadrons had changed as the war progressed. In the early years there'd been relatively few people flying on operations, and it was all about the spirit in the squadron. By the end many more airmen were flying, but there was an unspoken knowingness and consequent aloofness in the squadrons; now it was about the camaraderie within the crews. The apparently lively spirit of the squadron had become a transient, rather fragile mood, as Tom Wingham admits.

There was an emotional cut-off where people unconsciously isolated themselves from what was going on. As a crew you knew that you were fireproof, that you were going to survive, but you realised that there would be places missing in the mess next morning. Relatives ask me what it was like on a squadron during the war and I have to say, 'Yes, I knew your relative but I didn't *know* him.' You knew people in your crew. You sat and ate and drank with many other people on the squadron but you never *knew* them and you never got too close to them. You never knew what had happened to them because by the time information came through, you'd probably finished with your tour so they were people you just passed in the night.

Like most airmen, Peter Baker never doubted that he would complete his tour. 'We weren't really aware of the dangers and yet we knew the crews were going missing. Relatively few of us got through a tour, but we all expected to. It wouldn't happen to us. There's the old story of the group photograph and the squadron leader saying, "Take a look to your left and look to your right because you probably won't get a chance to see them again." It was that sort of atmosphere.'

The losses were also hard for the ground staff and WAAFs. They had made their own sacrifices: 1,479 of the male ground staff were killed during the war, and ninety-one WAAFs, usually following crashes or attacks at bomber stations. Some of the ground staff died as temporary aircrew, deputising as flight engineers, and a further fifty-two served time as POWs. It was the losses among the bomber crews which affected them more frequently, though. They too tried to create an emotional distance between themselves and the aircrews they worked with. The ground staff were invariably loyal, and they'd always be there to greet the returning crews, and ask them about the operation, but they also knew that the day might well come when that aircrew didn't return. Ricky Dyson had experienced it for himself as ground staff in the early part of the war, watching the crews go out and only a few aircraft limp home. 'It was pretty grim. Six went out, only two returned. Or a squadron went out and out of twelve aircraft, you only got, say, eight back.'

Experiencing the crews not returning only made the airmen even more edgy. There were cases of suicide, and suspected suicide. The superstitions grew stronger. Wireless operator Jim Rogers flew his last few operations as a 'spare bod', rather than with a regular crew. He was careful which crews he flew with, however.

> There were one or two occasions when I refused to fly with a crew. I used to get strong feelings about different crews. I would go to the wing commander and say, 'I don't wish to fly with that crew.' He'd ask, 'If I was to order you to, would you?' 'No. That's how strongly I feel about it.' I did that on two occasions, and each time the crew was shot down. I don't know whether it was a sixth sense but I felt I'd done enough trips to warrant some kind of say about who I was flying with.

Sixth sense or not, Rogers witnessed the psychological effects on a fellow wireless operator from the squadron who also used to fly as a spare, often accompanying the wing commander.

> We used to have what we used to call the 'acc room', where you put your accumulators on charge, which was on the perimeter. I was going out to the perimeter when I saw this chap coming out of the acc room looking very ill. Something wasn't right with him, so I said, 'What's the problem? You're not looking very well.' He replied, 'You'll never believe me,' and I said, 'Well, try.' Then he told me that while he was in the acc room, he had felt a door open and turned round, and standing in the doorway was his pilot, who was killed a year ago. I told him he must be hallucinating, but he said, no, he'd told him the target for tonight. This chap said that a year previously he had gone sick when they were going on a trip to a target in the Ruhr, and this pilot said to him, 'You're going there tonight and you'll be joining me.' I couldn't believe it. He told me the target was

Duisburg. Sure enough, when we went into briefing, it was the target and he was shot down that night with the wing commander.

There was a whole language for dealing with the death of aircrew. Nobody was 'killed' as such. Instead there were euphemisms, such as 'Charlie got the chop'. 'Johnson had a prang' meant that he'd had a crash. The Ruhr, which was so heavily defended, was called 'Happy Valley'. It was another way of avoiding the harsh truths of squadron life, as Bill Burke explains. 'Aircrew tended to have a range of vocabulary of their own. You never said anybody was "killed", that was too realistic. They'd "gone for a Burton" or "gone in" or "got the chop". A good attack would be a "wizard prang" or a "wizard show". This vocabulary was all very schoolboyish but you've got to remember that so many of the aircrew were little more than schoolboys.'

Towards the end of the war, Burke could see the unspoken strain in the aircrews as he looked around his squadron.

H. E. Bates was a very popular writer of the time, and he said that he'd gone into an aircrew mess and felt he'd wandered into a gathering of sixth-form boys who were prematurely aged. The thing that struck him most of all was their eyes, the way that this premature ageing had taken place. It was undoubtedly true. The thirty-trip tour evolved because Bomber Command decided that an average person could not tolerate more than thirty trips without suffering some degree of psychiatric illness. But that built up and you found guys who went entirely Flak happy. That was when the nervous tension and strains had reached the degree where people couldn't control their behaviour properly and would act in highly abnormal manners. They weren't of sound mind, and some had to be taken off flying. But the general thing was you developed things like a tic in the eye or a twitch. I had such a terrible twitch, I had difficulty in lighting a cigarette by the end of my tour.

No wonder some sought refuge in the bottle. Robin Murray admits he was among them. 'We were heavy drinkers on the squadron and after the war, there's no doubt about that. After the war years, I got in with a crowd of people who were heavy drinkers and I got the shakes. I realised if I didn't give it up, I wasn't going to be much good to anybody.'

Occasional stories emerged of airmen who had lost control of their alcohol consumption altogether. Maurice Flower remembers a case on his squadron. 'We had a rear gunner, who unfortunately was an alcoholic. They came back from a trip and the crew got out and were getting on the bus when they realised they were missing their rear gunner. They went to the turret and turned it round and he fell out. He was still drunk and he'd been drunk and asleep the whole trip.'

Admittedly such extreme cases were incredibly rare.

The beer was very weak in those days, I think it was a gesture rather than an attempt to get drunk. You could drink an enormous amount of it without getting drunk and it wasn't on a regular basis that we went boozing. In fact we'd sometimes go down to the Unicorn and sit and talk to Old Ma and maybe just have one pint all night and just chat. It was just a little relief from the horrible billets we were in and the sea of mud that Foulsham was. It was a horrible place really to live in.

Eventually, for the lucky ones, that final thirtieth operation would dawn. The last trip was approached with almost as much apprehension as the first, although apprehension of a different sort. The crew were so close to reaching the magic number, they'd survived for so long against the odds, and yet the risks were just as high as during every other operation. Completing even five or six trips was daunting; by the time a crew had passed twenty they were usually getting tired and edgy. Yet there were still another *ten* operations to go. Jim Chapman was shot down on his thirtieth operation, and he certainly wasn't the only member of Bomber Command to suffer this ironic fate. Bill

Burke had hoped for an easy operation to complete his tour. The tension was more potent than ever as he waited for the curtain to be drawn back in the briefing room. 'All you wanted was a nice, easy trip, where you flew over the Channel, dropped some bombs on a coastal town and then came back. When we saw the curtain pulled back, and we saw how easy the target was, it was Royan, all the crew felt a great sense of relief. We knew that we'd got through the tour, unscathed.'

Having conquered his anxieties, just about, Arthur Smith must have been looking forward to completing his tour more than most. He had reached his thirtieth operation, although at that time the Air Ministry had temporarily extended the length of the tour, so he knew he hadn't quite got there yet. As the crew took off for another night-time raid over Germany, a terrible accident would ensure that his thirtieth raid would be his last after all.

> After taking off, we were circling to gain height, and there was a bang from one of the engines. The starboard outer had caught fire. The pilot operated the switch to activate the fire extinguisher to put the fire out, but we only had three engines. We had a full bomb load; we hadn't even started, so we decided we'd better turn back. We tried to land. The first time we couldn't, the pilot didn't line up properly on three engines, so we went round again. The second time he was lined up but the aircraft wouldn't lose height properly. Suddenly we crashed. The next memory is scrabbling through the front of the aircraft. I got out, and one or two people got out with me. The flight engineer was yelling blue murder. He was caught by his flying boot in some flaming wreckage. We managed to get him out. We all got by a tree and realised two were missing. By this time the whole aircraft was a mass of flames, with ammunition going off, and the petrol tanks exploding. We couldn't get near it.

Smith's crew had barely got beyond the aerodrome, but there was nothing the emergency trucks could do. The wireless operator and rear air gunner were both killed. Smith was badly burnt, and spent the next three weeks in a convalescent home waiting for his injuries to heal. Then he had to pay one last visit to his squadron base.

> By that time, none of the rest of the crew were there. Two had been killed, the others had moved on. I had to go back to my Nissen hut, collect my kit, and the most harrowing part was walking into the Nissen hut completely empty, knowing two of them had been killed, to collect my stuff. No one had been in it since we left. It was dusty on the floor, a joke notice I'd put up had torn off and was lying on the floor, and that was the worst part of it.

There was the inevitable feeling of relief when Maurice Flower had completed his tour of thirty ops. His crew had also had to turn back shortly after take-off, owing to electrical failure, but they had managed to get back to their aerodrome. The flight commander asked the crew whether they still wanted to go. They did and took another aircraft out and returned to complete the tour. As his Canadian crew mates returned to their homes in Canada, Flower was sorry to see them go, but he had no desire to fly with another crew. Nevertheless, he felt not only elation at completing the tour, but also a sense that they had contributed something valuable to the war effort. 'The man in charge of 100 Group was Air Vice-Marshall Addison, and he was very effective at spreading the good news. Periodically he would send a letter round, saying due to our efforts we have had so many less attacks by German fighters and things like that. It did give you a sense of achievement, that we were doing something that was worthwhile and it was going to end the war.'

With the tour completed, airmen were entitled to a six-month rest period – resting from front-line operations, that is. They were still active members of the RAF, and 'resting' generally involved a period in the training schools, passing on their knowledge to the next intake of bomber crews. Some, including Adge

Boal, were transferred to Transport Command, or sent overseas to fly with the armed forces in the other theatres of war. After carrying bombs to Germany, Boal found himself ferrying anything 'from cabbages to people' around the Middle East, North Africa and the Indian subcontinent. He was proud that Bomber Command had continued taking the war to Germany when no one else could, and happy that, now that they had helped pave the way for D-Day, the army could get in and finish the war. Jim Rogers was dispatched to an Operational Training Unit in Abingdon, but it was then that the strain and mental fatigue from a tour of duty set in.

> I found as I was training crews that I was getting nervous. I was showing signs of nerves with trainee crews because 'sprog crews' did so many silly things. At times I'd find myself feeling for my parachute, so in the end the medical officer sent me to the RAF hospital at Horton to be assessed. They took me off flying completely and I was sent on an administration course to become the assistant adjutant for No. 75 Squadron at Mepal.

Not everyone was so relieved to get to the end of their tour. When Leonard Miller had been shot down, it had been on his thirty-second operation. 'We normally did thirty ops but I stayed on because some of my crew hadn't completed thirty ops. We were still in a crew all together and the loyalty was such that we didn't want to get split up. We were like brothers and you feel you have a great responsibility.'

Peter Baker had also allowed his first tour to be prolonged. 'I loved flying and I liked the excitement. I enjoyed the friendships of the squadron although they got less and less as I did more and more trips. We were operating at full capacity so nobody noticed I'd completed my thirty and I did four more. I suppose I did know but I began to lose count. I remember putting the thirty-fourth in my logbook and being a bit surprised that I'd done thirty-four on the squadron.'

It was only then that the squadron commander, who signed

the logbooks, also noticed. Baker also went off to an OTU, at Pershore, as an instructor, from where he also took part in the Thousand Bomber Raids. Now commissioned, Baker soon found himself signed up for a second tour of operations. 'The chief flying instructor asked me to go back with him. I was honoured. He selected four of the instructors to go back with him and we all went. I was very glad to go back to squadron life.'

It seems extraordinary to the contemporary mind that, having been through everything a first tour had to offer, any airman would offer to go through yet another twenty operations, the standard duration of a second tour on heavy bomber squadrons. Many did, though. 'It was a very glamorous life in some ways. It was very dangerous but you had a whole range of privileges. Aircrew got some petrol, you could have a car. You got leave every six weeks, you got flying pay. There was the feeling that Bomber Command was a *corps d'élite*. You could get hooked to some extent to the danger; you wanted the adrenalin to run and the relief which comes after it.'

After completing his first tour, Bill Burke also found himself missing operations. It had been a peculiar, exhausting, deadly dangerous, frightening experience, but he still didn't want to go to a job as an instructor in Training Command. He initially volunteered to be a navigator on fighters attacking enemy shipping, thinking it would be an easier life. He was refused, though, and was assigned to fly on Mosquitoes instead. Tom Wingham also flew as a navigator on Mosquitoes when he finally returned from Europe after evading capture. It had been on Wingham's second tour that he'd been shot down, but now his experience of living in enemy-occupied countries had only deepened his resolve to rejoin Bomber Command. 'I still felt I owed the Germans a thing or two. When I got back to this country, the most difficult thing was trying to get across to people the difference between living in freedom and living with an occupying force in your country.'

In the final months of the war, Bomber Command was larger

than ever. Thousands of volunteers coming through the training schools were joined by the many airmen completing second, even third, tours. As the invasion forces advanced the liberation across Europe, Bomber Command would be part of a last push to victory.

11

The Long March

'The destruction of Dresden remains a serious query against
the conduct of Allied bombing.'

Winston Churchill, 28 March 1945

John Whiteley standing in front of his Lancaster ready for
his next sortie.

The policy of area bombing was always going to be contro-versial, flying as it did in the face of all prior notions of the proprieties of aerial combat. It would be the raids conducted by Bomber Command in the final months of the war, however, after the outcome had ceased to be in any real doubt, which would fuel the angry debate about bombing that has continued to this day. It's easy to see why. In the period after D-Day, the Nazis may not have admitted it, but they were in retreat. Paris was liberated on 24 August 1944; the Allies entered Belgium in early September; by the end of the month, the first American troops had reached Germany itself. By this point the only question was when the war would be over, not who was going to win it. Bomber Com-mand had redirected its operational methods in the run-up and during the immediate aftermath of D-Day, concentrating on missions in direct support of the invasion and the land-borne forces. By the autumn, however, the bombers were not needed by the Allied armies for such direct assistance for so much of the time. As soon as he could, Harris reverted to his earlier strategy, raining destruction down on German cities, and their civilian populations.

The statistics make sobering reading. In the last three months of 1944, a larger weight of bombs would be dropped by Bomber Command than during the whole of 1943. In August 1943, the bomber forces had dropped 20,149 tons of bombs. It had been the highest monthly total so far in the war, and would remain the highest monthly total until April 1944, when preparations for Overlord were at their height. In the summer of 1944, the monthly totals rose sharply. In August, 65,855 tons of bombs were dropped. After that, the monthly totals fall back a bit, but never revert to the levels of 1943, the year of the Battles of the Ruhr, Hamburg and the start of the Battle of Berlin. The month with the heaviest bomb drops was yet to come. In March 1945, 67,637 tons of bombs were dropped by Bomber Command, now almost entirely over Germany. In fact, 46 per cent of the total tonnage of bombs dropped during the entire war by Bomber Command fell in the last nine months of the conflict. Yet surely the war was as good as over by then?

If Harris's reputation was to be permanently tarred by these statistics, it was to be further sullied by a debate that opened up even at the time about the use of the bombing forces. It would result in a bitter divide between Harris's headquarters and the Air Ministry, and stretch Portal's long-standing support of Harris to its limit. Portal and his colleagues in the Air Ministry wanted the crews to concentrate on targeting Germany's synthetic oil production plants. The Reich, after all, was desperately short of oil, and a sustained offensive here could leave the Wehrmacht and the Luftwaffe unable to continue, as well, of course, as avoiding the charge of civilian casualties. Such was their oil crisis that trainee German pilots were being trained on simulators, rather than fuel-guzzling real aircraft.

Pressure came too from the Allied commanders on the ground in Europe, urging Harris to bomb German transportation systems, to help the liberating armies' advance across France and the Low Countries. Harris, though, remained intransigent; the only targets he considered valid and valuable remained German cities. He saw no reason to be deflected from his main aim, the utter destruction of the German war machine through the pulverising of its civilian population. Harris was therefore dis-missive of the latest directive issued to Bomber Command on 1 November 1944, ordering the oil objective to be prioritised whenever weather conditions allowed. He dubbed them 'panacea targets', irritated by yet another directive for his command to change its strategy, yet another diversion from what he considered the bombers' principal function. Even as the war was reaching its final, bloody conclusion, he continued to send his squadrons again and again to the targets they had been pounding since the war's earliest days. He had promised to destroy the Reich single handed, and he was not about to stop trying now, not with final success so close.

Harris emerges uneasily from this debate, but to some extent he is judged unfairly. As throughout his career, he never held back in expressing his own opinion on any new policy, and was frequently a fierce and abrasive critic. Yet once a decision was taken, no matter how little he agreed with it, he would then follow it to the letter. Nor was his opposition to the policy simple bone-headed obstinacy. He remained only too aware that, despite the great advances in bombing technology now at his disposal, that old adversary the weather would still conspire against him. Under the heavy cloud that was abundant on so many nights, the levels of precision required by these oil targets remained simply unattainable to any reliable degree. Furthermore, despite his well-voiced reservations about the oil directive, Harris did send crews out to bomb as many synthetic oil production sites as possible, and as often as the conditions allowed. The records show that Bomber Command did in fact hit a large number of oil plants that winter, and often with great success, far more than Harris is generally given credit for. There were regular raids on transport and communication targets too: marshalling yards, airfields, railways, canals and shipping. It was in November 1944 that Lancasters drawn from Nos. 9, 617 and 463 Squadrons finally capsized the mighty German battleship the *Tirpitz*, blasting her with 12,000-pound Tallboy bombs, another innovation from Barnes Wallis. Hitler had called the *Tirpitz*, Germany's largest ship, 'the beast', her crews believed her to be unsinkable, and for years she'd been causing chaos for Allied shipping convoys, eluding the many attempts by both bombers and submarines to sink her. It was the ultimate moment of triumph in Bomber Command's prolonged battle against German shipping and U-boats, which over the course of the war had taken up to a quarter of the entire bombing effort.

So when the conditions were less favourable, the bomber force, now larger than ever, would carry on being dispatched to bomb German cities even in these final months of the war. For Harris, area bombing remained not only what his bombers were best equipped to do, but more importantly, even in the war's dying months, it remained as powerfully as ever *the* strategy most likely to bring the whole thing to a conclusion. Until the Germans capitulated, the war was still there to be won. For Harris, there was no halfway stage. In any case there was no one in power, not Portal, not even Churchill, powerful enough, or determined enough, to try to deter him. If there is a sense in which Harris was out of control that winter, it is balanced by a sense that, in their faltering indecision, his superiors condoned him.

Much of Germany's industry had, of course, already been destroyed; many of its cities were completely devastated. So while familiar targets continued to be visited by the bomber crews, Harris also continued his search for newer targets, ones that had hitherto escaped his attentions, even if their strategic importance remained questionable. Many of these were Germany's second-tier, medium-sized cities. They had been put on the list of targets compiled even before Harris had entered Bomber Command headquarters in 1942, but did that make bombing them at this late stage justifiable? Was this just a rerun of those earlier raids that had been mounted simply because they could be, like the attacks on Lübeck and Rostock? Darmstadt, for example, which had been the victim of several minor or failed raids, was virtually wiped out in September 1944. Clear weather conditions allowed an accurate raid in the city centre, and it's thought that as many as 12,000 people died out of a total population of 120,000. Was this the 'terror bombing' so angrily condemned by propaganda minister Goebbels? The city did have important railway communications passing through it, but it lacked major industries.

There was also the fact, of course, that by this stage in the war Bomber Command had acquired such a complement of men and machinery that after six years of continual combat there was a strategic momentum that made this type of bombing unstoppable, even if Harris had wanted to stop. Bomber Command had consumed a very considerable proportion of Britain's war expenditure, perhaps as much as a third. The crews could hardly be left idle now. By December 1944, the RAF had begun to cut back its vast training schemes, but this raised its own concerns. What if, as Churchill had warned was still possible, the war didn't finish in the next few months? Would there still be enough experienced crews to keep the bombing going for longer should it be necessary? The new crews were, of course, still pouring out of the OTUs, and new squadrons were still being formed to accommodate them. No. 186 Squadron, for example, was re-formed as late as October 1944 and would fly 1,254 operational sorties between then and the end of the war, dropping 5,773 tons of bombs and 12 tons of mines. Harry Smith, who had originally arrived at the Aircrew Reception Centre at Lord's cricket ground in 1943, was sent to No. 186 when he'd completed his training as a wireless operator. His first trip was to a synthetic oil plant at Kamen in February 1945, and later operations included Dortmund (also an oil target), Essen, Wesel, Kiel, Operation Manna and Operation Exodus.

As Bomber Command continued to grow, the largest raids got larger. In November 1944, Lancaster pilot John Whiteley led his crew on a major raid to Dusseldorf. Bomber Command sent out nearly a thousand aircraft that day. It was only Whiteley's fourth operation, and he was mesmerised by the experience of being in such a large bomber stream.

> I shall always remember this operation because there was Flak, there were night fighters, there were searchlights and quite frankly I hadn't got very much of a clue what was happening. As we got closer and closer, probably quarter of an hour from Dusseldorf, you could hear the master bomber marking the

target. We were about to run up to drop our bombs, when I suddenly saw these lights coming up. I asked the bomb aimer, 'Can you see those lights coming up?' and he replied, 'Don't be daft, Skipper, it's the target markers going down!' I hadn't got a clue. When I reoriented my sight, I realised it was the target markers going down. I never experienced that again but it was very uncomfortable at the time.

The bomber losses in the autumn and winter were considerably lower, proportionately at least, than they had been in the previous years of the war. The bombers were now simply overpowering the Luftwaffe's increasingly ragged defence system. The reality, however, was that this was a war that still had to be won. In hindsight, we may be tempted to think that after D-Day it was virtually all over bar the shouting, but that is not at all how it looked to the armies bogged down in the forests of the Ardennes during the Battle of the Bulge, Germany's great last counter-offensive, which caught the Allies completely off guard. It didn't look like that either to the advancing Red Army, which was still suffering simply astronomical losses at the hands of an army now comprising old men and boys, as well as Waffen SS veterans operating in small and lethal groups. Nor did the war look over to the 9,000 Allied troops who entered Arnhem, only 2,400 of whom would remain when the Allies were forced to withdraw towards the end of September 1944. To the Allies the prevailing view was simply that nothing short of total destruction would suffice to see the war finally end; the Germans would simply keep on rising out of the dirt until completely vanquished. The only way to ensure this happened would be to keep up the pressure, increase it even, right to the bitter end. In one sense they were right. The German armed forces had by now lost millions of men, yet still they kept going. The Luftwaffe was getting younger, and older, as a result of Hitler's conscription of an ever widening part of the Reich's male population. He was only sixteen at the time, but Horst Hirche had already been called up that August, and he was sent to join the Luftwaffe's anti-aircraft division.

I'd already left school and was an apprentice at the Signal Corps in Berlin. After 1944 it wasn't only high-school boys who were called up, but boys from technical schools were also enlisted to the anti-aircraft units. We were called up according to the years we were born. The apprentices who were born in 1928, high-school boys and grammar school boys who were born in 1926 and 1927 were called up. I hadn't expected to be called up as a Flak trainee, even though most of us already had some kind of military training because we'd been in the Hitler Youth. We were still rather surprised that we couldn't finish our training or our education. But that was not possible because the regular anti-aircraft personnel had been sent to the eastern front. This had already begun in 1943 and they were being replaced by Flak trainees.

The young trainee Flak gun operators continued to be indoctrinated with Nazi values in the regime's dying days.

We had a youth officer in every Flak battery. We were trained in recognising aeroplanes and we got political and military schooling. We were told, 'You are too weak and too few to be able to successfully fight off the many attacks but you have to shoot back so that the civilian population will see that there is resistance.' We took our duty very seriously and we were very competent. We were often praised by our superiors for our work. Our motto was that everybody had to give a hundred per cent and be able to do their job properly.

It was clear to Hirche that the defences against the bombers were not nearly as effective as they had been a year previously.

The attacking bombers did suffer some casualties. We did have some hits but very few. I can vividly remember on 18 March 1945, when we had two direct hits on the tower, that over thirty aircraft were badly damaged so we did have some kind of an effect, but it was minimal given the massive power we were up against. The Flak couldn't defend Berlin effectively. We were vastly outnumbered by the superior powers of both the Americans and the British bombers. During a large-scale attack there were sometimes a thousand aeroplanes or more if you included the escort in Berlin. We had a very narrow anti-aircraft belt in Berlin and these three anti-aircraft towers were the only ones equipped with the most modern guns. They could reach the necessary altitude but it was far too little to tackle this massive superpower. I only later found out about the damage and the hits we made. The Allies only suffered a tiny amount of damage.

Despite the German predicament, Hirche's determination to fight the Allies remained resolute.

We were not demoralised. We believed what we had been told for years about the wonder weapons that were still to come, that the war wasn't lost and to keep going. 'We will win the war' was the slogan that they bombarded us with constantly. I remember when I was still lying in the Luftwaffe hospital [after being injured], my battery commander visited me and I said to him, 'Lieutenant, when I am well again, I want to go back to my post.' That was how we had been educated and trained. Today I simply don't understand it, but back then that was all we knew.

It is also important to recall that this area bombing remained a joint Allied strategy, not just an obsession of Harris's. The Americans also escalated their rate of bombing during this period as much as the RAF did. The carpet bombing of Berlin, for example, which Horst Hirche found himself defending in 1945, was undertaken by USAAF aircrews. Bomber Command launched no major attacks on the German capital that year; indeed, its last major heavy bomber raid had been the 'Night of the Strong Winds' at the end of the Battle of Berlin in March

1944. Thereafter, Bomber Command sent only smaller Mosquito raids, but where Bomber Command had left off the USAAF came to complete this Armageddon over Hitler's great capital. Hirche was shattered to witness the resulting devastation.

> I was horrified when I saw the rubble and destruction in Berlin. I was overwhelmed and felt very angry at the attackers. Sometimes we used to walk around the bombed areas of the city and saw the havoc and destruction that had been caused. Only the façades of the buildings were left and only holes where the windows used to be. You would see burnt-out furniture. But the worst thing was to see the people, old people primarily, and children who used to sit in front of the rubble, and we couldn't help them. The people were bitter and it contributed to making sure that we took our duty to defend the population even more seriously than we did up to then.

It was clear to Hirche that Berlin's war was far from over.

> From the end of 1944 to March 1945, the attacks increased steadily. They were heavier and more frequent and happened during the day. The British also carried out a lot of disruptive attacks. They also flew over Berlin in smaller groups. The impression I had was that there was a certain tactic to instil fear in the population. We always had the advance warning, the people were always ready and packed. I had my suitcase packed at home with all the necessary documents you'd need in life, and we used to take these to the air-raid shelters.

After the Battle of Berlin, Luftwaffe pilot Peter Spoden had been sent to Hungary. When he returned to Germany towards the end of the war, it was all too clear to him how much had changed. The Luftwaffe no longer had control of the airspace over their country. 'During the Battle of Berlin, we were still successful as night fighters. Then the raids on Berlin stopped and we were transferred to the south, and later to Hungary. When I returned to Germany, things had changed completely. In the autumn of 1944, we didn't have much of an impact as fighter bombers. By the time of the terrible air raids on Pforzheim, Würzburg and Dresden, the air war had already long been lost.'

Of all the raids conducted by Bomber Command, it was the attack on Dresden which has become the most infamous, a synonym for *all* the criticism levelled at the bombing campaign. It too was a city that had been on the list of legitimate targets since 1942 but had been relatively untouched, largely because its geographical position had put it out of range of British bases. It was in fact not just an exquisitely beautiful baroque masterpiece, one of Germany's best loved cities, but a key industrial centre, its factories having long been turned over to war work. The Zeiss-Ikon camera factory, for example, was now manufacturing bomb sights; the cigarette factories were rolling out bullets. It was also a city that had participated as much as any other in propagating the Nazi regime, a stronghold of Hitler's grip on Germany, whose synagogue had been destroyed during Kristallnacht. Rear air gunner Jack Eveleigh was one of the airmen sent to Dresden on the night of 13 February 1945.

As far as we were concerned on the day, it was just another operation. When we arrived at the briefing room the pilots and navigators had already been pre-briefed so they would know where we were going. As we went into the briefing room, some of the navigators were larking around, with their arms folded, pretending to do the Cossack dance. Then we were issued with placards to hang around our neck in case we were shot down near the Russian lines, which said in Russian, 'I am a British aviator, please don't shoot me.' It also had a Union Jack.

As they set out from their squadron bases, what was daunting about Dresden for Eveleigh and the rest of the airmen was the distance involved. This was even farther than going to Berlin.

The actual time for our aircraft from take-off until landing was exactly ten hours, I can remember that quite clearly. On the run into the target, it's very rare that we had any remarks from the front other than the bomb aimer's instructions but on this occasion I do remember somebody said, 'What a target, look at those fires!' With the red glow from the fires, we could see the Lancasters around us quite clearly lit up, even at twenty thousand feet. There were fires from horizon to horizon, complete fire everywhere.

In Dresden, as in Hamburg in July 1943, the creation of a firestorm was not in itself a deliberate plan. What sealed Dresden's fate was a terrible combination of circumstances that would turn what by that point was a run-of-the-mill bombing raid into an apocalypse. Firestorms as such weren't deliberately engineered; they couldn't be because they relied on factors outside Harris's control. But the terrible truth is that the Dresden firestorm remains an example of what happens when everything went *right* in Second World War bombing, especially the round-the-clock variety visited on Dresden, the RAF night-time attacks being compounded by those of the USAAF during the day. The weather conditions were clear, allowing the vast majority of the bombers to reach the target and bomb with deadly and concentrated accuracy. City complacency had prevented the construction of enough air-raid shelters. They had willed themselves into believing that somehow they were exempt from Allied attack. They had even allowed their Luftwaffe defences, already below par, to be further weakened, with many Flak guns being redeployed to the Ruhr. The result was the wholescale destruction of the city centre, and the estimated loss of 50,000 lives.

If Dresden had been a legitimate industrial target in 1942, it is often suggested that by February 1945 that rationale had been superseded by the turn of events. It's true that the industrial imperative to destroy the city was considerably weaker (although certainly not eliminated), but there were other compelling reasons to target Dresden. It was a key communications centre, an important junction for major railway lines, and it had become a crucial conurbation for the Russian advance from the east. Jack Eveleigh recalls being briefed on the city as a strategic target on the afternoon of the raid. 'They told us Dresden was a very important rail, road and waterway junction. The Russians were having a hard time and to prevent reinforcements going up, this town needed to be obliterated because it was such an important transport area. We were told that the Russians had asked specifically for it.'

It is still not completely clear how important a factor to the Dresden raid the Soviet position actually was. It's likely that when the Allied leaders had met at Yalta at the beginning of February, the Red Army had requested that Dresden be attacked soon. It was also a target that had appealed to the Joint Intelligence Committee, Churchill and Portal, as part of Operation Thunderclap, designed as one last major bombing offensive. This was intended to help the Red Army, and would be an important demonstration to Stalin that the western allies were doing their bit. Churchill had written to Sir Archibald Sinclair, Secretary of State for Air, 'I asked whether Berlin, and no doubt other large cities in East Germany, should not now be considered especially attractive targets . . . Pray report to me tomorrow what is going to be done.' Berlin was the primary choice for Thunderclap, but when that looked unfeasible, Dresden was high on the list of alternatives. So the irony is that while Harris gets most of the condemnation for Dresden, it was actually he who questioned its appropriateness, at least from an operational point of view. It was Churchill who encouraged the attack; Harris was to write later, 'The attack on Dresden was at the time considered a military necessity by more important people than myself.'

So it is Churchill who should be most associated with the decision to attack Dresden. His position changed dramatically in the weeks after the raid. This was Churchill's political genius working at its macabre best. In the final weeks of the war, Churchill skilfully distanced himself from the controversy Dresden had started to provoke even then. Harris, who never flinched from a direct and honest appraisal of what the men under his command had done, was left standing alone to take the blame. There were many others involved in the decision-making in the Air Ministry and elsewhere, of course, but it was Harris who was the public face of Bomber Command, a role he never ducked, and it was Harris to whom the stigma of Dresden would later stick. He'd been a hero during the dark days of the war, bringing hope to the entire country by taking the war to Germany. There had been nothing ironic or snide about his popular nickname, 'Bomber Harris'. Now, as the post-war world started facing up to the shocking vision of what the bombers had done to Germany, it would be Harris who would be vilified. The 'Bomber Harris' label, once worn with pride, would become a smear. At the end of March 1945, Churchill issued a memorandum to the British chiefs of staff that makes his changed position all too transparent. 'It seems to me that the moment has come when the question of bombing of German cities simply for the sake of increasing the terror, though under other pretexts, should be reviewed . . . The destruction of Dresden remains a serious query against the conduct of Allied bombing.'

Stoking up civilian terror had *not* been official policy. Harris protested as much, but Churchill's priority was no longer how to win the war; that was in the capable hands of his generals. Churchill was now thinking more about his own post-war reputation, preferring to play down the uncompromising ruthlessness that had driven him throughout the war. The press reports on Dresden had been critical, questions were being asked. The memorandum was clearly influenced more by what was being said in the public sphere than by the history of the bombing strategy. Churchill the politician would soon be facing an election at home, and Churchill the international statesman was concerned about the state of the vanquished country that the Allies were about to take control of. Yet even now, in the period between Dresden and Churchill's memorandum, there would be more bombing; indeed, it would even increase in one final spasm of destructive wrath. The rumblings of discontent may have been beginning in London, but out on the squadron bases it was business as usual. Bill Burke was in the air on 16 March. 'I was on the Würzburg raid. It got a lot of adverse publicity. It was late in the war and there were questions as to whether it was an appropriate target, but for me it was a straightforward marking operation.'

Würzburg was an old cathedral city with virtually no industry. Little was left undamaged by the time the bombers had returned to their stations. The bombing raid had never been more potent, with an ever greater number of the best aircraft available, and little in the way of German defences to hinder the bomber crews. It was still far from guaranteed that crews would get back, though. A daylight raid on Essen in March 1945 served as a timely reminder to John Whiteley of the dangers that remained, even when the Luftwaffe's actions were so often in vain.

There seemed to be aircraft all over the place. It struck me at the time, because I didn't normally see what was happening. I saw one aeroplane, a Lancaster, drop its bombs on another Lancaster and knock its wing off on the port side. It was about half a mile away and a thousand feet below me. This aeroplane spun down and none of the crew got out unfortunately. At another point on the same operation, the mid-upper gunner said, 'For goodness sake, weave, Skipper! There's an aeroplane up above!' About two hundred feet above us was another Lancaster with its bomb doors open! So I had to do a quick manoeuvre to get out of the way. If it had been at night, I wouldn't have seen it.

By the time of these last big bomber raids, many of those airmen who had become POWs were being marched across Europe from one prison camp to another. It was part of the last desperate attempt by the Nazis to maintain their hold over the Reich as the enemy closed in around them. By moving the POWs, they deferred their liberation by Russian troops advancing from the east for as long as possible. The 'Long March', as it has become known, was one of the most gruelling periods for the POWs, and remains a particularly bitter memory for those who were part of it. For Robert Kee, it was certainly the worst part about being a prisoner of war. 'We were moved from our camp as the Russians came to another camp and there wasn't any food. That was the worst time, the only time one got no Red Cross parcels at all, because one lived on these Red Cross parcels we had been getting all the time.'

As it had become apparent to Robin Murray that the war was not going to go on for ever, he had begun to prepare for what he realised was going to be an arduous journey. He was still having great difficulty walking owing to the injuries sustained when his Wellington had crashed.

> We had a radio in the camp, and every evening after the parade at six o'clock, this letter used to come round to the compound with all the news from England. So we knew what was going on, and by that time the Germans knew the war was over. In the summer of 1944 I had realised that we were going to go, but nobody was going to come to pick us up. We were going to have to walk out of the camp. I had a pair of British army boots and I had clumps, in other words extra-thick sole and heels, put on them and I broke them in. I had got some Vaseline and put it all round the welts so that they were really waterproof. I used to walk round and round the compound to get into a bit of training, a bit of exercise, and when we did go out, we walked 882 miles, right across Germany. I didn't have any problems at all on the march.

After years of meagre diets in prisoner-of-war camps, few POWs were in a fit state for the physical endeavour involved in walking hundreds of miles, day after day. Without even the rations that had been available in the camps, the prisoners' diet became abysmal and they ate anything they could find, hoping to come across crop-laden fields they could plunder while their guards, who often weren't much better off themselves, weren't looking. Most of the POWs started walking in January, during the bitterest winter Germany had endured for half a century, with inadequate clothing and shelter. Thousands died on the way, from malnutrition, exhaustion or the diseases that quickly spread among the columns of soldiers, sailors and airmen. Those who survived watched their weight falling dramatically. Robin Murray, who'd always been known to his friends as Tubby, weighed just under eight stone when he was finally released. Jim Chapman, who at thirteen stone had been classed as a bit heavy for a rear air gunner, weighed six stone when he got back to Britain. As they were marched across Germany, there was one consolation. Harold Nash could see the hope of Allied victory in the skies above him. 'The Flying Fortresses were beginning to attack by day. Several times while we were walking, we saw the whole fleet of American bombers, roaring overhead, like silver fishes in the sunlight. This steady roar was a menace and it seemed to be awful, and then the distant gunfire of the German anti-aircraft fire. But you felt less lonely; you felt that the war was going your way.'

Many of the POW camps had been placed deep in eastern Europe, well away from the range of the bombers. Up on the Lithuanian border, Hal Croxson never heard the Allied aircraft going over his POW camp. Now he saw the bombers coming, but they brought with them one last, terrible danger for the prisoners of war.

When we were on the march, we began to get nearer to the western front and then we did see aircraft. They blew us up on one or two occasions. They'd see a column of people marching and from the air you could not possibly identify them. They would just belt in there and blow this lot out and there was nothing you could do. On one occasion, we were bombed in the barn we were sleeping in. We didn't know it at the time but earlier that day there had been a German unit there and they had all their trucks parked underneath the trees, along the road that was adjacent to this barn. So when it was dark, our night fighters came in and tried to blow the barn up and I think one chap was killed directly. Somebody else died later and there were about nineteen or twenty chaps with wounds.

It was another incident of what would now be termed 'friendly fire' which would provide Jim Chapman with his most terrifying memory from the entire war.

We were marching northwards. It was a forced march, at bayonet point. Some who lagged behind got shot. We'd been on the road for some time and waiting in a field where at an appointed hour we were supposed to have been supplied with Red Cross parcels. Food at last, instead of having to rely on taking eggs from fowl and digging into potato clumps on the way. We were all scattered about, waiting. There was much enemy troop movement around us and there was a motorcycle with a sidecar coming towards me, a chap in the sidecar and a chap on the bike with rifles slung across their shoulders. Suddenly, and I heard no sound, everything went silent and this motorbike took off and turned a complete somersault.

Overhead, Chapman could now hear the aircraft firing shells. They were RAF aircraft, six of them altogether.

Another one came in to attack. He thought he was attacking Germans, but there were POWs down there as well. I kept moving from place to place as each aircraft came in, until I got to a field which had got a drainage trench down the side of it. There was a chap in there with his head up against a big tree. He was an army chap who I'd met in the camp. I dropped in there. Another aircraft came over and again opened fire. When I got up, I saw that this chap had got his head blown off and my head had been lying by his neck. He'd been left with a great hole in his back. I moved over, I couldn't do anything because another aircraft was coming in. He didn't open fire, he'd recognised us. That was the most terrifying moment of my war. No matter what else I'd faced, I don't think about anything else.

In the disorganisation of the crumbling Reich, some prisoners tried to desert from the Long March. Robin Murray knew that it was still a considerable risk, but it didn't stop him from trying.

The second day out, two of us broke from the column and we hid and went across this bridge, hopefully to get away. This very large German military policeman stepped out and he was waiting for deserters from the Russian front but he picked us up. He took us to a little place which had been the prison for Hitler Youth who had misbehaved. There were about fifty or sixty of us in there and amongst them was a Pole who was due to be shot for killing a German officer, but we dyed his hair, put glasses on him and a RAF greatcoat and he came out with us. Then we were put into these open cattle trucks and taken to a big camp about forty miles away. We walked the rest of the way across to a place south-east of Kassel.

Eventually Murray would be liberated by the Americans.

When the Americans broke through at the Nijmegen bridge, they started to move us back again south-east, and after a time, I suppose about five days, two of us hid up in this barn. The Americans were sending out probes in these tank destroyers, looking for prisoners of war on the loose. The German farmer knew we were hiding in this barn because every evening he used to put out a big bowl of boiled potatoes for us and a jug of water. Eventually the Americans came through, picked us up and took us back to where they were based. From there, we gradually went back and acted as guards on their big trucks, with the German prisoners of war. We drove back to Gotha and flew to Le Havre. We were in a big American camp at Le Havre that was completely organised for the receipt of prisoners of war.

After the ordeal of the Long March, the camp at Le Havre seemed luxurious.

There were tents, six beds in a tent, and they had these mobile shower units, which were very useful because by this time we were as cooty as hell. We'd been sleeping in barns in straw and we were covered in lice. So we had to delouse ourselves – they had this powder which you sprayed over yourself to get rid of the lice, which was very effective. They took all our clothes away from us, deloused them, washed them and they all came back clean and pressed. From there we were flown across to Wing, which was an RAF aerodrome outside Aylesbury, and we went through the same procedure, delousing again. Then we went down to the big hotel in Euston where we were debriefed before being sent home on six weeks' leave.

Prisoners returning to Britain were entitled to double rations. After his leave, Jim Chapman was asked how he felt about going out to the Far East to join the forces based there. Understandably, he politely declined the offer.

By the end of April 1945, the war was finally coming to an end, but Bomber Command continued to operate until almost the very last day of the war. The last Lancaster to be shot down fell over Sweden on 26 April 1945. The crew were just short of their target, Tonsberg in southern Norway, where there was an oil refinery, when they became one last victim of the deadly cannon fire of *schräge musik*. A Junkers Ju-88 firing upward into the front turret seriously injured the bomb aimer, but the two gunners, Fred Logan in the mid-upper turret, and Jock Hogg in the rear, succeeded in shooting the fighter down. The pilot had managed to get the aircraft across to neutral territory, where the landscape also made landing conditions much more favourable, but both he and the flight engineer were severely frostbitten. Thanks partly to the advanced medical care available in Sweden for frostbite victims, all the crew survived.

One of the last major jobs for the bomber boys was to drop not bombs, but food parcels. While most of western Europe had been liberated, there was one area of western Holland that still lay under the control of German troops, and the population was fast approaching starvation. A truce was reached with the local German commander, and on 29 April, Lancaster crews from 1, 3 and 8 Groups began Operation Manna, a series of food drops for the civilian population. They were supported by Pathfinder Mosquitoes marking the dropping zones, and over nine days 2,835 Lancaster flights and 124 Mosquito flights were made before the Germans finally surrendered. More than 6.5 tons of food were dropped, along with medical supplies, before ships and road transport were once again allowed to enter the area. It's one of the operations that the airmen involved in it are proudest of, including Jack Eveleigh.

We were quite surprised that instead of loading high explosives and incendiaries, they were loading food into the Lancasters. We were told that several million people were now on the point of starvation. The Dutch government-in-exile had asked for assistance and the only way they could provide this was to load the bombers with food, and try and come to some arrangement with the Germans to have a ceasefire over a certain area where we could drop this food. There was a lot of trouble getting this ceasefire. There were a couple of days when it was a bit iffy whether or not they were going to fire at us.

As Eveleigh was briefed, he realised that the operations had been meticulously planned.

There would be a dropping zone designated, and it would be marked just as if we were marking a target. We had to fly at a very low altitude, about two hundred feet, as we didn't use parachutes for dropping this food. If it was any higher, it would probably have gone to pieces. We flew in over the coast, and having cleared the sand dunes, we saw the flooded areas with roads running along the dykes in between. There were people from all directions waving. I remember one chap on a push-bike fell off in fright! We flew in over the drop zone, dropped our supplies and flew out. I did six of these trips.

Those on the receiving end of Bomber Command's operations were for once thankful to see the aircraft overhead. These parcels were a vital lifeline in a desperate situation, and the people of Holland have demonstrated their sincere gratitude ever since, hosting regular reunions for the crews who took part in Operation Manna. By now, Operation Exodus had already begun, the bomber crews being used to bring back the thousands of prisoners of war from the continent.

With Hitler's suicide on 30 April 1945, Nazi Germany was finally at an end. Power had been handed over to Admiral Doenitz, but there was now no possible outcome other than complete German surrender. Even Bomber Command had ceased its activities, bar Operation Manna and the rescue of POWs. There had been no offensive operations since 26 April, but one last raid by Mosquitoes was ordered on 2 May. The target was the port of Kiel, where it was feared the Germans might gather together their remaining ships to take the remnants of the Wehrmacht to Norway, from where they could hope to continue the war. Thirty-six hours after the raid, Allied troops arrived in the town. It was on this raid that the last Bomber Command aircraft were lost in the war, when two Halifaxes from No. 199 Squadron crashed just south of the town. It's thought that they collided on their bomb runs; just three men survived from a combined crew of sixteen.

This last possible pocket of resistance destroyed, the German army finally admitted defeat. A surrender document was signed on 4 May for all German troops in north-west Germany, Denmark and Holland. Three days later, General Eisenhower accepted the unconditional surrender, on behalf of Britain, Russia and France as well as the USA, of all German forces on all fronts. Although this final surrender didn't come into effect until 9 May, the fighting was finally over. It had taken eleven months from the invasion for western Europe to be liberated, and five years and eight months since Neville Chamberlain had broadcast that 'this country is at war'. It had been a long war, and no more so than for Bomber Command. They had been there since the beginning in the fight against Nazism, and had played their part in its defeat. The war in the Far East would, of course, continue for a few months yet, and Bomber Command's squadrons would now be expected to help end the war there too. Thousands of airmen joined Tiger Force, but their training would be interrupted by the dropping of the atom bombs, bringing the Second World War to its terrible but conclusive end.

12

The Old Lags

'This was the greatest lost battle on the German side.'

Albert Speer, 1959

Jack Eveleigh among the aircrew and ground staff of 550
Squadron as they celebrate the 'V for Victor' Lancaster
completing its 100th operation.

Bomber Command's controversial reputation took form very quickly in the weeks after the end of the war, a reputation that had grown darker during the area bombing raids that Harris carried on mounting right up to the bitter end. While the rest of the armed services rejoiced in victory, the bomber boys were quietly sidelined. Churchill's 'VE Speech', broadcast on 13 May 1945, listed just about every major part of the war effort, but not the bombing campaign. Little was said, but it was all too clear that Bomber Command had become an embarrassment, and the snubs were barbed. Harris retired from the RAF with few of the honours enjoyed by those of equivalent stature elsewhere in the forces, and his 'old lags' as he called them were denied a campaign medal. There were, and remain, various official excuses for this slight, but none are particularly convincing. The fact remains that Harris did not dictate policy but enacted it, planning attacks according to the directives handed down to him by the Air Ministry which had been agreed by the Prime Minister and War Cabinet. His volunteer airmen carried out those orders to the best of their ability, determined to do their bit for the war effort, risking their lives in the process, just as members of every other branch of the armed forces did.

For sixty years, those volunteers have had to live with the legacy not only of their own personal war experiences, but the muted public response to them. It's as if the bombing campaign has become the gesture of concession, the acknowledgement that in the total warfare which cast such a shadow over the twentieth century, both sides are responsible for atrocities which in hindsight they have to atone for. In short, Bomber Command has become the symbol of a nation's collective guilt. It's not hard to see why. The early years of an ill-equipped bomber force that lost so many crews without the compensation of inflicting sufficient damage on the enemy; the hundreds of thousands of civilians who lost their lives as a result of an area bombing policy, in the worst cases during appalling firestorms; those final months of bombing that call into question the conduct of Allied leaders so close to victory. All of these are factors in the perception we now have of Bomber Command.

So much so that it has become hard to see the positive elements of Bomber Command's contribution to the Allied victory over Nazism. Fighter Command could point to the Battle of Britain, the British Army to the defeat of Rommel's forces in North Africa or the liberation of Europe in the aftermath of D-Day. For the bomber crews, though, none of their victories were so tangible. Their war had few moments of unequivocal glory. There's a sense that Bomber Command is damned on both counts; for failing to hit enough targets during the first half of the war, and for doing too much damage when they did, in the second half. There was a grim equation at work too, with 'success' tallied to the numbers of Germans killed, a fact too blunt for post-war celebration. In the absence of a single, decisive achievement, historians are left to analyse the complexities of the impact on German war production, the value of delaying the opening of the second front on the ground, and a supporting role in the bigger campaigns of Overlord and the Battle of the Atlantic. Furthermore, the truth was, no matter how awful the regime the Allies were fighting, the reality of bombing made it hard to take pride in Bomber Command's achievements. Adge Boal was challenged about the bombing even during the war.

I had a very religious aunt and I went home on leave once when the raids were causing a lot of damage and casualties. She laid the law down something terrible to me and said what a bad person I was and how disgraceful it was that we were destroying

German cities and people. I tried to explain to her what it was all about, and that we weren't going for German people at all. We went for the industries to try and stop the war. She asked, 'Don't you bother to think about the German people below?' I said, 'Of course I do, but our main battle is to release the bombs and then the fight is between ourselves; the fighters, the searchlights and the Flak.' The ruling we used to have when we were briefed was that you will take your aircraft to the target, you will bomb the target and you'll bring your aeroplane back. Those are the three priorities. If you achieved that, it was a successful raid.

So what did the bombing achieve? Firstly, there *was* a very significant impact on German industry. Although industrial production was able to increase as the war progressed, the fact is, the increase was far less than would otherwise have been the case. German factories were slow to reach full wartime capacity, so there were bound to be improvements in production, but there is no question that the impact of bombing was to curtail the levels that were attainable. Without the bombing, the Nazis would have been able to maintain their hold of the occupied areas of Europe for much longer. They would, surely, have been able to see off the Normandy landings of Operation Overlord. It was the slow war of attrition against Germany's wartime industrial production that Leonard Miller sees as Bomber Command's most valuable achievement: 'Bomber Command wore down the enemy. They cut off his industry, they cut off his supplies and it kept their heavy artillery fighting us as opposed to fighting the army and everybody else. They had a lot of people tied down on home defence.'

Industrial production was repeatedly disrupted. How many days of labour must have been consumed repairing the bomb damage rather than actually continuing the manufacturing process? How many resources were swept up in the need to constantly repair and rebuild factories and equipment, rather than creating additional industrial capacity? Such questions can only be answered speculatively, but it's impossible to examine the photographs of bombed factories without conceding that the diversion of resources to deal with the aftermath of the bombing must have been considerable. Jack Eveleigh believes that without the bombing, D-Day would have been postponed for around a year.

> We didn't destroy the armaments and the potential for the Germans to wage war but we must have slowed them down, we must have knocked them back. The day after the raids, the photographs we took over the aiming point would be on the wall and reconnaissance aircraft would have gone over in daylight and taken photographs of the damage. If you had succeeded in hitting your target, and you had some good photos, you felt quite chuffed about it.

Then, there is the part of industrial production and capacity that was diverted to build and maintain the aircraft, searchlight facilities and Flak guns that were needed to defend the Reich from the bombers. So much of the increase in industrial production was immediately absorbed into defending the very cities that produced it. Yet it still wasn't enough. In those final months, the RAF and USAAF effectively won air supremacy. Despite finally reaching full industrial wartime capacity, the Nazis were running out of equipment, oil and men. The conscription of all men aged between sixteen and sixty in September 1944 had been a desperate measure. Who was Hitler going to call on next? A large part of the Luftwaffe was forced into a sustained defence of the homeland, rather than being able to prolong the war in the east, attempt a second Battle of Britain or conquer other new territories. In 1959 Hitler's former minister for armaments, Albert Speer, recorded his understanding of the contribution of the bombing.

> The real importance of the air war consisted in the fact that it opened a second front long before the invasion in Europe. That

front was the skies over Germany. The fleets of bombers might appear at any time over any large German city or important factory. The unpredictability of the attacks made this front gigantic; every square metre of the territory we controlled was a kind of front line. Defence against air attacks required the production of thousands of anti-aircraft guns, the stockpiling of tremendous quantities of ammunition all over the country, and holding in readiness hundreds of thousands of soldiers, who in addition had to stay in position by their guns, often totally inactive, for months at a time. As far as I can judge from the accounts I have read, no one has yet seen that this was the greatest lost battle on the German side.

What of the civilians? Certainly civilian morale, though battered, never actually collapsed; there was no popular uprising against Hitler and his war, as had been thought a likely outcome of bombing. Even when the bombing reached its terrible apogee in 1945, there was still no serious threat to the regime from the German population. Indeed, the evidence from the bombing of Britain *and* Germany alike suggests that civilian resolve is only stiffened by bombs, not broken by them. Horst Hirche witnessed the continued resolve of the population, however bad the bombing became.

People who had lost everything would sit in despair in front of the rubble of their homes. But I was constantly surprised again and again how these people still had the discipline to go about their daily work after the heavy attacks. I'm talking here about the young woman or the mother who worked on the trams in Berlin. She went to her depot and worked. The factory workers went back to their factories. If the factories had been hit, after the rubble had been cleared, they went back to work. These construction teams were quickly on the scene, repairing and rebuilding the most important areas. Mr Harris deluded himself that he could demoralise the population that way, that the people would revolt or overthrow Hitler. It didn't happen.

If anyone wanted that to be part of the ambition behind Bomber Command (and in fact Harris didn't, although others did), they would have done well to listen to this prophecy from 1917 on the parameters of a future aerial war.

> It is improbable that any terrorisation of the civil population which could be achieved by air attack could compel the Government of a great nation to surrender ... In our own case, we have seen the combative spirit of the people roused, and not quelled, by the German air raids. Nothing that we have learned of the capacity of the German population to endure suffering justifies us in assuming that they could be cowed into submission by such methods, or indeed that they would not be rendered more desperately resolved by them.

Its author? None other than one Winston Churchill, at the time Minister for Munitions.

In total war, however, civilians are not just innocent bystanders to a distant conflict. The civilians of the industrial cities are the very people who make the war machine work. They run and operate the factories. It's from the civilian population that the military personnel are drawn, and never more so than during wartime conscription. Nobody rejoices in the deaths of civilians, but the disruption of their working lives, and the obstacles that bombing puts in the way of their contribution to the war effort can be legitimised as part of a total war effort. As Robin Murray points out, even when the bombing of the first few years of the war so frequently did little hard damage, it still had the effect of disruption.

> The bombing did keep the workforce out of their beds so that the next day they weren't able to do a decent day's work. That's where it did the damage, not so much the buildings but the people. It destroyed their will to work. They never knew where we were going to bomb next, they lived wondering what was going to happen that night. When the Americans came in and started daylight bombing, they were getting it twenty-four hours a day.

As the war progressed, Bomber Command's ability to disrupt the industrial workforce greatly increased. For Tom Wingham, it justifies the area bombing strategy.

> We were area bombing without a doubt and I don't think anybody should apologise for that. Most of the people in those towns were working to produce armaments to supply their troops. Therefore could they claim to be innocent civilians? Who should one target, the maker of the rifles or the people using them? The whole purpose was to cover the town in order to smash the factories and de-house the population which reduced their production.

Yet the plight of the civilians was of course much worse than that. Hundreds of thousands were killed, maimed or made homeless, many in appalling circumstances. It is our own contemporary awareness of this that makes it so hard to justify the bombing, even in the terms of the time. The line 'we only found out later' seems inadequate. After all, it was only a generation ago; could anyone really have been so naïve about the effects of area bombing of civilian cities? There seems no hiding place for the devoted armies of scientists employed by military leaders, under the orders of politicians, to develop an ever increasing array of weapons seeking to maximise destruction. So much has changed in a generation. It is precisely the legacy of the two world wars that has overturned the perceptions of warfare that had lasted for centuries. Terrible atrocities were nothing new; nor were civilians as the victims of warfare. Civilians had died in shocking ways for centuries, not least those who had been starved and slaughtered in siege warfare since ancient times. What changed was the scale of the warfare, the involvement of such large swathes of the world's population, and the visibility of the conflict. It is the potency of the images, often revealed years after the war, which has changed minds, and their widespread dissemination. Their immediacy too: the consequences of a bomb blast now can be seen across the world by millions of people within minutes on the television news, citizens in even far away countries able to draw informed opinions of a conflict as it is fought. The images seen by the bomber crews in the 1940s only told part of the story, and they only had their imagination with which to picture the scenes below. No imagination dreamed of the depth of suffering we now associate with the firestorms of Hamburg or Dresden. In the early months of the war, these later episodes were simply unimaginable. This was a war of lines crossed, of endless incremental increases, a war that ended up taking a form nobody could possibly have foreseen in 1939. With every passing year, the stakes got higher, and with every passing year, too, the nature of the war changed. It didn't only become global, and total, the Germans quite explicitly turned it into a war of annihilation, particularly in the east. The 'whirlwind' that the Germans would now reap, according to Harris, changed too, but once it was whipped up, it proved impossible to stop. In hindsight we can see that, but without the images and testimony that have shaped that hindsight, it was not so apparent at the time. The cities were, for Jack Eveleigh and many others, simply targets.

We looked upon things differently than today. You would look upon the town, the city or the factory as a target. This is your target. You have been trained, given some very expensive equipment and sent there with the sole purpose of flattening that target. I don't think we had too many qualms about the people and the conditions on the ground. I know this sounds very hard now but it was the attitude at the time. Remember we'd had four or five years of war and we had been bombed.

Besides, the crews had little time to contemplate the scenes below as all their energy was devoted to completing the operation. Arthur Smith was too preoccupied at the time to consider the impact of the bombing.

All you thought about was getting the bombs on the target, which was underneath the markers. Never once can I remember thinking of the damage I was doing. I didn't think about the lives that my bomb could have been ending, I only thought of that afterwards. While you're doing it your whole mind is on hitting what you've come out to bomb. You just don't think of casualties.

There is a further consideration. If the Allies had been right to take on the Nazi regime in the first place, then they had to do everything in their power to win that war, and as quickly as possible. There was no margin offered from which to show restraint, or reply in moderation to the full onslaught of the Nazi threat. Nor, finally, was it possible to dislocate that threat from the wider German population. It wasn't going to be possible to win *this* kind of war, and salve everybody's consciences. The prospect of a victorious Hitler, and the millions upon millions of future victims of his murder squads and unhampered death camps, simply removes that luxury.

So Harris's question remains a potent one: what exactly was the alternative? Without the distraction that the bombing provided, when German production reached full capacity, and was wholly directed towards the war, what could Britain, as the sole western European free and belligerent power, have done to hold back a fresh attempt at Operation Sealion? What resources would Russia have been able to fall back on in a prolonged campaign on the eastern front given the high price that had already been paid? Bill Burke has no qualms about what the bombing did, or the number of civilians that were killed. For him there was no question the ends *did* justify the means.

You've got to remember that the Germany of those days was not the Germany of today. That Germany was evil. They were prepared to kill six million people in the concentration camps. They killed twenty-five million people on the eastern front because they decided that the Russians were sub-human and could be treated like animals. It was the Germans who really pursued the idea of bombing cities. You can go back as far as the Spanish Civil War when the Condor Legion bombed Guernica, and then in 1940 the Luftwaffe hammered Rotterdam and Warsaw, in order to speed up their military victories. They tried the same here in cities such as Coventry and London. So far as I was concerned, Bomber Command was the only force at that time which was capable of attacking Germany and we did a marvellous job in building up the morale of the people at home, at a time when there was very little to celebrate.

There are no regrets for Peter Baker either: 'We were at war, we were fighting a very evil force and doing our bit, and doing what we were told to do.'

The criticism of the bombing angers Leonard Miller.

Everybody fastened their ideas onto Dresden but it deserved what it got. OK, a lot of architecture was destroyed in Dresden but that was unfortunate. Hitler was trying to bring back all the panzer divisions from the eastern front through Dresden, to throw them into the Battle of Berlin and against the Allies on the western front. It was a Gestapo headquarters and also a map-making section for all the army controls. I had no compunction in doing what I did. I feel that I contributed something to civilisation, I was defending my family and my country.

It is in this context that Britain's wartime leaders, in conjunction with their Allied colleagues, did what was necessary at the time to bring Nazi power to an end. No one showed more formidable leadership of his troops than Arthur Harris. He remains a complex character, and was never an easy man to lionise, with his lack of charisma and uncompromising bluntness. Not everyone is even agreed about his strategic acumen, particularly towards the end of the war. There are many occasions when he pursued area bombing even as the possibility of alternatives appeared. He was mocking of the 'panacea targets' such as the synthetic oil plants that were unambiguously military targets; he was sceptical about the development of the Pathfinder Force that promised the precision bombing that made attacks on strategically important military targets possible; he objected to the Dams Raid as it involved a fleet of Lancasters being diverted from the main campaign. The many achievements of Bomber Command beyond the cities – and during the course of the war, less than half the bomb tonnage dropped by Bomber Command was actually dropped on Germany's industrial cities – seem to belong to Harris far less than the area bombing. His war was the blasting of the cities.

Yet Harris was a remarkable leader of his men, someone who inspired loyalty and unending commitment in the face of adversity. That loyalty has endured through everything that sixty years of peacetime have thrown at the reputation of Bomber Command, and its veterans are almost universal in their admiration of Arthur Harris. Robin Murray is typical: 'Bomber Harris was a man of his times. He did what he had to do. At one time Bomber Command was the only command that was able to hit Germany at all, at any time. None of our land or sea forces were able to do anything.'

Jim Chapman is also full of praise for Harris: 'He was the man. We'd do anything for Butch and we did. He hit back. Bomber Command seemed to me to be the only people that were hitting back at our enemies and that did a lot for my morale, I think it did for most of us.'

Harris 'old lags' have been left to make their own judgements on their war, contemplating their legacy largely in silence. Arthur Smith has given the events of the 1940s much thought. 'Since the war ended, I've read a lot of books about various raids, and seen programmes on television, and heard other people's opinions, and realised what terrible carnage air bombers caused to targets and to human life. To me it was a war, we had to do it. I think the bombing was a terrible thing, but we were saving our country from Hitler, who was terrible, and if I had to do it again, I suppose I would.'

Some had the opportunity to see the damage properly for themselves soon after VE Day, when 'Cooks' Tours' were arranged so that ground staff could see the targets for themselves. It must have been a sobering experience for aircrew and ground staff alike to see those cities in the cold light of day for the first time. Robert Kee flew over Hamburg when he was brought back at the end of the war having spent more than three years as a POW. 'It must have been disturbing for the German population to realise that we could come and bomb Berlin and the other cities. I think it must have affected morale a bit. There was nothing there except ruins. This whole city was in ruins. It was pretty awful. Well, war is awful.'

Many have returned to those targets in the years since. In 2003, Adge Boal returned to Rouen. It was the first time that he had returned since the night his crew inadvertently released a bomb directly onto the French city's cathedral. That night still nags at his conscience.

> I actually stood in the centre of that cathedral, the very spot where our bombs landed. It was a very strange feeling, but things happened, and it wasn't intended. They spent twelve years rebuilding it and there's still work to be done. I saw an article on the history of Rouen Cathedral and one sentence read, 'On that terrible night'. I thought, 'Oh my goodness, that's me!' To stand there and know for sure that you are responsible for it is a pretty rotten feeling, it really is.

No veteran feels complete ease about the bombing, but it has affected Harold Nash more than most. At the time, he'd given it little thought, but years later the memory of the three ladies dressed in black trying to give him a piece of bread as he was taken on a train to POW camp came back to him. A chance remark at a party about Christ turning the other cheek triggered Nash to reassess what he'd been part of all those years earlier.

> The gesture of these three women came to mind. I'd tried to kill them five or six nights before and in return they'd offered me bread. This began to work on me and over the years it's

changed me. Why should I try to kill these three good women because of a swine and monster called Hitler? The whole farce of war seemed to descend upon me with such a clout. I became a pacifist. No government can be pacifists; that's a luxury which I as an individual can indulge. I'm not always happy about what we did, I'm not accusing any of my comrades, not one. I wouldn't have a word said against them. We were obeying orders but I'm not proud of the carpet bombing I did. Nobody deserves to suffer such a fate. But at the time when I was in that aircraft, I was a young man and all I thought of was my own skin. Those sparking lights on the velvet background, they weren't people to me, just the target. It's the distance and blindness which enabled you to do these things. I think the bombing was awful and unnecessary, especially Dresden. When they erected a statue to Bomber Harris, I protested but I found out that I was making a big mistake. It wasn't Bomber Harris so much, he was carrying out War Cabinet orders; it was Churchill who insisted on Dresden, together with Eisenhower.

Since that revelatory moment, Nash has been engaged in years of reconciliation work between Britain and Germany, particularly in Coventry and Dresden. He was awarded an Order of Merit for this work by the German government and is a fervent advocate of European harmony. He is rare in the extremity of his reaction to the legacy of the bombing campaign, but his sentiments are ones every veteran has to wrestle with for himself.

For many years after the war, most airmen were only too eager to forget the conflict. While a few made post-war careers with the RAF, the vast majority dispersed into civilian life. The pilots, navigators, bomb aimers, flight engineers, wireless operators and gunners became bank managers, teachers, lorry drivers, department store managers, industrial salesmen, publicans, factory workers, and engineers. They were young men, often still in their early twenties, and they had lives to get on with. Their priorities now were getting jobs, and settling down with families. Returning to civilian life wasn't always easy though. It had been an exhausting experience, and the fatigue had taken its toll on the war veterans. The post-war world would be a perplexing environment. Some of the bomber boys found that jobs they'd had before volunteering had been held open for them, but few wanted to return to the same position they'd been in all those years ago. Adjusting to life outside the forces was in any case enough of a challenge but John Holmes had never even known adult civilian life. 'When I came home from the service I was worn out. It's difficult to say or explain but I was literally worn out. No interest in anything, didn't want to do anything, didn't want to go anywhere. I was just burnt out. It took me six months to get over it and twelve months to accommodate myself to civilian life because I'd been in the service for twelve years. I didn't like civilian life. Not a bit.'

The war had not only bridged the gap between boyhood and manhood, it had greatly widened the gulf. A generation of boys who had started out with a curiosity for flight, and a straightforward patriotism had grown up with astonishing rapidity. Hal Croxson says, 'We weren't heroes, we didn't win any medals. We were just pink-faced little boys doing the job we set out to do, and growing up very quickly.' The old lags had all grown up quickly. There had been some profound lessons in life for John Holmes.

I went in the air force at twenty when one is not really developed into anything very much. I mean you're a bit raw at twenty, you really haven't got much idea about what life's like. It taught me very quickly what life was like and that it could be extremely unpleasant. The thing that I've never given up is the comradeship. It taught me that you have to depend on other people whether you like it or not and life is very much easier if you can. It also taught me that no man is indispensable. The crews went out and they didn't come back and what happened the next day? You got another crew. No man is indispensable. I like to think as a senior flight sergeant technician that I was indispensable but I doubt it very much. If they'd dropped a wing on me, they'd have found another flight sergeant somewhere.

It wasn't just the emotional challenges of peacetime. Many airmen experienced the psychological aftermath of warfare. There was no counselling or therapy, only perhaps a sympathetic doctor who would prescribe a 'tonic'. Quite a few former airmen were taking a 'tonic' for years afterwards, but there was a widespread silence about the war, nobody talked then of 'post traumatic stress' just as nobody talked about fear. Even among those who had emerged relatively untouched by the worst experiences, psychological complaints were an unexceptional occurrence. Bill Burke noticed the signs of a nervous disorder once the war was over: 'I had a terrible twitch so it was difficult to light a cigarette. I became conscious of things that made me nervous to a totally unreasonable degree. It took me several years to recover and to return to normality.'

Roy Finch suffered from similar symptoms. 'I would get on a bus, and then fumble about trying to get the right change, all fingers and thumbs. This started after I'd been back two or three months.' Fortunately, the problem didn't last for long. Such nervous twitches were common. So were nightmares. Maurice Flower recalls having horrible nightmares on a regular basis for several years after the war.

If the years of readjustment were hard enough for the airmen coming home to Britain, they could be even more difficult for those airmen returning to other parts of the world. When he got back to Australia after the war, Ron Pitt noticed the disparity in the reaction to war veterans in Britain and Australia, which was after all so far removed from the European theatre of war.

The family were very interested of course, but generally people weren't that interested. They thought you were having a good time in England because when we wrote home, we didn't write about the sad parts. We'd write about going into Cambridge and on the river at Cambridge and seeing a show in London. I think quite a few people got the wrong impression. They'd pass the word about, 'Oh, he's having a great time on leave,' and they didn't think about the hard part that we went through.

There is a lasting bitterness that the airmen have not been more widely and more publicly recognised. The 'old lags' had lost more than 55,000 of their comrades. Nearly 10,000 had been prisoners of war. Thousands more bore the permanent wounds acquired as a member of a bomber crew. Ground staff and WAAFs alike had died or been wounded, had seen friends and colleagues die and been deeply affected by their experiences. Bill Burke resents the lack of recognition for the bombers.

Nobody lost personnel at the speed that we lost them in Bomber Command and what recognition did we get? At the end of the war people wanted to disassociate themselves from what we'd done but what we had done was immense. We'd not only built up morale, we had diverted a million people to anti-aircraft defences of various kinds. Around two thousand night fighters had been diverted which could have flown on the eastern front. We did terrible damage to their industrial and civil and economic systems. We bombed Peenemünde which delayed the application of the V weapons. We attacked the V1 and V2 sites to save people dying in this country and we eliminated the V3 site which would have been even more dangerous. So we achieved an enormous amount, and even though we didn't win the war ourselves, it was a hell of a price to pay.

It's a resentment that Maurice Flower shares.

I feel very bitter about it. Bomber Command flew on the first day of the war and then every day until the end of the war. The light bombers went through some appalling conditions, shot out of the sky in hundreds in the early part of the war in France. I think Bomber Harris did a fantastic job. Bomber Command really was instrumental in winning the war. I think we deserved a bit better recognition than we did get, and especially Bomber Harris. Bomber Command should have had a medal.

A Bomber Command medal was eventually struck, but it was a private endeavour. As a commemorative issue, it has no official status. The veterans wear it with pride, but a pride tarnished by the Establishment's refusal to officially recognise their contribution to the defeat of the Nazis.

In the immediate aftermath of the war, most airmen chose to forget their experiences and move on. Crews who had been bound together by that extraordinary camaraderie quickly lost touch, in many cases as soon as they'd left their stations. It seems strange that men who'd been like brothers disappeared from each other's lives as suddenly as they'd arrived, but with the bombing over, no one wanted to dwell on it longer than they had to. Some still choose not to acknowledge their war service publicly, and are reluctant to talk about their experiences. As the years have gone on, however, the thoughts of many veterans have once again turned to the war. They know that if they don't put their experiences on record, future generations will be left with little understanding of the complexities of the bombing war. Since the 1970s, veterans have become more active, holding reunions under the auspices of the Aircrew Association and Bomber Command Association. In the past few years, many veterans have also begun to trace their former crew members; frequently it's the first time they've spoken since the war. It's too late to reunite many whole crews, but curiosity about what happened to the rest of their crews has finally taken hold of the bomber boys. Adge Boal was only recently reunited with one of his former crew mates.

We have a No. 514 Squadron reunion every year. About four years ago a fortnight before the reunion, I had a message from the organiser. He said I've had a guy on the telephone who thinks he knows you, but I'm not sure if you're the right guy or not. An hour later, this voice rang up, a deep gruff voice, 'Adge, boy, is that you?' I thought, Ronny Pitt! Brilliant, knew him straightaway. He's been back every year since and stays with us for a few weeks during the period of the reunion.

Despite the ambiguities and contradictions of their war, the veterans of Bomber Command are above all proud to have served their country. Jim Rogers believes that the bomber crews did a good job.

I was a very lucky person to have taken part in it and come through it. I feel we achieved something, I think we helped to cure what was Nazi Germany. I think we saved thousands of lives of troops on the ground by our bombing of the battle areas and the German equipment. So to me, it was worthwhile. I'm very proud of the fact that I was a member of Bomber Command and I think most of the people who were in it were proud of the fact. If it happened again, I would do it again.

Amongst the death and destruction, there were also positive elements of squadron life. Most of all, for John Holmes, it was the comradeship: 'I've thought about it over the years and it seems a strange thing to say but it's an experience I don't think I would want to have missed. You go through all the sensations that there are one way and another. I wouldn't want to do it again but I likewise wouldn't have missed it. The comradeship was – it still is – something else.'

The wartime spirit and comradeship is a cherished memory of Ricky Dyson.

People were very considerate of other people's needs, both civilians and military. There was a sense of patriotism, of the urgency to keep going through thick and thin. The older generation were very sensitive to what you were trying to achieve and there was never a thought that we were going to lose the war. I don't think anybody in this country ever thought they were going to lose, even when we were facing invasion. It was just a solid mass of support by everybody you came in contact with.

For Peter Baker, the war was an exciting time in his life. 'We were young, they were exciting days. Yes, I do look fondly back. In the Wellington era [on his first tour], everything was new and exciting. Your chances of getting through a tour were slightly remote, so you felt relieved if you had got through. It was sixty years ago and many of the experiences I remember as though they were yesterday. They were a great crowd.'

The thrill of flying has never left some of the volunteers. Even though almost all the veterans are now in their eighties, there are a surprising number who still fly today, Roy Finch among them. 'After my wife died eleven years ago, I took up flying again, in a way to try to make up for lost time. It was extremely frustrating coming down on my third op, it really was. I resented it bitterly. I've done far more hours now than I ever did in the RAF!'

Despite having been through the experience of a bomber crew, Adge Boal has never lost his enthusiasm for aircraft, and he too still flies today. 'When I left the air force, I went straight into the Volunteer Reserve and flew at weekends. I then took up gliding with the Cambridge University Gliding Club, became an instructor there and I also started flying the tow planes. It's entirely different, though, it's purely flying for the fun of it.'

Bill Burke can't help admitting a certain adrenalin-fuelled thrill from going on the bombing raids. 'There's nothing as exciting as dicing with death. Doing a marking operation on a target was just like having a ten-minute white-knuckle ride and nothing in life corresponds to that by way of excitement, or the relief afterwards.'

Nonetheless, there were always the sombre overtones to the raids.

Nothing by way of training prepares you for going into battle. I don't think there's any experience in life which matches going into battle. That sorts out the lads from the men. In just the same way as presumably people like the archers of Agincourt or the sailors at Trafalgar, when they were about to go into battle, thought to themselves, 'Shall I be alive on the morrow?' exactly the same applied every time you operated, particularly against German targets, in Bomber Command.

The lost comrades of Bomber Command are still remembered. The two crew lost when Robert Kee's Hampden crashed are regularly in his thoughts, and the loss of friends killed in such circumstances has never ceased to be a distressing memory. Adge Boal went to find the graves of his first crew after the war. Having trained with the six young Canadians, Boal had been called home because of his mother's illness just as they were due to go on their first operation. The rest of the crew picked up a spare wireless operator, but none of the crew returned. For him, looking at the grave of his replacement was the hardest part, knowing he'd been due to be in that crew. For Alan Bryett, the most poignant memory of all is of the pilot who saved his life as he struggled to get out of his Halifax over Berlin. 'The pilot couldn't get out, he couldn't pull his parachute and he couldn't save his life and he gave his life for me. It's something I think about every day. The whole of the last sixty years is through him, in that one moment of time, when he did what all captains of aircraft would do.'

Years later, Bryett named his son Kevin, after that pilot who so gallantly put the safety of his crew before his own life. Yet he too looks back on his Bomber Command days with a fond pride.

It's very strange but I wouldn't have missed it for anything. I wouldn't wish anyone to go through what I had to go through but looking back, I learned so much in those two years. I went in as a young, raw boy. I came out as a gnarled, old, cynical man in some ways. I learned a great deal and the experiences helped me through the rest of my life. I've done all sorts of jobs and quite harrowing jobs on occasions, but it's been a piece of cake really because I know I'm going to be alive at the end of the day and everything is quite simple. I've got a good bed to go to at night. I've got food.

Hal Croxson had lost comrades too when his Lancaster had been shot down.

I lost four members of my team. That is a very sad thing to me, because they were damned good blokes and we were doing a damn good job. On the squadron when we weren't flying, we used to have so much fun. We used to have a few drinks to drown some of the tensions, but yes there were many happy times with the rude songs that we used to sing and the laughter. It was a lovely time, we were a wonderful team.

The frustration of being shot down on his first operation is still felt by Fred Stearn, but he too is glad he was a bomber boy.

I feel very inferior to the rest of them. It wasn't our own fault but it was such a waste. It was one of the most devastating things, the feeling's never gone. I just feel that I didn't prove myself. It's something that I've never been able to come to terms with, but a lot of people got the chop on the first op. Still, I wouldn't have missed it for the world, it's a terrible thing but the comradeship and with what I achieved, I am proud. That we didn't all get a special medal upset quite a lot of people, but medals don't count, it's your own conscience and satisfaction that counts.

The debate about the role of Bomber Command, and the wider role of the Allied bombing in the Second World War, will no doubt continue, and so it should. Whatever conclusions we choose to arrive at, we can nonetheless draw a distinction between those who formulated policy, and those who carried it out. The men of the bomber crews were not fêted or celebrated as heroes, nor did they ever expect to be. It was always going to be their fate, that apart from a small number of exceptional figures, they would mostly remain anonymous, ordinary men, drawn from a broad social spectrum. They joined up in the innocence of youth, taken in by a passion for aircraft, and a visceral sense that stopping the Nazis was a mission worth putting their lives on the line for. They don't consider themselves to have been particularly brave, just doing a job they were given. Yet they were very real heroes. They all risked their lives night after night, and in many cases lost them. Many survived appalling circumstances, some on several occasions, all in the flower of their youth. Their dedication in spite of everything the war threw at them was unwavering to the end.

Today, sixty years later, the few veterans that survive from Bomber Command remain eloquent and sobering witnesses to one of the most terrible chapters of the Second World War. In Germany, too, a new awareness has grown, as a new generation comes to grasp that the wartime suffering endured by their grandparents can also now be acknowledged and addressed. As new alliances are forged across both Britain and Germany, and reconciliation has become the new watchword, it should surely now be possible to commemorate the thousands of RAF volunteers at the same time, and in the same breath, as contemplating *all* the victims of six years of conflict in the skies over the Third Reich. Everyone involved in that long and awful bomber war surely deserves that at the very least.

Acknowledgements

We would like to thank the very large number of people who have helped make 'Bomber Crew' possible. We hope that through this book, and the television series it accompanies, an important part of the history of the Second World War will be better understood, and the courage of those who were part of it better known. Every one of us will draw our own conclusions on the way that warfare was conducted between 1939 and 1945, but those conclusions should at least be based on an appreciation of the complexities involved, and a realisation of the sacrifices made.

The wealth of first-hand testimony contained in this book is thanks to the very large number of Bomber Command veterans who were willing to share their experiences with us. We were lucky enough to be able to talk to, and in many cases meet, nearly 300 veterans from the aircrews, as well as veterans from the ground staff and WAAFs. They all have their own stories to tell and many were generous enough to lend us fascinating personal accounts and artefacts relating to their wartime service. We were privileged that so many were willing to share with us what were often very personal and difficult memories. Inevitably, we were only able to formally interview a small selection of those we have spoken to, but we hope that our account of the history of the bomber crews will go some way towards reflecting their experiences as well.

Our particular thanks must of course go to the veterans we interviewed formally: Peter Baker, Adge Boal, Alan Bryett, Bill Burke, Jim Chapman, Hal Croxon, Ricky Dyson, Jack Eveleigh, Roy Finch, Maurice Flower, John Holmes, Robert Kee, Leonard Miller, Robin Murray, Harold Nash, Ron Pitt, Jim Rogers, Arthur Smith, Fred Stearn, John Whiteley, Dennis Wiltshire and Tom Wingham. Without exception, they welcomed us warmly into their homes, were generous with their time and highly supportive of our endeavours. Given the sensitivities surrounding the history of Bomber Command, we are especially appreciative of this generosity of spirit. The photographs in the book are all taken from the personal collections of the veterans who were kind enough to allow us to use them. We are also grateful to have been able to talk to Wolfgang Falck, Horst Hirche and Peter Spoden who gave us some sense of the German perspective on the bombing campaign.

We would also like to thank the various associations and individuals who put us in touch with the veterans. Doug Radcliffe, Tony Iveson and their colleagues in the Bomber Command Association have been supportive of the project from the outset, while the Aircrew Association's assistance was invaluable in letting many veterans know about the series and book through their extensive organisation of regional associations. Among the many individuals who passed on contacts, Jack Burgess, Stephen Darlow, Sydney Dale, Grahame Holloway, Linda Shepperd, Steve Vessey and George Wootton were particularly helpful.

Our own historical comprehension of the role of Bomber Command was shaped by the contributions of four experts: Dr Stephen Bungay, Sir Max Hastings, Professor Richard Overy and Frederick Taylor. All gave fascinating full-length interviews for the series. We would also like to thank Nigel Carver, Sebastian Cox, Vaughan Crossley, Jonathan Falconer, Jörg Friedrich, Lee Gale, Sid Gray, Harry Le Marchant and Mike Varley who at various points in our research process have given us many useful insights. We were extremely grateful for the opportunity to see Emily Mayhew's book *The Reconstruction of Warriors* before it was published, and Professor Edgar Jones's unpublished paper on LMF. Tom Docherty was an invaluable guide to the complex details relating to the training of the bomber crews.

While the selection of a 21st century bomber crew was of particular importance to the television series, that process provided a different and very illuminating perspective on the bomber crews as a whole. So it is impossible to distinguish where such insights were used for the series, and where they informed the book. We would like to extend our appreciation to Luke Alkemade, Tim Chambers, Tanya Marriott, John Nolan and James Smith whose journeys into the RAF careers of their grandfathers added an important dimension to our understanding of the legacy of Bomber Command. Eric Atkins of the Mosquito Aircrew Association, W. R. Chorley, Fred Parent and Jock Whitehouse were among those who aided our research into specific details relating to the background of the five grandfathers.

The opportunity for our 21st century crew to fly wouldn't have been possible without the enthusiastic cooperation of the team at the Imperial War Museum in Duxford, notably Tracey Woods and Rebecca Dalley. While the experience of the real bomber crews can never be replicated, Brendan O'Brien's tutoring of the crew ensured that during the filming period, they gained a genuine grasp of Bomber Command's contribution to the Allied victory over Germany. The use of the Harvard and Beech aircraft was courtesy of John Romain, Lee Proudfoot, John 'Smudge' Smith and their colleagues at the Aircraft Restoration Company, based at Duxford; Elly Sallingboe, Peter Brown, Steve Carter, Andrew Dixon and Jim Jewell of the B-17 Charitable Trust were kind enough to allow us to use the 'Sally B' B-17 Flying Fortress. Keeping vintage aircraft flying requires an endless cycle of fundraising, technical expertise and dedication on the part of a team of pilots, engineers and supporters and we are fortunate that each year these groups somehow manage to keep the few airworthy examples of Second World War aircraft that are left in the air. Thanks to another group of dedicated enthusiasts, led by Fred and Harold Panton, the 'Just Jane' Lancaster is preserved in East Kirkby, and they too were generous in allowing us to film the aircraft taxiing on the runway. Our 21st century crew were joined there by four veterans, Bill Burke, Jack Eveleigh, Steve Stevens and Tom Wingham, who travelled considerable distances so that the five grandchildren could learn about the Lancaster directly from Bomber Command veterans. We are obliged to the many other individuals and groups who took part in the filming process, including the Canadian Warplane Heritage Museum, Major John Conway, Adrian Kilby, George Puttock and his colleagues at the Ministry of Defence.

The series would never have been possible without the support of Channel 4 Television, in particular Hamish Mykura who commissioned the programmes. It was made thanks to the tireless dedication and expertise of our colleagues on the production team at RDF Media: Rob Coldstream, Joseph Maxwell, Diana Francis, Marie-Louise Frellesen, Janne Read, Zara Akester, Jessica Versluys, Lulu Lory, James Barker and Divya Pathak. Natasha Goodfellow, Wolf Gebhark and Michael Foedrowitz were invaluable in finding the German veterans. Much of their work has contributed to the book, sometimes unwittingly, but our thanks also go to the many other people who helped make the series.

In evolving the historical research that derived from the series into a book, we are particularly indebted to Rupert Lancaster who has been an encouraging and patient editor. His colleagues at Hodder and Stoughton, not least Hugo Wilkinson, have worked hard to ensure that the book has met a very tight publication deadline without compromising its ambition. Among their many colleagues, special thanks are due to Ian Paten, the copy editor, Clare Parkinson, the proof reader, Diana leCore, the indexer, and Mark Ecob who designed the striking jacket and the map. At RDF Media, Rachel Barke was integral to ensuring that there would be a book in the first place and she has been a supportive influence ever since, aided by Mark Lesbirel and Laura Owen. Jilly Lloyd provided the excellent transcriptions for the majority of our interviews, while Brigitte Downey translated and transcribed the interviews from the three German veterans.

Bibliography

Bird, Tony: *A Bird Over Berlin: A Lancaster Pilot's Story of Survival Against All the Odds* (Bognor Regis, Woodfield, 2001)

Bourke, Joanna: *An Intimate History Of Killing* (London, Granta, 1999)

Bowman, Martin W: *Boeing B-17 Flying Fortress* (Marlborough, Crowood Press, 1998)

Bungay, Stephen: *The Most Dangerous Enemy* (London, Aurum Press, 2000)

Chorley, W. R.: *In Brave Company: 158 Squadron Operations* (Salisbury, P. A. Chorley, 1977)

Chorley, W. R.: *RAF Bomber Command Losses Of The Second World War* (London, Midland, in 8 volumes from 1992)

Clutton-Brook, Oliver: *Footprints on the Sands of Time: RAF Bomber Command Prisoners of War in Germany 1939–45* (London, Grub Street, 2003)

Connelly, Mark: *Reaching for the Stars: A New History of Bomber Command in World War II* (London, I. B. Tauris, 2000)

Cox, Sebastian (ed): *The Strategic Air War Against Germany* (London, Frank Cass, 1998)

Darlow, Stephen: *D-Day Bombers: The Veterans' Story* (London, Grub Street, 2004)

Darlow, Stephen: *Lancaster Down! The Extraordinary Tale of Seven Young Bomber Aircrew at War* (London, Grub Street, 2000)

Darlow, Stephen: *Sledgehammers for Tintacks: Bomber Command Combats the V-1 Menace, 1943–1944* (London, Grub Street, 2002)

Davidson, Martin and Taylor, James: *Spitfire Ace* (London, Channel 4 Books/Macmillan, 2004)

Dee, Mike: *The Third Son As Night Bomber* (Catterick, Silver Quill Publications, 2002)

Deighton, Len: *Bomber* (London, Jonathan Cape, 1970)

Docherty, Tom: *Training For Triumph* (Bognor Regis, Woodfield, 2000)

Falck, Wolfgang: *The Happy Falcon: An Autobiography by the Father of the Night Fighters* (Eagle Editions, 2003)

Falconer, Jonathan: *Bomber Airfields of World War 2* (Hersham, Ian Allan, 1995)

Falconer, Jonathan and Todd, Richard: *The Dam Busters* (Stroud, Sutton, 2003)

Falconer, Jonathan: *Bomber Command Handbook 1939–45* (Stroud, Sutton, 1998)

Friedrich, Jörg: *Brandstätten* (Berlin, Propyläen, 2002)

Friedrich, Jörg: *Der Brand* (Berlin, Propyläen, 2002)

Hastings, Max: *Armageddon: The Battle For Germany 1944–1945* (London, Macmillan, 2004)

Hastings, Max: *Bomber Command* (London, Michael Joseph, 1979)

Kee, Robert: *A Crowd Is Not Company* (London, Eyre & Spottiswoode, 1947)

Mayhew, E. R.: *The Reconstruction Of Warriors* (London, Greenhill Books, 2004)

McCrea, Bill: *A Chequer-Board Of Nights* (Warrington, Compaid Graphics, 2003)

Middlebrook, Martin and Everitt, Chris: *The Bomber Command War Diaries* (Hersham, Midland Publishing, 1996)

Nichol, John and Rennell, Tony: *The Last Escape: The Untold Story of Allied Prisoners of War in Europe 1944–45* (London, Viking, 2003)

Overy, Richard J.: *The Air War 1939–1945* (London, Europa, 1980)

Overy, Richard J.: *Bomber Command 1939–45: Reaping The Whirlwind* (London, HarperCollins, 1997)

Overy, Richard J.: *Why The Allies Won* (London, Jonathan Cape, 1995)

Parfitt, Richard: *Bombs Gone: An Elvington Lad's War* (Maryland, Riverdale, 2001)

Pickering, Sylvia: *Tales of a Bomber Command WAAF* (Bognor Regis, Woodfield, 2002)

Potts, Phil: *Just A Survivor* (Bognor Regis, Woodfield, 2002)

Probert, Henry: *Bomber Harris: His Life And Times* (London, Greenhill Books, 2001)

Rees, Wing Commander Ken: *Lie In The Dark And Listen* (London, Grub Street, 2004)

Richards, Dennis: *RAF Bomber Command In The Second World War: The Hardest Victory* (London, Hodder & Stoughton, 1994)

Rolfe, Mel: *Flying Into Hell* (London, Grub Street, 2001)

Rolfe, Mel: *Gunning for the Enemy: Wallace McIntosh, DFC and Bar, DFM* (London, Grub Street, 2003)

Rolfe, Mel: *Hell on Earth: Dramatic First Hand Experience of Bomber Command at War* (London, Grub Street, 1999)

Bibliography

Rolfe, Mel: *Looking Into Hell: Experiences of the Bomber Command War* (London, Weidenfeld & Nicholson, 1995)

Rolfe, Mel: *To Hell And Back* (London, Grub Street, 1998)

Sebald, W. G.: *On The Natural History Of Destruction* (London, Hamish Hamilton, 2003)

Smith, Arthur Carlton: *Halifax Crew: The Story of a Wartime Bomber Crew* (London, Carlton Publications, 1983)

Spoden, Peter (trans. Peter Hinchliffe): *Enemy in the Dark: The Story of a Luftwaffe Night-fighter Pilot* (Bristol, Cerberus Publishing, 2003)

Starkey, Richard: *A Lancaster Pilot's Impression On Germany* (Warrington, Compaid Graphics, 1999)

Sweetman, John: *The Dambusters Raid* (London, Cassell, 1990)

Taylor, Frederick: *Dresden* (London, Bloomsbury, 2004)

Vancouver Island Branch of the Aircrew Association: *Listen To Us: Aircrew Memories* (Victoria, Victoria Publishing Company, 1997)

Webb, Alan: *At First Sight: A Factual and Anecdotal Account of 627 Squadron Royal Air Force* (Romford, Alan B. Webb, 1991)

Wiltshire, Dennis: *Pro Ardua, Pro Patria: Autobiographical Observations Of A World War Two Airman* (Bognor Regis, Woodfield, 2000)

Wright, Jim: *On Wings Of War: A History of 166 Squadron* (166 Squadron Association, 1996)

Index

Figures in italics refer to captions.

Index

Index

Index

Index

Index

Index